ELUSIVE COMPROMISE

To the memory of my grandparents,
Aleksandar and Slavka Obrenović
and Mihajlo and Radmila Djokić

DEJAN DJOKIĆ

Elusive Compromise
A History of Interwar Yugoslavia

HURST & COMPANY, LONDON

First published in the United Kingdom by
C. Hurst & Co. (Publishers) Ltd,
41 Great Russell Street, London, WC1B 3PL
© Dejan Djokić, 2007
All rights reserved.
Printed in India

A catalogue data record for this volume is available
from the British Library.

ISBNs
978-1-85065-851-1 *casebound*
978-1-85065-864-1 *paperback*

www.hurstpub.co.uk

CONTENTS

ACKNOWLEDGEMENTS

This book is based on my doctoral and postdoctoral research at the School of Slavonic and East European Studies, University College London, and at the Harriman Institute, Columbia University, respectively. I especially thank Wendy Bracewell and Peter Siani-Davies, my former PhD supervisors, and Stevan K. Pavlowitch (University of Southampton) and Anita Prażmowska (London School of Economics), who examined the thesis and recommended its publication. The final manuscript benefited from extremely helpful reports by two anonymous readers. Aleksa Djilas and Desimir Tošić read an earlier draft and offered characteristically selfless and expert comments, suggestions and criticisms. Without Dina Almuli and her parents, and without the late Vane Ivanović, I could not have started this work. Jasna Dragović-Soso and Dejan Jović spent endless hours discussing Yugoslavia with me while we were postgraduates, and, although all three of us now teach at different British universities, somehow we still find time for 'the topic'. I am fortunate enough to have been surrounded by good colleagues in London, New York and Nottingham: John Arnold, Mark Mazower (now at Columbia), Lucy Riall, Naoko Shimazu, Ruth Watson, and really everyone else at Birkbeck's School of History, Classics and Archaeology; members of the Department of History and the Centre for South-East European Studies at SSEES, UCL; Sumantra Bose (LSE); Ilaria Favretto (Kingston); Milan Nikolić (Surrey); Brad Abrams, Gordon Bardos, and John Micgiel at Columbia; members of the Department of Russian and Slavonic Studies and of the Centre for the Study of Post-Conflict Cultures, both at Nottingham. For their help and support, I am grateful to friends in Belgrade, especially: Maja, Nikola, and

Olgica Djilas; Ljubinka Trgovčević, Andrej Mitrović, and Professor Mitrović's many 'disciples', too numerous to list here; and in Zagreb: the Cipek/Marjanović family, Ines Lovrić, Tanja Rudež and Čedomir Višnjić.

Help of the staff of the following archives and libraries is gratefully acknowledged: in London: the British Library, the British Library of Political and Economic Science (LSE), the National Archives (formerly Public Record Office), and the library of the School of Slavonic and East European Studies (UCL); in Belgrade: the Archives of Yugoslavia, and the National Library; in Zagreb: the Croatian State Archives, and the National and University Library; and in the United States: the Bakhmetteff Archives at Columbia University, and the Hoover Institution Archives at Stanford University.

The book could not have been written without the Yugoslav Studies Fellowship and Research Bursary (both awarded by SSEES, UCL), the Scouloudi Research Fellowship (Institute of Historical Research, University of London), the Central Research Fund (University of London), the Naša reč Research Studentship (Belgrade), the Postdoctoral Research Fellowship (Harriman Institute, Columbia University), and the Dean of Arts' Fund, the Humanities Research Centre Small Research Grant, and the School of Modern Languages and Cultures Research Grant (all of the University of Nottingham).

I thank my London publishers Christopher Hurst and Michael Dwyer, of Hurst & Co., for deciding to publish a book that is not on Yugoslavia in a war.

I hope that sacrifices that my Serbian family has made for me are at least partly rewarded by this publication. Unfortunately, neither of my grandparents is alive to see the book about the country in which they grew up, and about events that shaped their lives probably without them noticing it much at the time. It is to their memory that this work is dedicated.

Needless to say, I am solely responsible for the book's shortcomings and for any remaining errors.

Washington, DC, April 2007   D.Dj.

A NOTE ON SPELLING, TRANSLATION AND PRONUNCIATION

(1) Yugoslav personal and place names are spelled as they normally appear in Serbo-Croat or Slovene. The exceptions are as follows:

Personal names. Names of rulers have been Anglicised—thus King *Alexander* (not *Aleksandar*) and Prince *Paul* (rather than *Pavle*), but *Nikola* Pašić, *Stjepan* Radić, and *Petar* Živković.

Place names. Exceptions to the standard Serbo-Croat spelling have only been made where an Anglicised alternative has become the norm. For example: *Belgrade*, not *Beograd*, but *Niš*, instead of *Nish*. *Herzegovina* is preferred to *Hercegovina*, as *Bosna*, *Hrvatska* and *Srbija* are spelled in English as *Bosnia*, *Croatia*, and *Serbia*, respectively. The northern Serbian province is spelled as *Vojvodina*, not the archaic *Voyvodina* (which, incidentally, means the same as Herzegovina—a Duchy). The same rule applies to names of rivers—the original spelling is used, unless there is an accepted Anglicised form. Thus, the river is *Danube*, but the *banovina* is *Dunavska* (not the Danubian *banovina*). When other authors are quoted the original spelling is kept.

(2) All translations from Serbo-Croat are mine, unless otherwise indicated.

(3) The following letters are pronounced in Serbo-Croat (more or less) as follows:
C, c: ts (as in nets)

Ć, ć: ch (softer sound than 'tch', not unlike 'tu' in 'tuna')

Č, č: tch (as in 'sketch')

Đ, đ (also spelled 'Dj', 'dj'): not unlike 'du' in 'duke'

Dž, dž: j (as in 'joke')

J, j: y (as in 'Yugoslavia')

Lj, lj: lu (as in 'solution') or lia (as in 'parliament')

R, r: pronounced not unlike the Scottish rolling 'r'

Š, š: sh (as in 'shoe')

Ž, ž: zh (as in 'Zhivago')

GLOSSARY OF SERBO-CROAT WORDS

ban – governor, viceroy
banovina – province
oblast – administrative region
sabor – Diet
skupština – assembly, parliament
sporazum – agreement

ABBREVIATIONS

AJ	Archives of Yugoslavia, Belgrade
BAR	Bakhmeteff Archive of Russian and East European Culture, Columbia University, New York
DS	Democratic Party
HDA	Croatian State Archives, Zagreb
HIA	Hoover Institution Archives, Stanford University
HSS	Croatian Peasant Party
HPSS	Croatian People's Peasant Party (renamed the HRSS in 1919)
HRSS	Croatian Republican Peasant Party (renamed the HSS in 1924)
FO	(Britain's) Foreign Office papers held at the National Archives
JF-1	*Jugoslovenski federalizam: Ideje i stvarnost. Tematska zbirka dokumenata* (compiled and edited by Branko Petranović and Momčilo Zečević) 2 vols, Belgrade, 1987, vol. 1.
JMO	Yugoslav Muslim Organisation
JNS	Yugoslav National Party
JRZ	Yugoslav Radical Union
KPJ	Communist Party of Yugoslavia
MPHSS-1	Ljubo Boban, *Maček i politika Hrvatske seljačke stranke. Iz povijesti hrvatskog pitanja, 1918-1941*, 2 vols, Zagreb, 1974, vol. 1.
MPHSS-2	ibid., vol. 2..
NRS	People's Radical Party
PPP	Papers of Prince Paul

SDK	Peasant Democratic Coalition
SDS	Independent Democratic Party
SKK	Serbian Cultural Club
SLS	Slovene People's Party
SZ	Agrarian Union (sometimes referred to as the Agrarian Party)
UO	United Opposition

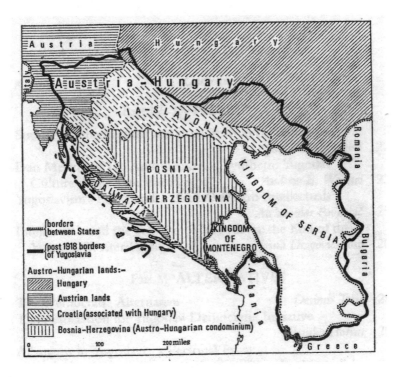

The Yugoslav lands on the eve of the First World War

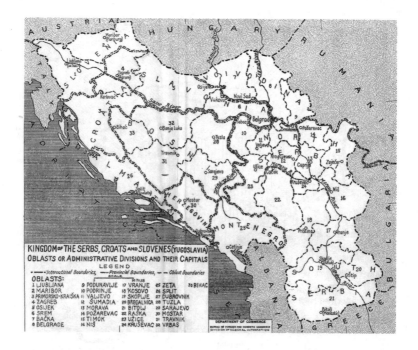

Yugoslavia in the 1920s

Yugoslavia, 1929-1941

INTRODUCTION

The origins of the crisis in Yugoslavia are to be found above all in the official policy, continuously implemented since the creation of this state. The Constitutions of 1921 and 1931 are nothing but results of this policy, the policy of hegemony of one region over all other regions. That policy has above all affected the Croats [...] At the same time, it is necessary to emphasise that although the Croats are the main opponents of the state policy and of this form of state, they are by no means alone and the only ones [in opposition]; a great majority of Serbs outside the borders of the old Kingdom of Serbia, namely the so-called 'prečani', are equally dissatisfied [with the regime] and empathise with the Croats.[1]

This book is about Yugoslavia between the Wars (1918-1941). Specifically, it analyses attempts to find a compromise on the form of state between Serbs and Croats during this turbulent period. Although ultimately a true compromise may have proved elusive, interwar Yugoslavia cannot be understood as a simple Serb-Croat dichotomy.[2] The emphasis on inter-ethnic conflict, favoured by most historians of Yugoslavia, fails to explain a number of developments during the period, most of which sought to achieve an agreement between the country's two largest groups. Because political contest often crossed ethnic lines, it cannot be simply reduced to its Serb-Croat dimension either.

---

1 'Jedan prijedlog za Nacrt Ustava', *Nova Evropa*, vol. 30, no. 7-8, 26 July 1937, 228-9.

2 Nor can the post-1945 Yugoslavia or even its violent disintegration be understood this way, as recent works by Dejan Jović (*Jugoslavija: Država koja je odumrla*, Belgrade and Zagreb, 2003) and Chip Gagnon (*The Myth of Ethnic War: Serbia and Croatia in the 1990s*, Ithaca, NY, 2004) demonstrate.

The book challenges the popular view that because of competing Serb and Croat national ideologies, formed before Yugoslavia had been created, a common state was doomed to failure. Despite the importance of historical legacy, the crisis in Yugoslavia was caused above all by the decisions made in the post-1918 period, as the passage quoted above amply illustrates, even if it fails to account for many Serbs from the old Serbian kingdom and many other non-Serbs who also opposed the regime.

The analysis centres on Serbs and Croats. Because of their numerical strength, geographical position, and historical role in the development of the Yugoslav idea and formation of the Yugoslav state, they held the key to Yugoslavia's unity and... disunity.[3] The aspirations and demands of other Yugoslavs, particularly the Slovenes, the only other recognised Yugoslav 'tribe' in the interwar period, and the Bosnian Muslims, whose religious distinctiveness was accepted but who were not regarded as a distinct 'tribe', would require separate studies and are only treated in passing.

The discourse of the main Yugoslav leaders receives due consideration. It is argued that their actions were not motivated by ethnic antagonism towards the 'other', although nationalism, sometimes in combination with political manoeuvring, did in many cases influence their actions. Although essentially a study of conflict management at the level of political elites, the book also provides insight into the impact of politics on 'ordinary' Yugoslavs. Finally, close attention is paid to detail, as the reader will undoubtedly soon realise. Such an approach has been necessary in order to illustrate

---

3 The best brief introduction to Yugoslavia and the peoples and territories that made it is Aleksa Djilas, *The Contested Country: Yugoslav Unity and Communist Revolution, 1919-1953*, Cambridge, MA, 1991, 1-14. Djilas convincingly argues that Serb-Croat relations were crucial for Yugoslavia's survival. This is a generally accepted view, though some scholars have argued that it was a Serb-Slovene, not Serb-Croat, axis that was central. (For example: Momčilo Zečević, *Na istorijskoj prekretnici. Slovenci u politici jugoslovenske države 1919-1929.*, I, Belgrade and Ljubljana, 1985; and Susan L. Woodward, *Balkan Tragedy: Chaos and Dissolution after the Cold War*, Washington, DC, 1995.)

the complexity of the period and to demonstrate the plurality of opinion, not only among Serbs and Croats generally, but also inside their main political parties.

Finally, this book indirectly suggests that the interwar Yugoslav state should be seen within a wider, European context, rather than as an anomaly, as Yugoslavia and the Balkans are often regarded. Europe between the Wars was beset by national questions, which did not go away following the creation of nation states at the end of the First World War. However, nationalism was not the only reason for Yugoslavia's instability. Like most Europeans, the Yugoslavs had to contend with unprecedented destruction brought about by the Great War. They faced the difficult task of the postwar rebuilding, not just of infrastructure, but also of destroyed families and societies. Yugoslavia was not even unique in being a new state, made up of a number of components, which had never previously come together. Like the Yugoslavs, many citizens of European states, especially those in East-Central Europe, experienced constitutional debate, the failure of democratic institutions to create stable governments, and their replacement by autocratic regimes. Yugoslavia could not remain immune to the post-1929 worldwide economic crisis, nor, most tragically, to the international crisis which by the end of the 1930s culminated in another World War: the war which also destroyed the South Slavs' first attempt to live in a common state.

The book has a chronological flow, but some chapters are organised thematically; a combined chronological-thematic approach seemed most appropriate. The arguments and conclusions are based on my research into primary sources: documents held in the Croatian State Archives in Zagreb, the Archives of Yugoslavia in Belgrade, National Archives (formerly Public Record Office) at Kew, the archives of Columbia University in New York, and the Hoover Institution Archives at Stanford University, as well as published documents, newspapers, pamphlets and memoir literature. In addition, extensive use has been made of the relevant secondary sources in English, Serbo-Croat and, in a few instances, Slovene.

The scene for the main part of the book is set in the first two chapters. The emergence of the Croatian question in the formative years of the Kingdom of Serbs, Croats, and Slovenes (as Yugoslavia was officially called between 1918 and 1929) is explained, and attempts by Serb and Croat political leaders to reach a compromise during the 1920s are traced. The Croatian question in this work is understood as the majority of Croats' refusal to accept fully the Yugoslav state centralist institutions and their determination to seek wide autonomy, even the status of a state within a state, for Croatia. Although the constitutional debate began even before the creation of Yugoslavia as a political contest between centralists and anti-centralists on what kind of constitution the new state should have, it eventually turned into what has generally been perceived as a Serb-Croat conflict. This debate marked the whole interwar period and was at the heart of the political contest in the Yugoslav kingdom.

The inability to find a solution to the Croatian question contributed to the failure of democratic institutions—a failure which culminated tragically with the murder of the Croat leader Stjepan Radić and two other members of his Croatian Peasant Party by a Serb deputy in the summer of 1928. However, already in the 1920s leading Serb politicians attempted to accommodate Croat demands for a de-centralised Yugoslav state.

In chapter three, attempts by King Alexander, Prince Paul and several prime ministers to deal with the Croatian question in the 1930s are explored. Following Alexander's assassination in 1934, organised and carried out by the Croat *Ustaša* group and the Internal Macedonian Revolutionary Organisation, gradual abandonment of integral Yugoslavism (an ideology which claimed that Serbs, Croats and Slovenes belonged to an ethnic whole) and relaxation of the dictatorship took place. Yet, neither the Crown nor the government was prepared to abolish or amend the 1931 Constitution, which would have been necessary in order to grant Croatia self-rule.

Cooperation between the major Serb political parties and the Croatian Peasant Party in opposition to the government—after 1935 formed by Serbs, Slovenes and Bosnian Muslims—is the subject of chapter four. The willingness of Serbian opposition leaders to support Croat demands was symbolised by their decision to choose the Croat leader Vladko Maček as head of the united opposition list in the 1935 and 1938 general elections. In November 1937 the Serb-Croat opposition formed the Bloc of National Agreement, which called for a return to democracy; in August 1938 Maček visited Belgrade, where he was greeted by tens of thousands of Serbs; and in December the same year the united opposition nearly defeated the government in general elections.

The relative success of the opposition in the December 1938 elections sent a powerful signal to Prince Paul that the time was ripe for a change of government. Prime Minister Stojadinović, whose personal ambitions were beginning to threaten the Prince Regent himself, was replaced by Dragiša Cvetković in February 1939. Cvetković soon proclaimed that the Croats had developed a separate identity and that the first aim of his government was to grant them autonomy within Yugoslavia. Events that led to the establishment of an autonomous Croatia in August 1939 are analysed and an assessment of the August agreement is provided in chapter five.

Although the Cvetković-Maček agreement may have settled the Croatian question, it also ended the Serb-Croat pro-democracy opposition. Because many Serbs were included in the newly formed *banovina* (province) of Croatia and because, unlike the Croats, the Serbs were given no autonomy, the agreement led to the emergence of a Serbian question. Serb opinion was not as homogeneous as the Croat, and there soon emerged a Serb-Serb debate over the agreement and over the meaning of Yugoslavia and Yugoslavism. The debate over the respective merits of democracy and dictatorship was thus virtually abandoned, as Serbs, like the Croats before them, turned to the national question.

The Serb question is analysed in chapter six. Many Serbs—both those living in autonomous Croatia and those in the rest of Yugoslavia—sought to 'rally together' all their compatriots in a Serbian province (Slovenes and Bosnia's Muslims also called for the creation of their own *banovinas*). However, there were prominent Serbs, both in the government and among intellectual circles, who supported the Cvetković-Maček agreement.

There are alternative interpretations of interwar Yugoslavia. Despite the dearth of English-language works on the period, two books stand out. Ivo Banac's seminal *The National Question in Yugoslavia*[4] primarily analyses the crucial interim period between the unification of 1 December 1918 and the promulgation of the (first) centralist Constitution in June 1921; it also provides a detailed account of the origins of South Slav national ideologies prior to 1918. Banac contends that the conflicting Serb and Croat ideologies, developed prior to the creation of Yugoslavia, laid the foundations for the country's instability. While the Croats preferred co-operation with other South Slavs, the Serbs promoted state-sponsored assimilation of non-Serbs. According to Banac, immediately after the unification 'the national question was still susceptible to other—more equitable and pluralistic—solutions', but after 1921, 'despite dictatorships and attempts at democratic renewal, occupations and wars, revolutions and social changes…hardly any new elements were introduced in the *set pattern* of South Slavic interactions.'[5] Attempts to achieve an agreement between Serbs and Croats in the 1930s may be seen as belated if not irrelevant in this context.

As this book—it is hoped—demonstrates, the way Yugoslavia was created did significantly influence interwar developments, but it is wrong to argue that a pattern of Serb-Croat relations was set

---

4 Ithaca, NY, 1984.
5 Ibid., 415. Emphasis added by D. Dj.

by 1921. Furthermore, it is debatable whether Serbian and Croatian nationalisms had been formed by 1918, and whether they remained immune to evolution following the creation of Yugoslavia.

The second key work on interwar Yugoslavia is Jacob Hoptner's *Yugoslavia in Crisis, 1934-1941*.[6] If Banac's book is more relevant for an understanding of the national ideologies and the politics of the early interwar years, Hoptner provides an authoritative study of Yugoslavia's international predicament in the second half of the 1930s. He points to an interaction between foreign policy and major internal issues, such as the Serb-Croat question.[7] Because of the Croats' and other non-Serbs' dissatisfaction, the Yugoslav government had to be wary of its revisionist neighbours, particularly Bulgaria, Hungary and Italy. Belgrade, backed by its traditional ally France, worked towards the establishment of the Little Entente and the Balkan Entente, in which Yugoslavia played a prominent part. Yugoslavia's foreign policy changed in the second half of the 1930s, with the re-emergence of a strong Germany. The country found itself in an increasingly delicate position, trying to maintain neutrality in a Europe of sharp ideological divisions. The external position tended to be influenced by internal discord, for which Hoptner blames Yugoslavia's political leaders, 'men of limited vision and even less flexibility who revealed no capacity for working together'.[8]

Yugoslavia in Crisis is heavily based on Prince Paul's papers, to which Hoptner had had exclusive access, and his conclusions often bear the mark of the Prince Regent's perspective.[9] Consequently, the

---

6 New York, 1962. Jozo Tomasevich's *Peasants, Politics and Economic Change in Yugoslavia* (Stanford, 1955), is another outstanding work on the period, but is left out of this analysis because it is not directly relevant to my argument.

7 Hoptner defines the Serb-Croat question as a conflict between centralism and federalism, arguing that 'It was the Serb-Croat divergence, although primarily an internal problem, that proved crucial in the formulation and operation of the new kingdom's foreign policy.' *Yugoslavia in Crisis*, 4.

8 Ibid., 297.

9 Because in the early 1960s Prince Paul's papers were still unavailable to other researchers, Hoptner refers to them in his book as 'Papers of Jacob B.

activities of the Serbian opposition, and its attempts to reach a compromise with the Croats, are somewhat neglected.

In terms of argument and the period it covers, the present book may be positioned somewhere between the works of Banac and Hoptner, although my understanding of Yugoslavia's internal dynamics is closer to Hoptner's. It is hoped that this work offers a fresh interpretation of Yugoslavia between the wars, and helps fill one of many remaining gaps in literature on the subject.[10]

This study would probably have been impossible without the foundation provided by historians of the interwar period based in former Yugoslavia. Yugoslav historians began seriously to research the history of the interwar Kingdom in the late 1950s, after a signal had came from above. In 1957, formally at the initiation of the Society of Historians of Serbia and Association of Historical Societies of Yugoslavia, a group of leading Yugoslav historians organised a seminar on the interwar history. The result was an edited volume which came out the following year; its authors stressed that the book represented only the first step toward future, 'proper' studies of the Kingdom of Yugoslavia.[11] As Vaso Čubrilović explained in the introduction, the book had two main aims: to fill an existing gap in the historical literature and to introduce the study of contemporary history, mostly in order

---

Hoptner' (JBH).

10 For example, students of Yugoslavia still await critical biographies of King Alexander and Nikola Pašić. Gligorijević's trilogy on King Alexander (see the bibliography) is overall very useful, but at times hagiographic and ultimately disappointing. Another significant gap, a study of the life and work of Stjepan Radić, has at last been filled by Mark Biondich's *Stjepan Radić, the Croat Peasant Party, and the Politics of Mass Mobilization, 1904-1928*, Toronto, 2000. Christian Axboe Nielsen's meticulously researched and unpublished doctoral thesis explores the impact on daily life of King Alexander's dictatorship, despite its title ('One State, One Nation, One King: The Dictatorship of King Aleksandar and His Yugoslav Project, 1929-1935', Columbia University, 2002).

11 Sergije Dimitrijević *et al.* (eds), *Iz istorije Jugoslavije, 1918-1945: Zbornik predavanja*, Belgrade, 1958, 5-6. The same year Ferdo Čulinović published his *Slom stare Jugoslavije* (The Collapse of Old Yugoslavia), Zagreb.

to 'raise future generations in the spirit of our People's Revolution'.[12] However, only one history of interwar Yugoslavia was ever published in Serbo-Croat, by the eminent historian Ferdo Čulinović. It came out in 1961 and, unsurprisingly, it presented the official view held in the socialist Yugoslavia of its royalist predecessor—that the 'Greater Serbian bourgeoisie', in some cases aided by its Croatian and Slovenian counterparts, established a hegemony and led the country to political and economic collapse even before the invasion by the Axis powers in April 1941.[13]

If the number of general histories of interwar Yugoslavia is scarce, studies on more specific aspects of the history of the period abound. From the mid-1960s onwards—coinciding with attempts by the authorities to introduce economic and political reforms—Yugoslav historians produced a number of invaluable books and articles on the interwar political parties and key developments.[14] Based on the then newly accessible archival records, these studies offered a wealth of information, while making sure the official interpretation of the period remained unchallenged. Such an approach to the writing of history was probably the only possible one. Official historiography, following the end of the Second World War, served the legitimisation of the new regime, and academic historians often sought refuge in medieval and early modern history, avoiding subjects concerned

---

12 Vaso Čubrilović, 'Uvod u istoriju Jugoslavije od 1918. do 1945.', in Dimitrijević et al. (eds.), *Iz istorije Jugoslavije*, 7-8. Apart from Dimitrijević and Čubrilović, other contributors included Ferdo Čulinović, Pero Damjanović, Edib Hasanagić, Dragoslav Janković, Bogdan Krizman, Jovan Marjanović and Pero Morača, the *crème de la crème* of Yugoslavia's official historiography. Some of these historians were probably also responsible for an earlier volume, a history of interwar political parties: *Istorija gradjanskih stranaka u Jugoslaviji*, Belgrade, vol. 1, 1952 (author(s) unknown). To the best of my knowledge, the projected second volume, which would have looked into the history of fascist and pro-fascist parties and movements among the South Slavs, was never published.

13 Ferdo Čulinović, *Jugoslavija izmedju dva rata*, 2 vols., Zagreb, 1961.

14 See the bibliography for details on secondary literature on the period produced in socialist Yugoslavia.

with the more recent past.[15] Although from the mid-1980s 'nation' increasingly replaced 'class' as the dominant ideology, the next generation of (mostly Belgrade-based) scholars continued with the well-established, largely positivist approach to Yugoslavia's interwar history, producing several key works on the period.[16]

My own approach acknowledges the importance of pre-1918 history, of ethnic rivalries and differences, and the significance of class, as well as of external factors. However, I consider political events as they developed after the unification as equally if not more important for an understanding of the period. Political actors were active rather than pre-programmed 'agents', who sometimes acted out of genuine beliefs, but sometimes out of pragmatism, and whose views, in many cases, evolved during the period. Benefits of such 'instrumentalist' approach will hopefully become clear to the reader as s/he engages with the book.

---

15 Stevan K. Pavlowitch, *The Improbable Survivor: Yugoslavia and its Problems, 1918-1988*, London, 1988, 129. In that respect Yugoslav historiography mirrored that of the Soviet Union, despite the 1948 split between Moscow and Belgrade. As Eric Hobsbawm wrote, '[i]f one was a serious Soviet historian, the best thing was to stick to the history of the ancient East and the Middle Ages, although it was touching to see how the modernists rushed to say (within the constraints of the permissible) what they knew to be true every time the window seemed to be slightly opened—as in 1956 and in the early 1960s.' *Interesting Times: A Twentieth Century Life*, London, 2003, 291. Nevertheless Yugoslav modern historiography produced some first class scholarship, such as the work by Ljubo Boban, Milorad Ekmečić and Andrej Mitrović (see the bibliography for references).

16 This type of transformation was of course not unusual in East-Central Europe and it mirrored—in some cases even preceded—the transformation of the political scene. Just like in the sphere of politics, the transformation is often not complete. Even in the works by more obviously nationalist historians, such as Vasilije Krestić in Serbia or the late Croatian president Franjo Tudjman, who had been a professional historian in the 1960s, old communist phraseology and even interpretations are visible.

INTRODUCTION

Most works dealing with interwar Yugoslavia address, in one way or another, the Croatian question. However, what is lacking in the existing literature is an analysis of Serb and Croat attempts to find a compromise vis-à-vis Yugoslavia and Yugoslavism and reach a solution to the Croatian question. A search for compromise and for a Serb-Croat agreement dominated the Yugoslav politics in the interwar period, and especially in the 1930s. What follows is a (hi)story of that search.

1
DEATH AND UNION

Too far are Belgrade and Zagreb from each other in the first months of 1919; even the fastest [Zagreb-Belgrade] trains regularly take 27 hours to reach their destination, and due to postwar conditions they are running late every day. A trip from Zagreb to Belgrade, and the other way round, is an uncomfortable journey; cars are not heated and windows are broken; people are reluctant to travel. This makes contacts [between Serbia and Croatia] very difficult.[1]

At 10.00a.m. on 27 November 1918, a special train left Zagreb's main railway station for Belgrade, the capital of Serbia, just liberated after three years of the Austro-Hungarian occupation. The train's sole passengers were delegates of the National Council, the government of the newly-formed, internationally unrecognised State of Slovenes, Croats, and Serbs. The sense of historic importance of their mission probably overwhelmed the fatigue and stress the group must have felt. The lengthy and intense debate over the unification with Serbia, which began on 23 November, had finally concluded around 11.00p.m. the previous night. The National Council convened at the time when the Habsburg Monarchy was rapidly disintegrating, Italian troops were moving into Dalmatia, and social unrest threatened the young state's authorities. Only neighbouring Serbia, with its revitalised and victorious army and its international prestige elevated,

---

1 Josip Horvat, *Politička povijest Hrvatske*, Zagreb, 1990, 2 vols, vol. 2, 158 (First published as *Politička povijest Hrvatske, 1918-1929*, Zagreb, 1938). Horvat, a journalist and a member of the Croatian Peasant Party, witnessed some of the most important events during Yugoslavia's formative period. His book is an invaluable and highly readable contemporary account of Yugoslavia in the 1920s.

whose aim since the early stages of the war had been the liberation
and unification of Serbs, Croats, and Slovenes, could provide a sense
of security and protection.

The train was forced to move slower than usual because of thick
fog, and the passing countryside reminded the delegates of the
devastation brought about by the war which had barely ended. The
delegation arrived around 11.00p.m. in Zemun, where it spent the
night, before crossing over the Danube to Belgrade the following
morning. There, the delegates were greeted by enthusiastic crowds of
Serbs and by the few political leaders present in the city.[2]

The Zagreb delegation travelled to Belgrade in order to invite
Serbia's leaders to proclaim the unification of South Slavs into one
state. The text of the invitation had been drawn up by the National
Council, during the historic session of 23-24 November. By the end
of the session the National Council had overwhelmingly voted for
unification with Serbia, but not before heated discussion. The main
arguments and concerns raised at the time, in hindsight, highlighted
the origins of subsequent debates on the institutional structure of
the Yugoslav kingdom and therefore deserve a close scrutiny. Before
examining the discussion in the National Council in more detail, it is
necessary to first sketch out the context in which it took place.

The First World War and the Yugoslav Question

For an independent and united Yugoslavia to be formed, the Ottoman and Habsburg monarchies had to give way. The Ottomans'
presence in Europe all but ended as a result of the First Balkan War
of 1912. The Second Balkan War of 1913 nearly doubled the territory
of Serbia and enhanced its prestige among the South Slavs living in
Austria-Hungary. When Archduke Franz Ferdinand, the heir to the
Habsburg throne, was assassinated in the Bosnian capital Sarajevo
on 28 June 1914, more than half of the future Yugoslavia was part of
Austria-Hungary: Slovenia, Croatia, Vojvodina, and Bosnia-Herze-

---

2 Ibid., 131.

govina. Only Serbia (which included what is today Kosovo and Macedonia) and Montenegro were independent states. The archduke's assassin was Gavrilo Princip, a twenty-year-old member of 'Young Bosnia', a revolutionary youth movement that campaigned for the breakup of the Dual Monarchy and the unification of its South Slavs with Serbia. Although Young Bosnians were armed and financially aided by the 'Unification or Death' (a.k.a. 'Black Hand'), a secret Serbian organisation led by Colonel Dragutin Dimitrijević Apis, official Belgrade was not behind the assassination. Nevertheless, for Vienna and Budapest the murder of the archduke presented an ideal opportunity to bring to an end Serbia's threat to the empire. When an ultimatum was rejected by Belgrade, Austria-Hungary declared war on Serbia on 28 July. This proved to be the beginning of the First World War.[3]

Serbia's war aims included territorial aggrandisement at the expense of the Habsburg Monarchy. In early September 1914 the Serbian coalition government of Nikola Pašić informed its allies that it would aim to create, 'out of Serbia, a strong south-western Slavonic state, that would include all Serbs, all Croats, and all Slovenes.'[4] On 7 December, the government, evacuated to the southern city of Niš, formally proclaimed its aim to 'liberate and unite all our unliberated brethren: Serbs, Croats, and Slovenes' into one state.[5] The

---

3   For a brief description of the formation of Yugoslavia see Slobodan Jovanović, *Ustavno pravo Kraljevine Srba, Hrvata i Slovenaca*, Belgrade, 1995 (first published by Geca Kon in 1924), 31-51. The road to unification and its international dimension are analysed in Kosta St. Pavlowitch, 'The First World War and the Unification of Yugoslavia', and Andrej Mitrović, 'The Yugoslav Question, the First World War, and the Peace Conference, 1914-1920', both in Dejan Djokić (ed.), *Yugoslavism: Histories of a Failed Idea, 1918-1992*, London and Madison WI, 2003, 27-41 and 42-56, respectively.

4   Milorad Ekmečić, *Ratni ciljevi Srbije 1914*, Belgrade, 2nd ed., 1990, 89. The government was formed by Pašić's Radicals, the Independent Radicals and the Progressives.

5   'Izjava kr.[aljevske] vlade u Narodnoj Skupštini', Niš, 7 December (24 November O.S.) 1914, *Dokumenti o postanku Kraljevine Srba, Hrvata i Slovenaca, 1914-1919* (compiled by Ferdo Šišić) [hereafter *Dokumenti*], Zagreb, 1920, 10.

Yugoslavism of the Serbian government was motivated by several factors. A large state would stand a better chance of confronting antagonistic powers such as the Habsburg Monarchy in future. Such a state could be best achieved by the unification of ethnically related South Slav peoples; the existence of the Yugoslav idea provided the necessary ideology. In addition to ethnic kinship, the South Slavs were connected by the common danger of pan-Germanic expansion. Finally, the unification should be carried out around Serbia, which had already emerged prior to the war as the centre of the South Slav liberation struggle.[6]

There was some confusion among Serbian cabinet ministers as to the exact meaning of Yugoslavism: was it above all an idea of Serb-Croat unity, or should the Slovenes—perhaps even the Bulgarians—be included, too? Other issues concerned the most appropriate name for the new nation and the new state, and whether the idea of pan-Serb unification (including plans for a union between Serbia and Montenegro) and Yugoslavism could go hand in hand.[7] Serbia's political elites accepted the Yugoslav idea much later then their Croatian and Serbian counterparts in the Habsburg Monarchy, where Yugoslavism originated in the first half of the nineteenth century. After the war started, the Serbian government consulted the country's leading intellectuals, who had showed considerably more interest in Yugoslavism in the years before the war.[8] The term 'Greater Serbia' was not used by Serbia's political leaders, at least not in official documents. Military leaders did refer to it, albeit often to describe Serbia's 'greatness' and 'glory', rather than a political pro-

---

6 Andrej Mitrović, *Srbija u Prvom svetskom ratu*, Belgrade, 2nd ed., 2004, 138.

7 Ibid., 139. For plans for the unification between Serbia and Montenegro see Dimitrije Vujović, *Ujedinjenje Crne Gore i Srbije*, Titograd, 1962.

8 See Ljubinka Trgovčević, *Naučnici Srbije i stvaranje jugoslovenske države, 1914-1920*, Belgrade, 1986, and her chapter 'South Slav Intellectuals and the Creation of Yugoslavia', in Djokić (ed.), *Yugoslavism*, 222-37.

gramme.[9] In fact, the term was used more often by Serbia's Western allies than by Serbs themselves.[10]

Serbia supported, morally and financially, the creation of the Yugoslav Committee, a group of exiled Habsburg South Slav politicians and intellectuals based in London from May 1915 until the end of the war. The committee's leaders were two Dalmatian Croats, Ante Trumbić and Frano Supilo, and its activities were largely propagandistic.[11] Following Serbia's military defeat in late 1915, King Peter I, the government, and a decimated army reached the safety of the Greek island of Corfu after an epic retreat through the mountains of Montenegro and Albania during the winter of 1915–16. The combination of such a precarious situation and pressure from the Entente powers to give up claims to Dalmatia and Istria in favour of Italy, in exchange for Rome's entry in the war on the Allied side—to keep a promise made to Italy by Britain, France and Russia in the secret Treaty of London of April 1915 - allegedly led Pašić to reconsider his government's 'maximalist' aim, Yugoslav unification. Instead, he had to be content, for the time being at least, with an enlarged Serbia that would include Montenegro, Bosnia-Herzegovina, and possibly Serb-populated parts of Croatia.

It would be wrong to conclude, however, that Pašić was offered a 'Greater Serbia' by the Powers. Serbia was not a signatory to the London Treaty, and Pašić learned of its contents indirectly, from Serbia's diplomatic representatives to Paris and Rome and from Supilo. Although in the summer of 1915 the British proposed to

---

9 Mitrović, *Srbija*, 141.

10 Ibid. An article on the formation of Yugoslavia published on 7 December 1918 in the London *Times* was entitled 'Greater Serbia: Regent accepts offer of redeemed Slavs'.

11 Trumbić and Supilo were among the few members of the Committee who chose to not receive financial support from the Serbian government in order to maintain an independent position. The Serbian government had a representative inside the committee (in later stages it was Stojan Protić, member of the Radical Party and the first Prime Minister of the Kingdom of Serbs, Croats, and Slovenes), while Dinko Trinajstić of the Yugoslav Committee was attached to the Serbian government at Corfu.

the Serbian government territorial compensation at the expense of the Habsburg Monarchy in exhange for Serbia giving up its share of Macedonia (parts of which Serbia gained at the expense of Bulgaria in the Second Balkan War), with which the Allies had tried unsuccessfully to entice Bulgaria to join the war on their side, similar bargaining with territories was not uncommon during the war. Until the later stages of the war, not many could have predicted the disintegration of the Habsburg Monarchy, let alone the war's outcome and the postwar map of Europe. Serbia's government would have preferred the creation of a large South Slav state and, in any case, it is debatable whether a viable alternative was available at the end of the war.[12]

Although Pašić did appear to backtrack on the issue of creation of a Yugoslavia in 1916, the Serbian Prince Regent Alexander continued to publicly support the Yugoslav option.[13] At a reception in London's Claridge's Hotel[14] in April that year, Alexander told his British hosts that the Serbian army fought for 'the ideal towards the attainment of which we have striven for centuries. This ideal is the

---

12 It is therefore incorrect to argue that the then Serbian leadership made a fatal mistake, or a noble sacrifice, by choosing Yugoslavia over an enlarged Serbian state, as it has been suggested in recent years in non-scholarly as well as some scholarly circles in Serbia. See the debate between Dubravka Stojanović and Kosta Nikolić, two Belgrade historians with opposing views on the issue, in the Belgrade weekly *Vreme*, no. 624, 19 December 2002, and no. 628, 16 January 2003.

13 Alexander was the second son of King Peter I and Princess Zorka of Montenegro, who died before her husband became king in 1903. He became heir to the throne in 1909, because his elder brother George's bad temper was deemed unsuitable for a future king. In June 1914 Alexander was proclaimed the Prince Regent and from then on ruled in the name of his ailing father, King Peter I. He became king upon Peter's death in August 1921.

14 The same hotel where in July 1945 Alexander's grandson and namesake would be born. An apartment in the hotel was proclaimed by the British government a Yugoslav territory for 24 hours, so that heir to the throne would be born in 'Yugoslavia'. At the end of the Second World War, the Yugoslav Communist-dominated authorities ousted the Karadjordjević dynasty and banned it from returning to the country.

union in one single fatherland of all the Serbs, Croats and Slovenes, who are one people with the same traditions, the same tongue, the same tendencies, but whom an evil fate has divided.'[15]

The suspicion that the Serbian government-in-exile was no longer firmly in favour of a Yugoslavia led to a conflict within the Yugoslav Committee. Supilo wanted the Committee to sever its relations with Pašić and his ministers, but Trumbić refused to take such a radical line. In this he was supported by other members of the Committee, who believed that the two sides must work together towards unification, while any differences would be worked out after the war. Supilo resigned from the Committee in protest, effectively ending his political career even before his untimely death the following year.[16]

The conflict between Trumbić and Supilo was not the only disagreement within the Committee. Its dependence on Serbia and the Entente, a lack of political legitimacy, and its mixed membership— the majority were Croats, but there were also Serbs and Slovenes—all created antagonisms. This internal disunity led Thomas G. Masaryk, after the war the first president of Czechoslovakia, to observe that 'already since 1916 [the Yugoslav Committee] was dangerously unstable', and Jovan Jovanović Pižon, the Serbian minister to London (and the future leader of the Agrarians), to write in his diary in May 1917, that '[because of internal divisions] the Yugoslav Committee

---

15 'Deputation to the Prince Regent: A Nation's Ideal', *The Times*, 6 April 1916. Alexander's statement provides not only an example of his early Yugoslavism, but also an insight into his understanding of Yugoslav nationhood. Following the proclamation of the royal dictatorship in January 1929, Alexander tried to impose 'integral' Yugoslavism from above. Like in 1916, he (and other 'integral' Yugoslavs) argued in the post-1929 period that Serbs, Croats and Slovenes belonged to a single, ethnic nation, which had been divided for centuries by foreign rule.

16 For more on the Yugoslav Committee, its relationship with Pašić's government, and its precarious international position, see Gale Stokes, 'The Role of the Yugoslav Committee in the Formation of Yugoslavia', in Dimitrije Djordjević (ed.), *The Creation of Yugoslavia, 1914-1918*, Santa Barbara, CA, 1980, 51-67.

was no longer functioning'.[17] It unquestionably weakened the Committee's position vis-à-vis the Serbian government and those South Slav leaders leaders who remained in Austria-Hungary.

The year 1917 proved to be particularly eventful. In February, a spontaneous uprising against the occupying forces broke out in the Serbian region of Toplica, only to be brutally suppressed the following month.[18] In May, the Habsburg South Slavs pushed for more autonomy within the Empire. During the spring a three-sided power struggle between Prince Regent Alexander and a group of officers loyal to him (known as the 'White Hand'), Colonel Apis and the 'Black Hand', and Pašić's Radicals came to a head. The 'Black Hand' was accused of conspiring against the government and even of plotting the assassination of the Prince Regent. Apis and two other members of the secret organisation were executed in June, after a show trial held in Salonika. Although Alexander got rid of a dangerous political opponent, the whole episode destabilised the government, damaged the relationship between Pašić and the Prince Regent, and somewhat marred Serbia's international reputation.[19] In hindsight, it was an early sign of the Prince Regent's autocratic tendencies.[20]

In the international arena, the entry of the United States of America into the war in April and Russia's withdrawal following the November (October O.S.) revolution provided two turning points. President Wilson of the United States championed the small nations' right to self-determination and opposed the policy of secret

---

17 Masaryk and Jovanović cited in Dragoslav Janković, *Jugoslovensko pitanje i Krfska deklaracija 1917. godine*, Belgrade, 1967, 131, and 185n, respectively. Jovanović was nicknamed 'pižon' (Serbian spelling of '*pigeon*' in French) by his Serbian friends while studying in France, because of his elegant dress sense and posture.

18 For more on the uprising see Mitrović, *Srbija*, 356-70.

19 The Independent Radicals and the Progressives resigned from the government in protest. For a detailed analysis of the trial see David MacKenzie, *The 'Black Hand' on Trial: Salonika, 1917*, Boulder, CO., 1995.

20 Mitrović, *Srbija*, 261.

treaties.[21] At the same time Pašić lost a powerful ally in Russia, which had viewed the Yugoslav unification with suspicion and would have probably preferred the creation of an enlarged Serbia instead.[22]

Arguably the most significant event of 1917 was the meeting in June-July between the Serbian government and the Yugoslav Committee on Corfu. They issued a joint declaration, announcing that after the war, Serbs, Croats and Slovenes, 'who are also known by the name of southern Slavs or Yugoslavs', would unite in one state, 'a constitutional, democratic, and Parliamentary Monarchy, under the [Serbian] Karageorgevitch Dynasty', which would be named 'the Kingdom of Serbs, Croats and Slovenes'.[23] The future state was thus predestined to become a monarchy, under the Serbian dynasty, even before it was created and before such vital decisions could be tested by democratic means.

In a debate with Pašić's Radicals in the mid-1920s, Trumbić argued that on Corfu he had resolutely rejected centralism.[24] However, he had also expressed reservations about federalism, stating during the Corfu meeting that, while in favour of wide regional autonomies, 'I do not have any illusions in respect to federal system of government, because I cannot see how it would benefit the progress of our national development.'[25] Most members of the Yugoslav Committee supported Trumbić and the concept of a unitary decentralised state, although some supported the Serbian centralist argument.[26] Therefore, although both sides formally rejected federalism, centralism was

---

21   As did Vladimir Ilich Lenin, though for different ideological reasons.

22   See Michael Boro Petrovich, 'Russia's Role in the Creation of the Yugoslav State, 1914-1918', in Djordjević (ed.), *The Creation of Yugoslavia*, 73-94.

23   For a detailed analysis of the Corfu Declaration, see Janković, *Jugoslovensko pitanje*, 189-207, 288-98. The text of the Declaration in English is published in *Yugoslavia through Documents: From its Creation to its Dissolution* (compiled by Snežana Trifunovska), Dordrecht, 1994, 141-2.

24   Ivo Banac, *The National Question in Yugoslavia: Origins, History, Politics*, Ithaca, NY, 1994, 124.

25   Janković, *Jugoslovensko pitanje*, 236.

26   Ibid., 237-40.

not its universally accepted alternative. Those opposed to centralism argued for a compromise solution, a system of government that was neither centralist nor federalist, but they did not fully elaborate what that would involve.

The Corfu statesmen failed to specify whether the future state should be a centralised or a decentralised one, and are often blamed by historians for this failure. After the unification the debate on what form of government was best for the country would be renewed. The centralist argument would eventually win, but only just; this, in turn, led to a long crisis, which plagued the interwar Yugoslav state throughout its existence. However, the differences at the Corfu meeting were less pronounced than has been subsequently assumed. It may be argued that both the centralists and anti-centralists left the conference believing that although the future system of government had not been decided, their arguments had effectively won.[27] Both sides agreed that the future state would be a monarchy, with the Serbian Karadjordjević dynasty at its helm. That the Serbs, Croats and Slovenes belonged to the same ethnic group was not even questioned. They were considered 'tribes' (*plemena*) of a single, 'trinominal nation' (*troimeni narod*).[28] The 'Serbo-Croat-Slovene' nation was also referred to as the 'Yugoslav' nation, or, in the jargon of the day, 'race', and occasionally even as a single 'tribe' (*jugoslovensko pleme* or *srpsko-hrvatsko-slovenačko pleme*), by advocates of a South Slav union.

Even before the war both opponents and proponents of Yugoslav unification regarded Serbs and Croats as a single nation. For instance, the 1910 Austro-Hungarian population census included among the Empire's nationalities 'Serbo-Croats'. The foremost British expert on South Slav history (and later a close supporter of the Yugoslav Committee), R.W. Seton-Watson, wrote in 1911 that Serbs and

---

27 Ibid., 244.

28 Ibid., 221-2. *Narod* in Serbo-Croat also means 'people'. Another Serbo-Croat word for nation, *nacija*, was used less frequently at the time. Bosnian Muslims were believed to differ from Serbs and Croats in religion only, while Eastern Orthodox Montenegrins and Macedonians were considered members of the Serbian 'tribe', although very few of the latter actually felt Serbian.

Croats belonged to one, Yugoslav, 'race' which would eventually unite, just like the Italian and German 'races' had done in the nineteenth century.[29] In September 1914, three months before the Niš Declaration, Seton-Watson praised *The Times* for its writing about 'our gallant Servian allies'. 'It is high time that the splendid qualities of the Serbo-Croat race should be more widely realized among us', he wrote, adding:

But it is not enough for us to consider Servia. The Southern Slav question as a whole is one of the most vital issues raised by this war; and the day is already drawing near when, in conjunction with our friends in Russia, we must endeavour to ensure its lasting solution. The whole future of the Serb, Croat, Slovene race is at stake. The movement for unity among the three kindred peoples has rapidly gathered strength during the last five years, and nothing can arrest its progress.[30]

Ironically perhaps, given the obstacle Italy posed to the creation of a Yugoslav state, the Yugoslav unification movement was often compared to the Italian one. Another prominent British historian, G.M. Trevelyan, recalled in the same newspaper his visit to Serbia before the war. Trevelyan had encountered young men who spoke of Serbia as a new Piedmont and saw books on the Italian *Risorgimento* displayed in Belgrade shops as well as 'on the table in the waiting room of their Foreign Office'. 'Servia is indeed now engaged in a war of liberation similar to that undertaken by Piedmont for the other Italian provinces.' wrote Trevelyan. 'And Russia is playing the part of Napoleon III.'[31]

---

29 R.W. Seton-Watson, *The Southern Slav Question and the Habsburg Monarchy*, London, 1911, 336.

30 'Southern Slav Patriotism', letter of R.W. Seton-Watson to the editor, *The Times*, 16 September 1914. Seton-Watson continued to regard Serbs and Croats (and sometimes Slovenes as well) as one nation in his later writings; see for instance his article 'The Background of the Jugoslav Dictatorship', *Slavonic Review*, vol. 10, no. 29, December 1931, 363-76.

31 'Aims of a Small Nation', letter of G.M. Trevelyan to the editor, *The Times*, 18 September 1914. Giuseppe Garibaldi and Italian revolutionaries provided inspiration to both Yugoslav and Serbian national movements. Mihajlo Pupin, the American scientist of Serb origin, remembered how in his Serbian village

The Slovenes were not regarded as identical to Serbs and Croats, chiefly because of their separate language, but during this period many Slovenes saw themselves—and were seen by others—as part of the Yugoslav nation.[32] Thus even those with a deep knowledge of South Slav affairs, such as Seton-Watson, in the passage quoted above, referred to both Serb-Croat and Serb-Croat-Slovene national unity. South Slav leaders sometimes overemphasised the unity of the three 'tribes', perhaps aware of the support in the United States for the principle of national self-determination. They often referred to Serb-Croat-Slovene linguistic unity, even though they must have known that Slovene was a separate language from Serbo-Croat.[33]

When the war broke out, Habsburg Yugoslavs had little choice but to declare their loyalty to the Monarchy. Anti-Serb riots following the Sarajevo assassination created an atmosphere of hostility not just against the Serbs but also against pro-Yugoslav Croats and Slovenes. However, as the war entered its later stages, things began to change. In 1917 South Slav members of the Vienna *Reichsrat* formed their own parliamentary group—the Yugoslav Club—just like Czech and Polish deputies had previously done.[34] On 30 May 1917 the Club, under the chairmanship of Anton Korošec, leader of the Slovene People's Party (and in the interwar period one of the

---

in southern Hungary (present-day Vojvodina) Garibaldi was known as 'the Karageorge of Italy'. The Pupins' living room was adorned, in addition to the icon of the family's patron saint, by pictures of Karadjordje (archaic spelling Karageorge, the leader of the First Serbian Uprising against the Ottomans in 1804-1813), the Russian Tsar, and Garibaldi. Pupin, *From Immigrant to Inventor*, New York, 1960 (first published in 1922), 8.

32 Mitja Velikonja, 'Slovenia's Yugoslav Century' in Djokić (ed.), *Yugoslavism*, 84-99, 86.

33 Janković, *Jugoslovensko pitanje*, 227-8. Nevertheless, the language was officially called Serbo-Croat-Slovene throughout the interwar period.

34 The most detailed and useful narrative of South Slav politics in the Habsburg Monarchy during the war, which concentrates on Serb-Croat relations and contains numerous quotations of primary sources, is Bogdan Krizman, *Hrvatska u Prvom svjetskom ratu: Hrvatsko-srpski politički odnosi*, Zagreb, 1989.

most influential figures on the Yugoslav political scene), issued a declaration, demanding,

On the basis of the principle of nationality and of the historical rights of the Croatian State, the unification of all those territories in the Monarchy inhabited by Croats, Slovenes, and Serbs into an independent and democratic state, free from domination by any foreign nation, under the sceptre of the dynasty of Habsburg and Lorraine.[35]

The May Declaration and the Corfu Declaration therefore differed in one crucial element: while the latter called for an independent Yugoslavia, the former envisaged the unification of Habsburg South Slavs *within* the Empire, partly on the basis of the Croat state right.[36] What the two declarations had in common was their reference to the principle of national self-determination, at the time championed by the United States.[37] The US rejected the politics of secret treaties and promoted the right to national self-determination, which, as it turned out, favoured Yugoslav unification.[38]

The declaration by the Yugoslav Club was warmly received in Croatia's *sabor* (diet). Ante Pavelić, a leading member of the Croat-Serb Coalition,[39] enthusiastically placed the declaration in the wider context of a Europe awakened by 'the democratic spirit of the great and enlightened Russia'.[40] The importance of the May Declaration lay not only in that it spread the pro-Yugoslav action within the

---

35 'Deklaracija Jugoslovenskoga kluba (Beč, 30. maja 1917.)', *Dokumenti*, 94.

36 An ideology which emphasised the continued existence of Croatian statehood on the basis of legal documents and the sabor. See Mirjana Gross, *Povijest pravaške ideologije*, Zagreb, 1973.

37 For an argument that the two declarations were not as mutually exclusive as is often believed see K. St. Pavlowitch, 'The First World War', 34.

38 This is convincingly argued in Mitrović, 'The Yugoslav Question', 46.

39 A coalition of the main Croat and Habsburg Serb political parties which advocated the 'national oneness' of Serbs, Croats and Slovenes and their unification into a single state. In 1906 it won the elections for the *sabor*, remaining its largest group until the diet dissolved itself in 1918. Ante Pavelić is not to be confused with the *Ustaša* leader of the same name.

40 Krizman, *Hrvatska u Prvom svjetskom ratu*, 109. Pavelić was, of course, referring to the Russian March (February, O.S.) Revolution.

Monarchy to Slovenia—hitherto regarded by Vienna as generally more loyal than Croatia—but also in that it alarmed the Serbian government and the Yugoslav Committee by showing that the initiative was slowly being taken by the Habsburg Yugoslavs.[41] Therefore, it is possible that the May Declaration accelerated the convention reached on Corfu several weeks later.

By September 1918, when Emperor Karl (who had succeeded Franz Josef in 1916) sent Count István Tisza to the southern parts of the Empire to report on situation on the ground, it was clear the Habsburg control over the South Slav territories could not be maintained for too long. Tisza was shocked by the hostility and anti-Habsburg sentiment he encountered, and yet he told the loyal Croatian General Stjepan Sarkotić that 'Hungary remains strong and will deal with its enemies!'[42]

The events of October and November 1918 took place in quick succession. The Serbian army successfully liberated the country, entering Belgrade on 1 November, expelling the last enemy soldiers two days later. On 8 October, Habsburg Yugoslavs formed the National Council—a *de facto* government based in Zagreb. Korošec was elected its president, while Pavelić and Svetozar Pribićević, the leading Croat and Serb in the Croat-Serb coalition, respectively, became its vice-presidents. On 29 October Croatia-Slavonia and Dalmatia declared the formation and independence of 'the unified national sovereign State of Slovenes, Croats, and Serbs on the whole ethnographic territory of that nation.'[43] The *ban* (governor) of Croatia Antun Mihalovich proclaimed that there was no longer need

---

41   K. St. Pavlowitch, 'The First World War', 33. In addition to Korošec, the Yugoslav Club was made up of another 22 Slovenes, 12 Croats and 2 Serbs. However, the two Serbs were not among the signatories of the May Declaration, for unclear reasons. Mitrović, *Srbija*, 432.

42   Krizman, *Hrvatska u Prvom svjetskom ratu*, 261; K. St. Pavlowitch, 'The First World War', 35.

43   Jovanović, *Ustavno pravo*, 34. The term 'ethnographic' (*etnografski*), often used at the time, was meant to emphasise the ethnic and territorial unity of the Serb-Croat-Slovene nation.

for the *sabor* to exist, as there was no more Croatia. The sequence of events illustrates well the legalistic way of thinking characteristic of the Habsburg tradition, which was not abandoned even during the revolutionary changes taking place in the disintegrating Empire.

Although some Croats tend to point out that it was only after they entered the union with Belgrade that Croatia lost its statehood, apparently preserved despite the *Pacta Conventa* with Hungary of 1102 and the incorporation into Austria in 1526-7, the Croatian *sabor* in fact dissolved itself, on its own will, more than a month before a united Yugoslavia was proclaimed. Serbia sacrificed its sovereignty upon entering the Kingdom of Serbs, Croats, and Slovenes on 1 December 1918, as did Montenegro by uniting with Serbia a week previously. But so did the historic Croatia, by giving up symbols of its medieval statehood upon entering the short-lived State of Slovenes, Croats, and Serbs on 29 October 1918.[44]

The act of 29 October was part of the same process which led to the proclamation of the union in Belgrade on 1 December. The State of Slovenes, Croats, and Serbs was in that sense a 'temporary' Yugoslavia, until the 'real' one, which would include Serbia and Montenegro, could be proclaimed. This point would be made in the National Council's address to the Prince Regent of Serbia, on 1 December 1918.

The leaders of the three organisations representing South Slavs—the Serbian government, the National Council and the Yugoslav Committee—met in Geneva in early November 1918, to discuss the terms of unification. The aim of the meeting, which was also attended by representatives of Serbia's opposition, was to produce

---

44 As Slobodan Jovanović explains: 'In the new state, the Croatian *sabor* could not exercise executive power; that is why at the same session [of 29 October]... the *sabor* proclaimed that it "recognises the supreme authority of the National Council of Slovenes, Croats, and Serbs." The *ban* [Mihalovich] declared, in the name of the Croatian government, that he completely accepted the position of the Croatian *sabor* and was therefore handing over executive power to the National Council. Thus, by the free will of the Croatian *sabor* and the Croatian *ban*, an independent Croatian state ceased to exist, in order for a new state of Austro-Hungarian Yugoslavs to be created.' *Ustavno pravo*, 34.

a declaration on Yugoslav unification to be presented to the Entente powers, but differences immediately emerged. While Pašić believed that Serbia was best placed to advocate the Yugoslav aim and should therefore play a leading role, representatives of the National Council argued that the State of Slovenes, Croats, and Serbs should be Serbia's equal partner. They were supported by the Yugoslav Committee and by the Serbian opposition, which apparently regarded Pašić as a greater threat than Croat-Slovene dualistic designs for the new state. Outnumbered, the Serbian Prime Minister reluctantly backed down. On 8 November he officially recognised the State of Slovenes, Croats, and Serbs, calling on the Entente to follow his example, and the following day a joint declaration was issued.[45]

The Geneva Declaration stipulated that the existing institutions of Serbia and the State of Slovenes, Croats, and Serbs should remain until a Constituent Assembly was formed, and envisaged a joint interim government. However, the Declaration came to nothing. The Serbian government on Corfu refused to ratify it after Pašić falsely claimed that Prince Regent Alexander opposed it too. There were dissenting voices in Zagreb, as well, where Pribićević in particular was critical of the Declaration. To speculate how different Yugoslavia's history might have been if the Declaration had been implemented would mean entering the realm of virtual history. What is beyond doubt is that as a result of the ultimate failure of the Geneva talks, over the next two weeks the relationship between Serbia and the State of Slovenes, Croats and Serbs was cold and tense.[46]

This was the context in which on 23 November 1918 the central committee (*središni odbor*) of the National Council convened to discuss unification with Serbia.

---

45 'Recognition of the National Council in Zagreb by the Royal Serbian Government', Geneva, 8 November 1918, *Yugoslavia through Documents*, 148-9. For the text of the Declaration in English see 'Geneva Declaration', Geneva 9 November 1918, ibid. 149-50. Dragoslav Janković provides a detailed discussion of the Geneva meeting in 'Ženevska konferencija o stvaranju jugoslovenske zajednice 1918. godine', *Istorija XX veka. Zbornik radova*, vol. V, 1964, 225-62.
46 Jovanović, *Ustavno pravo*, 36.

The November Session of the National Council

The session opened with a discussion about six proposals *for* unification submitted to the National Council. The most detailed was the proposal by the 'Provincial government of Dalmatia', authored by Josip Smodlaka and Ivo Krstelj. It stated that the 'vital interests of our [Serb-Croat-Slovene] nation' demanded immediate unification, 'especially because of [the need to organize] a defence against Italy and to [secure] order in the country'.[47] The provisional administration of the new state was to be entrusted to the King of Serbia,[48] an interim government and an interim parliament. The interim parliament would be based in Sarajevo and would be made up of all deputies from the National Council, 50 representatives of Serbia elected by the Serbian parliament, and five representatives from each of the Yugoslav Committee and Montenegro.[49] Similar proposals—that an *immediate* unification with Serbia, on the basis of the 1917 Corfu Declaration, be carried out—were issued by politicians grouped around three other Dalmatian Croat leaders: Edo Lukinić, Grga Andjelinović and Ante Tresić-Pavičić.[50]

---

47 'Sjednica Narodnog Vijeća od 23. novembra 1918: a) Predlog zemaljske vlade za Dalmaciju (Dr. Ivo Krstelj and Dr. Josip Smodlaka)', *Dokumenti*, 268.

48 This would in practice mean Prince Regent Alexander.

49 *Dokumenti*, 268-9; Horvat, *Politička povijest*, 121-2. It was not elaborated why Sarajevo was suggested as the seat of the interim government, but it was almost certainly in order to avoid rivalry between Belgrade and Zagreb and perhaps also to demonstrate the Dalmatians' neutral position vis-à-vis the Serbian and Croatian capitals. Sarajevo was the geographical centre of the new state, and the capital of Bosnia-Herzegovina, over which both Croats and Serbs claimed supremacy. By proposing Sarajevo for a Yugoslav administrative centre and possibly a future capital, the Dalmatians may have hoped to stress Serb-Croat unity. Interestingly, the Democratic Party (initially called the Democratic Union) was founded in Sarajevo, in February 1919, even though the majority of its founding members came from Belgrade, Zagreb and Ljubljana. How different might Yugoslavia's history have been had Sarajevo been the capital city?

50 'b) Predlog dra Lukinića i drugova', 'c) Predlog dra Andjelinovića i drugova', and 'e) Predlog dra. A. Tresića-Pavičića', *Dokumenti*, 270-71.

Another proposal was submitted by the Social-Democratic Party of Croatia-Slavonia, a former member of the Croat-Serb Coalition, which supported in principle the proposal of the 'Provincial government of Dalmatia'. However, 'in agreement with the comrades in Serbia', the Social-Democrats called for the creation of a Yugoslav republic, at least during the provisional period, until a more lasting solution was agreed.[51]

The small Croatian Peasant People's Party (HSPS) warned against a hasty unification. Its leader, Stjepan Radić, believed that a federal state best suited the 'ethnographically unified, [but divided by] different historical, cultural, and political developments...nation of Slovenes, Croats and Serbs'.[52] Radić argued that unification should be based on the Croat state right ideology and on the right of nations to self-determination. Because the creation of the State of Slovenes, Croats, and Serbs defied Hungarian historic and state rights, Croat state right could not provide legitimacy for the new state without making its architects self-contradictory. What the Croat Peasants' leader was proposing had elements of both the failed Geneva agreement and the 1917 May Declaration. According to Radić, the future state should be jointly run by a three-member regency consisting of the Prince Regent of Serbia, the *ban* of Croatia and the president of the Slovenian assembly. The regency would appoint a federal government made up of only three ministries: foreign affairs, defence and 'people's nourishment'. All other affairs should be left to regional administrations. Radić therefore envisaged Yugoslavia as a union of states, which he believed would best protect Serb, Croat and Slovene 'historical-national individualities', but did not elaborate on the issue of borders between the provinces.[53]

---

51 'f) Predlog socijalista', *Dokumenti*, 271-2. There were prominent Serb republicans other than Social-Democrats, mostly of liberal political orientation. See Ljubomir Stojanović, *Nekolike misli o našem novom državnom uredjenju*, Belgrade, 1919, and Trgovčević, 'South Slav Intellectuals'.

52 'd) Predlog Stjepana Radića', *Dokumenti*, 271.

53 'd) Predlog Stjepana Radića', *Dokumenti*, 271. Radić proposed 'autonomous state governments' for Serbia, Croatia, Slovenia and Montenegro and, somewhat

After a Serbian deputy from Vojvodina threatened the 'amputation' (*amputacija*) of Srem, Bačka and Banat (present-day Vojvodina) and an immediate unification with Serbia if Radić's proposal was accepted, many deputies felt a sense of unease.[54] Ivan Ribar of the Croat-Serb Coalition was far more concerned about the foreign threat than about Serb hegemony.[55] Pavelić even threatened to resign as vice-president of the National Council if similar rhetoric continued. The next few speakers mostly tried to calm down the atmosphere, emphasising their support for unification with Serbia. Smodlaka then warned that there was a serious danger of an Italian invasion of Dalmatia and appealed to all to stop arguing and finally reach a consensus. Although driven by different motives from Miladinović, Smodlaka issued a similar warning: 'If you gentlemen are not going to go to Belgrade, my [Dalmatian] comrades and I will go without you and will bring state unity to life', by uniting Dalmatia with Ser-

---

lower in the hierarchy, 'provincial governments' for Bosnia-Herzegovina, Dalmatia and Vojvodina. The regency would be responsible for the formation of a federal parliament which would consist of ten representatives from each of Serbia, Croatia-Slavonia and Slovenia, four from Bosnia-Herzegovina, and two from each of Montenegro, Dalmatia, Vojvodina and Istria. Independently of Radić, some Serbian intellectuals had at the time propagated the 'United States of Yugoslavia', organised as a federal republic. Trgovčević, 'South Slav Intellectuals', 234-5.

54 Horvat, *Politička povijest*, 125. The Serbian deputy was Žarko Miladinović, of the Independent Serbian National Radical Party, which had a power base in Vojvodina. They should not be confused with Serbia's Independent Radical Party (the so-called Independent Radicals), a group of younger, liberal-minded politicians who broke away in 1901 from Nikola Pašić's People's Radical Party; they were to form, together with members of the Croat-Serb Coalition and liberal groups from Slovenia, Serbia, Bosnia and other parts of the country, the Democratic Party in 1919-20. Vojvodina's Independent Radicals would join Pašić's Radicals after the unification.

55 During the interwar period Ivan Ribar (1881-1968) was a member of the Democratic Party and one of only a few leading Croat members of the party who did not leave in 1924 to join Svetozar Pribićević's Independent Democrats. He was the president of the Yugoslav Parliament in the early years of both the kingdom and the post-1945 socialist republic (during the Second World War Ribar joined Tito's Partisans, as did his two sons, who were both killed in the war).

bia.[56] Smodlaka's speech had a powerful and possibly decisive effect on the unification-leaning National Council. It was finally decided, on Smodlaka's suggestion, that seven members of the central committee should draft an address to Serbia's leadership, proclaiming the unification of Habsburg South Slav territories with Serbia. A compromise proposal was drafted quickly and was presented to the central committee in the evening of 24 November 1918.[57]

It was decided that a delegation of 28 members of the National Council would travel to Belgrade to proclaim the unification jointly with Serbia's leaders. An interim government and parliament should be formed as soon as possible by members of the National Council, the Serbian and Montenegrin governments, and the Yugoslav Committee. A constituent assembly must be convened within six months of the formal end of the war. Its delegates would draft a Constitution, decide whether the new state would be a monarchy or a republic, a centralised or decentralised state, and choose state symbols. In the meantime the head of state would be the King of Serbia. The final form of government would be determined by a national assembly, with two thirds of the vote being the necessary majority.[58]

The central committee of the National Council voted in favour of the proposal, but not before another heated debate, which took place the same evening. Radić criticised the proposal, repeating his federalist argument. Historians of Yugoslavia tend to consider Radić's speech as prophetic, and given the subsequent events it is hard to

---

56 Horvat, *Politička povijest*, 126.

57 The following deputies were elected to the committee: Ante Pavelić, Svetozar Pribićević, Izidor Cankar, Josip Smodlaka, Vilim Bukšeg, Hamid Svrzo and Mate Drinković. *Dokumenti*, 274. Although all members of the committee had a Yugoslav identity, Pavelić, Smodlaka and Drinković were Croats, Cankar and Bukšeg Slovenes, Svrzo was a Bosnian Muslim, and Pribićević a Serb.

58 *Dokumenti*, 274-6. The delegation was representative of all 'tribes' and regions, and included Izidor Cankar, Mate Drinković, Halid Hrasnica, Vitomir Korać, Anton Korošec, Albert Kramer, Matko Laginja, Ivan Lorković, Edo Lukinić, Ante Pavelić, Dušan Popović, Svetozar Pribićević, Stjepan Radić, Josip Smodlaka, Hamid Svrzo, Ante Tresić-Pavičić, and Ante Trumbić.

argue against this verdict.[59] The speech provided an early insight into Radić's understanding of Yugoslavism. Moreover, it clearly revealed that he was primarily concerned with Croatia, rather than with Yugoslavia as a whole. The speech betrayed an able and emotional speaker, who did not hesitate to hurl verbal abuse at his political opponents. Finally, it showed another of Radić's trade marks—his unpredictability and self-contradiction.

Radić criticised all previous speakers for failing to consider Croatian interests, and for 'competing to erase and destroy Croatia'.[60] He was in favour of an agreement with Serbia, but was against Serbia dominating the new state. Less than a month previously, Radić had enthusiastically supported the creation of the State of Slovenes, Croats, and Serbs and had talked of the 'unification and liberation of the whole of our *nation* of Slovenes, Croats and Serbs'.[61] In his proposal *for* unification with Serbia, presented on 23 November, he talked about '*ethnographically unified*, [but divided by] different historical, cultural, and political developments...*the nation* of Slovenes, Croats, and Serbs'.[62] The following day, Radić reminded his audience that he had always, 'publicly and openly, firmly and fearlessly defended *our national oneness—oneness of all South Slavs*, but above all of Croats and Serbs—even then, twenty and more years ago, when

---

59   However, Josip Horvat, a member of the Croatian Peasant Party, did not reproduce Radić's speech of 24 November in his book, although the book contains numerous other speeches and documents, including Radić's speech of 29 October, when the State of Slovenes, Croats and Serbs was proclaimed. Instead, Horvat merely provides a brief summary of the speech (Horvat, *Politička povijest*, 128-9). Could this be because Radić's speech was not considered so significant by contemporary observers such as Horvat, and only gained in significance when analysed retrospectively?

60   Stjepan Radić, 'Govor na noćnoj sudbonosnoj sjednici Narodnoga vijeća dana 24. studenoga 1918.', Stjepan Radić, *Politički spisi: Autobiografija, članci, govori, rasprave*, Zagreb, 1971 (compiled by Zvonimir Kulundžić), 323-35, 323.

61   Stjepan Radić, 'Posljednji govor u Hrvatskom Saboru dana 29. listopada 1918.', ibid, 310-15, 314 (emphasis added by D. Dj.).

62   'd) Predlog Stjepana Radića', *Dokumenti*, 271 (emphasis added by D. Dj.).

doing so carried personal risks, when one could have easily ended up in prison.'[63] However, towards the end of the same speech he declared that 'we are three brothers, Croat, Slovene and Serb, *but we are not one.*'[64]

Radić's rhetoric should not be understood as a criticism of Serbs and Serbia only. He did not oppose the unification, but warned against making rushed decisions and criticised the fact that the new state would be a centralised monarchy, instead of his preferred federal republic. As he said in the often quoted part of the speech:

Gentlemen! It is still not too late! *Don't rush like geese into the fog!* Don't form a unified government with the kingdom of Serbia just yet, if for no other reason than because there are no [Serbia's representatives here], except a telegram [of support from Belgrade]. Do not act the way you have intended, because tomorrow you Slovenes, you Serbs from Vojvodina and Bosnia, and you, our Croats from Dalmatia, but above all you, our own Croatian Serbs, may be accused of gathering today to betray the people, and above all to betray Croatia and Croats.[65]

Deputies of the Croat-Serb Coalition regarded Radić as a separatist.[66] Dragutin Hrvoj, one of few Radić's supporters, objected to this equation between unitarism and centralism. 'The German nation was united in a federation. Why couldn't we be united that way, too?' Hrvoj asked, but the question remained unanswered.

The vast majority of deputies, both Croats and Serbs, supported the proposal drafted by the central committee. Mate Drinković, a leading Croat in the Coalition, argued that Croat demands had been more than met, perhaps even at the expense of 'national [Serb-

---

63 'Govor na noćnoj sudbonosnoj sjednici Narodnoga vijeća dana 24. studenoga 1918.', in Radić, *Politički spisi*, 332-3 (emphasis added by D. Dj).

64 Ibid., 334. Emphasis in original.

65 Ibid. Emphasis in original.

66 For instance Dušan Popović, one of the leaders of the Coalition, accused Radić of separatism. It is telling that Popović used the term 'separatist', even though Yugoslavia was not yet created. Ironically, both Radić and Popović had indeed been separatists, from the point of view of Vienna and Budapest.

Croat-Slovene] principles'. Drinković's words caught the prevailing mood in the National Council:

We are forming neither a Greater Serbia, nor a Greater Croatia, nor a Greater Slovenia, but a large, strong and powerful Yugoslav state. However, we should admit loudly that the Serbian kingdom is a victor in this war, whereas we are on the defeated side. Common sense and honesty demand every patriot today to support national and state unity [of Serbs, Croats, and Slovenes].[67]

At the end of the session, the compromise proposal was overwhelmingly accepted, even by the Social Democrats, who were satisfied by the inclusion of a stipulation leaving the final form of government open. Only Radić and Hrvoj voted against.[68] Radić later argued that the proposal for the unification would have been rejected had it been presented to all members of the National Council, rather than just its central committee.[69] However, this seems unlikely, given the dominance of the Croat-Serb Coalition in the National Council and the pressure by the Dalmatian politicians for immediate unification. The delegation boarded the train to Belgrade in the morning of 27 November, joined by a small group of financial experts, but without Radić, who refused to go.

In spite of Radić's boycott and despite the intense debate of the last few days, the delegation travelled to Belgrade safe in the knowledge that the National Council was overwhelmingly in favour of unification. They could not have known, however, that during the session of 23-24 November they had raised some of the issues that would form the essence of the political debate during the 1920s and 1930s. Most of these would revolve around one crucial question: what should be the extent of central power vis-à-vis regional autonomies? As in the National Council in November 1918, political divisions in

---

67 Cited in Horvat, *Politička povijest*, 129. Drinković was one of several prominent Croats who later supported King Alexander's dictatorship, and was a minister in several post-1929 governments.

68 *Dokumenti*, 278.

69 Branislav Gligorijević, *Parlament i političke stranke u Jugoslaviji, 1919-1929*, Belgrade, 1979, 275.

the interwar Yugoslavia were complex and did not always reflect the Serb-Croat divide.

The unification

Upon its arrival in Serbia, which had previously united with Montenegro on 26 November, the delegation was received by Stojan Protić, the most senior member of the Serbian government then present in Belgrade.[70] Protić objected to the text of the address because it did not state unconditionally that the new state would be a monarchy. His fears were unfounded. According to a contemporary observer, 'Men from the delegation of the National Council were genuinely, both for emotional and rational reasons, in favour of the monarchy, as the only possible form [of government] of the future state.'[71] Nevertheless, the address was slightly rewritten by Pribićević, Pavelić and Smodlaka to omit any reference to a republic.

In the evening of 1 December, Pavelić read the address in front of Prince Regent Alexander. He began by praising the role of the Serbian army in creating the conditions necessary for unification, before declaring the National Council's decision to unite the State of Slovenes, Croats, and Serbs with Serbia. The address noted the temporary nature of the State of Slovenes, Croats, and Serbs, the creation of which was only a first step towards pan-Yugoslav unification:

We are happy to be able to greet Your Royal Highness, in the name of the National Council of the Slovenes, Croats and Serbs, in the capital of liberated Serbia, as the Commander-in-Chief of the victorious *national* Army, which in the common struggle side by side with the Armies of our mighty

---

70 Thus, strictly speaking, Montenegro entered the Yugoslav state as part of Serbia. At the same session when it decided to unite with Serbia, the overwhelmingly pro-Belgrade Montenegrin assembly overthrew King Nicholas and the Petrović dynasty. 'Odluka Podgoričke skupštine', Podgorica, 26 (13 O.S.) November 1918, *Dokumenti*, 258-61, 260. Serbian municipalities in Bosnia and Vojvodina also voted for unification with Serbia in late November, putting additional pressure on the National Council in Zagreb.

71 Horvat, *Politička povijest*, 132. Horvat knew personally most if not all members of the delegation.

Allies has created the conditions necessary for the accomplishment of the great ideal of our *national* union. The Slovenes, Croats and Serbs, who have effected a revolution on the territory of the former Austro-Hungarian Monarchy, have *temporarily* constituted themselves [as] an independent *national* State. Imbued with the idea of national unity and on the strength of the great principles of democracy which demand that every people should have the right to determine its own destiny, they have declared already in the proclamation of the National Council on October 19, that they wish and are determined to unite with Serbia and Montenegro in one joint *national* State of the Serbs, Croats and Slovenes, [...] to embrace all the continuous ethnographic territory of the Southern Slavs.[72]

The address also stated 'that the power of the Sovereign throughout the whole territory of the now united State shall be vested in His Majesty King Peter, respectively in Your Royal Highness in his stead as Prince Regent.'[73] It outlined the delegation's proposal for the creation of interim institutions, before issuing a plea to the Serbian Prince Regent to defend Dalmatia from Italy, and to make sure that all 'ethnographic territories' of the Yugoslav nation be included in the new state. The address thus revealed the desperate situation in which the State of Slovenes, Croats, and Serbs found itself and its sense of dependency on Serbia:

With complete confidence we cherish the hope that your Royal Highness together with our whole nation will strive that in the end [...] frontiers of our state be drawn in such a manner as to agree with our ethnographic boundaries, in accordance with the principles of national self-determination as proclaimed by President Wilson of the United States of America [...] and by all the Entente Powers.[74]

Replying to the invitation, Alexander promised to be 'King only of the free citizens of the *State* of Serbs, Croats and Slovenes', and to 'always remain faithful to constitutional, parliamentary and broad

---

72 'Proclamation of the Kingdom of Serbs, Croats and Slovenes', Belgrade, 1 December 1918, *Yugoslavia through Documents*, 157-60, 157. Emphasis added by D. Dj.

73 Ibid., 157.

74 Ibid., 158.

democratic principles, based on universal suffrage. [...] May our *Kingdom* of Serbs, Croats and Slovenes be ever happy and glorious!'[75] Therefore, he made it clear that so far as he was concerned, Yugoslavia would be a kingdom, before the provisional institutions could make a decision on the form of government. As already indicated, the opposition to monarchy was not strong and it was almost certain that after an interim period of state formation, the Serb-Croat-Slovene union would remain a kingdom under the Karadjordjević dynasty. However, the way Alexander imposed his vision of Yugoslavia did not bode well for the future of South Slav democracy.

Quite apart from Alexander's autocratic tendencies, admittedly more obvious with the benefit of hindsight, the emerging Yugoslav state faced a number of obstacles. Serbia in particular had been devastated by the war. Its enormous human losses—around 1 million dead—often overshadow a destroyed infrastructure and crippled economy.[76] The area of what became the Kingdom of Serbs, Croats, and Slovenes had not only been among the poorest and least indus-

---

75 Ibid., 160. Emphasis added by D. Dj.

76 Historian Andrej Mitrović estimates that nearly 370,000 Serbian soldiers, more than half the number of those mobilised (707,000), were killed or died of disease or hunger during the war, while some 600,000 civilians lost their lives. (Mitrović, *Srbija*, 509). When the war broke out Serbia's population was around 4.5 million, around 3 million of whom lived on the territory of pre-1912 Serbia. Another historian, John Lampe, estimates that 150,000 Serbs died of a typhus epidemic during the war, and that overall one half of Serbia's male population aged 18 to 55 perished between 1914 and 1918. Around 8 million South Slavs living in Austria-Hungary lost a similar number of soldiers as Serbia (many of them fighting the Serbian army). John Lampe, *Yugoslavia as History: Twice There was a Country*, Cambridge, 2nd ed., 2000, 109. To put these figures in a wider context, Niall Ferguson (*The Pity of War: Explaining World War I*, London, 1998, 295) estimates that Russia lost over 1.8 million men, France nearly 1.4 million, Britain 723,000 (not counting nearly 200,000 dead soldiers from the British Empire), Romania 250,000, and the USA 114,000. In total, the Allies lost over 5.4 million men (Ferguson's estimate for Serbia is 278,000 dead soldiers). As for the Central Powers, Germany lost just over 2 million men, Austria-Hungary 1.1 million, while Bulgaria lost 88,000 soldiers. Total loss for the Central Powers was just over 4 million men. For a brief summary of economic consequences of the war in Serbia see Lampe, *Yugoslavia as History*, 109-10.

trialised in Europe, but in some cases its various composing parts had little or no history of mutual trade.[77] The international recognition of the new state would not be achieved for another several months, and even then Italy, Hungary, Bulgaria and Albania would contest Yugoslavia's borders throughout much of the interwar period. Scholars working on former Yugoslavia tend to point out distinct cultures and histories of the peoples which made up the country at the time of the unification as a major (if not *the* major) reason for the country's instability, but there were clearly other, just as serious problems.

If we accept the notion of the 'national oneness'—as many contemporaries did—Yugoslavia was a nation-state, in which the South Slavs formed more than 80 per cent of the country's population.[78] It was not an entirely new state like Czechoslovakia, because its eastern half was made up of the previously independent Kingdoms of Serbia and Montenegro. Although Serbia was in many ways the core of the new state, the Kingdom of Serbs, Croats, and Slovenes was not simply an enlarged pre-war kingdom like Romania, nor was it a restored state like Poland. The historian Joseph Rothschild has argued that 'by virtually every criterion—history, political traditions, socioeconomic standards, legal systems, religion and culture—Yugoslavia was the

---

77 According to Lampe, a leading authority on Balkan economic history, 'barely one percent of Serbia's and Croatia-Slavonia's foreign trade was one with the other.' Lampe, 'The Two Yugoslavias as Economic Unions: Promise and Problems', in Djokić (ed.), *Yugoslavism*, 184.

78 The 1921 census did not distinguish between the South Slavs in terms of ethnicity, but only in terms of religion and language. Statistician Bogoljub Kočović estimates that out of 11,985,000 people living in Yugoslavia in 1921, there were 4,813,000 (40.1 per cent) Serbs (including Montenegrins), 2,797,000 (23.3 per cent) Croats, 1,020,000 (8.5 per cent) Slovenes, 740,000 (6.2 per cent) [Slav] Muslims, and 465,000 (3.9 per cent) Macedonians, or in total 9,835,000 (82 per cent) Yugoslavs. (Kočović provides round figures). Kočović, *Etnički i demografski razvoj u Jugoslaviji od 1921. do 1991. godine (po svim zvaničnim a u nekim slučajevima i korigovanim popisima)*, Paris, 1998, 2 vols., vol. 2, 332-3. According to the census, there were 5,593,057 (46.7 per cent) Eastern Orthodox, 4,708,657 (39.3 per cent) Roman Catholics and 1,345,271 (11.2 per cent) Muslims, while 8,911,509 (74.4 per cent) people listed Serbo-Croat as their mother tongue and 1,019,997 (8.5 per cent) spoke Slovene.

most complicated of the new states of interwar East Central Europe, being composed of the largest and most varied number of pre-1918 units.[79] Yet, it may be argued that in many respects the Yugoslav kingdom did not stand out in the generally complex mosaic which emerged following the disintegration of Austria-Hungary.

The existence of national, cultural and historical differences between the South Slavs in 1918, and economic and social problems, combined with external pressure, can only partly explain events in interwar Yugoslavia. The country's stability—and instability—rested very much on post-1918 internal political developments, and in particular on Serb-Croat relations.

79 Joseph Rothschild, *East Central Europe between the Two World Wars*, Seattle and London, 1974, 201.

2
THE VOLATILE TWENTIES

The unity of the Yugo-Slav states is a 'fait accompli', and all differences have been wiped away. The new Cabinet in Belgrade comprises representatives of all Serb, Slovene, and Croat parties, including a socialist member. The one party not represented in the Cabinet is that of Mr. Raditch. The party is composed of a few peasants, all Extremists and without any constructive programme. It is merely a small 'bolchevik' movement of no importance and with very few sympathisers. It is a great satisfaction to me that all misunderstandings and petty quarrels between the Yugo-Slav National Council and the Serbian Government died a natural death the moment the main idea of national unity was realized.

Milan Pribićević to R.W. Seton-Watson, January 1919 [1]

Now a number of people, not merely open enemies of the new order, but ordinary intelligent people who follow events as best they can in the daily press, have been asking themselves recently whether such events as the Skupshtina murders of last June or the *coup d'état* of this month are not a proof that Jugoslavia is an artificial structure, foredoomed to failure and wrongly laid in the first instance. My first contention to-night is that this is a complete misapprehension of the facts. What is wrong is not the events of 1918, but those of 1920 onwards.

R.W. Seton-Watson, January 1929 [2]

---

1 Milan Pribicevich [Pribićević] to R.W. Seton-Watson, Zagreb, 24 January 1919, *R.W. Seton-Watson and the Yugoslavs: Correspondence, 1906-1941*, 2 vols, London and Zagreb, 1976, vol. 2, 23.
2 'Jugoslavia and Croatia (Address given on January 29th, 1929)', *Journal of the Royal Institute of International Affairs*, March 1929, 118.

Although Milan Pribićević, the brother of Svetozar,[3] may have rendered the predominant feeling in Zagreb in the weeks after the unification, certainly among supporters of the union, in his letter to Seton-Watson, political events of the first interwar decade would prove him wrong on at least two counts. Differences between the Serbian government and (some) South Slav leaders from the formerly Habsburg territories were not 'wiped away'. The jubilation of the first weeks following the unification was followed by a long period of hangover. Passionate statements and tactless actions by some Yugoslav leaders inflamed the volatile political scene. This was particularly true of Milan's brother Svetozar, the first Yugoslav Minister of the Interior (between 7 December 1918 and 19 February 1920), and Stjepan Radić, the emerging leader of the 'hard' opposition.[4] Not long after the unification the relationship between Belgrade and Zagreb became one of mutual mistrust; by the end of the decade an almost perpetual political crisis would lead to the proclamation of the royal dictatorship. Despite Radić's ill-advised trip to Moscow in 1924, the accusation that the Croatian Republican Peasant Party (HRSS) was Bolshevik was unfounded. Moreover, rather then being 'composed of a few peasants', the HRSS would emerge as the strongest Croatian party after the November 1920 elections.

---

3 Svetozar Pribićević (1875-1936) had three brothers: Valerijan (1870-1941), an Orthodox bishop, shot by Italians at the beginning of the Second World War in Yugoslavia; Milan (1877-1937), a Habsburg officer who defected to Serbia in 1904, from where he campaigned for Yugoslav unification and fought in the Balkan Wars and the First World War as an officer in the Serbian army; and Adam (1880-1957), leader of the Independent Democrats between 1936 and 1938, who committed suicide as an émigré in Canada after the Second World War. Milan retired from the army as a colonel in 1919 in order to devote his life to politics, but eventually became disillusioned with how events in Yugoslavia unfolded. Both Adam and Milan became involved in peasant politics and both settled in Kosovo as colonist farmers in the 1920s.

4 To use Ivo Banac's phrase. Banac distinguishes between 'hard' and 'soft' opposition, which did not boycott the state institutions. See his *The National Question in Yugoslavia: Origins, History, Politics*, Ithaca, NY, 1994 (first published in 1984).

Nevertheless, Milan Pribićević was also correct in two respects. In January 1919 Yugoslavia was a *fait accompli*, formed by the Yugoslavs and not by the Great Powers at the Paris Peace Conference in 1919-20, as is sometimes wrongly claimed. That same conference refused initially to recognise the Kingdom of Serbs, Croats, and Slovenes, referring to its delegation as 'the delegation of the Kingdom of Serbia'.[5] Inside the new country, an attempt was made by Yugoslavia's leaders to have all 'historic provinces' and political groups proportionally represented in the provisional institutions. Whereas ministers in the Provisional Government were selected on the basis of party membership,[6] each 'historic province' was allocated a quota of delegates for the Provisional Parliament.[7] The size of the quotas

---

5 For more on the Yugoslav delegation at the Peace Conference see Andrej Mitrović, 'The Yugoslav Question, the First World War and the Peace Conference, 1914-1920', in Dejan Djokić (ed.), *Yugoslavism: Histories of a Failed Idea*, London and Madison, WI, 2003, 42-56, 45-6.

6 The following parties and coalitions were represented in the Provisional Government: Croat-Serb Coalition (2 ministers), Starčević's Party of Rights (1), Social-Democratic Party (1), Croatian National Union (1), Slovene People's Party (1), Yugoslav Democratic Party (i.e. Slovene liberals, 1), People's Radical Party (3), Independent Radical Party (2), [Serbian] Progressives (1), Independent Radicals (1, a dissident Radical group led by Marko Trifković, not to be confused with the Independent Radical Party), [Bosnian] Muslims (1) and two non-party figures, Ante Trumbić and General Rašić. Gligorijević, *Parlament i političke stranke u Jugoslaviji, 1919-1929*, Belgrade, 1979, 336. Ten ministers were Serbs, four Croats, two Slovenes and one was a Bosnian Muslim.

7 Slovenia was represented by 32 deputies, Croatia-Slavonia, including Rijeka and Medjumurje, by 60, Istria by 4, Dalmatia by 12, Bosnia-Herzegovina by 42, Vojvodina by 24, pre-1912 Serbia by 84, Macedonia and Kosovo (territories added to Serbia after the Balkan Wars) by 24, and Montenegro by 12. Banac, *The National Question*, 381n. At the same time, the Yugoslav delegation to the Peace Conference was headed by Nikola Pašić, a Serb, but his deputy was the Croat Ante Trumbić, Foreign Minister in the Provisional Government and its sole representative in the delegation. The other five members of the delegation were: Milenko Vesnić (Serb), Ivan Žolger (Slovene), Mateja Bošković (Serb), Josip Smodlaka (Croat), and Otokar Ribarž (Slovene). Žolger's inclusion in the delegation raised objections from the Powers, particularly Italy, because he was a Minister without portfolio in the last Austrian government, but the Yugoslavs resisted the pressure to withdraw Žolger from the delegation. Mitrović, 'The

depended on the province's size and 'historic' significance—a decision which was bound to cause controversy.[8] However, the generally recognised leading role of Serbia—an independent kingdom prior to the unification, and a 'hero' and 'victim' of the struggle for 'liberation and unification'—and the Serbs' numerical supremacy (albeit based on a pre-war census) meant that Serbia and Serbs received the most significant posts and had a majority of delegates in the Provisional Parliament.

The gist of the pre-unification debate was transferred to the Provisional Parliament. The argument between centralists and decentralists gradually turned into a Serb-Croat disagreement.[9] Yet, even then the lines of conflict and cooperation were not so clear. On the one hand, it was a dispute between Belgrade, or the pre-war Serbian tradition on the one side, and the former Habsburg territories of the new state on the other side.[10] On the other hand, it was a conflict between different beliefs about what was best for the new country. Protić, the first Prime Minister of the Kingdom of Serbs, Croats, and Slovenes, argued in favour of local autonomies, while Pribićević, a Croatian Serb, was among the staunchest centralists. Protić only became the Prime Minister because Prince Regent Alexander had blocked Pašić's election to the post.[11] This was not only another early

Yugoslav Question', 46. In the years after the unification, Yugoslavs considered Istria as theirs, although it was under the Italian control.

8   See Banac, *The National Question*, 380-81.

9   How a political and constitutional debate came to be perceived as a Serb-Croat conflict is well described in Josip Horvat, *Politička povijest Hrvatske*, 2 vols, Zagreb: August Cesarec, 1990, vol. 1, 158-98. Banac provides a concise analysis of 'The Twenty-one Months of the Interim Parliament' in his *The National Question*, 379-87. See also Gligorijević, *Parlament*, 17-65.

10   As Banac argues: 'Of all the many differences between the political culture of Serbia and of the lands united to it in 1918, those in the area of state institutions were most evident.' *The National Question*, 141.

11   Their relationship was strained since the Salonika trial and the controversy over Pašić's misrepresentation of Alexander's position on the Geneva Declaration.

omen of the future King's undemocratic tendencies, but also a good example of an intra-ethnic (i.e. Serb-Serb) conflict.

Nor were the alliances inside the Provisional Parliament established along Serb-Croat lines. The parliament was dominated by two groups: the Democratic-Socialist Bloc and the Parliamentary Union. The main party within the Bloc was the newly-established Democratic Party (DS).[12] The Democrats were joined by the Social Democratic Party of Croatia-Slavonia and a group of pro-unification Montenegrins.[13] In total, the Bloc had 137 deputies, a majority of whom (114) were members of the Democratic Party. The Parliamentary Union consisted of the People's Radical Party (NRS), the National Club (formed by Croat members of the former Croat-Serb Coalition who did not join the DS), the Yugoslav Club (mostly Korošec's Slovene Clericals) and 11 deputies belonging to two small groups of Serbian liberals. In total it had 130 deputies, with the Radicals as the single largest group with 74 deputies, followed by 26 deputies of the National Club and 19 deputies of the Yugoslav Club.[14]

Two main factors led to the formation of the parliamentary blocs. The first was the conflict between the Democrats and the Radicals over the extent and speed of the agrarian reform, with the former favouring more radical policies. The second was the prewar inter-party rivalry carried over into the new state. Davidović's former Independent Radicals and Pašić's Radicals continued to see each other as major rivals, as did Pribićević's followers and the Vojvodina Radicals, who integrated into the NRS after the unification. Similar rivalry existed between Slovene liberals who joined the DS and the Korošec-led

---

12 For the formation of the Democratic Party see Branislav Gligorijević, *Demokratska stranka i politički odnosi u Kraljevini Srba, Hrvata i Slovenaca*, Belgrade, 1970, 15-56, and *Istorija gradjanskih stranaka u Jugoslaviji*, Belgrade, 1952, 146-50. Banac provides a detailed analysis of ideologies of all the main political parties in *The National Question*, Parts II-IV.

13 Serbian Social-Democrats, like the Croatian Peasants, decided to boycott the Provisional Parliament because they felt they deserved more seats than they were allocated. Gligorijević, *Parlament*, 30.

14 Ibid., 43-8.

Yugoslav Club, and between the two groups from the former Croat-Serb Coalition, one of which integrated into the Democratic Party, while the other formed the National Club.[15] Overall, it could be said the Democrat-Socialist Bloc was a liberal group, while the Parliamentary Union represented a conservative political option. During the period of provisional institutions, the two blocs both spent time in power, but neither was able to form a long-lasting, stable administration. This, too, would be one of the features of Yugoslav politics during the two interwar decades.[16]

The most important debate within the Provisional Parliament concerned the issue of centralism-unitarism.[17] Unitarist Croat and Slovene deputies, who supported 'national oneness' Yugoslavism but opposed centralism, criticised both Democrats and Radicals for confusing the two concepts and using them interchangeably.[18] For Svetozar Pribićević, the Interior Minister throughout much of the formative period, calls for regional autonomy and federalism were tantamount to separatism. Ironically, though one of the leaders of the pre-war Croat-Serb Coalition, he did much to worsen Serb-Croat relations after the war. Stjepan Radić was detained on Pribićević's orders in late March 1919; Hinko Hinković, once of the Yugoslav Committee, was monitored by the police; and several

---

15 Ibid., 43-5.

16 But not just in Yugoslavia. East-Central Europe, as well as most of Europe, underwent a series of political crises in the 1920s and 1930s. For a standard history of interwar East-Central Europe see Joseph Rothschild, *East Central Europe between the Two World Wars*, Seattle and London, 1974 and relevant chapters in Richard Crampton's more recent *Eastern Europe in the Twentieth Century—and After*, London and New York, 2nd edn, 1997.

17 By unitarism I mean the understanding of Yugoslavia as a Yugoslav nation-state, whereby Serbs, Croats and Slovenes were three 'tribes' of one, Yugoslav nation. Centralism, in this context, refers to a political system where decision-making occurs in one centre.

18 Slobodan Jovanović, *Ustavno pravo Kraljevine Srba, Hrvata i Slovenaca*, Belgrade, 1995, 94.

Croat publications were banned, apparently because of their support for 'separatism'.[19]

Pribićević clashed with Serb politicians, too, accusing the Radical Milan Srškić of Serbian nationalism because of his involvement with organisations of *Četnik* veterans in Bosnia, and was generally critical of the Radicals for their cooperation with the National Club. Dismissing Pribićević's criticism that the National Club's policies contained 'seeds of separatism', Protić explained that calls for local autonomies by his party's Croat allies were in fact similar to the Radicals' well-known championing of local 'self-government'.[20] Moreover, Protić warned, Pribićević mistakenly believed that:

The unification and unity of Serbs, Croats and Slovenes must be carried out in such a way that all separate identities, all regional and historic traditions and individualities should merge together! I must say, gentlemen, that this represents an exaggeration dangerous for our national unity, especially in these early days of our new national and state life.[21]

Protić's views notwithstanding, the Radicals would eventually reach a consensus with the Democrats over the issue of centralism. Following the November 1920 elections for a constituent assembly, where the Democrats and the Radicals emerged as the two strongest political parties in the country and formed a coalition government, a centralist Constitution would be voted in. In the aftermath of the First World War, centralised, compact and preferably ethnically homogeneous nation states were generally viewed as more viable than former multinational empires such as Ottoman Turkey and Austria-Hungary. This trend, combined with the Serbs' and some non-Serbs' inclination towards centralism, meant that advocates of a federal

---

19   Hrvoje Matković, *Svetozar Pribićević: Ideolog, stranački vodja, emigrant*, Zagreb, 1995, 86.

20   'Ministar unutrašnih dela i vladina politika. Govor g. Stojana M. Protića na zboru radikalnom od 2. novembra ove godine', in Stojan M. Protić, *Naša spoljna i unutrašnja situacija (Konferencija održana u Klubu beogradskih Radikala 2-X-1919)*, Belgrade, 1920, 29.

21   Ibid., 30.

form of state in Yugoslavia (mostly, but not exclusively, non-Serbs) faced an uphill battle from the start.

Yet, as is often the case with Yugoslavia, things were not so simple. Apart from the Democrats and Radicals, who in the November elections won 92 and 91 parliamentary seats respectively, all other major parties were opposed to centralism. The Communists came third with 51 seats, closely followed by Radić's party, which secured one seat less. Korošec's Slovene People's Party and Mehmed Spaho's Yugoslav Muslim Organisation won 24 seats each, while the predominantly Serbian Agrarians received 15 parliamentary seats.[22]

The new Constitution was based on the old Serbian Constitution and made Yugoslavia a centralised monarchy divided into 33 administrative regions (*oblasts*), governed from the centre in Belgrade. However, the centralists only just won, thanks to a boycott by the Croatian Peasants, the fourth largest party, and votes from the Yugoslav Muslims, to whom Pašić had promised political and economic concessions in exchange for supporting the constitutional proposal. At the end, 223 deputies voted for, while 35 voted against; 161 deputies did not vote.[23] The vote took place on 28 June 1921, St Vitus' Day (*Vidovdan* in Serbo-Croat), so the Constitution came to be known as the *Vidovdan* Constitution. Because St Vitus' Day is the anniversary of the medieval battle of Kosovo and is closely connected with the Serbian Kosovo myth, the date was chosen somewhat unfortunately, because it only contributed to an overall impression among non-Serbs that the new country was dominated by Serbs.[24] How many

---

22 Banac provides a critical assessment of the elections and the Constitution in *The National Question*, 387-403. The source for figures showing distribution of parliamentary seats throughout the 1920s is Gligorijević, *Parlament*.

23 For more details see Banac, *The National Quesiton*, 387-403; Charles A. Beard and George Radin, *The Balkan Pivot: Yugoslavia. A Study in Government and Administration*, New York, 1929, 44-56; Gligorijević, *Parlament*, ch. 2; and Jovanović, *Ustavno pravo*, 65-71.

24 For an analysis of the (mis)use of the myth of Kosovo, which at the time had also been used by champions of Yugoslavism, see Dejan Djokić, 'Whose Myth? Which Nation? The Serbian Kosovo Myth Revisited', *MittelalterStudien*, forthcoming.

remembered in 1921 that the date was also the anniversary of the assassination of Archduke Franz Ferdinand seven years previously, which eventually paved the way for the creation of Yugoslavia?

The Serb primacy in the new state was also reflected in the country's official name: the Kingdom of Serbs, Croats, and Slovenes. The paradox was that the centralists, who strongly opposed any territorial divisions of the country, wanted the state name to preserve the 'tribal' identities, while the anti-centralists, who argued for the protection of individual identities, preferred the name 'Yugoslavia'.[25] Pašić in particular was in favour of the three-part name for the country, with Serbs mentioned first, arguing that this was common practice in European history. The Radical leader was of course mistaken: Piedmontese accepted the name Italy for the united Italian state, while Prussia, Bavaria and other German principalities came together to form Germany.[26]

Alternatives to the Radical-Democrat centralist constitutional proposal were considered. Inspired by the 'English system of government', Protić proposed a compromise between centralism and federalism.[27] The country would be divided into nine provinces that vaguely corresponded to the old historic regions.[28] Each province would enjoy wide autonomy, and would be responsible for its own

---

25 Jovanović, *Ustavno Pravo*, 89-90.

26 Andrej Mitrović, *Srbija u Prvom svetskom ratu*, Belgrade, 2004, 408.

27 *The Balkan Pivot*, 45. When Frano Supilo asked Protić in 1914 whether he was for 'centralism or autonomy', Protić replied: 'I am, Mr. Supilo, for the English system [...] In the English system you have the national unity—one parliament, one head [of state], one legal system—but you also have local autonomies', 'Ministar unutrašnjih dela i vladina politika. Govor g. Stojana M. Protića na zboru radikalnom od 2. novembra ove godine', in Protić, *Naša spoljna i unutrašnja situacija*, 30-31. By 'English' Protić in fact meant 'British'.

28 Serbia; Old Serbia (i.e. Kosovo and Sandžak) and Macedonia; Croatia-Slavonia with Rijeka, Istria and Medjumurje; Bosnia; Montenegro, Herzegovina, Boka and the Littoral; Dalmatia; Srem and Bačka; Banat; Slovenia with Prekomurje. 'Ustavni nacrt Stojana Protića', JF-1, 98-102. Although Istria was part of Italy, Yugoslav politicians continued to refer to it in the years after the unification, for reasons not entirely clear.

laws, providing these did not violate central laws or the Constitution. A governor general, appointed by the central government with 'supervisory' powers, would make sure any such violations were avoided. Central government would enjoy considerable powers, similar to those of British government.[29] The proposal was supported by a large number of Radical deputies; some genuinely desired a compromise with Croats, while others simply wished to oppose the Democrats' centralism although the two parties were together in the government at the time. However, Pašić urged the party to back the centralist Constitutional draft, convincingly arguing that it was in the country's best interests.[30] Because Protić did not fully accept federalism, his programme appealed neither to the National Club nor to the Yugoslav Club.[31] Despite advocating the preservation of the existing 'national individualities', he also failed to attract Radić's support. Protić and Radić met several times in the summer of 1921, but their visions of Yugoslavia remained too far apart for an agreement to be achieved.[32]

The National Club and the Yugoslav Club presented separate, yet similar constitutional drafts. Central government would be in charge of foreign policy, defence, tariffs and commerce, currency, posts and railways, indirect taxation, maritime commerce and business affairs, while the central parliament would have two houses: the upper house of provinces and the lower house, elected 'on a general democratic basis'. All other powers, including civil and criminal law would rest

---

29 Ibid.; Beard and Radin, *The Balkan Pivot*, 45-6; Jovanović, *Ustavno pravo*, 66-7.

30 Gligorijević, *Parlament*, 96-7.

31 Stojan M. Protić, *Uoči Ustavotvorne skupštine*, Belgrade, 1920, 68.

32 See Djordje Stanković, 'Neuspeh Stojana Protića u okupljanju političkih snaga radi rešavanja hrvatskog pitanja 1921. godine', *Istorijski glasnik*, no. 1 (1971), 7-34. Politically isolated, Protić took part in the March 1923 general elections as the leader of a small, dissident Radical group, but failed to get re-elected. He died a few months later.

with the provinces.[33] Both groups proposed the country's division into six provinces, with the Yugoslav Club arguing for a Catholic-Orthodox balance.[34] Smodlaka also proposed a federation of twelve provinces enjoying limited legislative power under a governor appointed by the King.[35] Potential conflicts between provincial and central authorities would be resolved by a state council. The central parliament would have two chambers: the upper house would consist of delegates elected by provinces and others elected by trade and occupational organisations, while delegates in the lower house would be elected indirectly by popular vote.[36]

While the three 'Croat-Slovene' proposals preferred federalism but supported monarchy, not all Serb politicians were centralists or even monarchists. Two small Serbian parties, the Socialists and the Republicans, presented their own constitutional proposals which both advocated a 'decentralised republic',[37] while the predominantly Serb Agrarians wanted 'a semi-presidential, semi-parliamentary system in monarchical dress, with regional autonomies.'[38]

---

33 Beard and Radin, *The Balkan Pivot*, 46-7, 49; Jovanović, *Ustavno pravo*, 76.

34 Slovenia, Croatia-Slavonia, Dalmatia, and, curiously, Bosnia-Herzegovina would be predominantly Catholic; Serbia, Montenegro and Vojvodina predominantly Orthodox provinces. This probably reflected the thinking of Korošec's Clericals, the dominant group within the Yugoslav Club. The National Club proposed the following six provinces: Serbia, Old Serbia and Macedonia; Croatia-Slavonia, Dalmatia, and Medjumurje, Istria and the islands; Montenegro; Bosnia-Herzegovina; Vojvodina (Bačka, Baranja and Banat); and Slovenia.

35 In some respects, King Alexander's *banovinas* of 1929 were to vaguely resemble Smodlaka's plan. Smodlaka proposed the establishment of the following provinces: Dunavska [Danubian] Serbia (with Belgrade as its capital); Vojvodina (Novi Sad); Slavonia (Osijek); Croatia (Zagreb); Slovenia (Ljubljana); Dalmatia (Split); Krajina (Banja Luka); Bosnia (Sarajevo); the Littoral (Dubrovnik); Raška (Novi Pazar); Moravska [Moravian] Serbia (Niš); and Macedonia (Skopje).

36 Beard and Radin, *The Balkan Pivot*, 50; Jovanović, *Ustavno pravo*, 78-81.

37 Jovanović, *Ustavno pravo*, 83-5.

38 Stevan K. Pavlowitch, *Yugoslavia*, London, 1971, 63.

The Croatian Peasants, who boycotted the Constituent Assembly, called for a 'neutral peasant republic of Croatia'. The borders of the republic were to be those of the so-called *Banska* Croatia (i.e. Croatia-Slavonia with Medjumurje), where the majority population voted for Radić at the November 1920 elections.[39] It is not clear whether the Croatian 'neutral peasant republic' was envisaged as an independent state, or as a confederate unit within Yugoslavia. Radić had elsewhere called for a 'Croat state within the Yugoslav unity',[40] while in a February 1921 memorandum to Prince Regent Alexander, Croatian Peasant deputies stated that all Slavs formed 'not only a linguistic but also a moral and spiritual whole', before adding that, nevertheless, Croats and Serbs were not 'one people in the political sense of that word.'[41] In the early years after the unification Radić was presented with a dilemma: self-determination within Yugoslavia or 'nothing [to do] with Belgrade'.[42] Did the latter mean independence for Croatia? According to an authoritative study, while the Croat leader was in favour of Yugoslavia in 1918-19, 'his correspondence reveals that he was in fact committed to outright independence (a neutral Croatian peasant republic) in 1919-20 and only gradually moved [back] towards Yugoslav (con)federalism.'[43]

---

39 As the text of the 'Constitution' specified, among the deputies coming from the territory of Croatia-Dalmatia, there were 59 republicans and 34 monarchists. Because the 'neutral peasant republic' was to be based on the principle of national self-determination, Croat-populated areas in Dalmatia and Bosnia-Herzegovina could unite with the 'republic' if their populations decided so by plebiscite and if relevant regional governments agreed. 'Državno uredjenje ili Ustav neutralne seljačke republike Hrvatske', Zagreb, 1 April 1921, JF-1, 113-20.

40 Stjepan Radić, 'Hoćemo u jugoslavenskom jedinstvu svoju hrvatsku državu', *Politički spisi: Autobiografija, članci, govori, rasprave* (compiled by Zvonimir Kulundžić), Zagreb, 1971, 319-22. In the same article Radić argued that 'we, Croats, Slovenes and Serbs really are one nation, both according to our language and our customs.'

41 Biondich, *Stjepan Radić, the Croat Peasant Party, and the Politics of Mass Mobilization, 1904-1928*, Toronto, 2000, 162.

42 Banac, *The National Question*, 238.

43 Biondich, *Stjepan Radić*, 161.

Radić concentrated his activities on getting as much autonomy for Croatia as possible. His refusal to cooperate with the small [Serb] Republican Party on the grounds that its programme was Serb, not Yugoslav, was disingenuous.[44] Radić's relationship with the mostly unitarist, if not centralist, Croatian bourgeoisie was not much better at the time. This would change only in May 1921, with the formation of a supra-party Croatian Bloc that included the Peasant Party, the Croatian Club (formerly the National Club), the Party of Rights and a small Croat Workers' Union.[45] Owing largely to the universal male franchise introduced in the new state and, arguably, greater political freedoms than in former Austria-Hungary, the Croatian Republican Peasant Party was transformed from a relatively small party into the leading force within Croatian politics and the main opposition to the government in Belgrade.

In the meanwhile, the Communist Party stepped up its activities during the summer of 1921. There was an unsuccessful attempt at the Prince Regent's life on 29 June, after Alexander had sworn the oath to the Constitution. The Interior Minister, Democrat Milorad Drašković, the chief architect of anti-Communist legislation, was murdered several weeks later, while on a break in the Croatian countryside. This prompted the government to enact the Law for the Protection of the State, which made the Communist Party illegal. The regime's act was more than a mere reaction to Drašković's murder. Following the second Russian Revolution, fear of Bolshevism spread across Europe, and Yugoslavia was no exception. The country provided refuge to many White Russian refugees, including General Wrangel and his army; neighbouring Hungary had been temporarily taken over by Béla Kun's revolutionaries in 1919; and the Communist Party of Yugoslavia did well at the November 1920 elections. A clampdown had begun even before the summer of 1921, but the

---

44 Ljuba Stojanović to Stjepan Radić, Belgrade, 20 March 1922, *Korespondencija Stjepana Radića* (compiled and edited by Bogdan Krizman), Zagreb, 1972-73, 2 vols, vol. 2, 554-7.

45 Biondich, *Stjepan Radić*, 179-80.

Yugoslav authorities' fear of a Bolshevik revolution in the early 1920s proved to be unfounded. A year after it was made illegal, the Yugoslav Communist Party all but disappeared.[46]

Early attempts to reach an agreement, 1922–1924

Changing alliances between the main political parties as well as inter- and intra-party rivalries suggest that Yugoslav high politics during the 1920s was dominated by a struggle for political influence and power, as much as, if not more than, competing nationalisms. Genuine political motives mixed with a dose of pragmatism existed, too. In 1922, Davidović's faction within the Democratic Party began to call for a 'third way' between the Croat boycott and the hard-line approach practised by the government, of which the Democrats were a part. Davidović proposed a combination of 'cultural unification and decentralized administration' as a way out of the crisis.[47] Davidović's thinking was in line with pro-Yugoslav intellectuals who met twice in 1922 to discuss the political crisis and Serb-Croat relations (in a Sarajevo suburb in June, and in Zagreb in September) and who called on the country's political leaders to reach a compromise, by revising the Constitution.[48]

---

46 A young Communist named Milovan Djilas met the King's would-be assassins, Lajoš Čaki and Spasoje-Baćo Stejić, in prison in the 1930s. The two men were broken physically and mentally after years in solitary confinement, but both still hated the King and were pleased when they heard the news of Alexander's assassination in Marseilles in October 1934. (Djilas, *Memoir of a Revolutionary*, New York, 1973, 161, 203-05.) Djilas would become one of the key figures in the Communist Party of Yugoslavia which reemerged in the late 1930s and under Josip Broz Tito's capable leadership led a successful resistance movement during the Second World War, seizing power in 1945. After the war Djilas was one of Tito's three closest collaborators, in charge of ideology and propaganda, until he was purged in January 1954 for calling for an end to one party rule. With the publication of *The New Class* in 1957, Djilas, who was a political prisoner in both royalist and socialist Yugoslavia, became perhaps the best-known dissident in the world.

47 Pavlowitch, *Yugoslavia*, 66.

48 That same year the leading Belgrade intellectual magazine *Srpski književni glasnik* (Serbian Literary Herald) carried out a survey on Serb-Croat relations.

In October and November representatives of the Croatian Peasants and the Democrats met to discuss possible cooperation.[49] Radić's willingness to negotiate with a party so closely associated with unitarism-centralism was not so surprising. By late 1922 he realised that only through cooperation with 'liberal and moral elements' with a 'progressive national [...] and social orientation', such as the Democrats, could a Serb-Croat agreement be achieved.[50] By forging closer links with Davidović, Radić also hoped to neutralise the influence of Pribićević's faction within the Democratic Party. As Davidović's reservations towards centralism—though not unitarism—grew, Pribićević gradually moved closer to Pašić. Davidović's motives were ideological—a belief in a Serb-Croat agreement—and pragmatic: he hoped to isolate the Radicals by establishing closer cooperation with Radić.[51]

The main obstacle to cooperation between the two parties was Radić's refusal to end his boycott of parliament. In late November 1922, the Croat leader assured Davidović that his aim was 'an honest and long-lasting Croat-Serb agreement', but:

[Because] this regime is hated in Croatia to such an extent my trip to Belgrade would provoke [...] fears and complaints among the Croatian people, which [...] I represent as president of both the HRSS and HB [the Croatian Bloc] ... [Otherwise], instead of writing this letter, I would have instantly come to you [...], to tell you in person that [...] you belong to those representatives of the Serbian people in whom we Croats have absolute confidence.[52]

For the full text of the Zagreb resolution of 10 September 1922 see 'Rezolucija kongresa javnih radnika', JF-1, 228-30.

49 Gligorijević, *Demokratska stranka*, 297-9. See also the same author's article 'Politička previranja u Demokratskoj stranci na pitanju taktike prema Hrvatskom bloku u drugoj polovini 1922.', *Istorija XX veka. Zbornik radova*, vol. VIII, 1966, 165-269.

50 Biondich, *Stjepan Radić*, 187.

51 Ibid., 186-7.

52 Radić to Davidović, Zagreb, 27 November 1922, *Korespondencija*, 565-6. Emphasis added by D. Dj.

On 1 December, the fourth anniversary of the unification, Radić wrote again to Davidović, explaining that although in principle he was in favour of 'parliamentary action', preferred by the Democrats' leader, under the circumstances a joint action against the government was possible only outside parliament.[53]

Davidović, however, believed in parliamentary politics. Although the Democrats left the government in December 1922, they remained in parliament to continue the new political course. The Radicals clung to their other coalition partner, Mehmed Spaho's Yugoslav Muslim Organisation, and the King approved Pašić's request to dissolve the parliament and call for fresh elections. The elections, held in March 1923, were practically fought as a referendum for or against the Constitution.[54] The Democrats, who called for a compromise, were bound to suffer in such a contest of sharply polarised visions, while the Radicals and Croatian Peasants emerged stronger. The Croatian Republican Peasant Party became the second largest party in the country with 70 deputies,[55] behind the Radical Party, which won 108 seats, 17 more than in 1920. The success encouraged Radić to step-up the campaign against Pašić and Pribićević, the most high-profile exponents of centralism. At the same time, however, the Radicals' growth at the expense of the Democrats, which made them the largest Serb party and enabled them to form a purely Radical government (and ditch the Yugoslav Muslims), moved Radić closer to Pašić.[56] The Croat leader believed that he should seek an agreement with whoever represented most Serbs. His successor Vladko Maček shared this belief throughout the 1930s.[57] However, neither

---

53 Radić to Davidović, Zagreb, 1 December 1922, ibid., 567-8.

54 Pavlowitch, *Yugoslavia*, 66.

55 Although Radić's party boycotted the parliament, it regularly took part in elections. The Croatian Peasant deputies were organised in a 'Croatian National Representation', a quasi-parliament which periodically met in Croatia.

56 Biondich, *Stjepan Radić*, 189-90.

57 And even as an émigré in the United States after the Second World War. In 1948 he wrote to Dragiša Cvetković—with whom he had successfully negotiated the creation of autonomous Croatia in August 1939—who was

in the 1920s nor in the 1930s would there be a Serbian equivalent to the Croatian Peasant Party.

Fearing that if the Croatian Republican Peasant Party suddenly decided to end the boycott of the parliament, the so-called 'Federalist Bloc' consisting of the Croatian Peasants, the Slovene People's Party and the Yugoslav Muslim Organisation could bring down the government, the Radicals struck a deal with Radić. In exchange for a pledge by 'Federalists' not to cooperate with the Democrats, Pašić agreed to halt the 'parcelling out' of Croatia, Bosnia and Slovenia by the 1921 *oblast* system, paving the way to a partial revision of the Constitution.[58] The Croatian Peasants also agreed to continue the boycott, securing the Radicals' majority in parliament. The agreement, signed in April 1923, became known as 'Marko's protocol', after the first name of the first (and the oldest) signatory, the Radical Marko Djuričić.[59]

When they realised that Pašić did not intend to revise the Constitution, the 'Federalists' turned towards the Democrats once again. In order to strengthen the parliamentary opposition to the Radicals, Radić finally ended the boycott in February 1924, also ending the Radicals' majority in the parliament. The following month Davidović, Radić, Korošec and Spaho formed the Opposition Bloc, which campaigned against the government and the Constitution. Differences between Davidović and Pribićević became irreconcilable and they

---

in exile in France, that if a Serb-Croat agreement was to be achieved, it was necessary for émigré Serbs to unite around one party, like the Croats had done around the Croatian Peasant Party. HIA, Dragiša Cvetković Collection, Maček to Cvetković, [Washington, DC ?], 27 January 1948. Maček seemed to forget that the days when his party was supported by virtually all Croats were long gone. Even in émigré circles, many Croats sympathised with the *Ustašas*, not with Maček. Maček and Cvetković corresponded regularly until Maček's death in 1964. Cvetković died five years later.

58 *Oblasts* cut across old, historical borders, except in case of Bosnia. Mehmed Spaho, leader of the JMO, had secured that Bosnia remained 'visible' within the *oblast* system by supporting the centralist Constitution in 1921.

59 'Kominike o pregovorima—Markov protokol', Zagreb, 14 April 1923, JF-1, 191-2.

finally parted ways. Pribićević's breakaway Independent Democratic Party joined the Radicals in what became known as the first P[ašić]-P[ribićević] government. The government was short-lived, but when Davidović was given a mandate by the King on 15 April, he was unable to form a cabinet, so Pašić, with support from Pribićević, returned to office once again. During this period Alexander was in a dilemma whether to lend his full support to Pašić - with whom he did not enjoy a good relationship, but who remained the ablest politician in the country - and the volatile Pribićević, or to Davidović, who increasingly criticised the Constitution and who moved closer to the even more volatile Radić. Alban Young, the then British minister to Belgrade, reported to London that the Yugoslav King was nervous and even feared that the ongoing political crisis could endanger the position of the Crown.[60] Did the King begin to consider a dictatorship at this point, as a Yugoslav historian later proposed?[61]

While the shifting alliances of the first few months of 1924 weakened Davidović, Radić's decision to send his party's deputies to the parliament did not lead to any significant opposition within the party, as he had once feared.[62] However, several members of the party objected when Radić enrolled it in the Comintern-controlled Peasant International (Krestintern) during his stay in Moscow in the summer

---

60 FO 371/9955, Young to the FO, 'Political situation in Jugo-Slavia', Belgrade, 15 May 1924. The British minister reported apparently growing republicanism across the country. FO 371/9955, Young to the FO, 'Political Situation in Jugo-Slavia', Belgrade, 8 July 1924.

61 Branislav Gligorijević, 'Uloga vojnih krugova u "rešavanju" političke krize iz 1924. godine', *Vojnoistorijski glasnik*, vol. 23, no. 1, 1972, 174.

62 Biondich, *Stjepan Radić*, 195-6. Ante Trumbić, once of the Yugoslav Committee and the first Foreign Minister of the Yugoslav state, who had joined Radić in the early 1920s, broke away in early 1926 with a small group of dissidents to form the Croatian Federalist Peasant Party. Trumbić would rejoin the HSS in 1928, following tragic events in the summer of that year (about which more later). The future *Ustaša* leader Ante Pavelić also briefly joined the HSS in 1928, before fleeing the country.

of 1924.[63] Radić had apparently hoped that Soviet support would speed up an agreement with Serbs, and this was not the first time he went abroad to champion the Croat cause. The previous summer he had toured Vienna, Paris and London, but without much success. Radić's visit to Moscow coincided with the Comintern's Fifth World Congress held in June-July 1924, which issued a resolution calling for the dissolution of Yugoslavia, seen as an imperialist, Versailles creation. Although there is no evidence to suggest that Radić attended the Congress, it is highly unlikely he was unaware of the resolution.[64] The Croatian leader specified to his hosts that he stood for a 'neutral peasant republic of Croatia' *inside* Yugoslavia, but his claim that there was no Yugoslavia, only 'a militaristic and plundering Great Serbia under the formal name of "Kingdom of Serbs, Croats and Slovenes"',[65] was not only contradictory, it also fed suspicions in Belgrade that Radić was a separatist.[66] Upon returning home in August 1924, Radić reiterated his support of Davidović, who had formed a Democrat-Yugoslav Muslim-Slovene Clerical coalition government after Pašić had been forced to resign in July.[67] Possibly in order to counter the bad publicity the Moscow trip had created,

---

63 Ibid., 196. Before the trip Radić wrote that 'we Croats respect and love this Bolshevik Russia incomparably more than the forever deceased Imperial Russia', because the Bolsheviks supported the right of nations to self-determination. However, the decision to join the Krestintern proved too much for Rudolf Horvat, Tomo Jalžabetić and Vinko Lovreković, who favoured cooperation with Belgrade and who eventually left the party. Ibid., 196-7; Gligorijević, *Demokratska stranka*, 388.

64 Biondich, *Stjepan Radić*, 192-3; Pavlowitch, *Yugoslavia*, 68.

65 Biondich, *Stjepan Radić*, 197.

66 Radić was closely monitored by Yugoslav secret agents while on his trips abroad. Mihailo Banković, a member of the Yugoslav intelligence service, wrote to Prince Paul years later to describe how Radić was spied on in Vienna, Berlin, London and Moscow. BAR PPP, box 12, Banković to Prince Paul, Vienna, April 1935.

67 Biondich, *Stjepan Radić*, 199; Pavlowitch, *Yugoslavia*, 68. Apart from the political instability caused by the conflict between the Pašić-Pribićević government and the Opposition Bloc, the government had difficulties dealing with the economic crisis, as the outgoing Finance Minister Milan Stojadinović

Radić pointed out that his party supported a Serb-Croat agreement, and that by entering parliament, it was moving closer to recognising the monarchy.[68]

The visit and its timing infuriated Belgrade, especially the strongly anti-Bolshevik King Alexander. After a series of talks between the Democrats and the Croatian Peasants in September 1924, Radić apparently appeared willing to accept the monarchy and the Constitution—two preconditions for the Croatian Peasants entering the government. Davidović, on his part, was critical of centralism and appeared more flexible on the issue of unitarism. However, the King did not trust Radić's motives and blocked the inclusion of the Croat party in the government, despite initially supporting the idea.[69] Alexander's mistrust of Radić was fed by Pašić and Pribićević's daily denunciations of the Croat leader's alleged 'Bolshevism' and republicanism. The opposition even argued that Serbs in Croatia would be physically endangered if the Radićists entered the government, and encouraged rumours that the army was distributing weapons to Serb civilians in Croatia.[70] Davidović's 'one-hundred-day' government fell in October, after General Hadžić, the Defence Minister, resigned, apparently infuriated by Radić's criticism. Although Radić's denunciation of Hadžić was tactless and 'explosive', the resignation

---

(the future Prime Minister) admitted in a letter to the King. Gligorijević, *Demokratska stranka*, 385-6.

68 Gligorijević, *Parlament*, 177.

69 Gligorijević, *Demokratska stranka*, 390-400, 409-10. The following members of Radić's party would have entered the government: Vladko Maček, Josip Predavec, Juraj Krnjević and August Košutić. For a detailed account of the negotiations between the government and the Croats see the same author's article 'O pitanju ulaska predstavnika HRSS u Davidovićevu vladu 1924. i o krizi i padu te vlade', *Istorija XX veka. Zbornik radova*, vol. VII, 1965, 345-406.

70 Gligorijević, *Demokratska stranka*, 411-18. The impact of rumours on Yugoslav politics during the period is still to be explored. Numerous contemporary sources, both Yugoslav and non-Yugoslav, that I came across while researching for this book refer to 'rumours', often taken as a good indication of impending developments.

was probably orchestrated by the King, who never fully supported Davidović, and who now turned again to Pašić and Pribićević.[71]

The political crisis of 1924 was one of the most serious crises of the 1920s, even if King Alexander clearly exaggerated several years later when he told a group of French ministers that the events of 1924 were more testing than those of the summer 1928, when Radić was shot.[72] The 1924 crisis put Serb-Croat relations to a serious test; the British Minister to Belgrade described the crisis as a 'struggle between Serbism and Croatism'.[73] However, the crisis represented a multi-layered political contest between the King and the main political leaders, between Pašić and Radić, Pašić and Davidović, Pribićević and Radić, and between Davidović and Pribićević. It was largely caused by the ongoing disagreement over the Constitution, opposed by Croats but, increasingly, by some Serbs, too.

The Pašić-Radić agreement

The new Pašić-Pribićević government, formed in November 1924, decided to neutralise the threat posed by the opposition by hitting at the obvious target—Radić. Pribićević believed that a hard-line policy would force the Croatian Peasants into submission, while Pašić thought an anti-Radić campaign was opportune before the new elections, which had been called for February 1925.[74] According to the regime's propaganda, Radić and his party symbolised the two greatest threats to Yugoslavia: separatism and Bolshevism. Arguing that the HRSS was working for the 'Communist International', the government banned the party in December 1924, using the same Law for the Protection of the State which had been enacted to ban the Communists three years previously. The Croat party leaders

---

71 Biondich, *Stjepan Radić*, 199-200; Gligorijević, *Demokratska stranka*, 421-4; Pavlowitch, *Yugoslavia*, 68-9.

72 Gligorijević, 'Uloga vojnih krugova', 169.

73 FO 371/9956, Young to MacDonald, 'Political situation in Jugoslavia', Belgrade, 30 October 1924.

74 Pavlowitch, *Yugoslavia*, 69.

were arrested in early January 1925, though all except Radić were soon released and kept under house arrest. The Democrats, Yugoslav Muslims and Slovene Clericals strongly condemned the regime's crackdown, but were unable to prevent it.[75]

Despite being formally banned, the Peasant Party was allowed to take part in the elections, while Radić orchestrated the election campaign from prison.[76] The Croatian Peasants were not affected by the regime's action, repeating the success of the previous elections by winning 67 seats (down by only 3 seats). The Radicals did even better, winning 142 seats in a 313-seat parliament. As for the Democrats, Pribićević's defection showed: they lost many votes in formerly Habsburg territories and were down from 51 to 37 seats. The Independent Democrats secured 21 seats in the new parliament, while the Slovene Clericals and Yugoslav Muslims lost three seats each, with 21 and 15 seats respectively.

Following the February 1925 elections, the parties of the old Opposition Bloc agreed to work together against the government, forming the Bloc of National Agreement and Peasant (People's) Democracy.[77] However, Radić also began secret negotiations with Pašić from prison. He told an envoy of Pašić that 'Ljuba Davidović is honest and intelligent...Ljuba Jovanović [a Radical dissident] is honest and intelligent...but Pašić is honest and intelligent and a [capable] politician, which is most important. That is why we would rather go [together] with the Radicals.'[78] On 27 March Radić's nephew

---

75 Biondich, *Stjepan Radić*, 201.

76 In retrospect, this was an early sign of what was to come in the 1930s, when political parties, despite being banned in 1929, would be allowed to resume activities and take part in election campaigns, while even imprisoned politicians were often able to continue with political action.

77 'Izjava Ljube Davidovića o formiranju Bloka narodnog sporazuma', Belgrade, 22 March 1925', JF-1, 242. Twelve years later the Democrats and Croatian Peasants played a key role in forming the opposition Bloc of National Agreement, together with the Independent Democrats, Agrarians and Stanojević's Radicals. The Slovene Clericals and Yugoslav Muslims would be in the government then, together with Stojadinović's Radicals.

78 Milan Marjanović, *Stjepan Radić*, Belgrade, 1937, 158.

Pavle Radić told the stunned parliament that his party recognised the existing political structure, including the Constitution and the dynasty; the party would from then on work towards revising the Constitution in order to help achieve a lasting 'national agreement [*narodni sporazum*] within the nation of Serbs, Croats and Slovenes [*naroda Srba, Hrvata i Slovenaca*].'[79] The following month Stjepan Radić issued a statement, declaring that his party recognised unconditionally the monarchy and the Constitution. 'We shall do nothing in future that would pose an obstacle to an agreement between Serbs and Croats,' Radić stated, before adding:

Serbs and Croats complement each other so much that they must go [forward] together. If the Serbs are better military leaders and better diplomats, we [Croats] are better at building roads and schools. Serbs are...warriors, while we are peacemakers. Both [skills] are important. Let us at last start working together. [...] Therefore, *we no longer demand the revision of the Constitution*, but accept Mr Pašić's view that the Constitution should remain for a year, two, three or more, before it is revised according to the people's needs, if that proves to be necessary.[80]

In July 1925 a 'Serb-Croat agreement' between the Radicals and Croatian Peasants was formally announced. Radić denounced republicanism, dropping the word from the party name, accepted the monarchy and the Constitution, and was duly released from prison. 'Long live all our peasant people, long live our peasant and people's

---

79   Ibid. 157-8; For a full transcript of Radić's speech see 'Reč Pavla Radića u Narodnoj skupštini', JF-1, 245-55. '*Narod*' and '*narodni*' may also be translated as 'people' and 'people's', respectively. Significantly, Pavle Radić referred to the nation/people of Serbs, Croats and Slovenes, though he did not use the more obviously singular form '*srpsko-hrvatsko-slovenački narod*' (Serb-Croat-Slovene nation/people). Radić would be tragically murdered in the same parliament only three years later by a Radical deputy.

80   'Izjava S. Radića o prihvatanju monarhije i centralizma', Zagreb, April 1925, JF-1, 256. Radić's words offered a good example of mutual stereotyping among Serbs and Croats, which survive to this day, despite Croatia, practically speaking, defeating Serbia militarily in the 1990s, and in spite of Serbia's cultural scene being arguably superior during the same period.

king,' the Croat leader declared.[81] The Independent Democrats re-signed from the government in protest against the Pašić-Radić rap-prochement. They were duly replaced by members of the Croatian Peasant Party (HSS), which entered the government for the first time on 17 July.[82] Radić himself joined in November as Minister of Education.

During the summer it seemed as if the Serb-Croat conflict was finally coming to an end. Before entering the government, Radić was sent to Geneva as a Yugoslav delegate to the League of Nations, thus fulfilling his long-held wish to convey his views on the international scene. This time, though, Radić emphasised the unity of the state and praised the Serb-Croat rapprochement. For the first time, he spent some time with Pašić when the Prime Minister was in Geneva. The two apparently got on well, though the pious Radić was some-what disappointed to find out that Pašić was not overtly religious.[83] In mid-August the Croatian Peasant Party organised in Zagreb the millennial celebrations of the establishment of the medieval Croatian kingdom under Tomislav, using the occasion for two purposes: to emphasise its undisputed leadership among the Croats and to pro-mote the newly achieved Serb-Croat agreement.[84] King Alexander and Queen Marie[85] visited Zagreb, where they were greeted by Radić

81 'Hrvatsko-srbski sporazum i nova vlada' (Croat-Serb agreement and the new government), *Dom*, 22 July 1925, cited in Biondich, *Stjepan Radić*, 207.

82 Pašić was prepared to sacrifice Pribićević, as Radić made it clear he would much rather join a government that did not include the Independent Democrats.

83 Marjanović, *Stjepan Radić*, 163-4. Pašić had been a socialist in his youth, while a student in Zurich.

84 Ibid. 164-5.

85 Queen Marie was born in 1900 as the second daughter of King Ferdinand of Romania and Queen Marie (née Princess Marie of Saxe-Coburg-Gotha). She was a granddaughter of Alfred, Duke of Edinburgh and great-granddaughter of Queen Victoria, and was also closely related to the Russian Imperial family, as her grandmother was daughter of Tsar Nicholas I. She married Alexander in 1922, giving birth to Peter (1923-70), Tomislav (1928-2000) and Andrej (1929-90). When Alexander made his fateful trip to Marseilles by sea, Marie travelled

with enthusiasm normally reserved in the past for verbal attacks on Belgrade.[86]

The new cabinet was dubbed by contemporaries the P-R [Pašić-Radić] government, but its PR was not up to standards. In its tenure of less than two years, internal conflicts between the Radicals and the Croatian Peasants destabilised the cabinet and began seriously to discredit parliamentary democracy in the eyes of the public. Two strong personalities, Pašić and Radić clashed. The latter even joined the opposition-led criticism of the government's alleged role in a corruption scandal that involved Pašić's son Radomir-Rada. As a result, Pašić was forced to resign in April 1926. In December that same year the eighty-one-year-old politician died, allegedly not long after a bitter row with the King. With both Pašić and Protić gone, the decline of the Radicals, Yugoslavia's *de facto* government party during the 1920s, began, although the Radical-Croat coalition survived for almost another year, under the premiership of the Radical Nikola Uzunović.

The Radić–Pribićević agreement and the June 1928 tragedy

The Radicals coped with the resignation of the Croatian members from the Uzunović cabinet in February 1927 by forming a coalition government with the Slovene People's Party, lured into the government by a promise of a free hand in Slovene areas. However, the government could not maintain a majority in parliament, where the

---

separately by train, because of rough seas and her poor health; this probably saved her life. After the assassination she kept a low profile, moving in 1938 to Britain, where she died as an émigrée in 1961.

86 The royal couple's second son, born in January 1928, was named Tomislav in honour of the medieval king of Croatia. To further symbolise national unity, the baby was christened with a mixture of waters from the Danube, the Adriatic Sea, and the Vardar river in Macedonia. All major political leaders, including Radić, except Svetozar Pribićević, who was not even invited, attended the ceremony. H.W. Kennard, the British minister in Belgrade, acted as the godfather in the name of King George V. 'The new Yugoslav Prince', *The Times*, 26 January 1928.

opposition was bolstered by the Croatian Peasant Party. Uzunović resigned in April, but King Alexander gave a mandate to another Radical, Velimir Vukićević. New elections, held in September 1927, showed a decline in support for both the Radicals and the Croatian Peasants, and a Democrats' recovery. The Radicals were down to 112 seats, the Croatian Peasants down to 61 seats, while Davidović's party secured 59 seats in the new parliament. However, the outcome of the elections was overshadowed by the formation of the Peasant Democratic Coalition by the Croatian Peasant Party and the Independent Democratic Party in February 1927—an event even more surprising than the rapprochement between the Radicals and the Croatian Peasants two years previously. Whereas the Pašić-Radić 'Serb-Croat agreement' in government failed, the Radić-Pribićević 'Serb-Croat agreement' in opposition was to be the longest lasting coalition of the interwar period, surviving throughout the 1930s.

The Independent Democrats' support largely came from Serb-populated areas of Croatia and Vojvodina, even if many *prečani*[87] Serbs there voted for the Radicals. The Independent Democratic Party, however, was not simply a Serb party. Its leadership included prominent non-Serbs, such as Hinko Krizman, Većeslav Vilder, Gregor Žerjav, Prvislav Grisogono and Juraj Demetrović (before the latter two defected to the government side after 1929).[88] All except Žerjav, who was a Slovene, and Vilder, an ethnic Czech, were Croats,

---

87 *Prečani* means 'those from across' (*preko*). This is how Serbs of pre-1912 Serbia referred to Serbs and other South Slavs who lived across the border in Austria-Hungary.

88 Once close personal and political friends from the days of the Croat-Serb Coalition, Grisogono and Pribićević found themselves not only on opposing sides, but also in drastically different predicaments. Grisogono served as Yugoslavia's minister to Prague while Pribićević was in exile there in the 1930s. In another twist of fate, Grisogono would end up as an émigré in London after the Second World War, at the time when the Yugoslav Communist authorities posthumously 'rehabilitated' Pribićević, or at least that period of Pribićević's career when he opposed the King. In 1953 Pribićević's book on Alexander's dictatorship was for the first time published in Yugoslavia, in Serbo-Croat, twenty years after it first came out, in French.

but all had a strong Yugoslav identity.[89] Although the Independent Democrats remained a unitarist party, its turn against centralism made the coalition with the Croatian Peasants possible. That Radić objected to centralism more than to unitarism also contributed to the unlikely alliance.

After an unsuccessful attempt by Vukićević to entice the Croats into his new cabinet—Radić would only enter along with Pribićević, to whom the Radicals objected—the new coalition government included, apart from the Radicals, the Slovene Clericals, Yugoslav Muslims and several Democrats.

Parliament became almost paralysed by a constant fight between the Radicals and the Peasant Democratic Coalition. In Stevan Pavlowitch's succinct words:

Accusations of irregularities, corruption, and police brutality flared up. That year, parliament turned into an arena for verbal and gymnastic displays. Obstructionist tactics altered with fisticuffs. Insults, threats, and blows were exchanged in an alarming *crescendo* between Radicals, on the one hand, and deputies of the Peasant Democratic bloc, on the other. More and more sittings were suspended because of disorders. While tension increased in parliament to breaking-point, extremist Frankists[90] in Croatia talked openly of the need to break away, and Radich invited the king to step in, as arbiter, to

---

89 Maček provided another good example that what mattered was not 'real' ethnicity, but the declared one: the father of the Croat leader was a Slovene while his mother was half-Polish. Maček, *In the Struggle for Freedom*, University Park and London, 1957, 14-15.

90 'Frankists' were followers of Josip Frank (1844-1911), a former disciple of Ante Starčević's, whose nationalism and anti-Serbism led to a conflict with Starčević's successors who formed the Croat-Serb coalition. The *Ustašas* originated from this group, although not all Frankists were *Ustašas*. During the interwar period all forms of extreme Croat nationalism were often referred to as Frankist, including the *Ustašas*. For more on Frank and his ideology see Banac, *The National Question*, 94-5. For more on the ideology of the *Ustašas*, who were responsible for a number of terrorist activities during the 1930s, including the assassination of King Alexander in 1934, and who ruled the Independent State of Croatia during the Second World War, see Aleksa Djilas, *The Contested Country: Yugoslav Unity and Communist Revolution, 1919-1953*, Cambridge, MA, 1991, 103-27.

appoint an extra-parliamentary government under a general, to make clean sweep, and start afresh from scratch.[91]

Parliamentary chaos tragically culminated on 20 June 1928 when Puniša Račić, a Radical deputy, shot dead two Croatian Peasant deputies—Pavle Radić and Djuro Basariček—and wounded three: Stjepan Radić, Ivan Grandja and Ivan Pernar. Pribićević was lucky to escape unscratched, even though Račić had allegedly aimed at him, too.[92] After an operation necessary to remove the assassin's bullet was carried out in Belgrade, Radić went back to Zagreb by train. The Croat leader, who had refused to board the train going to Belgrade in late November 1918 with other delegates of the National Council, was greeted along the route like a king by Croat crowds, during what would turn out to be his last journey. Anti-Belgrade sentiments were not publicly proclaimed, on strict orders of the leadership of the Peasant Democratic Coalition, who did not wish to give the government pretext to claim that Croats were against Yugoslavia.[93] Although the Coalition deputies, both Serbs and Croats, left Belgrade immediately after the murders, severing all relations with central institutions, they appealed for calm. Despite the terrible tragedy, the leaders of the Peasant Democratic Coalition did not turn against the idea of a common South Slav state. On 1 August they issued a resolution which condemned Belgrade hegemony and called for a federation that would 'secure full equality of all [...] individualities' within Yugoslavia.[94]

Radić, who suffered from diabetes, initially appeared to have recovered, but he died on 8 August of complications caused by the operation. His funeral was attended by some 200,000 people. Central

---

91 Pavlowitch, *Yugoslavia*, 72.

92 'Kako je spasen život g. Pribićeviću', *Riječ*, 22 June 1928. One may wonder what the effect on Serb-Croat relations it would have been if Pribićević, a Serb, had been murdered too. Račić, the assassin, was a Serb, while all victims were Croats.

93 'M. Raditch home again', *The Times*, 10 July 1928.

94 'SDK za novo državno uredjenje', *Riječ*, 2 August 1928.

Zagreb witnessed an emotional and dignified ceremony which lasted almost a whole day. Leaders of the Peasant Democratic Coalition repeated the calls for autonomy, but almost nobody from Belgrade was there to hear them; politicians from Serbia were advised not to attend. The King's wreath, carried by four army officers immediately before the coffin,[95] was the only reminder that Radić's death was mourned in Belgrade and Serbia as well.

Only days before his death, Radić told a German journalist that Serbs and Croats were two different peoples, of different traditions and cultures: 'The Croats are a people of European culture, the Serbs of an Eastern and Byzantine culture'.[96] Radić argued that Yugoslavia could not be a centralist-unitary state, but instead Croatia and Serbia should be connected through a personal union, under King Alexander and a 'neutral' (i.e. non-party) government.[97] When the King visited Radić in hospital in the immediate aftermath of the bloodshed in the parliament, the Croat leader stated that now that parliamentary democracy had collapsed only the King and the people remained.[98] The boycott by the Peasant Democrat deputies and the collapse of yet another government, headed by Korošec (the only non-Serb Prime Minister in the whole interwar period), gave Alexander an opportunity to take matters into his own hands.

Proclamation of the royal dictatorship

Just over ten years after he led the 28-member delegation of the National Council to Belgrade, Pribićević took the same train, again in order to meet Alexander Karadjordjević. This time, however, he was accompanied by Maček, the new leader of the Croatian Peasant Party, and the circumstances could not have been more different. In early January 1929 Alexander invited the country's leading political

---

95 'M. Raditch's funeral', *The Times*, 13 August.
96 'Croat Separatism: M. Raditch on his party's policy', *The Times*, 7 August 1927.
97 Ibid.
98 Pavlowitch, *Yugoslavia*, 72.

and public figures to consult them about the ongoing crisis. Leaders of the Zagreb opposition believed that federation was a solution, with 'a common King, common state borders, common army, common foreign affairs, common financial policy and common customs and trade policies.'[99] However, to Alexander anti-centralism amounted to anti-Yugoslavism and was therefore unacceptable. In the immediate aftermath of the June tragedy, the King apparently also threatened the 'amputation' of Croatia (minus its Serb-populated territories), but given the obvious impracticalities of such an action, it is not clear how seriously he considered it.[100] Anyhow, instead of dissolving the country, Alexander opted to integrate it through his personal rule. If the politicians could not unite the nation, the King hoped a strong state apparatus under his control would. On 6 January 1929, the Orthodox Christmas Eve, he dissolved parliament, abolished the Constitution, banned political parties and declared that 'the moment has arrived when there can, and should, be no intermediary between nation and King'.[101]

The Sixth-of-January dictatorship was meant to put an end to the country's disunity by enforcing an integral Yugoslav identity from above. The initial discourse blamed political, not inter-ethnic conflict for the crisis in the country. In his proclamation of 6 January, Alexander berated the country's politicians, saying that their

Blind *political* passions have begun to misuse the parliamentary system…to such an extent that it has become a hindrance to any fruitful work in the State…It is my sacred duty to preserve the unity of nation and State by all

---

99 AJ 335/15 (Papers of Vojislav Jovanović Marambo), Minutes from a meeting of the Executive Committee of the SDK, 21 Dec.[ember, 1928].

100 The King allegedly told Pribićević that he would rather opt for the 'amputation' of Croatia than a federation, but both Pribićević and Radić resolutely opposed this idea. Pribićević, *Diktatura Kralja Aleksandra*, Belgrade, 1953, 73-5.

101 For an English translation of the 6 January 1929 proclamation see 'Royal proclamation abrogating the Constitution and dissolving the Parliament of the Serb-Croat-Slovene Kingdom', Belgrade, 6 January 1929, *Yugoslavia Through Documents: From its Creation to its Dissolution* (compiled by Snežana Trifunovska), Dordrecht, 1994, 190-91.

means; and I am determined to fulfil this duty to the end without hesitation.[102]

The royal proclamation was initially supported by the Croat leadership. Maček issued a statement welcoming the abolition of the Constitution and expressing his belief that thanks to 'the great wisdom of His Majesty the King' the Croats would now achieve autonomy.[103] In declaring his support for the royal dictatorship in January 1929, the leader of the Croatian Peasants had perhaps betrayed a degree of political naivety, as it soon became evident that the King had no intention of decentralising the state and allowing autonomy for Croat (or any other) areas.[104] However, Maček's initial reaction reflected the prevalent mood within his party and also among the Croat population at large. A member of the Executive Committee of the Croatian Peasant Party later recalled that he could see 'satisfaction on everyone's face' at a party meeting on 7 January 1929, because 'everyone was convinced that the King's act of 6 January 1929 meant victory for the Croat position'.[105] Even Trumbić, who had in the meantime grown bitterly disillusioned with the Yugoslav state, allegedly believed that the royal dictatorship was 'perhaps the only way to

---

102 Ibid. Emphasis added by D. Dj.

103 Horvat, *Politička povijest*, 362. In this statement Maček used the then well-known metaphor 'the waistcoat (*lajbek*) is unbuttoned', arguing that in 1921 it was badly 'buttoned', and that the King's Manifesto presented a chance to now 'button' Serb-Croat relations all over again, 'properly' this time. The metaphor was originally used by Ferenc Deák, the Hungarian politician, to describe the Austro-Hungarian Compromise of 1867. Could Maček's use of it be seen as another indication that he saw Yugoslavia as a dual Serb-Croat state, resembling the former Austria-Hungary? The Croat leader often openly stated the dualistic idea—see for instance Stenographic notes from Maček's trial, Belgrade, 11 March 1933, in *Vodja govori: Ličnost, izjave, govori i politički rad vodje Hrvata Dra. Vladka Mačeka* (compiled by Mirko Glojnarić), Zagreb, 1936, 178-83.

104 In his memoirs, Maček fails to mention his initial support for the dictatorship: Maček, *In the Struggle for Freedom*, 124-6.

105 Ljubomir Maštrović, 'Hrvatska politika od 20. VI 1928. do danas', *Dom*, no. 34, 21 August 1935.

find a solution [to the country's instability]', providing the King was up to the task.[106]

According to contemporary accounts, the King's view that political parties and their leaders were to be blamed for political instability was shared by many 'ordinary' Yugoslavs, including Croats. A report from the town of Jastrebarsko, near Zagreb, caught the popular mood in the aftermath of the dictatorship. It stated that people thought 'politicians had managed to compromise themselves over the last ten years', and that with the royal proclamation 'a knot was cut off, so there will be no more demands made in the party name, and what is most important there will be no more party arbitrariness and terror.' The same report offers a useful analysis of the reaction of local politicians. The Croatian Peasants and Independent Democrats welcomed the abolition of the Constitution and believed that Radić's wish, that there should be only the King and the people, had now been achieved.[107]

Maček was aware that the Peasant Democratic Coalition was not in a position to achieve its main goals—the revision of the Constitution and decentralisation of the country—in the parliament, because other political parties were strongly opposed to them. Both Pribićević and Maček preferred a radical solution to parliamentary stalemate,[108] which may explain the latter's initial endorsement of the dictatorship. The two leaders of the Zagreb opposition, but Pribićević in particular, believed that joint action with Serbian parties was impossible because the latter rejected their policies as too radical, but he was equally against cooperation with the Royal Court. Maček, however, preferred to deal directly with the Crown rather than with Serbian parties. As there was not a Serbian equivalent of the Croatian Peasant Party—a single political party supported by the

---

106   Ivan Meštrović, *Uspomene na političke ljude i dogadjaje*, Zagreb, 1993, 183.

107   HDA XXI/26/1559, Sreski poglavar Grubić, Jastrebarsko, Velikom županu zagrebačke oblasti, Zagreb, 'Proklamacija novog stanja, raspoloženje naroda', Jastrebarsko, 9 January 1929.

108   MPHSS-1, 47.

majority of Serbs—he did not consider any Serbian party, not even the Radicals who were divided into several factions following Pašić's death, as representative enough of Serb opinion. Maček hoped that a deal with the King would leave Serbian parties with no option but to accept it.[109]

Foreign diplomats were also of the opinion that the failure of political institutions had put Alexander in an impossible position where something had to be done. Howard W. Kennard, the British minister in Belgrade, wrote to Austen Chamberlain, the Foreign Secretary, a few days after the King's proclamation:

Quite apart from the questionable manner in which this absolute autocracy has been introduced, it was essential, as I have frequently reported in recent despatches, that some drastic action of a radical nature should be taken to free the Administration from the *political* incubus which has crippled it and finally brought it so low a level that it was hardly functioning at all.[110]

However, the prime goal of the dictatorship was to solve the national question. On 3 October 1929 the country's official name was changed to the Kingdom of Yugoslavia, and it was divided into nine *banovinas* (provinces), which cut across old historic borders and were, at least in theory, based on geographical, rather than ethnic criteria.

---

109   See Ljubo Boban, 'Iz historije odnosa izmedju Vl. Mačeka i Dvora u vrijeme šestojanuarskog režima (Odnosi do oktroiranog Ustava od 3. IX 1931.)', *Historijski zbornik*, vol. XVIII, 1965, 47-88. Throughout the 1930s Maček negotiated with the Crown, while maintaining contact with the opposition in Serbia.

110   FO 371/13706, Kennard to Chamberlain, Belgrade 14 January 1929. Emphasis added by D. Dj. Kennard also expressed his doubts over General Živković, the new Prime Minister, writing in the same despatch that 'one must doubt whether the King has chosen the best instrument with which to purge the Augean stable.' The new Prime Minister, General Petar Živković (1879-1947), was among King Alexander's closest confidants. Although he took part in the conspiracy against King Alexander Obrenović and Queen Draga in 1903, he later found himself opposed to Colonel Dragutin Dimitrijević Apis, one of the leaders of the 1903 regicide, as a member of the so-called 'White Hand' group of officers. Živković was one of the organisers of the Salonika trial. During the Second World War he was briefly a Minister without portfolio in the government-in-exile in London; he died as an émigré in Paris after the war.

Nevertheless, Dravska was a *de facto* Slovenian *banovina*, Savska and Primorska put together resembled the territory of Croatia-Slavonia-Dalmatia, while six out of nine provinces had a Serb majority.[111] By naming all but one *banovina* after large rivers, the regime sought to emphasise the unity of the state, as rivers are meant to symbolise fusion.[112] The new official name for the country was more than just an act of convenience, given that the state had already generally been called 'Yugoslavia'. It was meant to reflect 'the complete state and national oneness [...] and to express symbolically the idea of total unity, equality and brotherhood of us South Slavs—Serbs, Croats and Slovenes', in the words of the Prime Minister, General Petar Živković.[113] Looking back at the significance of the October 1929 changes, a government manifesto issued the following year stressed that:

The ethnic and ethical substance of our historical and national development has definitely been formulated by the [new] name of our Kingdom, which has been accepted throughout the country with great enthusiasm. The administrative division [into 9 *banovinas*] has forever erased historic borders and [removed] all obstacles to our national formation and development [...]This Law [of 3 October 1929] has laid foundations for the following absolute principle: *a single nation and single sense of national belonging*.[114]

The creation of large provinces was meant to satisfy demands for federalisation, but the country remained as centralised as it had been throughout the 1920s. Instead of gradually decentralising power, the King believed that centralism and unitarism were essential for the

---

111 Dragoljub Jovanović, a leading member of the Agrarian Party and a Serb, believed the regime intentionally created a Serb majority in six *banovinas*, as the Serbs were considered most loyal to the state. Dragoljub Jovanović, *Političke uspomene*, Belgrade, 1997, 7 vols, vol. 2, 172.

112 Unlike mountains, which are apparently symbols of separation. According to Jovanović (ibid.), the idea was borrowed from the French. The only *banovina* not named after a river was Primorska (Littoral).

113 'Obrazloženje predsednika vlade Petra Živkovića zakona o nazivu države Kraljevine Jugoslavije—3 oktobra 1929', *Politika*, 4 October 1929.

114 'Historički zaključci Ministarskog Savjeta', *Novo doba*, 5 June 1930. Emphasis in original.

country's survival. As he told his ministers at the New Year's Eve dinner party in 1929, new Yugoslavia was to:

Represent that higher synthesis of our national expression and character, which would in our internal harmony enable the development of all beautiful distinguishing features of our race, while showing to the outside world the strength of unity and unyielding will of the same-blooded [Yugoslav] nation. In such a Kingdom of Yugoslavia, [only] those institutions, state government and state structure which are best suited to general needs of the nation and of state interests, will be established.[115]

In practice that meant that there would be no longer Serbs, Croats or Slovenes, but only *Yugoslavs*. Alexander's 'integral' Yugoslavism placed more emphasis on unitarism and represented a slight shift from the pre-dictatorship Yugoslavism, when internal sub-identities within the nation were tolerated, as reflected in the country's pre-1929 official name.

Yugoslavia thus turned to authoritarian form of government before the first interwar decade was over. Despite the initially widespread belief that the royal dictatorship would be temporary, democracy would not be restored until 1990, just before the Yugoslav state disintegrated.[116] The Serb-Croat rivalry, political conflicts irrespective of ethnic, cultural and historical divisions, the inability of the country's leaders to find a lasting compromise, and the King's autocratic tendencies, combined with democracy's retreat across Europe, were the main reasons for the tragic turn of events in 1928-9. The origins of the crisis of the 1920s lay not in a distant past of 'ancient ethnic hatreds' between the Yugoslav 'tribes', not even so much in the nineteenth century, when the competing South Slav nationalisms emerged, but largely in the post-1918 period. As R.W.

---

115 AJ 74/38/56 (The Royal Court Papers), 'Govor na večeri', 31 December 1929.

116 In retrospect, a whole set of new legislation and changes introduced following the proclamation of the dictatorship, including the abolition of the Chair of Constitutional History at Belgrade University on the grounds that there was no longer any such thing as Constitution, should have been a clear sign that the dictatorship was there to stay for some time.

Seton-Watson argued in January 1929, with much insight: 'What is wrong [with Yugoslavia] is not the events of 1918, but those of 1920 onwards.'[117] How did events in Yugoslavia—in particular the political rivalries and the search for a Serb-Croat compromise—unfold in the 1930s, the decade that would bring even more challenges, both domestically and internationally?

---

117 Seton-Watson, 'Jugoslavia and Croatia', 118.

3

COMPROMISE WITH THE DICTATORSHIP?

On 20 January 1934 Ivan Šubašić received an invitation to meet King Alexander in Belgrade five days later.[1] The two men had met twice before: at the Salonika front in 1917-18, where Šubašić had fought as a volunteer in the Serbian army, and in Zagreb in 1920, when Šubašić had greeted the then Prince Regent in the name of Croatian students.[2] Šubašić was a member of the Croatian Peasant Party, which, like other parties, continued to operate semi-legally after 1929. He was among emerging and moderate members of the party, together with Ivan Andres, Ilija Jukić and Juraj Šutej.[3] Although in January 1934 Vladko Maček was in prison for alleged anti-state

---

1 MPHSS-1, 122.

2 BAR PPP, box 11, Prerad Preradović to King Alexander, September [?] 1934. A lawyer from Podravska Slatina and a Serb from Croatia, Preradović liaised between the Royal Court and the Croatian Peasant Party, as well as the Serbian opposition (Stanojević's Radicals in particular), throughout the 1930s. His reports offer an invaluable insight into the relationship between some of Yugoslavia's leaders and the way the political negotiation and decision-making was conducted in the interwar period. Preradović fought alongside Šubašić at the Salonika front and the two remained friends after the war. They were among many Habsburg Yugoslavs who joined the Serbian army, sometimes as liberated POWs and deserters. Among them was Alojzije Stepinac, future Archbishop of Zagreb, whose relationship with Belgrade in the second half of the 1930s was however strained.

3 Moderate in the sense that they were in favour of an agreement with Serbs and were considered generally pro-Yugoslav. Mihailo Konstantinović, *Politika Sporazuma. Dnevničke beleške, 1939-1941. Dnevničke beleške, 1944-1945*, Novi Sad, 1998: Šubašić: 111; Andres: 76; Šutej: 170.

activities, the King had come to realise that only an agreement with the Croat leader would lead to the solution of the Croat question.[4] His sources suggested that five years after the dictatorship was introduced, Maček was supported by virtually all Croats, including the more extreme elements around the Catholic Church, but that Maček and the majority of Croats were not opposed to the Yugoslav state.[5] Šubašić, who was one of the sources, was to be Alexander's link with Maček.[6]

Alexander's invitation to Šubašić was not the first approach he made towards the Croatian Peasant Party, nor had it been his only attempt to solve the Croat question since the dictatorship was introduced. The King had at first attempted to sideline Maček and his party by inciting eminent Croats—both those who were members of the party and those who were not—into the government. He was also behind supposedly spontaneous 'greeting delegations' from Croatia. When these attempts failed to bring any significant results, Alexander tried to solve the Croat question by negotiating with Maček. The King's 'successor' Prince Regent Paul and several prime ministers also negotiated, either directly or indirectly, with Maček. It was mostly at the regime's initiative that the contacts were made. The Croats' leader, who spent part of the period in prison, was

---

4 Branislav Gligorijević, *Kralj Aleksandar Karadjordjević*, Belgrade, 2002, 3 vols, vol. 3, 224.

5 BAR PPP, box 11, Prerad Preradović to King Alexander, September [?] 1934.

6 Šubašić's close relations with both the Radić and Maček families did not harm his rise within the party. The fact that he occupied a uniquely vital position—a leading member of the HSS who enjoyed the confidence of both Maček and the Karadjordjevićs, due to his war record and moderate position—certainly helped, too. However, in early 1934 Šubašić probably could not have imagined where his political career would take him. Five and a half years after the meeting with Alexander, he would become the first (and, it would turn out, the only) *ban* of the *banovina* of Croatia, while in 1944 he would become the Prime Minister of Yugoslavia, albeit for a brief and largely symbolic term. (The real power would soon rest with someone with an even more remarkable career: Josip Broz Tito, the General Secretary of the Communist Party of Yugoslavia and the leader of the victorious National Liberation Movement, or the Partisans.)

generally interested in the overtures from Belgrade, but, for various reasons, rejected them.

Sidelining Maček and the Croatian Peasant Party

The government of General Petar Živković, who was Prime Minister between January 1929 and April 1932, included, at one time or another, ten Croats, several of whom were former members of the Croatian Peasant Party.[7] Not since 1925-7 and not until the 1939-41 Cvetković-Maček government were more ethnic Croats included in Yugoslav cabinets than during the 1929-31 period. Moreover, by appointing Croats in charge of ministries such as Agriculture, Finance, and Trade and Industry, the regime clearly hoped to counter the widespread belief, encouraged by the HSS, that Croats were being economically exploited in the new state.

When in early 1930 Dragutin-Karla Kovačević, a leading member of the HSS, broke away from the party and openly sided with the King, it looked as if the regime was gradually succeeding in weakening the Croat party.[8] Kovačević had been, together with Maček, one

---

7 Mate Drinković (he was successively the Minister of Trade and Industry; Minister of Social Policy; and Minister without portfolio), Želimir Mažuranić (Trade and Industry), Stanko Švrljuga (sometimes spelt Šverljuga, Finance; Trade and Industry; without portfolio) had all three been members of the Croatian Union, the so-called *zajedničari*; Drinković, together with Josip Smodlaka, was instrumental in persuading the National Council to send a delegation to Belgrade to ask Prince Regent Alexander to proclaim the unification in 1918). Other Croat ministers included Juraj Demetrović (Trade and Industry), the SDS dissident, and Otto Frangeš (Agriculture; without portfolio), without party affiliation. Former HSS members among the ministers in Živković's various cabinets were: Stanko Šibenik (Agriculture), Mirko Najdorfer (also spelled Neudoerffer, Agriculture; without portfolio), Nikola Preka (also spelled Precca, Social Policy; without portfolio), Ivan Švegl (without portfolio) and Pavao Matica (without portfolio).

8 It is not clear why Kovačević left the party to side with the regime. In his memoirs, Maček only mentions that 'the regime managed to undermine the good faith of several of Croatian Peasant Party's national deputies', comparing the defectors to 'branches of a tree' broken in 'a heavy storm'—'once no longer attached to the tree that gave them life, they would dry up.' (Maček, *In the*

of four vice-presidents of the party under Radić's leadership. After Radić's death, he was not considered for the party leadership because he was too old and was not an 'intellectual' but a peasant, though he had certainly enjoyed considerable prestige among the Croats.[9] Kovačević was joined by several other Croatian Peasant dissidents, including Ivan Radić, the late leader's nephew, and Andrija Berić, formerly of the party's Main Committee. The dissidents tried to portray themselves as authentic followers of Stjepan Radić. The editorial of the first issue of their weekly *Seljački glas* (Peasant Voice), written by the paper's editor Ivan Radić, reminded the reader of Stjepan Radić's proclamation—issued just before his death—that only 'the King and the people' remained. The author of the editorial believed that the late Croat leader, if he had been alive, would have called on all Croats to work for the good of their Yugoslav homeland and support the King:

Stjepan Radić had taught us for 30 years how to work for the homeland and we have therefore begun working in the spirit of his pacifist Slav ideology...we clearly see that our national future is with the King, for whom Stjepan Radić said at Bled in July 1925 ... [that] *'There is no King like ours—there are no people like ours.'*

Glory to the dead [!]—the Croatian peasant soul is grieving over the graves of all our great leaders—but since crying [over the graves] will not help, that same Croatian peasant soul is also proclaiming: *the living, to work!* Therefore, my peasant brothers, think carefully, gather your voices, unite, and you will see that the Kingdom of Yugoslavia under [the leadership of] King Alexander, himself the son of a peasant, will be powerful and mighty; the whole

---

Struggle for Freedom, University Park and London, 1957, 133.) However, he does not mention Kovačević (or other defectors) by name, let alone offer an explanation for his defection. A combination of factors may have motivated Kovačević, including personal disagreements with Maček, a hope that with the help of the King he might be able to sideline the HSS leader and take over the party, and possibly even a genuine belief that only by cooperating with Belgrade would the Croats achieve their aims.

9 Another vice-president, Juraj Valečić, was also a peasant.

peasant nation will have everything it needs and that glorious Slav dream of all our great leaders—peace, education and welfare—will be fulfilled.[10]

In a move clearly designed to reassure the Croats in the monarch's goodwill, Alexander announced a visit to Zagreb soon after the January coup, but the visit had to be cancelled. Even before the assassination of Toni Schlegel, a pro-government journalist, in April 1929, a number of incidents involving sympathisers of the newly formed exile *Ustaša* organisation made the situation too risky for the visit.[11] The King had to be content with receiving at his palace in Belgrade delegations of leading Croats, mostly businessmen close to the government, as well as 'ordinary' Croats. The delegations were to demonstrate publicly the Croats' support for the King and his regime and their loyalty to Yugoslavia. Alexander's increased interest in the Croat question became obvious when Minister Drinković started to visit Zagreb once a week, in order to observe the situation in the Croatian capital following the proclamation of the royal dictatorship and to talk to leading 'non-politicians' among Croats about possible cooperation with Belgrade.[12] Through Drinković, the King befriended Svetozar Rittig, a parish priest and a highly respected member of the local government in Zagreb.[13] Rittig, who frequently visited Belgrade and who spoke highly of the King, told the sculptor

10 Ivan Radić, 'Slava mrtvima—živi na posao', *Seljački glas*, no. 1, 2 February 1930 (emphasis in original). Ivan Radić refered to 'the peasant nation', perhaps because it could have been interpreted both as a reference to the *Yugoslav* nation—the official line—and to the *Croatian* nation, the (separate) existence of which was advocated by Maček and the HSS. King Peter I, Alexander's father, was not a peasant, but the Karadjordjevićs liked to portray themselves as people's dynasty, successors of Karadjordje Petrović, who prior to leading the Serbs in the First Uprising (1804-13) was a pig farmer.

11 MPHSS-1, 48.

12 Ivan Meštrović, *Uspomene na političke ljude i dogadjaje*, Zagreb, 1993, 184, 190.

13 During the Second World War Svetozar Rittig (1873-1961) would join the communist-led Partisan resistance. Today, an institute for the study of history and culture of ancient Slavs, which Rittig founded in Zagreb after the war, is named after him.

Ivan Meštrović that Alexander asked him to bring to Belgrade 'forty, or twenty respected Croats [not linked to any party], so that I could show to Serbians that Croats, too, want this state'.[14]

One of the first delegations was made up of representatives of Croat municipalities, businessmen, bankers, merchants and members of leading cultural societies. The delegation arrived in the capital on 17 December 1929, on the occasion of Alexander's birthday. It gave its birthday wishes to the monarch and declared its support for the King's attempts to safeguard the unity of the state, but also presented a list of demands in the form of a declaration.[15] The delegation was made up of federalist-minded, pro-Yugoslav Croats whose requests were mostly centred around proposals for casing centralism and granting more autonomy to Croat-populated territories. Although the King promised to take these seriously, he ultimately ignored them. Failure to secure concessions led to strong criticism of the delegation and Rittig in particular from both the Croatian Peasants and Frankists.[16] 'The "greeting delegation" brought some small success to the regime,' Meštrović recalled, 'but it represented a total disaster for members of the delegation.'[17] The regime rejected granting autonomy to Croatia out of ideological considerations, though Prime Minister Živković apparently also feared that if the delegation's demands had

---

14 Meštrović, *Uspomene*, 190. Ivan Meštrović (1883-1962) was perhaps the most famous Yugoslav artist in the first half of the twentieth century. Among the most enthusiastic proponents of Yugoslavism, and indeed one of its chief ideologists both before and after the unification, he eventually grew disillusioned with Yugoslavism in practice, becoming increasingly critical of Belgrade and Serbs in general. Although his memoirs offer an invaluable insight into the interwar period, they are not always reliable and must be read with special care. For more on Meštrović's Yugoslavism see Andrew Wachtel, 'Ivan Meštrović, Ivo Andrić and the Synthetic Yugoslav Culture of the Interwar Period', in Dejan Djokić (ed.), *Yugoslavism: Histories of a Failed Idea, 1918-1992*, London and Madison, WI, 2003, 238-51.

15 The King and Živković had been previously informed by Rittig about the declaration's contents, of which they apparently did not disapprove. Ibid., 191.

16 MPHSS-1, 49, 62n.

17 Meštrović, *Uspomene*, 191.

been published in full, the Serbs might have responded by sending their own delegations and making demands on the King and the government.[18]

Such delegations primarily served to publicise the apparent support of 'ordinary' Croats for the new regime. In October 1929 a group of 150 peasants from Zagorje wrote to the King asking to be received. The letter, sent through Marko Ćertić, the editor of the Zagreb-based pro-government publication *Novo vrijeme*, stated that:

The Croatian peasant, who for ten years had been led off course by the leaders of political parties [which had] finally brought him to a blind alley, greeted with a particular joy their great King's act of 6 January [...] Among the peasants of this region there is now a new feeling of clear-headedness and respect towards His Majesty the King because of the great historic act which will bring happiness and welfare to the whole homeland.[19]

In what was an obvious evidence of Alexander's eagerness to receive Croat supporters, Ćertić received a positive reply within days; the delegation would be received as early as 10 November.[20]

Although the King's opponents—in most cases correctly—tended to dismiss these delegations as organised by the regime and not representative of the real mood among the people, not all initiatives were disingenuous. How else to explain that the King was too busy to receive some delegations? A request by Dušan Ogrizović from Crikvenica in the name of 35 peasants to be received by the King[21] was rejected, and so was another one from Franjo Mežnarić, sec-

---

18 Ibid.

19 AJ 74/195/273 (The Royal Court Papers), Marko Ćertić Maršalatu Dvora, Zagreb, 19 October 1929.

20 AJ 74/195/273, Maršalat Dvora Ćertiću, Belgrade, 24 October 1929.

21 AJ 74/195/273, Dušan Ogrizović Kralju Aleksandru, Crikvenica, 30 December 1929. An explanation for the negative reply may be that Ogrizović was probably a Serb judging by his name (although this is by no means certain; Roman Catholics, i.e. Croats, formed the vast majority of Crikvenica's population—Bogoljub Kočović, *Etnički i demografski razvoj u Jugoslaviji od 1921. do 1991. godine (Po svim zvaničnim i u nekim slučajevima i korigovanim popisima)*, Paris, 1998, 59, gives the figures for Crikvenica from the 1931 population census). Despite, or because of, the King being a Serb, and the state being Serb-

retary of the Peasant Society of Zagreb.[22] He wrote in the name of 223 peasants from the Podravina region, '95 per cent of whom are Radićists (*Radićevci*)', but was told that the King was too busy to receive another delegation and anyhow, the monarch did not wish 'to interrupt the peasants in the midst of their field work'.[23] Mežnarić replied to the King reassuring him that he fully supported the new order and that if he had heard rumours to the contrary those were untrue.[24] Whatever the reason for the King's refusal to see Mežnarić, this example suggests that one of the motivations for members of these delegations was to indicate loyalty to the new regime.

Besides attempting to erode Maček's support, both at the grass-roots level and at the level of high politics, the authorities also tried to intimidate the leadership of the main Croatian party. Following Schlegel's murder, several leaders of the party, including Maček, had been questioned by the police but no link between them and the murder could be established. Maček was arrested and imprisoned in early January 1930 on suspicion of being behind a 'terrorist attack' on the members of a 'greeting delegation' which had gone to Belgrade.[25] Two of the arrested 'terrorist' leaders were indeed members of Maček's party. Under interrogation, they admitted to receiving financial aid from their party leader. However, it seems extremely unlikely that Maček was aware of their real intentions. The evidence against Maček was dubious, and even Živković conceded that placing the Croat leader under investigation was 'a rushed decision'.[26]

---

dominated, the monarch was mostly interested in appeasing the Croats, not Serbs.

22 AJ 74/195/273, Maršalat Dvora Mežnariću, Belgrade, 7 February 1930. Mežnarić's name indicates he was an ethnic Croat.

23 Ibid.

24 Ibid.

25 Maček, *In the Struggle for Freedom*, 127-9.

26 MPHSS-1, 62n. In order to strengthen its case against Maček, the regime tried to prove his alleged anti-state policies with a cartoon published on the first page of the HSS organ *Dom* (Home), which depicted a Christmas card with

Maček was kept in a Belgrade prison throughout the trial, which began on 24 April and ended on 14 June, when he was found not guilty and released at once. The members of the 'terrorist group' were sentenced to between one year and 15 years in prison.[27] Although imprisoned, Maček was treated fairly. Of the trial he later wrote that 'influenced by the liberal-mindedness of the chairman [of the court], the former Radical deputy and Minister of Justice, Jovan Subotić, the court had taken an impartial attitude.'[28] More interesting is his recollection of a conversation with a prison sergeant, who secretly delivered Maček the Belgrade newspaper *Politika* on a daily basis during the trial (so that the Croat leader could be informed of the proceedings of trial of others accused, something the authorities wanted to prevent). Maček wrote that,

When I tried to express my gratitude to this Serbian guard in the form of a sum of money, I discovered that I should not have judged him by his fellows. He categorically refused the offer and explained with finality: 'It is my firm conviction that you are an honest man. How good it would be if all our politicians were like you! I know that, instead of sitting here in this cell, you could have become a minister in the government if you had only wished, but you are here, and I respect you for it.' I received many compliments before and after this one, yet none lifted my spirits as high as the simple words spoken by this Serbian gendarme.[29]

The attitude of many Yugoslavs towards the country's politicians, irrespectively of their 'ethnic' background, is well illustrated by this example. The coup of 6 January 1929 initially enjoyed popular support because political parties and their leaders had been largely discredited by the late 1920s. Apparently, not much had changed a year

---

the Yugoslav coat-of-arms surrounded by a wreath, but with a thorn cutting through the Croat part of the coat-of-arms.

27 Maček, *In the Struggle for Freedom*, 132.

28 Ibid. The Justice Ministry was also in charge of prisons, which meant that although harsh, the treatment of prisoners had been probably fairer than it would have been if prisons had been under the control of the Interior Ministry. Milovan Djilas, *Memoir of a Revolutionary*, New York, 1973, 160.

29 Maček, *In the Struggle for Freedom*, 131.

and a half after the dictatorship was introduced. The story also shows a Serbian gendarme's respect and willingness to help the Croat opposition leader at the time when tensions between Serbs and Croats were allegedly high, and the gendarmerie was regarded by critics of the regime as a symbol of 'Serb oppression'.[30]

Maček's short spell in prison signalled the regime's intentions towards the opposition. Dragoljub Jovanović, one of the leaders of the (Serbian) Agrarian Union, was detained in early April following a public lecture at Belgrade university in which he criticised the government's national and social policies,[31] while Pribićević had been interned since May 1929, for his outspoken criticism of the King and the new order.[32] Therefore, the message from Belgrade was that any opposition to the regime and the King would be regarded as opposition to the state. Alexander regarded himself as the embodiment of the state and of the nation, taking quite literally the pledge to remove any 'intermediaries' between him and the people, made on 6 January

---

30 It is not argued, however, that even in this example one cannot detect any animosity between Serbs and Croats. Maček's admission that he 'should not have judged him [the Serb gendarme] by his fellows' is indicative of the Croat leader's view not just of the predominantly Serbian gendarmerie, but also of most Serbs, whom Croats often considered to be 'treacherous', 'corrupt', 'Byzantine', and 'dishonest'. Both Maček's and Meštrović's memoirs contain examples of similar stereotypes, while Dragoljub Jovanović recalled that Maček did not have confidence in the Serbian electorate, because '[to him] they are all Vlachs and are all unreliable.' Jovanović, *Političke uspomene*, Belgrade, 7 vols, 1997, vol. 5, 42. ('Vlach' is a pejorative sometimes used in Croatia for Serbs, although in Dalmatian towns it is used to describe anybody who comes from 'outside'. Vlachs are a Romance-speaking people scattered across the Balkans.) It is possible that the Serb gendarme was disappointed by Maček's attempt to bribe him, which may well have confirmed his own prejudices. Serb stereotypes about Croats (and Slovenes) included the belief that they were 'cunning', 'arrogant', 'cold', 'calculated', and generally not to be trusted.

31 Jovanović was released after only one night in prison, though a trial was scheduled for 18 October (but began exactly one month later). The verdict was 'not guilty'. Judge Subotić, whom Maček described as 'fair', interpreted Jovanović's lecture in a surprisingly favourable light. Jovanović, *Političke uspomene*, vol. 2, 173.

32 Svetozar Pribićević, *Diktatura Kralja Aleksandra*, Belgrade, 1953, 149-51.

1929. The regime's action was probably also meant to make Maček more cooperative. However, the Croat leader informed Alexander through Rittig that his position had not changed since they met last, in early January 1929—a Serb-Croat agreement was only possible if the King accepted Croat autonomy.[33]

In September 1931 Alexander 'granted' a new Constitution, which described him as 'the guardian of the unity of the nation and of the integrity of the state'.[34] Because it was imposed by the King and because it institutionalised the royal dictatorship, the Constitution was not received with much hope by the opposition. Until then the regime had appeared to be temporary, at least in form. Although, 'once again, no one considered these arrangements final, but merely a first step towards a further change', it was clear that a return to democracy was much further away than most had hoped in 1929.[35]

In a further attempt to make the dictatorship appear more 'democratic', the regime called for general elections in the autumn of 1931. However, only country-wide lists were allowed by the electoral law, which effectively ruled out all but the government's list.[36] The list was headed by Živković, who was also the leader of the newly-formed government party, the Yugoslav Radical Peasant Democracy (which

33 Curiously, Maček does not mention the conversation with Rittig in his memoirs. According to Živan Peršić, Rittig's close collaborator, Rittig was sent by the King to discuss with Maček ways of 'at least temporarily [...] minimising the Croat-Serb conflict. Maček's reply to Rittig was that he maintains those same conditions with which he presented [to the King] at the historic audience on the eve of the dictatorship.': Peršić papers, MPHSS-1, 51.

34 Stevan K. Pavlowitch, *Yugoslavia*, London, 1971, 81-2. The Constitution introduced a two-chamber parliament. Members of the upper chamber (Senate) were to be partly appointed by the King and partly elected, while members of the lower chamber were to be elected by universal male suffrage. The government was responsible to the King, who appointed and dismissed ministers.

35 Ibid., 82.

36 Every party or coalition entering the elections needed to have candidates in each municipality in the country. Paradoxically, such an electoral law encouraged the cooperation among Serb and Croat opposition parties in 1935 and 1938.

later transformed into the Yugoslav National Party).[37] The opposition parties had decided to boycott the elections, although the Croatian Peasants briefly considered taking part. If the opposition parties presented a joint list, their country-wide support would have made them eligible to take part in the elections, but it was decided that conditions were not right for the opposition to contest the government.

Early contacts between the King and Maček

During this period of political changes King Alexander established indirect contacts with Maček. Alexander had clearly become aware that despite the regime's clampdown, Maček remained the undisputed Croat leader. Somewhat ironically, the King's contact with Zagreb during the period was Stanko Švrljuga, one of those Croats who, the King had initially hoped, would sideline Maček and his party.[38] Švrljuga's own envoy, Živan Bertić, a Zemun-based lawyer, met Maček and Trumbić in Zagreb on several occasions in 1931 and in early 1932. According to Trumbić's recollections, Švrljuga claimed that Alexander was genuinely unhappy with the results of the dictatorship, particularly as regards the Croat question. The King seemed willing to introduce changes, but it was very hard to know for sure, as 'nobody knows what will happen, because the King never tells anyone anything.'[39]

According to Švrljuga, it was exclusively the considerations of domestic politics that impelled the King to reach an agreement with the Croatian Peasant Party. From Alexander's point of view, Maček was a far better partner than Pribićević. The King was convinced that it was impossible to reach an agreement with the Independent Dem-

---

37 The Yugoslav Nationalists would join the Maček-led Serb-Croat opposition in 1938. For a brief history of the Yugoslav Radical Peasant Democracy and the Yugoslav National Party see *Istorija gradjanskih stranaka u Jugoslaviji*, Belgrade, 1952, 362-76.

38 In addition to his career in politics, Švrljuga was also a former banker and head of the Zagreb stock exchange.

39 Trumbić papers, note of 19 January 1932, MPHSS-1, 69-70, 132n.

ocrats' leader, 'despite his [Yugoslav] ideology, which would have made him Prime Minister on 6 January 1929 rather than P.[etar] Živković, [if he had not joined the opposition],' as Alexander allegedly said.[40]

Maček's reply was the same: he had told the King his position in early January 1929 and nothing had changed since then, except that in the meantime his democratic right to represent the people who elected him had been withdrawn by the King. Therefore, Maček argued, he was no longer a legitimate representative of his people, and he could not speak or indeed negotiate with Alexander in a private capacity.[41] The Croat leader, however, was somewhat disingenuous, as he continued to run the party after 6 January 1929. Maček was referred to by others as the 'president [of the party]'[42] and as 'the Leader'.[43] But, more importantly, democratic principles, while

---

40 Ibid., 71. Following his U-turn in 1927, Pribićević became a fierce critic of King Alexander, harsher in his criticism than either Radić or Maček. He was the first leading politician whose freedom was confined for criticising the post-6 January order (in May 1929). Thanks to President Masaryk's intervention, Pribićević was allowed to leave the country, settling first in Czechoslovakia and then in France, where he wrote his damning account of Alexander's dictatorship.

41 Ibid.

42 Although, strictly speaking, he remained the party's vice-president, who ran the party in Radić's name. A statement issued by the HSS soon after Radić's death stated that Radić had 'not ceased to be the National Leader following his physical death.' (MPHSS-1, 4) The understanding of a collective as a community of the living and the dead was not confined to the Croatian Peasant Party: the Ustašas and the Romanian Iron Guard followed the example of the Spanish Falange Española, whereby names of dead members of their organisations were read at meetings, and those no longer alive were proclaimed 'present'.

43 Vodja in Serbo-Croat. Maček had also organised a paramilitary guard, the Croatian Peasant/Urban Defence. See Vodja govori: Ličnost, izjave, govori i politički rad vodje Hrvata Dra. Vladka Mačeka (compiled by Mirko Glojnarić), Zagreb, 1936. Some members of the Defence joined the Ustašas during the Second World War. Milan Stojadinović also liked to be addressed as vodja, but gave up the idea owing to strong criticism from the opposition and also the fact that when repeated several times vo-dja sounds like dja-vo, meaning 'devil'. Stojadinović later claimed unconvincingly that it was Cvetković's idea for the government's supporters to greet the Prime Minister with vodja, but

significant, were not Maček's imperative. In his reply to Bertić, the HSS president stated: 'The first and foremost question is the Croatian question. To Croats this is the most important *political* question. The question of dictatorship, civil liberties and political freedoms comes second, even if it is of the utmost importance.'[44]

Such a view disappointed Serbia's opposition parties, whose primary goal was the democratisation of the country. Only when democracy was restored, they argued, would it be possible to solve the Croatian question.[45] After a meeting with Maček in Zagreb, Bertić went to Belgrade, where he met the Independent Democrat Milan Kostić and Božidar Vlajić, Secretary of the Democratic Party. When Bertić explained Maček's position, Vlajić in particular was frustrated, arguing that if anyone lacked legitimacy, it was the regime, not the banned political parties.[46]

Apart from Maček, King Alexander also sought to establish contacts with Trumbić, who had in December 1928 rejoined the largest Croatian party.[47] While Maček was in prison, Trumbić was effectively running the party in his name—something the authorities were probably aware of.[48] When Meštrović told Alexander in August 1930 that Trumbić was under surveillance, the King appeared surprised that it was still going on. According to Meštrović, he said:

---

that he objected, among other reasons because it sounded like *djavo*. Milan M. Stojadinović, *Ni rat, ni pakt: Jugoslavija izmedju dva rata*, Rijeka, 1970, 534.

44 MPHSS-1, 72. Emphasis added by D. Dj.

45 Their dogmatic belief that only democracy could solve the national question was, arguably, not unlike the Communists' belief that the establishment of a socialist federation was the only possible way of solving the national question in Yugoslavia.

46 MPHSS-1, 72, 134n.

47 Maček, *In the Struggle for Freedom*, 116.

48 Although Josip Predavec was the party's vice-president, Maček instructed the party membership from prison that Predavec and Trumbić would jointly run the party. The old rivalry between Maček and Predavec may have been the reason for sidelining the party's vice-president. Maček had on another occasion instructed the party leadership not to make any important decisions without Trumbić's consent. MPHSS-1, 143n.

They are fools, idiots, why do they need it!? Trumbić is not going to run away across the border...Why didn't he [Trumbić] listen to me when I told him after [the Treaty of] Rapallo [of 1920, between Italy and Yugoslavia] that he should not join any political parties? This era [of official Yugoslavism] would have been ideal for him. Yugoslavism for which we fought in the war could not be implemented immediately [after the unification], there were obstacles. [But] now is the time. If he had listened to me, he would now be one of the leading [political figures].[49]

Alexander was probably genuinely interested in a rapprochement with one of the main symbols of Yugoslav unification. Although the King believed that Trumbić had turned into an 'extreme Croat nationalist', he acknowledged that nevertheless he 'had done a lot for this country.'[50] Alexander must have been aware that Trumbić, like many other Croats, had initially supported the dictatorship. He also appeared pleased when Rudolf Giunio, one of his contacts with Trumbić, told him, rather misleadingly, that the former leader of the Yugoslav Committee had only two fundamental beliefs: 'the state and the monarchy'.[51]

Paradoxically, it was in 1933, the year of Maček's second trial and imprisonment, and in early 1934 that Alexander was most actively trying to reach an agreement with the imprisoned Croat leader. His foreign policy gave the King some reason for satisfaction. Yugoslavia was a member of the Little Entente (together with Czechoslovakia and Romania), and Belgrade played a leading role in the formation of the Balkan Entente in February 1934. Besides Yugoslavia, the organisation included Greece, Romania and Turkey. In a series of meetings with King Boris of Bulgaria, Alexander did much to improve relations with the neighbouring country, despite Sofia's

---

49 Cited in Ljubo Boban, *Kontroverze iz povijesti Jugoslavije*, Zagreb, 1987-90, 3 vols, vol. 2, 28. Boban's source is Trumbić's diary (entry for 29 August 1930). Meštrović does not mention this conversation in his memoirs.

50 Meštrović, *Uspomene*, 190.

51 Boban, *Kontroverze*, vol. 2, 28. Giunio later told Trumbić that he had the impression that the King was 'yearning' to reestablish 'direct and personal contacts' with Trumbić.

revisionism in respect of Yugoslav Macedonia. Nevertheless, he became increasingly disappointed with the results of the dictatorship in regard to domestic politics. 'I know that the only...serious problem [remaining] is the solution to the question [of relations] between Serbs and Croats,' the King told Meštrović. 'Despite the problems with Italians, in external affairs I can [claim I have] achieve[d] a total success, but in internal [affairs], I have to admit, I have failed.'[52] As Švrljuga told Bertić, it was the fear of continued internal instability that prompted Alexander to try and solve the Croat question.[53] This time the intermediary between the King and Maček was to be Ivan Šubašić.

The 'Šubašić mission'

King Alexander received Šubašić on 25 January 1934. After they had briefly reminisced about their previous meetings, the conversation moved on to Maček. The King considered Maček 'politically too extreme', and a 'stubborn' and 'senile' man who had no desire to work towards the common good of the country. He claimed that all the information suggested Maček was either against the 'consolidation' of the state or surrounded by people who were against the state unity.[54] Šubašić strongly rejected these charges, arguing that Maček was both approachable and willing to cooperate, and that it was out of question that he could be pressured by anyone to work against the state. On the contrary, Šubašić told the King, 'Maček wants to work towards the consolidation of the state'. 'I know who you are, you were a volunteer [in the Serbian army], and I have very positive

---

52 Meštrović, *Uspomene*, 233.

53 MPHSS-1, 71.

54 Alexander told Meštrović, when the two met for the last time, in December 1933, that he admired Maček's 'character and courage', but that all his sources 'claim that Dr. Maček's aim is the complete secession of Croatia.' Meštrović reassured the King that the Croat leader was for 'Yugoslav state unity' and that the King's advisers were 'lying' to him. 'Well, can I do anything in such surroundings, if they are all lying to me?' the King asked. Meštrović, *Uspomene*, 233.

information about you,' the King replied. 'Therefore I have to ask you: can you guarantee to me what you just said [about Maček]?' Šubašić replied that his conscience and a sense of duty would not allow him to speak anything but the truth, insisting that the King had been misinformed about Maček.[55]

Šubašić had an ally within the King's circle—General Živković. He decided to stay in Belgrade for another day to meet Živković, who promised to arrange a visit to Maček in prison. Živković believed that the King was considering gradually re-introducing democracy. The General suggested that Maček should first enter the government; several key ministries, including the Interior, would be given to his party, and Maček would be able to select the *ban* of Savska *banovina*. Once this was agreed, the new government would call for fresh elections. Živković also told Šubašić that after reading Maček's speech at his trial, he was confident that 'there was not a single issue which he and Maček could not solve'.[56] Živković was one of the most influential figures around the King, not only as former Prime Minister and the Commander of the Royal Guard, but also as Alexander's personal friend. While it is almost certain that his message to Maček, through Šubašić, was sent on his own initiative, he would not have done so had he feared Alexander would fundamentally disagree.[57]

Šubašić visited Maček in prison on 1 March 1934, but they could not speak in private. The president of the court insisted he should be present during the meeting, so the two men were forced to whisper. Šubašić described to Maček his meetings with the King and with Živković. Živković's proposition apparently appealed to Maček. Maček secretly sent a letter to Šubašić soon after their meeting, stating that:

---

55 MPHSS-1, 122.

56 Ibid., 124, 151n. Stenographic notes from Maček's trial are published in *Vodja govori*, 163-92.

57 Although it is hard to imagine the King would have agreed with Živković's proposal that the Croatian Peasant Party should receive the Interior Ministry in a future cabinet.

It would be a mistake if I took such a position which would suggest that I am against an agreement within the borders [of Yugoslavia]. However, it would be even more catastrophic if those [ruling] forces were to be led to believe that I have 'softened' in prison [...] therefore, if you wish to help our common goal, and I know that you do, you must not show that you need them [...] you must not now go to Belgrade, but home to Zagreb, and if they need you, they will find you. The most important thing is that they know that the Croatian people are still with me...[The people] will remember me this Easter by sending me cards from *all* regions [emphasis in original], although I know I won't be able to see them. [But] the important thing is that they [the regime] see them [the cards].[58]

Despite Maček's instructions, Šubašić went straight back to Belgrade. He told Alexander that Maček had not been cooperative because he could not trust the government, but, in Maček's words, 'there is one person with whom one could talk, because he was not a member of any [old] political party, and because he only did what the King asked him to do, as his highest officer—[that person is General] Petar Živković.'[59] Maček preferred a non-party, army person to lead the government; this was Radić's wish in 1928, and it was clearly Alexander's preferred choice after January 1929. He also knew that Živković was Alexander's closest confidant.[60]

Neither Maček nor Alexander thought it wise to hold talks while the former was imprisoned. Maček often stated that Radić's biggest mistake was to negotiate with the regime while in prison. The King, on the other hand, did not wish to be seen as taking advantage of Maček's predicament, but at the same time he could not quite trust

---

58 MPHSS-1, 124.

59 Ibid., 125.

60 When Živković and Božidar Vlajić discussed this period of Yugoslav history in April 1941 in Jerusalem, which both had reached after fleeing the occupied country on their way to Britain, the former Prime Minister admitted to Vlajić that he had no decision-making powers and that he was merely an executioner of the King's orders. I am grateful to Desimir Tošić, who in the late 1930s led the youth section of the Democratic Party and who was a close friend and collaborator of Vlajić's during their émigré years in Britain after 1945, for this information.

Maček. On several instances he asked Šubašić if he could personally guarantee that Maček was genuinely interested in an agreement. Maček, on his part, told Šubašić that he refused to compromise and to renounce any of his previous statements, including the 'Zagreb points', for which he had been sentenced. The Croat leader believed it was up to the King to decide on this matter and take an initiative. The King apparently replied to Šubašić: 'Is that what Mr. Maček said? Now I am even less sure what do to.' He continued:

You know, Šubašić, we are all human, and we all make mistakes, including myself. I make many mistakes, and I always admit my mistakes when I realise I am wrong; however, when I see that I am not wrong, although others may think otherwise, I tend to justify my position. I personally did not put Dr Maček in prison, and I don't want him to be there, and above all I cannot allow for him to be maltreated there, but what am I to do? What am I to do? I am now even less sure what to do.[61]

Although Alexander personally did not put Maček in prison, such a major decision could not have been taken without his approval. He could have released Maček if he had wanted. Alexander realised that Maček was against a Serb-Croat agreement within the bounds of integral Yugoslavism, and suspected that he had regular contacts with Croat émigrés. Šubašić explained that Maček was in touch with August Košutić and Juraj Krnjević, his party colleagues who had moved abroad following the proclamation of the dictatorship, but not with Pavelić and the *Ustašas*. The King, however, did not seem convinced. 'See, that is one of the key questions that Dr Maček and I have to clarify,' he told Šubašić. Possibly because Šubašić firmly insisted that Maček was not in contact with the extremist émigrés and was genuinely interested in an agreement with the Crown, Alexander asked Šubašić to continue working on the matter, and to feel free to come and see him any time he wished, without the usual formalities.[62]

Alexander expected Maček to make a gesture and persuade him, as well as hard-liners in the government, that Croats were genu-

---

61 MPHSS-1, 125.
62 Ibid.

inely interested in an agreement with Belgrade. The Justice Minister Božidar Maksimović was among those unconvinced. The King was furious when he learnt from Šubašić that he was again unable to speak to Maček alone, complaining that 'Boža [Maksimović] likes to put his nose everywhere'.[63] Alexander wanted Maček to state publicly from prison that he supported the King and the dynasty and that he was not against Yugoslavia. It is safe to assume that had this happened the Croat leader would have been immediately released. Moreover, Alexander wanted Maček's party to enter the government. Paradoxically, while the post-6 January order was in its essence opposed to political parties, because they allegedly represented sectarian interests, at the same time it sought to secure legitimacy by including representatives of all the major former parties in the new government.[64]

While privately not against the state, nor against the King and the dynasty, Maček refused to make any statements while he was held in prison. In other words, neither the King nor Maček wished to make a first decisive move. Each feared that the other would exploit it and fail to keep his side of the bargain. Because of this lack of trust, the regime and the Croat opposition were locked in a vicious circle which could not be resolved easily without at least one side making significant compromises. It seemed as if both sides preferred the status quo to making significant concessions.

The Croatian Peasant Party leadership was not against a united Yugoslav state; it merely wished the 'Yugoslav contract' renegotiated. Krnjević and Košutić believed Yugoslavia should be reconstructed as

---

63 Ibid., 126. Maksimović was the Interior Minister in several Radical governments in the 1920s and earned a nickname 'Rifle butt' for his brutal methods against the opposition, particularly the HSS. Yet, when he went over to the opposition, Maček unsuccessfully tried to persuade his Serbian counterparts to cooperate with Maksimović.

64 The King, however, only managed to secure the support of Korošec's Clericals (before the two men fell out in 1930). All other cabinet ministers were either dissidents from their own parties or non-party personalities, such as the Prime Minister.

a dual monarchy, although they advised Maček to avoid using that analogy directly for fear of upsetting Belgrade:

The territory of Croatia is out of any discussion: Croatia-Slavonia-Dalmatia. In Bosnia-Herzegovina there should be a plebiscite whether it should go as a whole to Croatia or Serbia. If an agreement cannot be reached, then [we should] suggest that Bosnia-Herzegovina's position within Yugoslavia be the same as that of Croatia within Austria-Hungary. As for Vojvodina, [we should] ask for the triangle Subotica—Sombor—B.[ačka] Palanka—Ilok.[65]

The two exiled Croat leaders also recommended Maček to avoid discussing, if at all possible, the status of Montenegro and Macedonia. These had been considered by the Croats to be within the Serbian 'sphere of influence'.[66]

The King's visit to Zagreb in late December 1933 was aimed to coincide with both his birthday and the Roman Catholic Christmas. Alexander had hoped to meet as many 'ordinary' Croats as possible, but was unable to do so because the police again warned of a danger of assassination by Ustaša 'terrorists'.[67] After Zagreb, he went to Bled, a lake resort in Slovenia, where he wrote his last will, probably prompted by the discovery of the assassination conspiracy. On his way back to Belgrade he returned briefly to Zagreb, which turned out to be his last visit to the city.

In September 1934 rumours circulated that the King would grant Maček an amnesty. Maček was half-way through the four-year sen-

---

65 MPHSS-1, 128. Croatia was effectively divided within the Habsburg Monarchy between Budapest and Vienna. In the aftermath of the First World War 'complex' states such as former Austria-Hungary were seen as weak states. It is not clear whether Krnjević and Košutić believed that in the Yugoslav case a mini dual monarchy could prove to be more successful than the Austro-Hungarian Dual Monarchy.

66 This 'gentlemen's agreement' was respected after the war, among the émigré circles. See for instance HIA, Dragiša Cvetković Collection, Maček folder, Maček to Cvetković, Washington, DC, 27 January 1948.

67 FO 371/18456, MacRea [British consul in Zagreb] to Neville Henderson [British Minister to Belgrade], Zagreb, 19 January 1934.

tence and an early release was possible under existing legislation.[68] Alexander told Šubašić he would release Maček from prison after returning from France in October, and settle the Croat question once and for all: 'Tell Dr. Maček that I shall free him as soon as I return from France. But then I shall deal with him in person.'[69] How he was planning to do so remains unclear, although Meštrović claims that Alexander told him in December 1933, when the two met for the last time:

Dr Maček must be freed by the time I return [from France] and put my feet on our soil. Please make arrangements for a meeting between me and Dr Maček and also for the meeting to take place in your house. I shall solve the Serb-Croat problem with him. Upon returning from France I shall go straight to Zagreb from Split. I am confident that Serbs from Serbia do not lack reason, but they lack good-will for the solution of this problem. I shall divide the country into two halves: Serbian and Croatian. The latter will include Savska, Primorska and Vrbaska *banovinas*, the region of Baranja and the Croatian part of the region of Bačka with Subotica. Some corrections will be made in Srem, but Croatia cannot have Zemun, which is across [the river] from Belgrade, and which Maček wants [for Croatia]...Croatia will have its own parliament and will send its representatives to meetings of the common delegation, which will run common affairs.[70]

If faithfully reported, these words marked a significant shift towards compromise on the part of the King. Only several years previously, in the aftermath of the proclamation of his dictatorship, Alexander told Meštrović that he would never accept Croat demands for 'a state within a state'.[71] Despite the evidence that suggests that in 1934 Alexander had apparently changed his mind, it remains unclear how was he going to reconcile the ideology of integral Yugoslavism

---

68 The so-called 'Irish system' of prison sentences, whereby if a prisoner's behaviour 'improved' they would be eligible for an early release after half a sentence was served. Although in theory this was a liberal system, in practice it often made prisoners even more at the authorities' mercy. Djilas, *Memoir of a Revolutionary*, 157.

69 Maček, *In the Struggle for Freedom*, 154.

70 Meštrović, *Uspomene*, 236.

71 Ibid., 184.

with a decentralised state advocated by Maček. The King wrote in his testament that in internal politics the Yugoslav course must be maintained, while 'particularism and separatism' were to be prevented.[72]

King Alexander was assassinated on 9 October 1934, while on a state visit to France. The French Foreign Minister Louis Barthou was also murdered. The assassination was organised by the *Ustašas* and carried out by a member of the Internal Macedonian Revolutionary Organisation.[73] The King's death provoked a reaction opposite to the one his assassins had hoped for. Instead of the country breaking up, the Yugoslavs appeared more united than ever since 1918, if only for a brief period. Croats, Serbs, Slovenes and others were swept with a mixture of sorrow, anxiety and fear.[74] All sections of Croatian society strongly condemned the murder. The pro-Maček *Hrvatska revija* (*Croatian Review*) published an obituary, apparently written by Trumbić and Filip Lukas, president of the cultural organisation *Matica Hrvatska*, in which the late King was praised and Yugoslavia and Yugoslavism were described in a positive light.[75]

Other attempts to solve the Croat question

Although a dictator, Alexander was not in total control of his cabinet ministers' actions. His complaint about the treatment of Trumbić by the police is a good example. However, the King played a decisive role in the formation and resignation of governments. Potential

---

72 BAR PPP, box 1, King Alexander to Prince Paul, Bled, 5 January 1934. Alexander also recommended that the army's morale and combat level be kept high, and that there should be no influence of religion in state affairs. As for his funeral, he wished a small, modest military ceremony, without the presence of foreign dignitaries.

73 For a contemporary account see Hamilton Fish Armstrong, 'After the Assassination of King Alexander', *Foreign Affairs*, vol. 13, no. 2, January 1935, 204-25.

74 HDA/XXI/58 contains a number of reports from Croat-populated areas on the mood among the people after the assassination.

75 BAR PPP, box 11, Report on the reaction to the assassination in Croatia, unknown author, ca. late 1934.

prime ministers followed the King's line on most important affairs. Because the Croatian question was deemed the most pressing domestic issue, prime ministers were appointed partly in view of their potential ability to deal with the complex Serb-Croat relations. In the early 1930s three main factions emerged around the King. One was Živković's circle, which had strong support in the army and which had, initially at least, enjoyed the King's support. Another was led by Milan Srškić, a hard-line Radical from Bosnia. The third faction was a group of moderates around the Democrat dissident Vojislav Marinković. Marinković understood the dictatorship as a temporary measure, necessary only in order to stabilise the country. Once the dictatorship was over, Marinković believed, there should be a return to democracy and the Croat question could be solved by accepting the demands for federation.[76]

Marinković was aware of the growing opposition to the dictatorship throughout the country and knew that the Croat question could only be solved in a 'genuine agreement with the Croats'.[77] He became Prime Minister after Živković's resignation in early April 1932, but his was a short-lived cabinet even by the standards of interwar Yugoslavia.[78] Apart from the change at the helm, the cabinet remained

---

76 MPHSS-1, 77.

77 Kosta St. Pavlović, *Vojislav Marinković i njegovo doba, 1876-1935*, 5 vols, London, 1955-1960, vol. 5, 8. Marinković's views on the Croat question and the dictatorship were clearly not dissimilar to the views of his former colleagues in the Democratic Party.

78 The official explanation for Živković's resignation was that as a non-party premier he managed to calm down tensions caused by inter-party rivalries and secure the unity of the state, and the time was now ripe for a politician to take over the government ('New Prime Minister of Yugoslavia: Dr. Marinkovitch Appointed', *The Times*, 5 April 1932). However, by appointing Marinković Alexander indirectly admitted that his internal policies were failing, while sending a signal to Yugoslavia's democratic allies, France in particular, that he appeared willing to relax the dictatorship. For an insider's account of the 'ninety days' of Marinković's government see Pavlović, *Vojislav Marinković*, vol. 5, 5-17. Pavlović was Marinković's private secretary and worked closely with him between February 1928, when Marinković was appointed Yugoslavia's Foreign Minister, and Marinković's death in September 1935.

virtually unchanged; Živković even kept his other post as Minister of the Army and Navy (and was reinstated as the commander of the Royal Guard). Nevertheless, Marinković's appointment was seen as a step forward, and there was an immediate feeling of relief across the country.[79] Unlike Živković, who as a soldier had no political legitimacy and may even have had dictatorial pretensions, Marinković was a parliamentarian. He was elected first to Serbian and then to Yugoslav parliaments at every election since 1906, and even his political opponents respected his democratic credentials.[80] Marinković's democratic ideas could not be reconciled with the dictatorship for very long. After a speech at Niš in May 1932, when he openly called for a referendum on federation,[81] his days as Prime Minister were numbered. Marinković resigned in early July, after a clash with Milan Srškić, the Interior Minister,[82] who soon replaced him as head of government.

Although Srškić was rightly regarded by many non-Serbs, as well as by later historians, as a Serbian nationalist, especially because of his views about Bosnia,[83] even he thought the solution of the Croat

---

79 Ibid., 7.

80 Ibid., 6-7.

81 Ibid., 8; Todor Stojkov, *Opozicija u vreme šestojanuarske diktature 1929—1935*, Belgrade, 1969, 140. Stojkov argues that Marinković's speech represented a 'tactical move', rather than a genuine political belief, but this is somewhat unconvincing, because it is unclear how the public statement in favour of a federation could have strengthened the Prime Minister's position.

82 According to Pavlović, Marinković and Srškić clashed over the latter's decision to intern Korošec (*Vojislav Marinković*, vol. 5, 10-12). Stojkov, on the other hand, believes that wider disagreements, chief among which was Srškić's criticism of Marinković's understanding of 'national and state unity' were the reason for the conflict (*Opozicija*, 142-3).

83 John Lampe, in whose opinion Srškić was 'Aleksandar's poorest choice for prime minister', cites Srškić as saying that 'Bosnia-Hercegovina, both as a regional individuality and a geographic concept, must disappear forever.' *Yugoslavia as History*, 170. But Srškić was not a very popular figure among Serbs either, particularly among those from the pre-war Serbian kingdom. According to Trumbić's diary, Marinković was very angry because of the King's choice for the new Premier, while everyone in Belgrade 'hates Srškić, especially now [that

question to be a priority. There are indications that Srškić met with Juraj Šutej of the Croatian Peasant Party to discuss the reorganisation of the country into five *banovinas*, borders of which would be drawn according to non-ethnic criteria, but which would have a greater autonomy.[84] 'The opposition cannot be disarmed more effectively by any other means than by an urgent [law on] self-rule in the *banovinas*,' Srškić argued.[85] However, his proposal on local self-rule never reached the parliament for approval because Alexander did not believe it would be enough to satisfy the Croats. If Srškić could not solve the most burning domestic issue, could he last as Prime Minister?

Throughout 1933 rumours circulated that the Srškić government would fall because of its inability to solve the Croat question.[86] Bogoljub Jevtić, the Foreign Minister, was mentioned as a possible successor. Aware of these rumours, Jevtić sent two emissaries to Zagreb: a certain Marković, his best man, and a Croatian journalist named Jurinjak. However, neither was able to establish a direct contact with the Croat leadership. Trumbić, running the party in Maček's absence, decided that no one should see Marković. 'He must have been sent by Jevtić, in which case it would be good if we appeared uninterested [in negotiations]; and if he hasn't [been sent by Jevtić],

---

he has become the Prime Minister]. [The Serbians] would have easier accepted a donkey from Serbia [as the Prime Minister]. Nobody knows why the King has done this.' Trumbić papers, 'Diary', entry for 18 July 1932, MPHSS-1, 136n. Following the assassination of King Alexander in October 1934 Srškić retired from politics, and died prematurely in 1937, aged just 58. The *Times* obituary described him thus: 'Of patriotic Bosnian-Serb stock, he was a great gentleman, a true representative of Bosnian and Herzegovinian Serbs'. 'Dr Serskitch, Former Prime Minister of Yugoslavia', *The Times*, 15 April 1937.

84   BAR PPP, box 11, Draft of a *sporazum*, no date. Srškić and Šutej are mentioned in the document as two key negotiators. It is likely that the meeting took place during Srškić's premiership.

85   MPHSS-1, 78-9.

86   The following section is based on, and all citations are taken from, ibid., 100-03.

who cares about some Marković?', Trumbić said to explain his decision to party colleagues.

Not discouraged by this failure, Jevtić made another attempt to contact Maček, this time through another Croat ally (and another journalist) named Juretić. Juretić, who visited Maček in his prison in Sremska Mitrovica, carried the following message: there was a good chance that Jevtić would be asked to form a government. Should that happen, the main aim of the new government would be an agreement with Croats, and Jevtić's first move would be to release Maček. The message was sent secretly to Maček, but the Croat leader was mistrustful of Jevtić's intentions and refused to be involved in any speculations about a future government.

Trumbić, together with two other HSS leaders, Ivo Pernar and Jakov Jelašić, decided not to inform their Independent Democrat coalition partners of Jevtić's initiative. The Independent Democrats, particularly Vilder, were much more willing to negotiate with Belgrade. They were also keen to secure Maček's release as soon as possible for at least two reasons: they disliked Trumbić's increasing influence over the party and, if Maček was released, they would also demand an amnesty for Pribićević. The group around Trumbić was also careful not to inform other members of the party known to be in favour of a compromise with the regime (such as Šubašić and Ljubomir Maštrović) about the various initiatives for reconciliation coming from Belgrade.

Actions by Srškić, Živković and Jevtić seem to confirm that the King sought to achieve an agreement with the Croats. The most important requirement for a potential Prime Minister, in addition to being loyal to the King and to the official ideology, was an ability to show potential for solving the Croat question. The problem was that Maček's main demands—federalisation of the country and the recognition of separate Croat identity—were not acceptable to the King and his allies. Without the acceptance of those, however, Maček and the group around Trumbić refused even to negotiate with the regime. Another obstacle to a Serb-Croat agreement was posed by those individuals close to the King who opposed any concessions to the Croatian Peasant Party. (One of them was the Croat Ivo Perović, *ban* of Primorska and a future royal regent.) Opponents of a compromise with the HSS believed that the main Croat party was in a difficult position and that the opposition in general was too disorganised and divided to pose any serious challenge. Therefore, in their view, the regime needed to adopt a tough, uncompromising line.

Srškić resigned as Prime Minister in late January 1934, his lack of a clear political course and disagreements within the government over a new financial policy cited as the main reasons. *Ban* Perović was apparently considered as the next Prime Minister by the King, but Marinković was offered a mandate again. However, Marinković conditioned his acceptance on permission from the King to call fresh elections and to begin the democratisation of the country. Because this was deemed unacceptable to Alexander, it was the Radical Uzunović who was given another mandate to form a government. Uzunović enjoyed a similar hard-line reputation as Srškić, so this choice did not represent a major shift in policy.

General Živković and negotiations with the Croats

In the spring of 1930 secret negotiations between Živković and eight leading members of the Croatian Peasant Party allegedly took place. The Croats argued that the only way towards an agreement was a division of the country into three autonomous units: Slovenia, Croatia and Serbia. They also demanded that Maček be released from prison. The latter demand was met soon, but proposals for the country's internal division proved unacceptable to the government. Although it is by no means certain that such a meeting ever took place,[87] it is not inconceivable that if it had taken place the Croats would have demanded the federalisation of the country and Maček's release and that the regime would have rejected the former. Roughly at this time,

---

87   MPHSS-1, 51, 63n.

in May 1930, four members of Maček's party did enter the government, but without the party's consent. Whereas the claim by the Belgrade daily *Politika* that the event represented a major coup for the government, and a signal that Croats were abandoning the HSS en masse, was a gross exaggeration, it certainly represented a serious blow for Maček, at the time when he was imprisoned by that same government.[88]

Following King Alexander's assassination, in an atmosphere when the cult of the King-Martyr dominated the official discourse in Yugoslavia, the first Prime Minister of the 6 January regime emerged again as a leading political figure. Živković was generally recognised, among his friends and foes alike, as the only person who could keep the army under control, something considered essential during the post-assassination crisis.[89] Although he posed a potential threat to Paul's authority, Živković was deemed by the Prince Regent to be less dangerous inside the government than outside it, so he was appointed Defence Minister. (Two other of Alexander's former Prime Ministers, Marinković and Srškić, were included as well in Uzunović's reshuffled cabinet.) Živković was one of the dominant figures in the government, and after the resignation of Uzunović in late 1934, he was widely expected to return to the post of Prime Minister. However, Jevtić, who as Foreign Minister had accompanied Alexander on his trip to Marseilles and was the 'messenger' of the King's alleged last words ('Preserve Yugoslavia'), was given the mandate. The choice of Jevtić as the new Prime Minister was approved by Živković. The two men were distantly related and Živković

---

88 See *Politika*, 21 May 1930.

89 Even Alexander felt that he needed Živković because to him 'the army was the only pillar' in a country where political parties were so bitterly divided and in opposition to each other and the regime. 'There is no common view even among Serbian parties, they would all like to take the power...They could not care less about the state,' the King allegedly told Meštrović in 1929. Meštrović, *Uspomene*, 190.

possibly hoped to run the government through the younger and less experienced colleague.[90]

In early April 1935, only a month before the first elections held under the Regency, the recently released Maček and Živković held a secret meeting.[91] They met at Maček's farm at Kupinec, near Zagreb, while Živković was visiting the area in order to prepare election lists. Maček did not mention the meeting even to his closest political allies, including Trumbić. From a few available sources, we know that the two spoke about the Croat question and that Živković maintained that the Constitution could not be abolished or changed until King Peter II had come of age, in September 1941, on his eighteenth birthday. In all likelihood, Živković also talked about the possibility of the HSS entering a new government, as he apparently criticised Jevtić's premiership strongly.[92] It seems that Prince Paul knew about the meeting, as did the British minister to Belgrade, Neville Henderson (who probably found out from Paul). Henderson believed that Jevtić's government was not popular in Croatia because the Prime Minister continued to work with those Croats who discredited themselves because of their cooperation with the late King; that a majority in Croatia was for a Yugoslav state; and that if one Serb was considered acceptable to Croats as a future Prime Minister, it was Živković.[93] Although nothing came of the meeting, it is significant that it took place barely a month before the elections in which Maček led the united opposition list.

The results of the elections which took place on 5 May 1935 would determine Jevtić's destiny. Challenging the government was the united front of the Peasant Democratic Coalition, the Democrats,

---

90   As implicitly suggested by Stojadinović (*Ni rat, ni pakt*, 303). Jevtić's wife and the wife of Živković's brother, General Dimitrije Živković, were sisters.

91   One of the first moves by the regency was to release Maček from prison.

92   FO 371/19575, Henderson's memo to the Foreign Office, Belgrade 13 April 1935. For the conflict between Jevtić and Živković see Stojadinović, *Ni rat, ni pakt*, 302-03.

93   FO 371/19575, Henderson's memo to the Foreign Office, Belgrade 13 April 1935.

the Agrarians and the Yugoslav Muslims, headed by Maček. The opposition did relatively well—it received just over one million votes, against 1.7 million votes for the government list headed by Jevtić.[94] Jevtić's supporters celebrated the victory by greeting the Prime Minister with authoritarian-sounding chants of '*vodja!*'[95] (meaning 'leader'; this practice was later adopted by followers of Jevtić's successor Stojadinović). However, Prince Paul believed Jevtić was no longer the man for the job, and duly replaced him with Stojadinović.

Maček, in the meantime, maintained contacts with Živković. After the elections, he complained through Stanko Šibenik, his former party colleague, about the police terror in Croatia during the election campaign. Živković replied that he could do nothing about it, as he was in a difficult position in the government and only had influence over army affairs.[96] Until Maček inexplicably turned against Živković by the time he met Prince Paul in November 1936,[97] the Croat leader believed the General to be the only Serb, the Prince Regent aside, who could help achieve a solution to the Croat question.

Prince Paul and Maček

When Prince Paul became the Prince Regent following the assassination of his cousin King Alexander (he was the first regent in a three-

---

94 The exact results of the elections of 5 May 1935 were: Jevtić's list: 1,746,982 votes; Maček's list: 1,076,345 votes. However, the electoral law was unfavourable to the losing side, as the winner received three fifths of seats in parliament, regardless of the victory margin, while the remaining seats were then distributed according to the results. This prompted the opposition to boycott the parliament. For more on the elections and their aftermath see the following chapter.

95 A British journalist reported that following the elections 'the Yevtitch deputies were returned to Parliament, where they greeted the Prime Minister with cries of "Vodz!" [*sic*] or "Leader!" so infectious in these days are the methods of National Socialism and Fascism.': 'The Yugoslav Regency: Is Reconciliation in Sight?', *The Times*, 10 July 1935.

96 MPHSS-1, 172.

97 BAR PPP, box 5, Prince Paul's diaries, 8 November 1936. Did Maček consider Živković no longer useful, with the General's influence at the Royal Court in decline?

man regency that also included two non-political figures, Radenko Stanković and Ivo Perović), there was a renewed hope throughout the country that the new regime would be more receptive to the voices of opposition. In early November, a group of Croatian-based public figures sent a memorandum to the royal regents. They stressed that the Croats were not against the common state and urged the regents to restore democratic government and release Maček from prison. The signatories were not members of the Croatian Peasant Party, and they included Meštrović, Rittig, Švrljuga, Preka, Archbishops Bauer and Stepinac, eminent university professors, including the rector of Zagreb University, and the editor of the respected journal *Nova Evropa*, Milan Ćurčin.[98] Although the text of the memorandum was clearly written with the best possible intentions and its signatories could not be seen as anti-Yugoslav, the document was ignored by the regime. At the same time, disturbances broke out at the University of Zagreb when pro-regime students organised demonstrations against the rector for signing the memorandum.[99]

The Prince Regent released Maček on 22 December 1934. Upon the release, Maček sent a telegram to Paul, thanking him for his 'regained freedom' before adding: 'I hope and I believe that your act is the first sign of a new and more correct approach to the Croatian problem.'[100] Even before he was released Maček wondered whether an agreement could be achieved with the Prince Regent. Lujo Shaller, Maček's prison physician, informed Prince Paul of his conversations with the Croat leader. Maček told Shaller, apparently unaware that his words would reach Paul, that he could not envisage Croatia outside Yugoslavia. Although he wished that Croats had lived in ethnically compact areas like Slovenes, he could not ignore the fact

---

98 HIA, Dragiša Cvetković Collection, Prince Paul folder, Memorandum, Njegovom Kr. Visočanstvu, Knezu Namjesniku Pavlu, Zagreb, 5 November 1934.

99 BAR PPP, box 11, Kr.[aljevska] banska uprava u Zagrebu Milanu Antiću, 7 November 1934.

100 Maček, *In the Struggle for Freedom*, 156.

that Croats and Serbs lived mixed together. Maček recognised the Yugoslav state and the monarchy and did not wish a return to the pre-1929 order; he had supported the royal proclamation of 6 January 1929, but was opposed to politicians who had surrounded King Alexander.[101]

The Prince Regent, whose decision to release Maček from prison signalled the beginning of relaxation of the dictatorship—if not a return to democracy—was hopeful that the Croat question would quickly be solved. Maček did not waste time in reassuring Prince Paul of his loyalty to the state and the monarchy. Not long after Alexander's assassination, Šubašić contacted the Royal Court, asking to be received by Prince Paul in order to continue talks over the Croat question, which he had began with the late King.[102] Then in early 1935 Šubašić told his contact with the Crown that Maček was against centralism, but not against the state, and that he did not insist on federalism, but saw Yugoslavia as a state of Serbs, Croats and Slovenes—not Yugoslavs—and wanted wide autonomy for Croatia.[103] After a meeting with the Reuters Belgrade correspondent in January, Paul wrote in his diary:

Tea with Sir N. Harrison[104] [who] saw Maček who expected to be sent for; round table conference; desires interview with *Daily Mail*; would like to see Jevtić; wishes his friends to be released before coming here; on the whole much more reasonable than ever before. [Večeslav] Vilder backs Maček as long as he is reasonable. No Croats talk of separation. They want things to be given by mutual consent and not imposed. Mignon and Tommy expected

---

101 BAR PPP, box 11, Shaller to Prince Paul, Zagreb, 21 October 1934.

102 BAR PPP, box 12, a handwritten note by Prince Paul, no date (probably November-December 1934).

103 BAR PPP, box 11, Prerad Preradović to Dragutin Kojić [Justice Minister], January [?], 1935.

104 Harrison reported from Yugoslavia from 1922 until 1937, when the Yugoslav government refused to renew his *permis de séjour*, probably because of his balanced reporting on the 1937 Concordat crisis. See 'Processions Banned in Yugoslavia: Journalist to Leave', *The Times*, 22 July 1937.

to live there. Zagreb has become town of 1st magnitude whereas in the past it was only of 6th rate importance.[105]

Only ten days after the May 1935 elections Maček once again sent a message of loyalty to the Prince, this time through Stanko Šibenik.[106] Soon afterwards, Paul was updated on Maček's views through Ivo Belin, President of the Zagreb Stock Exchange, who had seen Maček and whose message from the Croat leader was as follows: the only way out of the current political impasse was for the Prince Regent to engineer a cabinet crisis, something which Maček believed could easily be done. Paul would then invite Maček, as the chief opposition leader, for consultations and the two would negotiate a solution to the Croat question. Even if an agreement could not be achieved at once, Maček believed that the establishment of personal contact between the two men would be a significant first step towards it.[107] There is no evidence whether Paul replied, but the Jevtić cabinet soon fell and Maček and the Prince Regent finally met.

The meeting took place on 21 June 1935. Not surprisingly, Maček was highly impressed with the man whose first significant step after becoming the Prince Regent was to release him from prison. Prince Paul, Maček later wrote, 'revealed himself as a man to whom aristo-

---

105   BAR PPP, box 5, Prince Paul's diaries, 15 January 1935. 'Mignon' and 'Tommy' were the Queen Mother and Prince Tomislav, whose presence in Zagreb would presumably symbolise Croatia's special position within the state. Similar, and similarly unsuccessful, proposals were made in the 1920s that Alexander should be crowned in Croatia as well as Serbia and that Prince Paul and Princess Olga should move to Zagreb. The Croats' Habsburg experience - Austrian Emperors were also crowned as kings of Croatia - meant that such moves would probably have been welcomed there. Although the fate of the old Empire was presumably one the Yugoslav leaders wished to avoid, it is still to be regretted, with the benefit of hindsight, that their vision was not greater and that the Karadjordjević dynasty did not do more to symbolically emphasise the importance of Croatia, even if that could have contradicted somewhat the ideologies of national oneness and integral Yugoslavism.

106   BAR PPP, box 5, Prince Paul's diaries, 15 May 1935.

107   BAR PPP, box 12, Milan Stojadinović to Prince Paul, 22 May 1935.

cratic thinking and aristocratic bearing were innate and who, in spite of a certain aristocratic streak, was thoroughly cultured in the best European tradition.'[108] But what impressed Maček most was that, in his view, the Prince Regent 'was free of even a trace of that Serbian chauvinism which, unfortunately, was noticeable in his late cousin, King Alexander.'[109] Maček recalled that,

Prince Paul made no effort, either, to conceal a certain disinclination toward some Serbian politicians. While we were enumerating and comparing the respective advantages of a monarchy and a republic, I did not conceal my republican views—but I readily conceded that I and many Croats would not object to a monarchy on the British pattern. At this he smiled sympathetically and replied: 'Rest assured that I, too, regard the British form of the monarchy as most desirable. But, to begin with, I should like to ask whether —————— (here he mentioned several familiar Serbian politicians) appear very British to you!' I was obliged to admit that there was little chance for the gentlemen in question to be taken for British.[110]

Although other sources also suggest that the two men shared a mistrust of many Serbian politicians,[111] the Prince Regent was not exactly enthralled by the Croat leader. This was not so much because Maček himself was not free of (Croat) chauvinism and it was debatable whether he could be compared to a British-style democrat. The Oxford-educated aristocrat looked down on the Croatian Peasants' leader (as he did on many other Yugoslavs). Paul described Maček to Campbell, the new British minister to Belgrade, as 'a nice little man', apparently with an emphasis on 'little'.[112] Both Prince Paul and Stojadinović looked upon Maček's provincial image with certain disdain. According to Stojadinović, the Prince Regent talked of

---

108 Maček, *In the Struggle for Freedom*, 178.

109 Ibid.

110 Ibid.

111 For example FO 371/21197, Conversation between Prince Paul and Mr [Terence] Shone, Belgrade, 1 September 1937, and Meštrović, *Uspomene*, 243.

112 FO 371/21196, Campbell to Eden, Belgrade, 4 January 1937.

Maček's ignorance of international politics, stubborn insistence on Croat demands, and appalling table manners.[113] During the June meeting, Maček proposed the abolition of the Constitution and free elections for a constituent assembly, to be overseen by a non-party government of civil servants under the premiership of General Živković.[114] Essentially, Maček repeated his old demands: only a return to 1918 and the formation of the state on a federal or quasi-federal basis would solve the Croat question.[115] 'Do the Croats want this state?' Paul asked. Maček replied that at first the vast majority was for Yugoslavia, but because of the politics of the late King Alexander, most were now in favour of a separate Croat state. However, he, Maček, was opposed to separatism and his main aim was to achieve equality for Croats *within* Yugoslavia.[116] Was this a genuine statement or Maček's tactic designed to emphasise the crucial role he could play in settling the Croatian question within Yugoslavia? Probably a bit of both, although Maček's significance as the undisputed Croat leader was obvious to both sides. Paul certainly knew that in any negotiations between Belgrade and Zagreb the key role would be played by the HSS leader.[117]

After the audience Maček met Živković, but despite the latter's eagerness to solve the Croat question, the gap between their respective positions was too wide. Živković allegedly proposed the formation of a new party, by merging the Croatian Peasants, the [Serbian] Radicals, the Yugoslav Muslims and the Slovene Clericals. He also claimed that he would accept a federation, providing the army remained united. Nevertheless, neither of these ideas appealed

---

113 Stojadinović, *Ni rat, ni pakt*, 466-7, 513. Stojadinović wrongly claims that Maček and Paul met for the first time in November 1936.

114 BAR PPP, box 5, Prince Paul's diaries, 21 June 1935.

115 Maček, *In the Struggle for Freedom*, 122; Maček to Seton-Watson, Zagreb, 24 February 1932, *R.W. Seton-Watson and the Yugoslavs: Correspondence, 1906-1941*, 2 vols., London, 1976, vol. 2, 220.

116 Trumbić papers, 'Diary', entry for 23 June 1935, MPHSS-1, 176.

117 Neil Balfour and Sally Mackay, *Paul of Yugoslavia: Britain's Maligned Friend*, London, 1980, 109.

particularly to Maček and the meeting, perhaps not surprisingly, proved to be fruitless.[118]

However, the Croat leadership appeared to believe the situation was more favourable for an agreement than it had been for a long time. In July 1935 Košutić wrote to R.W. Seton-Watson describing Prince Paul as 'a man of culture and not an enemy of the Croats'. According to Kosutić, the Prince Regent was willing to compromise, but one should not expect him to take the initiative. Maček thought that Paul did not appear particularly interested in high politics, preferring to talk about Croatian history, culture and arts, and his and Maček's families.[119] Košutić added that Živković was ready for a compromise so long as the army, dynasty and foreign policy remained outside any negotiations. Stojadinović, on the other hand, while generally in favour of an agreement, was aware that the Croats would not make many concessions. His tactic was to isolate Maček by including Spaho and Korošec in the government.[120]

Maček and Paul met again on 8 November 1936, at the Prince's winter retreat at Brdo, near Kranj, in Slovenia. Maček called for a constitution which would recognise Croat autonomy. He would cooperate with any government appointed by the Prince Regent, so long as that government was entrusted with organising elections for a constitutional assembly. The government could be formed by a general, providing he was not Živković, but no explanation was offered for this turn against the former Prime Minister.[121] Maček also expressed his dissatisfaction with Regents Perović and Stanković, suggesting that they should be replaced by the Queen Mother and Paul's father, Prince Arsen. Paul admitted he did not like his fellow regents, either, but that he could not follow Maček's suggestion,

---

118 Trumbić papers, 'Diary', entry for 23 June 1935, MPHSS-1, 176.
119 Košutić to Seton-Watson, Vienna, 4 July 1935, *R.W. Seton-Watson and the Yugoslavs*, 310-11.
120 Ibid., 311.
121 BAR PPP, box 5, Prince Paul's diaries, 8 November 1936. The meeting lasted between 12 noon and 3:30pm.

because that would have been in breach of Alexander's will. Besides, 'Prince Arsen was too old and Queen Marie was—a woman!'[122]

The Prince Regent repeated that the Constitution could not be changed until King Peter II came of age. Instead, he proposed step-by-step changes that would gradually lead to an agreement between the Crown and the Croatian Peasant Party and ultimately to the solution of the Croat question. He also hoped that the recent improvement in relations between Belgrade and Rome might make Maček less uncompromising,[123] but he was wrong, just as Maček's hopes that Paul might compromise on the issue of the Constitution were misplaced. Although the public was informed of the meeting, its proceedings were kept secret. When journalists asked Maček upon his return to Zagreb what Prince Paul and he had talked about, Maček replied with a question: 'Can you keep a secret?' When they responded with an enthusiastic and hopeful 'Yes', Maček said: 'So can I.'[124]

Over the following two years Maček's cooperation with the Serbian opposition parties would increase, leading to the formation of the Bloc of the National Agreement in October 1937, Maček's triumphant visit to Belgrade in August 1938, and the relatively successful elections of December 1938, when he headed the Serb-Croat opposition coalition. Yet, he also continued to maintain contact with the regime during this period. Dragiša Cvetković, the Minister of Social Policy, who established contacts with Maček and the Croat leadership in the summer of 1936, reported from Zagreb in January

---

122 MPHSS-1, 198. Therefore, even the 'sophisticated' and 'European' Prince Paul was not so liberal-minded after all (at least by today's standards). The Prince noted in his diary that Maček suggested that Paul and the Queen Mother should be the two regents (co-regents?), and believed the idea came from Mrs Švrljuga (who was close to Alexander's widow). BAR PPP, box 5, Prince Paul's diaries, 8 November 1936.

123 Balfour and Mackay, *Paul of Yugoslavia*, 132. The implication is that the Croat leader could not blackmail Belgrade by threatening to negotiate with Italy, Yugoslavia's most powerful revisionist neighbour.

124 MPHSS-1, 211n.

1937 that the Croats were in favour of an agreement.[125] In late August 1937, Paul learned from Šubašić that Maček wished to reassure the Prince of his 'goodwill and personal devotion'.[126] During the autumn, despite the improving relations with the Serbian opposition, the Croatian Peasant Party continued sporadic negotiations with the Crown and the government. In November 1937 Prince Paul was told that Maček sought to continue their talks.[127] According to Maček, he met the Prince Regent two more times, in 1937 and 1938, but they again failed to reach an agreement and hardly talked about politics anyhow.[128]

In a conversation with an official of the British legation in Belgrade, Prince Paul complained about 'Serbian politicians in general', saying that they were 'hidebound and tactless and that but for them he could have reached agreement long ago with Dr Maček on the Croat question.'[129] Perhaps the Prince Regent was right as far as 'Serbian politicians' in the government were concerned, but those outside the government were evidently capable of cooperation with Maček. Paul was not uninterested in the relationship between the Serbian and Croatian opposition, and had been aware that their relationship was not without its problems. After a rare visit by a Serbian opposition leader, the Democrat Milan Grol, in September 1935, the Prince Regent wrote in his diary:

No agreement with M.[aček] has been reached yet. C[roats] difficult people and the problem can only be resolved gradually...Croats have a different

---

125 HIA, Dragiša Cvetković Collection, Prince Paul folder, Milan Stojadinović to Prince Paul, Bled, 9 [?] August 1936; AJ 37/1/5 (Stojadinović papers), Cvetković to Stojadinović, Zagreb, no date (ca. January 1937). Cvetković had been previously the Mayor of Niš and briefly Minister of Religious Affairs.

126 BAR PPP, box 5, Prince Paul's diaries, Conversation with Dr Šubašić, 29 August 1937.

127 BAR PPP, box 5, Prince Paul's diaries, Cvetković to Prince Paul, 16 November 1937.

128 Maček, *In the Struggle for Freedom*, 178.

129 FO 371/21197, Conversation between Prince Paul and Mr [Terence] Shone, Belgrade, 1 September 1937.

mentality, of a people long under [foreign] rule...Fears for the future and that Croats might turn towards the [extreme] Left...They [Croats] hate the Slovenes and Korošec...Economic and financial situation [in the country] desperate. An honest government that would calm down the tensions needed. Maček under threat from the Frankists and Pavelić.[130]

However, the main obstacle to an agreement between the Crown and the Serbian opposition was not that the latter could not work with the Croats. It was the Serbs' insistence on the abolition of the Constitution and a return to democracy. Although Prince Paul argued that the Constitution could not be changed under the regency, he did consider revising it. In late 1936 he sought advice from Yugoslavia's four leading constitutional experts on whether the Constitution could be changed by the royal regents and whether a return to parliamentary monarchy and decentralisation would not reduce the King's power. All four answered that the regents could indeed introduce such changes within existing legislation, and that those would not be to the King's detriment.[131]

Stojadinović and Maček

When Milan Stojadinović was appointed Prime Minister in the summer of 1935, there was a general expectation that the dictatorship would be further relaxed, and that the country would be stabilised both economically and politically. He appeared more capable of solving the Croat question than his immediate predecessors. As a former Finance Minister in the Pašić governments of the mid-1920s, Stojadinović had close links with Zagreb industrialists, and

---

130   BAR PPP, box 5, Prince Paul's diaries, 16 September 1935. Grol recommended his party colleague Božidar Vlajić as an expert on the Croat question and suggested that the Prince Regent received him, too. He also spoke of Dragoljub Jovanović as a 'bad and unreliable man', whose messages from the opposition to Maček had to be double-checked as they were rarely correct.

131   BAR PPP, box 2, Anton Korošec to Milan Antić, Belgrade, 16 January 1937. The four experts were Professors Slobodan Jovanović and Mihajlo Ilić of Belgrade University, Ivo Krbek of Zagreb University, and Laza Kostić of the Faculty of Law in Subotica (Vojvodina).

was also well regarded among the British, whose opinion Prince Paul respected. The new Prime Minister was also (reluctantly) supported by Živković.[132] The creation of the new government by Stojadinović's Radicals,[133] Korošec's Clericals and Spaho's Yugoslav Muslims was followed by the merger of the three parties into a single one, named the Yugoslav Radical Union (JRZ).[134]

In the Prime Minister's view, only the Croatian Peasant Party was missing.[135] Stojadinović often used the 'three-legged chair' metaphor to argue that to achieve a full stability his government and the country needed the fourth, Croat, leg. 'The weakness of the new organisation [the JRZ],' Stojadinović wrote in his memoirs, 'was in the fact that Croats, a majority of them, stayed outside it...I called our party the three-legged chair (*tronožac*), on which it was possible to sit, when necessary, although a chair with four legs is far more stable.'[136]

Although the regime often accused the opposition of anti-Yugoslavism, Stojadinović was not necessarily a firm believer in integral

---

132 Stojadinović, *Ni rat, ni pakt*, 303-05.

133 Following the proclamation of the dictatorship the Radicals split into two groups: a majority, led by Uzunović and Srškić supported the regime, while the party's Main Committee, led by Aca Stanojević and Miloš Trifunović, went to opposition. Stojadinović, previously supportive of the Main Committee, joined and took over the pro-government faction in 1934-5. Although at one stage it seemed as if the party might reunite, and although rumours to this effect circulated throughout the second half of the 1930s, the split between Stanojević and Stojadinović appeared definite in 1935. BAR PPP, box 12, Stojadinović's personal notes, 8 November 1935; Stojadinović to Prince Paul, Belgrade, 16 December 1935; Aca Stanojević to Miša Trifunović, Knjaževac, 30 November 1935; and Stanojević to Anton Korošec, Knjaževac, 23 December 1935. See also HIA, Dragiša Cvetković Collection, Stanojević folder, Razgovor g. Dragiše Cvetkovića sa g. Acom Stanojevićem, 14 December 1935.

134 For details on the formation of Stojadinović's government and of the government party see Stojadinović, *Ni rat ni pakt*, 317-22. For a brief history of the JRZ see *Istorija gradjanskih stranaka*, 389-414. The government's opponents nicknamed the new party *Jereza*, because it sounded similar to the Serbo-Croat word for 'heresy'.

135 In a sense this mirrored Živković's plan for a supra-party created by the merger of the four parties.

136 Stojadinović, *Ni rat, ni pakt*, 318.

Yugoslavism either. He told Maček that he favoured the 'crystallisation of the peoples' wishes on national bases' and that he wished that Stojan Protić's constitutional proposal, which provided for wide regional autonomies, had been accepted when Yugoslavia was being formed.[137] Stojadinović wrote in his memoirs that in the 1930s he personally believed that 'Yugoslavia contained three national elements: Serbs, Croats, Slovenes.'[138] In the context of general relaxation of the dictatorship following Alexander's death, the Yugoslav Radical Union made demands for wider local autonomies and self-rule, which echoed the Radicals' programme of the late nineteenth century,[139] but was not compatible with the late King's understanding of Yugoslavia and Yugoslavism. Stojadinović, though the Yugoslav Prime Minister, also wished to be seen as a Serb leader, just as Maček, Korošec and Spaho were leaders of the Croats, Slovenes and Bosnian Muslims, respectively.[140] The Prime Minister was a member of the old Radical Party, which throughout the 1920s supported state centralism, but was never genuinely unitarist. His logic should therefore be understood in the context of his political background. Yet, unlike Croats, Slovenes and Bosnian Muslims, the Serbian electorate was not homogeneous, and it was difficult for Stojadinović or any other Serb politician in the interwar period to claim leadership over the largest Yugoslav 'tribe'.

Stojadinović and Maček met on 16 January 1937, in a hunting lodge near Brežice, on the border between Croatia and Slovenia. Contact between the two had been encouraged by Prince Paul,[141]

---

137 Ibid., 514, 516.

138 Ibid., 533.

139 Todor Stojkov, *Vlada Milana Stojadinovića, 1935-1937*, Belgrade, 1985, 55.

140 As he implicitly suggests in his memoirs (*Ni rat, ni pakt*, 533). After the Cvetković-Maček agreement of August 1939, Stojadinović's discourse became openly pro-Serb, and he would briefly lead a new party: the Serbian Radical Party.

141 BAR PPP, box 12, Prince Paul to Stojadinović, Belgrade, 19 December 1936.

and facilitated by Zagreb industrialists with whom Stojadinović was close, including Josip Krasnik, the president of the Chamber of Trade and Commerce in Zagreb. The hunting lodge belonged to another industrialist, Deutsch-Maceljski. The meeting lasted for three hours and was followed by a lunch. According to Stojadinović, Maček presented his 'well known views', while the Prime Minister had a number of comments and objections. They agreed that they should keep in contact and meet again if necessary.[142] Stojadinović apparently sympathised with Maček's views, but did not think a change of Constitution was possible or even desirable, certainly not until the King came of age. They agreed that fresh elections should be held in a near future, and the Prime Minister encouraged Maček to work closely with the Serbian opposition so that two blocs—a unitarist and a federalist one—could be established, 'like in Great Britain, on the question of Ireland.'[143] According to Maček, Stojadinović refused even to discuss constitutional changes, while Maček firmly insisted that he would only cooperate with a government that announced elections for a constituent assembly.[144] The meeting was a failure. Maček, who had never hidden his unwillingness to cooperate with Stojadinović,[145] preferred to negotiate with Prince Paul and later with Cvetković. Stojadinović, on the other hand, looked down on the Croat leader and failed to make a sustained effort to reach an agreement with the Croatian Peasant Party.

---

142 BAR PPP, box 12, Stojadinović to Milan Antić, 16 January 1937.

143 Stojadinović, *Ni rat, ni pakt*, 516. Stojadinović claims that Maček and he agreed much more when they discussed the international relations. For more on Stojadinović's view of the Croat question see AJ 37/10/59 (Papers of Milan Stojadinović), 'Vlada Dra. Stojadinovića i Hrvatsko pitanje', unknown author, ca. October-December 1938, and also chapter 5 of this book.

144 Maček, *In the Struggle for Freedom*, 178-9.

145 BAR PPP, box 12, Prerad Preradović to Milan Antić, Podravska Slatina, 20 October 1936.

The Brežice meeting was preceded by talks betweeen Cvetković and Ivo Pernar.[146] Pernar and Maček did not get along, but Maček was careful not to antagonise him, because he enjoyed considerable prestige among the Croats, having survived Puniša Račić's bullets in June 1928. Pernar told Cvetković that the HSS was divided into two factions: a moderate one, in favour of an agreement, and a hard-line faction. Although Pernar did not specify, he implicitly suggested that Maček was closer to the moderate position.[147] The view was shared by Cvetković, who thought the situation was favourable for a Serb-Croat agreement.[148] Cvetković reported that Pernar was 'very much inclined towards a compromise and is doing everything to achieve that aim.'[149]

Cvetković believed the Croatian Peasant Party would demand a revision of the Constitution and the formation of a 'concentration government' (a government of national unity)—although this was apparently the Independent Democrats' proposal and the HSS would not insist too much on it if it proved unacceptable to Belgrade. Cvetković thought the Croats were more interested in form than content: 'I believe that now is the best moment for an agreement and that the Croats would be satisfied with a certain form, which would paint the agreement in bright colours, while the content could offer less than their maximalist demands.'[150]

---

146 AJ 37/1/5, Cvetković to Stojadinović, Zagreb, no date (ca. 7 January 1937).

147 Nor did Pernar specify whether the hard-liners were for Croatia's separation from Yugoslavia.

148 Cvetković wrote in the same report about the animosity between Stjepan Radić's family and Maček. Vlatko Radić, the late Stjepan's son, told Cvetković at a dinner that 'Maček may be at the helm of the [Croat] peasant movement, but he is not its leader'. Radić argued that 'they all carry forward the movement'. Ibid.

149 Ibid. If true, this represented a shift in Pernar's views, as he had previously been supportive of Trumbić's hard-line approach to Serb-Croat relations.

150 Ibid.

Cvetković's assessment is confirmed by another contemporary source. Before the Brežice meeting, Stojadinović sent Šefkija Behmen, Minister without portfolio and representative of the 'Yugoslav Muslim component' of the government, to Zagreb to explore the political climate. Behmen held talks with Hinko Krizman and Juraj Gašparac, both Independent Democrats, as well as with Milivoj Dežman, a Croat close to the Crown, about the possibility of an agreement. Like Cvetković, Behmen believed that Maček was in favour of an agreement, and that Belgrade must not reject out of hand the possibility of a revision of the Constitution, because that was the minimum the Croats were prepared to accept.[151]

Although Maček maintained contacts with the Crown, he turned again to the Serbian opposition. The cooperation between the Peasant Democratic Coalition and Serbia's United Opposition would reach its peak in 1937-8 and very nearly bring down the government.

---

151   MPHSS-1, 202.

4

THE SERB-CROAT OPPOSITION

It is not only speculative, but also completely wrong, to suggest that the unity and progress of the state are dependent on, or even closely related to, centralism...I have therefore not hesitated to advocate—first among active politicians on this [Serbian] side, if I am not mistaken—a *complex state*, and to declare myself in favour of restructuring of state government so that [demands of] certain regions, above all Croatia and Croats, are satisfied.

Ljubomir Davidović, 1935[1]

Equality and parity is the starting point, a precondition for a political dialogue. Croats and Serbs, or, if you would prefer, Serbs and Croats, who form the spine of this state, need to reach an agreement so that each [group] is given their full rights, [their] peace and stability. Without an agreement between them, based on equality, it won't be possible to settle their relations, to calm the situation down, and to achieve security and freedom in this common state of ours. Therefore, to reach an agreement means to solve the Croat question, and, at the same time, the question of the [form of] state.

Vladko Maček, 1935[2]

What struck him [the author] most of all was the absolute unanimity among men of the most conflicting views, as to the extreme urgency of ending the internal deadlock, and the shortness of the time available for that purpose. In

---

1 'Iz ankete zagrebačkog časopisa *Nova Evropa* o unutrašnjoj politici, 1935', JF-1, 524. Emphasis in original. By 'complex state' Davidović meant a federal state, as opposed to a 'simple' (centralised, nation-) state. *Složena država* (complex state) and *prosta država* (simple state) were terms commonly used in Yugoslavia during the period to describe what today are normally called a multi-national federation and a centralised nation-state, respectively.

2 Ibid.

one sense this was reassuring, for it meant that the political atmosphere was more favourable to a *détente* between Serb and Croat - which is of course the point round which every problem of Jugoslav home and foreign policy has revolved ever since the Union - and that even in political and military circles hitherto averse to action the dangers of drift were at last realised.

R.W. Seton-Watson, 1937[3]

During the night of 4-5 January 1930, exactly a year after the audience with King Alexander, Vladko Maček was transferred to a Belgrade prison in order to face the Court for the Defence of the State.[4] He had been arrested in December, together with 24 other people, on suspicion of supporting a 'terrorist attack' on a 'greeting delegation' of Croats loyal to the regime.[5] Soon after the transfer to Belgrade, Maček received an unusual gift—a home-made cake. It was sent by Dragoljub Jovanović, one of the leaders of the Agrarian Party, who taught sociology at Belgrade University, and his wife Dana, also a member of the party. It is hard to guess who was more surprised: Maček or Prime Minister Petar Živković, who found out about the cake from the police, when they intercepted Maček's note thanking the Jovanovićs.[6]

Živković used the incident to accuse the staff of Belgrade University of a lack of loyalty to the regime. When around the same time the university rector, accompanied by a group of professors, met Živković and presented their demand for a pay rise, the Prime Minister replied: 'I see what the University demands, but I don't see what it has given so far and what it intends to do for the new order. I only know that you are sending cakes to Maček in his prison

---

3 'Jugoslavia and the Croat Problem', *Slavonic Review*, vol. 16, no. 46, July 1937, 102.

4 Svetozar Pribićević, the other co-president of the Peasant Democratic Coalition, who had also been invited by the King for discussions in early January 1929, had been interned since May 1929.

5 Vladko Maček, *In the Struggle for Freedom*, University Park and London, 1957, 129.

6 Dragoljub Jovanović, *Političke uspomene*, Belgrade, 1997, 7 vols, vol. 2, 176.

cell.'[7] The rector and his colleagues protested in astonishment that they had not sent any cakes. 'But Dragoljub Jovanović has,' Živković said, probably happy to be presented with such a good opportunity to turn down their demand, 'and you tolerate that.'[8] The delegation left the meeting empty handed, unable to raise the issue of the pay-rise again. The whole matter was discussed at a staff meeting several days later. Dragoljub Jovanović remembered later that two of the most respected professors, Slobodan Jovanović and Živojin Perić, both supported him, even though they rarely saw eye to eye.[9]

Although the incident presented Živković with a good excuse to reject demands for salary increases by the dissatisfied university professors, we do not know whether he was seriously concerned by Jovanović's symbolic act of support for a fellow opposition leader. In all likelihood, he was not. In early 1930 the Serbian opposition—the Democrats, the Agrarians and the Main Committee of the Radical Party[10]—and the Peasant Democratic Coalition were poles apart, and not only geographically. As Dragoljub Jovanović later recalled, Serbian opposition leaders did not think joint action was possible or even desirable, under the circumstances.[11] If the regime could not

---

7 Ibid., 176-7.

8 Ibid.

9 This suggests that some of the leading Serbian academics supported cooperation between the Serbs and Croats. Slobodan Jovanović apparently giggled throughout the meeting and Dragoljub Jovanović believed that the old professor could not wait for the meeting to be over so that he could tell the gossip to his publisher Geca Kon. (Ibid.) The two Jovanovićs maintained a warm relationship even though their political views would diverge by the late 1930s.

10 As explained in the previous chapter, the Main Committee of the People's Radical Party, led by Pašić's old collaborator Stanojević, stayed in the opposition throughout the 1930s, splitting from the rest of the party which joined the post-1929 regime. The party's majority under Stojadinović (who had previously been close to the Main Committee) merged into the Yugoslav Radical Union (JRZ) in the summer of 1935.

11 Dragoljub Jovanović, *Ljudi, ljudi...Vol. 2: Medaljoni 46 umrlih savremenika (sa fotografijama)*, Belgrade, 1975, 63-4.

claim that it had 'neutralised' the Croatian Peasant Party, the Serbian opposition was undoubtedly disorganised and divided.

However, Živković would have been worried if he could have foreseen events of the next decade. The united Serb-Croat opposition would seriously challenge the government in the two quasi-democratic parliamentary elections of May 1935 and December 1938. The opposition front was formed around two common goals: the solution of the Croat question and a return to democracy. The Croatian Peasants believed that the Croat question must be solved first, before the democratisation of the country could take place, while the Serbian opposition and the Independent Democrats argued that a return to democracy was a necessary precondition for the solution of the Croat question. They were nevertheless able to work together towards the achievement of both goals.

Because of the opposition's relative success at the two general elections, it may be presumed that the population at large opposed the dictatorship and favoured a Serb-Croat compromise.[12] Maček's triumphant visit to Belgrade in August 1938, when he was greeted by tens of thousands of people from across Serbia, possibly represented the highest point in Serb-Croat relations since the euphoria of 1918. (As it turned out, it also represented the beginning of the end of the Serb-Croat opposition.) Yet, as already suggested, a sustained and relatively successful joint Serb-Croat political action looked less than likely at the beginning of the 1930s.

Opposing the dictatorship? The early years, 1929-31

It may be argued that the Serb-Croat cooperation in the 1930s symbolically started with the 'cake affair', since Dragoljub Jovanović, together with his party boss Jovan Jovanović Pižon (no relation) and Ljuba Davidović, leader of the Democratic Party, was instrumen-

---

12 The turnout was high both times: in 1935 74 per cent (just over 2,880,000 out of 3,908,313 registered voters participated, *Politika*, 23 May 1935), while three years later 74.5 per cent of the electorate voted (Joseph Rothschild, *East Central Europe between the Two World Wars*, Seattle, 1974, 257).

tal in overcoming the mistrust which had existed between the opposition groups in Zagreb and Belgrade.[13] In June 1931 Dragoljub Jovanović went to Zagreb to meet Maček. This was only their second meeting ever, but the Serbian politician enjoyed a reputation among Croats as someone who genuinely supported their demands. Maček was impressed with Jovanović's courage and willingness to criticise the dictatorship publicly over the Croat question, which had brought him into trouble with the authorities.[14] Jovanović left Zagreb confident that Maček was in favour of a common state. He also believed that Belgrade and Zagreb must cooperate in opposition to the dictatorship, despite Maček's reserved stance.[15] Jovanović had proposed a joint boycott of the forthcoming elections, but the Croat leader

Neither rejected, nor accepted [the idea]. He was not even interested in contents [of the call to boycott] that the Belgrade opposition would draft. It seems as if he wanted us to work separately, to show our [respective] strengths, so that after the elections he would be free to work with a winner [on the Serbian side]—therefore, with the King, if the [opposition's call for a] boycott fails among the Serb electorate.[16]

However, if Jovanović was disappointed with Maček's non-cooperative attitude towards a boycott and rightly suspicious that the Croat leader might still make a deal with the Crown, the rest of their conversation greatly encouraged him. When Jovanović suggested that Maček was nowadays working together with Frankists, he vehemently denied this: 'I do not work with Frankists, they work with me!' He explained:

We shall remain side by side while the struggle against Belgrade goes on. When the time comes to settle the state question (*državno pitanje*), they [Frankists] will demand an independent Croatian state, even if that meant

---

13   See Todor Stojkov, 'O stvaranju Bloka narodnog sporazuma', *Istorija XX veka. Zbornik radova*, Belgrade, vol. VI, 1964, 245-301.

14   Maček, *In the Struggle for Freedom*, 158n. For a mini portrait of Jovanović, see Desimir Tošić, *O ljudima*, Belgrade, 2000, 176-92.

15   Jovanović, *Ljudi, ljudi*, vol. 2, 64. Jovanović mistakenly puts the meeting with Maček in 1930, instead of 1931.

16   Ibid.

making a deal with the Devil, but we shall be working on a common state with Serbs, even if the struggle for our rights lasts a hundred years.[17]

To Jovanović, 'these words were in that moment more important than the elections and a common opposition action'.[18]

One of the reasons for the lack of cooperation between the two opposition centres was that the Belgrade parties opposed the dictatorship, but their understanding of Yugoslavia as a united, strong state was not unlike King Alexander's own. The King's Yugoslavising policies were the main cause of Zagreb's dissatisfaction with the new order, not so much the fact that it was undemocratic. In this respect, the Independent Democrats were closer to Belgrade's opposition than to the Croatian Peasant Party, as it, too, primarily objected to the regime's 'absolutism'. However, despite disagreements with Maček's party over tactics and ideology, the Independent Democrats remained loyal to their coalition partners. They were aware that a democratic platform alone was not enough, as Croat opposition was predominantly nationalist, while *prečani* Serbs increasingly protested against the 'hegemony' of Serbs from Serbia (*Srbijanci*).[19] As Većeslav Vilder, one of the leading Independent Democrats, admitted in a letter to Pribićević, democratic ideas were 'still weak and undeveloped' and 'paralysed by nationalism—both Serbian and Croatian'; therefore they could not, by themselves, bring down the regime.[20]

---

17   Ibid. Maček's prophecy that Frankists would be prepared to make a deal 'with the Devil' in exchange for Croatia's independence was of course fulfilled in April 1941, when a former Frankist, the *Ustaša* leader Ante Pavelić, was installed by Nazi Germany and Fascist Italy as the *poglavnik* [Leader] of the Independent State of Croatia. Maček had previously refused to collaborate, so Berlin and Rome turned to Pavelić instead.

18   Ibid.

19   'Pismo V. Vildera i Vl. Mačeka Sv. Pribićeviću, [Zagreb], 27 February 1932', reproduced in Ljubo Boban, *Kontroverze iz povijesti Jugoslavije: Dokumentima i polemikom o temama iz novije povijesti Jugoslavije*, Zagreb, 3 vols, 1987-1990, vol. 1, 11-14, 12.

20   Ibid. The author of the letter was Vilder, but he wrote it in Maček's name, too. Maček added a hand-written postscript, as a brief reply to a letter from Pribićević which he had just received.

The Independent Democrats, nevertheless, believed that democracy offered the ultimate solution to Yugoslavia's problems. Vilder, ethnically neither a Serb nor a Croat, thought that the Yugoslav political scene was defined by a struggle between two 'ill nationalisms...the Serbian one, which suffered from megalomania, and the Croatian one, [which was ill with] a dispiriting scepticism'. He argued that 'it would be easy to reach a lasting agreement between these two nationalisms', if only 'there was a will for a genuine return to democracy.'[21]

Serbia's opposition parties were unpleasantly surprised by Maček's initial endorsement of Alexander's proclamation of 6 January 1929. Although the Croat leader soon grew disillusioned with the new order, his continued contacts with the regime led to suspicion among the Belgrade opposition circles.[22] The Serbian opposition considered the dictatorship a temporary measure—like almost everyone else at the time—and initially preferred to wait for a more favourable political climate before taking concrete action.

The cooperation between the Belgrade-based parties was not always very good either, especially in the initial period following the royal proclamation. Indeed, the first months of the dictatorship were marked by a Radical-Democrat argument, with both sides accusing each other of contributing to the failure of the democratic institutions and the establishment of the dictatorship. The Radicals were particularly critical of the Democrats' role in bringing down Korošec's government in 1928—an event they believed paved the way for the dictatorship. The Democrats, on the other hand, believed the Radicals were responsible for the political crisis of the late 1920s

---

21 BAR PPP, box 12, Poverljivi izveštaj dostavljen g. Lukoviću, šefu CPB, Zagreb, 13 December 1935. Vilder (1878-1961) was a Czech, but had both a Croat and a Yugoslav identity. He ended up as a political émigré in London, where he continued to be occupied with the question of Serb-Croat relations. See his *Bika za rogove. Gde je izvor spora srpsko-hrvatskog? Gde je rešenje?*, London, 1957.

22 Todor Stojkov, *Opozicija u vreme šestojanuarske diktature 1929-1935*, Belgrade, 1969, 101.

and the ultimate collapse of the democratic institutions.[23] Mutual antagonism between the two predominantly Serb parties, which in some respects had marked the Yugoslav politics in the 1920s and which continued through much of the first half of the 1930s, is usually overlooked by historians who concentrate on the Serb-Croat conflict. This antagonism would only be overcome, to a degree, in the second half of the 1930s.

The leaderships of the Serbian opposition parties had been aware that only together with their counterparts in Zagreb could they hope to undermine the regime.[24] Nevertheless, the cooperation between the opposition centres in Belgrade and Zagreb during the first two years of the dictatorship was reduced to sporadic contacts and marked by mutual mistrust.[25] In the early 1930s, the Democrats, Radicals and Agrarians established relatively close cooperation with Spaho's Yugoslav Muslims and, after they left the Živković government in September 1930, with Korošec's Slovene Clericals, but not with the Peasant Democratic Coalition.[26] If the largest Bosnian Muslim and Slovene parties had not rejoined the government by 1935, there would have quite probably emerged two strong opposition blocs—the Croat-Serb one based in Zagreb and the Belgrade-Sarajevo-Ljubljana one. If this had happened, perhaps significant political changes would have taken place long before 1939.

In August 1931, Davidović, Jovanović Pižon and Aca Stanojević, leader of the Radicals' Main Committee, asked Maček what his position would be if the King gave the opposition a mandate to form government. Would he enter such a government? To make a potential offer more attractive, the Serbian parties promised that in the event the post of the deputy prime minister would go to the Peas-

---

23 Ibid., 89n.

24 Ibid., 89.

25 Ibid., 105-09; MPHSS-1, 58-9; and Stojkov, 'Gradjanska opozicija i skupštinski izbori od 8. novembra 1931. godine', *Istorija XX veka. Zbornik radova*, Belgrade, vol. IV, 1962, 251.

26 Stojkov, *Opozicija*, 89; MPHSS-1, 58-9.

ant Democratic Coalition, as well as six other portfolios.[27] Maček, however, was in no rush to accept any offer from Belgrade. 'We have time,' he told his Serbian counterparts. 'We don't mind the dictatorship so much; let people get stronger and [as if made] of steel. Please act as you think is best, I [prefer to wait and] see how it all goes and then answer your questions.'[28]

Maček believed that his was a morally superior position. If Belgrade—both government and opposition—desired an agreement, it would have to act first, and it would have to meet Croat demands for autonomy before any further cooperation could be discussed. The King, however, never asked the democratic opposition to form a government. Instead, Alexander promulgated a new Constitution on 3 September 1931—an event which rather than signalling a gradual return to democracy only confirmed widespread fears that the dictatorship was there to stay.

When the regime announced fresh elections for November 1931, opposition parties from Belgrade, Zagreb, Ljubljana and Sarajevo began discussions over common action. The first dilemma they faced was whether to take part in the elections or not. The predominant mood was in favour of a boycott; Maček, alone among the opposition leaders, thought the opposition should participate.[29] He suggested that Stanojević head the united opposition list, but the Radical leader declined.[30] Because the Croatian Peasants did not stand a chance if they participated alone—the Independent Democrats favoured the boycott, too—Maček eventually backed down.[31]

The question of a common resolution calling the population to boycott the elections arose next. The text of a declaration drafted

---

27 This was virtually identical to the offer the SDK received (and accepted) in August 1939. Then, Maček became Dragiša Cvetković's deputy, the HSS received another five portfolios, while the SDS received one.

28 Cited in Stojkov, *Opozicija*, 119.

29 MPHSS-1, 59; Stojkov, 'Gradjanska opozicija', 267-8.

30 Jovanović, *Političke uspomene*, vol. 5, 47.

31 Stojkov, 'Gradjanska opozicija', 268.

jointly by the Belgrade parties, simply stating that the opposition was seriously disadvantaged in the post-1929 order and therefore refused to take part in the elections, was rejected by Maček and Pribićević as 'too soft'. In the end, the 'Belgrade declaration' was signed by Stanojević, Korošec, Jovanović Pižon, Davidović and Spaho, while a postscript was added stating that the Peasant Democratic Coalition, too, would not take part in the elections and that its leaders would soon issue a statement to that effect.[32] A separate declaration by the Independent Democrats was first published in the Czechoslovak press on 21 October (through Pribićević, who lived in Prague at the time), just two and a half weeks before the elections, because Maček and Pribićević had not been able to agree on its contents. The declaration stated that the 'absolutist rule' introduced following Radić's murder meant that conditions for free elections did not exist, and that the 'people would not feel obliged to respect the authority of the [future] parliament'.[33] The two coalition partners issued separate leaflets, which the regime described as both anti-Yugoslav. The Independent Democrats called on their mainly Serbian electorate to listen to 'all the Serb leaders' Pribićević, Davidović and Stanojević, and boycott the elections. Leaflets distributed by the Croatian Peasant Party stressed this party's 'battle for the Croatdom of the last 13 years', emphasising Radić's martyrdom for the Croat cause.[34]

Despite all the differences, the opposition parties' decision to boycott the elections, and especially the emergence of a Serb-based opposition bloc supported by Sarajevo and Ljubljana, sent a clear signal to the regime that its position was not as powerful as it might have seemed only a few months previously. However, the inability of Belgrade and Zagreb to issue a joint declaration also meant that the government's opponents remained seriously divided.

---

32 For a full text of the declaration see ibid., 271n.

33 Ibid., 273-4n. Stojkov believes that the declaration was issued with the outside world in mind.

34 Ibid., 284-6.

The 'Zagreb points' and the aftermath

Although one of the most significant political manifestos of the 1930s, the 'Zagreb points' were not meant for public use and were drafted quickly, without much prior preparation and discussion. They resulted from crisis talks of the Executive Committee of the Peasant Democratic Coalition held in Zagreb between 5 and 7 November 1932. The aim of the meeting was to discuss the relationship between the two coalition partners, at the time when the Independent Democrats were putting pressure on the Croatian Peasants to pursue a more active opposition to the dictatorship.[35] Moreover, the former shared the view of the Serbian opposition that a return to democracy should be given priority over any demands for territorial autonomy—Maček's main aim—even though they had publicly supported federalism since at least the summer of 1928.[36] As Većeslav Vilder, who presided over the meeting which took place in his house, explained, the meeting's main aim was 'to find out whether we can establish a common policy'; even if no agreement on common action was reached, it was important to demonstrate to the regime that the coalition still existed and functioned.[37] Despite some reservations as to the usefulness of such a meeting, Maček accepted the idea as he was eager to maintain the coalition, fearing that otherwise the Independent Democrats might return to unitarism, especially with Pribićević in exile.[38]

Maček's fears were not unfounded. During this period differences emerged inside the leadership of the Independent Democrats.

---

35 Maček, *In the Struggle for Freedom*, 137; Ljubo Boban, 'Zagrebačke punktacije', *Istorija XX veka*, vol. IV, Belgrade, 1962, 327.

36 When Pribićević called for the creation of seven 'historical provinces': Slovenia, Croatia, Bosnia-Herzegovina, Vojvodina, Serbia, Montenegro and Macedonia. Svetozar Pribićević, *Diktatura kralja Aleksandra*, Belgrade, 1953, 131. With the exception of Vojvodina, which became an autonomous province within Serbia, the other territories would become federal republics of socialist Yugoslavia.

37 Boban, 'Zagrebačke punktacije', 328.

38 Maček, *In the Struggle for Freedom*, 137-8.

Pribićević's shift away from integral Yugoslavism led to calls from within the party for him to resign, which he successfully resisted. The pressure came mostly from non-Serbs. Maček believed that Vilder and Hinko Krizman, not Pribićević, were most likely to lead the party back to centralism-unitarism. This is particularly significant because centralism-unitarism was usually linked exclusively with Serb politicians. Prvislav Grisogono and Juraj Demetrović—two prominent Croat Independent Democrats—had joined the regime because they disagreed with the party's new course, while Gregor Žerjav, a Slovene, also left the party.[39] 'I have lost all the confidence that under the leadership of Mr Svetozar P.[ribićević] things will get better […] We must decisively go back to the pure Yugoslav basis', Žerjav wrote to Krizman in March 1929, shortly before resigning from the party.[40]

At the November meeting the Croatian Peasant Party was represented by Maček, Trumbić, Predavec and Šutej.[41] Vilder, Krizman, Sava Kosanović, Father Dušan Kecmanović and Dušan Bošković represented the Independent Democrats.(Kecmanović represented Bosnian Serbs and Bošković Serbs from Vojvodina). Mile Budak, a writer and a prominent Frankist, also attended the meeting. Boban explains Budak's invitation as part of Maček's strategy to control the Frankists, but could this demonstration of cooperation with an openly anti-Yugoslav party also be explained as an implicit warning by Maček to his coalition partners that he had other political options?[42] In the spring and summer of that year the *Ustašas* managed

---

39 Hrvoje Matković, *Svetozar Pribićević i Samostalna demokratska stranka do šestojanuarske diktature*, Zagreb, 1972, 231-2. Žerjav had serious disagreements with the King, but remained a genuine integralist Yugoslav.

40 Ibid.

41 Ibid., 138. Trumbić only attended after Maček personally invited him (Boban, 'Zagrebačke punktacije', 328), which suggests that he was something of an outsider, close to Maček but not so much to the party.

42 Boban, 'Zagrebačke punktacije', 328. During the First World War Budak was a non-commissioned officer in the Austro-Hungarian army who, after being captured by Serbian troops, was among Habsburg prisoners of war who crossed the mountains of Albania in the winter of 1915-16, together with the Serbian army and government. Budak described this experience in *Ratno roblje. Albanski*

to smuggle small arms from Italy into Croatia, in order to prepare for an uprising against Belgrade. A group of peasants from the Lika region in Croatia, led by Juraj-Juco Rukavina, attacked a gendarmes' station in September 1932, but the 'uprising' was quickly suppressed. One of the attackers was killed and the rest were arrested, including Rukavina. The gendarmes, many of whom were brought in from Serbia, responded brutally to the attack; those interrogated and arrested were tortured and beaten up.[43] The *Ustaša*-organised 'Lika uprising' may have failed, but it showed that some Croatian peasants were ready to follow means of resistance other than the peaceful one favoured by Maček. Moreover, it provided another example of the regime's insensitive and counterproductive response to opposition.

At the end of the Zagreb talks a joint resolution was drafted by Trumbić. In a nutshell, the resolution blamed centralism for the country's political crisis, the only way out of which was a return to

---

križni put austrougarskih zarobljenih časnika, Zagreb, 1941 (reprinted several times since 1991). Budak would become a minister in the wartime *Ustaša* government, and was infamous for initiating anti-Serb and anti-Semitic legislation. He was sentenced to death as a war criminal in 1945 by the new, Communist authorities. After Croatia seceded from Yugoslavia in the early 1990s, the government of Franjo Tudjman attempted to rehabilitate Budak.

43   Milovan Djilas shared a cell with Rukavina and the two men became good friends. Friendship and even cooperation between the Communists and *Ustašas* in the prisons of interwar Yugoslavia was not uncommon. Although ideological enemies who fought bitterly against each other in the Second World War, in the early 1930s the two groups shared a common enemy, and the Communists supported in principle the *Ustaša* struggle for national liberation. A former Austro-Hungarian officer, who had briefly joined the Serbian army at the end of the First World War, before being discharged after a clash with a Serbian superior, Rukavina resumed his military career in the Second World War as an *Ustaša*. He was responsible for mass massacres of Serbs, whom he hated more than Communists. According to Djilas, Rukavina did not report former Communist prison mates when he recognised them in the street during the war. Nevertheless, he was shot by the Partisans at the end of the Second World War. Djilas provides an excellent short portrait of Rukavina and a typically insightful brief analysis of the Croat discontent with Belgrade among the peasants of Lika (*Memoir of a Revolutionary*, New York, 1973, 131-7).

1918 and a renegotiated, federal union.[44] Unlike in the summer of 1928, when the Peasant Democratic Coalition issued a resolution similar in tone and content, the regime responded firmly, by arresting Maček on 31 January 1933.[45] The context in which the 'Zagreb points' appeared was different from the timing of the 1928 resolution. In 1928, when Radić lay in hospital, an immediate crackdown on the Zagreb opposition was unthinkable. Four years later the situation was far calmer. Besides, despite the authorities' claim to the contrary, the 'Zagreb points' were not the sole reason for Maček's arrest.[46] In the aftermath of the resolution, the Croat leader gave several interviews to the foreign press, strongly criticising the regime and giving the impression that Croatia wished to secede. This embarrassed the Independent Democrats and annoyed the Serbian opposition.[47] Maček's interview in *Le Petit Parisien*, published in January 1933, caused much stir in Belgrade. 'To us Croats it is of secondary importance whether our freedom will be labelled "independence", whether Croatia will be a sovereign state, or a state within a [larger] union … a "federation", a "confederation", [or] an "empire",' Maček told the French paper.[48]

---

44 For the text of the resolution see Boban, *Kontroverze*, vol. 1, 34-5, and JF-1, 322-3. An English translation is provided in Maček, *In the Struggle for Freedom*, 139-40.

45 Maček, *In the Struggle for Freedom*, 142.

46 'Optužnica protiv predsjednika HSS dr. Mačka', *Vodja govori: Ličnost, izjave, govori i politički rad vodje Hrvata Dra. Vladka Mačeka* (compiled by Mirko Glojnarić), Zagreb, 1936, 162. When Maček demanded an explanation for his arrest, Stanoje Mihaldžić, chief of the Zagreb police (and the Interior Minister in the Cvetković-Maček government of 1939-41), confronted him with a text of the November resolution and asked if he was responsible for it (*In the Struggle for Freedom*, 142). Like Šubašić and Stepinac, Mihaldžić had fought as a volunteer with the Serbian army during the First World War. He was from a mixed Serb-Croat marriage: his mother was Švrljuga's sister. Mihaldžić was respected by both the Serbs and Croats, including the HSS leadership (Milan Jovanović Stoimirović, *Dnevnik, 1936-1941*, Novi Sad, 2000, 322).

47 MPHSS-1, 89-90.

48 Cited in ibid., 90.

The Independent Democrats sought to reassure their Belgrade colleagues. A memorandum drafted by Budisavljević emphasised Maček's commitment to Yugoslavia, though it admitted the interview was ill-advised and that it only benefited the regime-sponsored propaganda.[49]

Yet, the main reason why Maček was arrested was the reaction the November resolution triggered across the country. The 'Zagreb points' were followed by Korošec's 'Ljubljana points' of 31 December 1932, Spaho's 'Sarajevo points' and Davidović's 'Letter to a political friend' (the latter two were both issued in January 1933), as well as by declarations by smaller groups such as the Serb Republicans and Montenegrin Federalists.[50] Because all these resolutions supported the Zagreb resolution in principle, the regime was worried that a countrywide opposition front was emerging.

The Serbian parties could not agree on a joint statement, because their verdicts on the 'Zagreb points' differed.[51] The Radicals issued their resolution in April 1933. It criticised the post-1929 order and called for 'a *sporazum* between Serbs, Croats and Slovenes', in a unitary state which allowed local autonomies.[52] The Agrarians decided not to issue a statement at all, perhaps because the party felt there was no need for it. Dragoljub Jovanović had already in early 1932 issued a '16 point resolution', which called for the federalisation of the country.[53]

The most significant of the 'Serbian' resolutions was Davidović's 'Letter to a political friend'. Davidović in principle supported the 'Zagreb points', but disagreed with the suggestion that country should return to the *tabula rasa* of 1918. He proposed that the country be reorganised into four units, arguing for a federation in all but name:

---

49 Ibid., 90-91.
50 For the texts of the key resolutions see Boban, *Kontroverze*, vol. 1, 41-54.
51 MPHSS-1, 80-82.
52 JF-1, 333n.
53 Mira Radojević, *Udružena opozicija 1935-1939*, Belgrade, 1994, 27-33.

Due to being forced to live separately in the past, [but] *especially due to mistakes made in recent years*, there have developed feelings for wider autonomies, wider both in terms of territory and content. [...] satisfactory agreements for a free development of cultural-historical distinctiveness of Serbs, Croats and Slovenes must be reached. ... [It is therefore necessary to establish] large communities around great national-cultural centres in Belgrade, Zagreb and Ljubljana, and a fourth one, between these communities, in the transitional Serb-Croat zone.[54]

The 'fourth community' in the 'transitional Serb-Croat zone' was clearly Bosnia-Herzegovina. The creation of such a community, according to Davidović, would play a crucial role in the solution of 'our national problem' in two respects. 'First, it [would] remove the danger of a clear-cut and violent territorial division between Serbs and Croats.' Secondly, it would mean that Yugoslavia's internal divisions would not be entirely drawn according to 'tribal' (ethnic) boundaries.[55]

The significance of Davidović's proposal cannot be overestimated, even if it remained merely a proposal. It shows that one of the main opposition parties, the predominantly Serbian Democratic Party, had as early as January 1933 called for the federalisation of the country, and for the establishment of a Bosnian entity, on a par with Serbia, Croatia and Slovenia. Davidović's thinking may have been largely pragmatic—after all he was primarily concerned with avoiding a potential Serb-Croat conflict over Bosnia—and he did not regard Bosnian Muslims as a distinct Yugoslav 'tribe'. However, he had recognised the impossibility of Bosnia's division, which could not be said of Maček, Cvetković and Prince Paul, who effectively divided

---

54 'Deklaracija Ljubomira Davidovića', January 1933, JF-1, 327-31, 329 (emphasis added by D. Dj.). The declaration is usually referred to as '[Davidović's] Letter to a political friend', because it began with 'Dear friend', like most other declarations written by Davidović.

55 Ibid.

Bosnia in 1939.[56] The Radicals therefore remained alone among the major Serb opposition parties to continue to reject federalism. The three Belgrade-based parties could not agree easily on a joint statement condemning Maček's arrest either. Davidović drafted a statement which criticised not just the arrest, but also the government, the King, and state centralism. While the Agrarians accepted it, the draft was rejected by the Radicals.[57] When a joint statement, acceptable to all, was eventually issued on 23 April, it strongly condemned Maček's arrest and accused the regime of creating an even deeper gulf between Serbs and Croats, but fell short of blaming the centralist institutions for the political crisis.[58] Like the government, the Radicals' Main Committee believed that a compromise must be sought within the bounds of centralism. A year and a half later, Stanojević wrote to the Royal Court, stressing his party's support for 'unity between the state and the people, monarchy and the Karadjordjević dynasty', but urging the King to pursue the policies of 'rapprochement and agreement' between Serbs and Croats as the main principles of Yugoslavia's internal politics.[59]

The elections of May 1935

Dragoljub Jovanović travelled to Zagreb again in early February 1935. The purpose of his trip was to invite Maček, in the name of the Democratic Party and the Agrarian Union, to lead a joint opposition list in the elections, called for 5 May.[60] Maček, apparently unsure

---

56 Not to mention the majority of Croatian and Serbian politicians in the 1990s; some of the Serbs among those claimed to be Davidović's ideological successors.

57 MPHSS-1, 105.

58 AJ 37/10/60 (Stojadinović papers). The statement was signed 'collectively' by 'Representatives of the People's Radical Party, Democratic Party, [and] Agrarian Party'.

59 BAR PPP, box 11, Stanojević to Milan Antić, Knjaževac, 21 August 1934.

60 Maček, *In the Struggle for Freedom*, 158-9; Stojkov, *Opozicija*, 295; Stojkov, 'O stvaranju Bloka narodnog sporazuma', 249. At a public gathering of DS supporters in Kruševac in July 1935, Davidović said that the suggestion to ask

of the reaction of the Croatian population, asked Jovanović to give him a few days to consider the offer.[61] Years later, Jovanović told the historian Todor Stojkov that he had the impression that the Croat leader feared the regime's reaction.[62] Whatever the reasons for it, Maček's initial reluctance to accept the Democrat-Agrarian proposal did not last long. A few days later he accepted the Belgrade proposal, but faced opposition from within his own party. Trumbić was against any cooperation with Belgrade, as he bluntly told Jovanović.[63] In his memoirs Maček recalls that soon after the meeting with Jovanović, he was visited by a Frankist delegation which 'rallied around Ante Trumbić' and expressed its opposition to joining forces with the Serbian parties.[64] However, Maček's reasons for participating in the elections jointly with the Democrats and Agrarians were apparently so convincing that Trumbić not only changed his mind, but also volunteered to help in the campaign.[65]

While Maček initially hesitated, the Independent Democrats were instantly attracted by the proposal. Vilder told Jovanović that he was enthusiastic about the initiative, complaining that in comparison to Belgrade, Zagreb seemed 'politically dead'.[66] The party's exiled leader

---

Maček to lead the opposition came from a 'friend of Maček's', while the Croat leader was still in prison. The proposal was immediately accepted by Davidović and Jovan Jovanović Pižon, but rejected by Miloš Trifunović of the Radicals' Main Committee. Stojkov, 'O stvaranju Bloka narodnog sporazuma', 249n.

61 Maček, *In the Struggle for Freedom*, 159.

62 Stojkov, *Opozicija*, 295.

63 Trumbić remained firm even after Jovanović confessed that he only became a convinced Yugoslav after he heard a lecture on the Yugoslav question by Trumbić in Paris in 1918. Trumbić's only comment was: 'Bless you. I wish you success.' (in original: 'Živjeli. Želim Vam uspjeha.') Stojkov, *Opozicija*, 296n.

64 This example suggests that links between the HSS leadership and the Frankists were closer than Maček was prepared to admit.

65 Maček, *In the Struggle for Freedom*, 161. Unfortunately, Maček does not elaborate on reasons why he accepted to lead the united Serb-Croat opposition, after the initial hesitation.

66 Stojkov, *Opozicija*, 295n. Vilder's remark suggests that disagreements between the SDS and HSS over the tactics continued after the 'crisis talks' of

Pribićević feared the regime's manipulation of election procedures, but was swayed by reports that the population 'was putting such pressure on political leaders to take part [in the elections] that it was impossible to resist.'[67]

On 7 February, Maček wrote to Dragoljub Jovanović formally to accept the offer to lead the united opposition. He regarded the Serbian opposition's gesture as a 'personal honour' and 'a great step towards mutual understanding, and with it, [towards] the final solution of the Croat question *within the borders of this state.*'[68] The last line must have been music to the Democrats' and Agrarians' ears. Maček's leadership of the largest opposition party was not the only reason why Davidović and Jovanović Pižon had asked him to head the united opposition at the elections. They were also impressed by his courageous and dignified bearing during the trial following the publication of the 'Zagreb points', when Maček made it clear that he was not against Yugoslavia.[69] Strongly denying the prosecution's charge that the 'Zagreb points' challenged Yugoslavia's unity, Maček stated that,

[We] have above all sought to find a way and means to solve the Croatian question inside the borders of this state, to the satisfaction of Croats and Slovenes, and to the satisfaction of Serbs, but especially those Serbs living side by side with us Croats, who will continue to live [with us].[70]

Maček was sentenced to three years' incarceration, but was to serve only about half of it. In a telegram sent to the Prince Regent on 21 December 1934 to thank him for setting him free, Maček expressed hope that his early release was 'an act of good will to approach correctly the solution of the Croat question—within the borders of our common state.'[71] The Democrats and Agrarians now seemed con-

---

November 1932.

67 Maček, *In the Struggle for Freedom*, 161; Stojkov, *Opozicija*, 297n.
68 *Vodja govori*, 207. Emphasis added by D. Dj.
69 Stojkov, *Opozicija*, 295.
70 *Vodja govori*, 164.
71 Ibid., 195.

vinced that Maček was genuinely interested in working towards the good of the whole country, despite the mixed signals he gave in the foreign press. By asking him to lead the united Serb-Croat opposition list they also wanted to send a clear signal to both the domestic and the international public that the leader of the Croats was not a separatist. Davidović explained before the elections that common action between Belgrade and Zagreb was in the country's best interests. 'One of those interests,' Davidović argued, '[was] cooperation with the Croats, whose abstention [from state institutions] has been interpreted by our external enemies not only as a protest against the regime, but as separatism and indifference to the destiny of this state as a whole.'[72] Emphasising Maček's loyalty to Yugoslavia, Davidović stated that:

The representative of the vast majority of Croats, Dr Maček, has all this time been very open and resolute in respect of that issue [Croat loyalty to the state]. In the statement before the court [in 1933] and in the telegram thanking the Prince Regent [for releasing him from prison], Dr Maček always repeated that his was a struggle for the fulfilment of Croat demands *inside the borders of our common country.*[73]

On the eve of the elections the opposition was broadly divided into three groups: first, the Peasant Democratic Coalition of the Croatian Peasant Party and the Independent Democrats; second, the Democrats and the Agrarians, who were looking to join forces with Zagreb; the Radicals' Main Committee and the Slovene People's Party belonged to the third group. The Yugoslav Muslims were close to the Radicals and Slovene Clericals, but were not considered to be firmly inside their camp because of their links with the Democrats and Agrarians.[74]

After accepting to lead the united opposition list, Maček was keen to widen it as much as possible. He asked Davidović and Jovanović Pižon to try and persuade Korošec and Spaho to join the coalition.

---

72 AJ 37/3, Ljubomir Davidović, 'Pismo prijatelju', April 1935.
73 Ibid. Emphasis in original.
74 Stojkov, *Opozicija*, 293-4.

The Croat leader was in favour of the Radicals joining in, too, but left it to the Democrats and Agrarians to decide whether their differences with the Radicals' Main Committee could be reconciled. He also instructed his followers to help the former minister Božidar Maksimović, now in opposition, collect enough signatures to be able to present a country-wide list, hoping thus to weaken Jevtić.[75] (Maksimović and Dimitrije Ljotić, leader of the small, pro-fascist party *Zbor*,[76] presented their own election lists.) Only Spaho agreed to join the Maček-led list. The Clericals and the Radicals decided to boycott the elections, but maintain contacts with Prime Minister Jevtić.[77] Therefore, not only was the line dividing the government and the opposition not drawn along Serb-Croat divisions, but even the divisions within the opposition were clearly not 'ethnic'. The conflict between the Democrats and Agrarians on one side and the Radicals on the other dated back to the early 1920s, and was renewed by the Radicals' tacit support of Jevtić and their brief (ultimately unsuccessful) negotiations about joining his government.[78]

It was the Radicals' flirtation with the regime that brought the party closer to Korošec's Clericals, who also positioned themselves nearer to the regime than to the opposition. At the same time, Spaho's Yugoslav Muslims were somewhere in between the Radical-Clerical position and that of the Peasant Democratic Coalition and the Democrats and the Agrarians. Spaho too had negotiated with Jevtić over entering the government in December 1934.[79] In fact, it was their belief that by joining their forces Korošec, Stanojević

---

75 AJ 83 (Papers of Sava Kosanović), Maček to Kosanović, 10 May 1935. Maček would employ the same tactics three years later, before the 1938 elections.

76 The support base of *Zbor* was tiny, but well organised, extending beyond Serbia. Ljotić was briefly Justice Minister in 1931, but resigned in protest at the King's rejection of his constitutional proposal. For more on Ljotić and the *Zbor* see Miloš Martić, 'Dimitrije Ljotić and the Yugoslav National-Movement Zbor, 1935-1945', *East European Quarterly*, vol. 14, no. 2, Winter 1981, 219-39.

77 Stojkov, *Opozicija*, 297-8.

78 Ibid., 287-8, 294.

79 Ibid., 288.

and Spaho would be entrusted by the Prince Regent with forming a new government bringing the three leaders closer together.
In mid-November Korošec and Stanojević held talks in Knjaževac
(Stanojević's home town in eastern Serbia), which resulted in the
so-called 'Knjaževac protocol'.[80] The 'protocol', also referred to as the
'Stanojević-Korošec agreement', envisaged the creation of a coalition,
perhaps even the merger of the two parties—'a political union'—and
it was agreed that Spaho's Muslims should also be invited to join.[81]
In late February 1935 Korošec told a group of journalists that a Yu-
goslav National Union might be formed by the Radicals, the Slovene
People's Party and the Yugoslav Muslim Organisation.[82]

The question of participation in the elections was another bone
of contention between the Radicals' Main Committee and the other
two Serbian-based opposition parties. There were two main reasons
why the Democrats and the Agrarians decided to take part in the
elections. First, the dictatorship was evidently relaxed following Alexander's assassination and the political parties were able to carry out
their activities relatively freely. Second, there were strong indications
that the population at large wanted elections; to boycott the ballot could mean losing badly needed popular support. As Davidović
explained in April 1935:

The first and the basic reason [for taking part in the elections] is that the
people, who are fed up with the [current] situation, demanded action at all
costs. Impoverished and ruined, [the people] have nothing to lose and they
no longer fear a public ballot and [the regime's] intimidation.[83]

Davidović's claim about public pressure on political parties to take
part in the forthcoming elections was not merely rhetorical and limited to Serbia, the Democrats' power-base. As already mentioned,

---

80 Ibid., 285-6.
81 'Sporazum A. Stanojevića i A. Korošca', Knjaževac, 16 November 1934,
JF-1, 335-6.
82 BAR PPP, box 12, Nedeljni izveštaj, Ministarstvo unutrašnjih poslova,
Kraljevina Jugoslavia, Vrhovna policijska uprava, Belgrade, 26 February 1935.
83 AJ 37/3, Ljubomir Davidović, 'Pismo prijatelju', April 1935.

Pribićević also initially favoured a boycott, but allegedly changed his mind when he heard reports from the country that the population at large was in favour of elections, particularly in Croat-populated areas.[84] This prompted him to write to Maček a letter that began: 'Hats off to the Croats!'[85]

The opposition formed a technical coalition, and no common political platform was put forward before the elections. One of the reasons for the failure of the opposition parties even to issue a joint political statement was Maček's insistence that this must include the phrase 'the long-suffering Croatian nation'—something the other parties, including the Independent Democrats, opposed.[86] The only joint statement, signed by Maček, Davidović and Jovanović Pižon, was issued in early March, two months before the elections. It simply announced that the opposition would present a joint list, headed by Maček, stressing that 'existing political, economic and social difficulties can only be overcome through the freely manifested will of the people and in the spirit of national unity.'[87]

The regime was aware of the disunity within the opposition camp and its parties' different tactics. 'While in regions with a predominantly Serbian population [the opposition] campaigns with openly nationalist slogans, in other areas it secretly agitates using [slogans inspired by] tribal separatism, federalism and even...the creation of an independent Croatia,' a police report written before the elections stated.[88] The authorities responded with intimidation of opposition supporters, which did not help calm down tensions caused by a seri-

---

84 Maček, *In the Struggle for Freedom*, 161; Stojkov, *Opozicija*, 297n. According to Maček, Pribićević was sent results of opinion polls conducted by the HSS, which made him change his mind.

85 Maček, *In the Struggle for Freedom*, 161.

86 Stojkov, *Opozicija*, 301n.

87 Cited in ibid, 301.

88 BAR PPP, box 12, Izveštaj za Njegovo Kraljevsko Visočanstvo Kneza-Namesnika iz Vrhovne policijske uprave, no date, ca. Spring 1935. In interwar Yugoslavia, unlike in its socialist successor, Yugoslav patriots were described as 'nationalists'. After 1945, 'nationalists'—either Serb 'unitarists' or non-Serb

ous incident that took place in February 1935, when the gendarmerie clashed with a group of Croat peasants in and around Slavonski Brod, in north-east Croatia. In two separate incidents twelve peasants were killed, six were wounded, and a number of them were arrested, while three gendarmes were wounded. The incident started when the gendarmerie arrested three persons who allegedly shouted anti-Yugoslav slogans on the Pope's Day celebrations.[89] Despite high tensions, the violence did not escalate.

. The opposition supporters in Serbia were also intimidated, although there were no armed clashes.[90] Despite the government's election victory there, the authorities' policies had been in some cases counter-productive. A pro-government candidate for Orašac, central Serbia, complained directly to Prince Paul that many of his electorate voted for the Maček list in protest at the regime's policies.[91]

The intimidation was not one-sided, however. Police reports from Savska reveal a number of incidents in which the perpetrators were opposition supporters and the victims those suspected of pro-government sympathies. Although the regime's accusations that the opposition was carrying out 'acts of terrorism' against supporters of the government were exaggerated, incidents included the destruction of

---

'separatists'—were singled out as the greatest threat to the unity of the Yugoslav socialist federation.

89   BAR PPP, box 12, Nedeljni izveštaj, Ministarstvo unutrašnjih poslova, Kraljevina Jugoslavia, Vrhovna policijska uprava, Belgrade, 26 February 1935. Celebrations among Croats, and other Roman Catholics, commemorating the anniversary of the current Pope's accession (in this case the accession of Pope Pius XI in February 1922) are known as the Pope's Day (*Papindan*). They are clearly not to be confused with the so-called Pope's Day celebrations in Boston, Massachusetts, where those commemorating the anniversary of the English Gunpowder Plot in the 17th and 18th centuries carried effigies of the Pope.

90   BAR PPP, box 11, Jovan Jovanović Pižon to Prince Paul, Belgrade, 28 March 1935, 6 April 1935, and 1 May 1935 (three separate letters from Jovanović to Paul).

91   BAR PPP, box 11, Dr Milojević to Prince Paul, Belgrade, 31 May 1935.

property, the burning of vineyards and haystacks, the killing of cattle, and the distribution of anti-government leaflets.[92]

The Jevtić list won the elections, receiving 1.7 million votes or 60 per cent of the vote. The Maček-led opposition won only in Savska and Primorska—the two predominantly Croat *banovinas*—but lost in all other *banovinas*. It did well in Vrbaska, with just over 43 per cent, and reasonably well in Drinska, where it received 30 per cent of the vote. In total, Maček's list received just over 1 million votes (37 per cent). The other two opposition lists, headed by Maksimović and Ljotić, failed to win a single seat in parliament.[93] According to the electoral law, the winner, regardless of the margin of victory, received three-fifths of the scats, while the remaining two-fifths were allocated according to their percentage of the vote received. Thus the government, which won 60 per cent of the vote, received 303 seats in a 370-seat parliament, while the united opposition, with almost one third of the vote, was given only 67 seats.[94]

In the aftermath of the elections the opposition announced that it did not intend to participate in the new parliament. It explained that it had decided to take part in the elections as a single list aware that only by joining its forces could it replace the regime, which it regarded as 'a national disaster'.[95] However, the unfair electoral law and the manner in which the elections had been carried out left the opposition no choice but to boycott parliament. 'The state unity of Serbs, Croats, and Slovenes is an unavoidable historical necessity,'

---

92 HDA XXI/61/4006, Sresko načelstvo u Slav. Brodu, Kraljevskoj banskoj upravi savske [*sic!*] banovine, otseku za državnu zaštitu [Zagreb], Mesečni izveštaj o radu opće uprave za april 1935.g., Slavonski Brod, 14 May 1935.

93 The final results were as follows: Jevtić list 1,746,982 votes (60.64 per cent of the vote), Maček list 1,076,345 (37.36 per cent), Maksimović list 32,726 votes (1.18 per cent), and Ljotić list 23,814 (0.85 per cent). A minimum of 50,000 votes was needed to secure a seat in parliament. For a detailed analysis of the elections see Stojkov, *Opozicija*, 289-320.

94 Stojkov, *Opozicija*, 311.

95 BAR PPP, box 12, Draft of the opposition resolution, 22 May 1935. The resolution was formally declared on 30 May. See also *Vodja govori*, 212-3.

but the only 'real salvation' for Yugoslavia lay in 'true democracy', which alone could solve the country's problems 'to the satisfaction of Croats, Serbs and Slovenes', the opposition leaders stated.[96] However, the regime prevented the opposition's victory by intimidating its supporters and by exploiting a highly favourable electoral law. The leaders of the main opposition parties vowed to continue their joint action, as 'all problems in our state—political, economic and social—can only be solved in a free society and only if there is an agreement (*sporazum*) between the Serbs, Croats and Slovenes.'[97] In separate statements Ljotić and Maksimović also complained about intimidation of their supporters by the police, while Archbishop Bauer of Zagreb and another senior Catholic priest sent a memorandum to Prince Paul complaining about the regime's often violent election campaign.[98]

Tensions did not go away after the election results were announced. Because the ballot was open it was easy to find out how everyone voted, especially in villages and smaller towns. Although serious incidents preceded the elections and continued after they were over, and even though tensions between the authorities and population in predominantly Croat areas ran high, it would be wrong to see those simply as examples of Serb-Croat conflict. In areas where the opposition enjoyed majority support, anyone who voted for the government was potentially in danger of intimidation, regardless of their ethnicity. Equally, members of the gendarmerie were often victims of physical attacks, whether they were Croat or Serb or for that matter Slovene.

The incident that took place on 19 May 1935 in the village of Kravarsko, in Zagorje, offers a particularly good example. It started when Pavao and Josip Zagorac and Ivan Sremić (all ethnic Croats) were beaten up by a group of villagers because they had voted for the Jevtić list, and a group of local gendarmes tried to protect them and pacify

---

96 Ibid.
97 Ibid.
98 Stojkov, *Opozicija*, 312-3.

what was rapidly turning into an anti-government protest. A crowd of around 1,000 protesters refused to back down, instead throwing stones and other hard objects at the unfortunate gendarmes, who were lucky to escape with injuries. One of them, Hašim Meštrović, was seriously wounded, after being hit by an axe on the head.[99] The gendarmes barricaded themselves in a local restaurant and kept the crowd at a distance by shooting into the air. Only after two local priests, Andrija Busija and Leopold Vernik, intervened did the mob gradually lift the siege and head home.[100] The appropriately named priests[101] had been asked to help by the gendarmes' commander Ferdo Roth. They were not supporters of the government: the same police report states that they 'agitated' for Maček's list before the elections.[102]

The state clearly did not have full control of predominantly Croat areas, where the Croatian Peasants (and the Independent Democrats, to a degree) represented the highest authority. However, *de facto* control over the situation on the ground in Croat areas was not Maček's main aim. The Croat leader demanded full territorial autonomy for Croatia as well as the recognition of the Croats' separate identity. Maček was openly opposed to the belief that there was a single Yugoslav nation, as argued by 'integralist' Yugoslavs. He essentially understood the nation as a primordial community, believing that it was too late to forge a new national identity made up of Croat, Serb and Slovene 'elements'. In an interview with a Bulgarian journalist, Maček stated:

---

99 HDA XXI/62/4049, Kraljevska banska uprava savske [sic!] banovine, Otsek za državnu zaštitu, telefonski izveštaj Odelenju za državnu zaštitu, Ministarstva unutrašnjih poslova u Beogradu, Zagreb, 20 May 1935. The seriously wounded gendarme's name suggests he too was a non-Serb.

100 Ibid.

101 Busija means 'ambush', while Vernik is 'believer'.

102 HDA XXI/62/4049, Kraljevska banska uprava savske [sic!] banovine, Otsek za državnu zaštitu, telefonski izveštaj Odelenju za državnu zaštitu, Ministarstva unutrašnjih poslova u Beogradu, Zagreb, 20 May 1935.

There existed a Croatian nation, a Serbian nation, a Slovene nation and a Bulgarian nation, each with a developed national consciousness...nations are created and abolished by God, and not by ministers or dictators. Only what springs from the people can be long lasting.[103]

In another interview, this time with a Slovak newspaper, he explained that:

The ideology of national oneness was based on the notion of linguistic unity. But life has taught us that linguistic unity is not enough for national unity... *English and Americans share the same literary language. Danish and Norwegians as well.* And yet no one claims that they are the same *nation*.[104]

The Peasant Democratic Coalition confirmed at the beginning of June its earlier decision not to participate in parliament, demanding its dissolution and fresh elections.[105] The Democrats and Agrarians now hesitated, unsure how to explain to their voters any decision to boycott parliament. However, partly out of solidarity with their Zagreb counterparts, and partly because they too deemed the electoral law undemocratic, the two Serbian parties followed suit.[106] Despite promising the electorate to continue a 'joint action', the Yugoslav Muslim Organisation entered the new government of Milan Stojadinović in June 1935. The government was formed around a (Serbian) Radical - (Slovene) Clerical - (Bosnian) Muslim axis. This resembled the old Stanojević-Korošec plan, except that the Main Committee of the Radical Party was 'replaced' by the Radicals' pro-government faction. With the creation of the new government,

---

103   *Vodja govori*, 229.

104   Ibid., 268-9; emphasis in original.

105   AJ 37/10/60, 'Rezolucija Udružene opozicije', Zagreb, 2 June 1935.

106   This was a good example of the difference of approach to politics in Serbia and Croatia. While supporters of the HSS, as well as the SDS, were accustomed to their political leaders' policy of abstention, the Serbian electorate was less used to boycott as a political tool.

Stanojević's Radicals moved closer to the Democrats and Agrarians, and to the Peasant Democratic Coalition.

At the time of the formation of the Yugoslav Radical Union, in the summer of 1935, rumours circulated that the opposition would also unite in a single political party. Maček issued a denial:

There will be no two [main] parties, if for no other reason than because it would mean adopting Stojadinović's favourite political system, [based on] the American two-party system, whereby the Croat question, which is today known to the whole world as a national question, would be minimised. I believe that [such a party system] would suit gentlemen in Belgrade, but it would not suit us Croats. We Croats follow *Croatian national politics*, not party politics.[107]

Nevertheless, throughout the 1930s various ideas about the formation of supra-parties circulated. The failure of the democratic system in the 1920s was blamed largely on the inability of numerous political parties to work together. The dictatorship, although relaxed after 1934, was not working either and some Yugoslav leaders clearly believed that political stability might be achieved if there were fewer parties with countrywide bases. During their meeting in January 1937, Stojadinović encouraged Maček to work closely with the Serbian opposition parties, so that a federalist bloc would emerge.[108] As Maček had argued, Stojadinović had hoped the Belgrade-based parties and the Peasant Democratic Coalition would eventually unite into a single party, thus forming an opposition counterpart to the Yugoslav Radical Union:

On the one side the unitarists—the JRZ and others who support that line—and on the other the federalists—the HSS, [Ljuba] Davidović's Democrats, Pribićević's Democrats, [Jovan] Jovanović's Agrarians…[on the one hand] Slovenes and Bosnian Muslims together with the Serbian Radicals, [on the other hand] Maček's Croats together with the Serb opposition parties—that

107 *Vodja govori*, 247.

108 Stojadinović, *Ni rat ni pakt: Jugoslavija izmedju dva rata*, Rijeka, 1970, 516. See the previous chapter.

would provide an ideal recipe for the final solution of our internal problems and the consolidation of the state.[109]

Unlike Maček, Stojadinović did not see divisions between the government and opposition as strictly 'national' (i.e. Serb-Croat) but as 'political' (i.e. centralism vs. federalism). At this time the Croat leader once again hoped to negotiate an agreement with the regime, albeit with Prince Paul rather than with Stojadinović. Only after he had failed to achieve any concessions would he turn again to the Belgrade opposition. The two opposition centres re-established close cooperation in 1937 and for a year and a half they worked together. This was also the period when Serbia's United Opposition emerged.

The United Opposition

In the second half of the 1930s the Democratic Party, the Agrarian Party and the Main Committee of the People's Radical Party established close cooperation which, nevertheless, was not free of disagreements. Their informal coalition was usually referred to by contemporaries as the United Opposition (UO).[110] The parties of the UO were in a difficult position even without the differences that existed between them, because they were placed between the government and its somewhat reluctant partners in Croatia. When Dragoljub Jovanović visited Maček in Zagreb in August 1935, he rightly concluded that the Croat leader did not want to be too closely associ-

---

109 Ibid., 318. The Yugoslav Muslims' participation in the government throughout the second half of the 1930s is somewhat paradoxical: while the government, in form at least, sought to preserve the ideology of integral Yugoslavism, there were opposition parties, such as the Democrats, which had been prepared to grant Bosnia an autonomous status in the event of coming to power. Unlike Maček, Spaho was willing to join the government and work within the bounds of the 1931 Constitution, believing that the cooperation with the government would be more beneficial than cooperation with the opposition. Korošec was probably led by similar motives; after all, his was the only party which formally joined the post-6 January regime.

110 Mira Radojević (*Udružena opozicija*) offers the most extensive treatment of the activities of the United Opposition.

ated with the Agrarians, or with any other opposition party, because at the time he still hoped for an agreement with the Crown.[111]

Because the regime accused the Serbian opposition of being anti-Yugoslav by virtue of its cooperation with the Croatian Peasant Party, Serb leaders were compelled to prove not only that they were more patriotic than the government, but also that the Croatian Peasants were not an anti-Yugoslav party. The regime failed to understand that there could be more than one version of Yugoslavism. One of the legacies of the 1920s and of the dictatorship was that those who rejected centralism-unitarism were regarded as anti-Yugoslav. The opposition centres in Belgrade and Zagreb came closer together partly because the Democrats and Agrarians had gradually come to reject integral Yugoslavism. In his 'Letter to a political friend' of January 1933, Davidović publicly opted for federalism, and by the end of 1935 he appeared to have abandoned the notion that the South Slavs were a single (ethnic) nation.

During an opposition meeting in the Serbian town of Šabac in October 1935, an argument broke out between the Croatian Peasant Žiga Šol and the Democrat Mihajlo Škorić, over whether a single Yugoslav nation existed. Davidović sided with Šol, who argued that it did not exist. The Democrats' leader admitted he felt a Serb, not a Yugoslav. According to him Serbs, Croats and Slovenes were kindred peoples, but they were not the same. However, he hoped that in future a real Yugoslav identity would be forged.[112] Milan Grol, Davidović's eventual successor as the party leader, similarly believed that Serbs, Croats and Slovenes were not a single nation, although he too hoped that they would eventually develop into one.[113]

On the other hand, Lazar Marković, one of the leading members of the Radicals' Main Committee, wrote in June 1937 that separate

---

111 Nadežda Jovanović, *Život za slobodu bez straha. Studija o životu i delu dr. Dragoljuba Jovanovića*, Belgrade, 2000, 207-8.

112 Radojević, *Udružena opozicija*, 159. See also Ivan Ribar, *Iz moje političke suradnje (1901-1963.)*, Zagreb, 1965, 282-3.

113 Radojević, *Udružena opozicija*, 159, 163.

Croat, Serb, and Slovene identities only existed *within* the 'national oneness' ideology. 'If those two concepts can be reconciled we are ready to accept them. If, however, the recognition of Croat individuality means the negation and abandonment of the Yugoslav national thought, we cannot accept that.'[114]

The three Serbian parties were often unable to present a common platform. For instance, the Agrarians, themselves disunited, sought alternative political action, outside the United Opposition. Jovanović Pižon had hoped to form a common 'agrarian front' with other peasant parties in Yugoslavia, including the Croatian Peasant Party.[115] He believed that his party could achieve an agreement with the Croats much quicker if it acted independently of the Democrats and Radicals.[116] This led the other two parties of the UO to accuse the Agrarians of treason.[117]

The Concordat crisis

Differences of opinion within the United Opposition were to be put aside during the Concordat crisis of July and August 1937. In July 1935, thirteen years after they had first started negotiations, the Yugoslav government and the Holy See signed a Concordat regulating the position of the Roman Catholic Church in Yugoslavia.[118] The government hoped to attract Croat support at the expense of the Croatian Peasant Party and saw the Concordat as a way of solving the Croatian question. As Stojadinović told the parliament in summer 1937, 'The Concordat means agreement (*sporazum*). Who with, gentlemen? With the Holy See. Who does the Holy See represent?

---

114 Cited in ibid., 166-7.
115 Ibid., 110-11.
116 MPHSS-1, 299; Radojević, *Udružena opozicija*, 173.
117 Radojević, *Udružena opozicija*, 173; Stojkov, *Opozicija*, 279.
118 For details see AJ 37/25/195, 'Projekt zakona o Konkordatu izmedju Sv. Stolice i Kraljevine Jugoslavije', Belgrade, 20 July 1937.

It represents 400 million [Roman] Catholics, 5 million of whom live in our state.'[119]

Stojadinović delayed submitting the document to the parliament for ratification, but when he did so in July 1937, two years after the agreement was signed, his government nearly fell. The Serbian Orthodox Church instantly complained that the Concordat was concluded at its expense.[120] It argued that although there were more Orthodox than Roman Catholic believers in Yugoslavia, the latter were put in a favourable position by the state. Among other complaints, the Serbian church pointed out that under the terms of the Concordat children from mixed marriages where one parent was a Roman Catholic were to be raised as Catholics; and that the state had only 30 days during which to object to the Vatican's nominations of Catholic Bishops in Yugoslavia, while in the case of Orthodox bishops no such deadline existed. Roman Catholics were allegedly given special privileges in education and the army, and the Vatican would be free to spread its propaganda in Yugoslavia.[121]

Street demonstrations led by Orthodox priests broke out in Belgrade and other Serbian towns, while Stojadinović and Serbian members of the government were excommunicated by the Church. Suddenly, shouts of *djavo* ('devil' in Serbo-Croat, a play on '*vodja*' (leader), as Stojadinović liked to be called) and *Jereza* (a nickname for the JRZ, which sounds similar to Serbo-Croat for 'heresy') gained additional meanings. Demonstrators were joined by Živković's and Ljotić's supporters, and even by the Communists, but the Democrats, the Agrarians and Stanojević's Radicals kept a relatively low

---

119 AJ 37/2/9-11, draft of Stojadinović's speech to the *Skupština* [Belgrade], 23 July 1937.

120 See *Primedbe i prigovori na projekat Konkordata izmedju naše države i Vatikana*, Sremski Karlovci, 1936.

121 The Concordat crisis received significant attention in Britain, where some leading members of the Anglican Church sided with the Serbian Orthodox Church. See Nugent Lincoln's (The Bishop of Lincoln) letter to the editor, *The Times*, 7 July 1937.

profile.[122] Particularly violent was the so-called 'bloody litany' of 19 July, when a procession praying for Patriarch Varnava's health (he was seriously ill at the time) turned into anti-government demonstrations. Serbian churches displayed black flags, church bells tolled intermittently, while crowds shouted 'the police have killed our bishop!' when the news spread that Bishop Simeun, one of the leaders of the procession, had been taken to a Belgrade hospital after a gendarme hit his metal episcopal crown and allegedly damaged his skull.[123] The Bishop luckily did not die—it turned out he had only received minor injuries—but other casualties were reported. The gendarmerie responded with violence, charging with bayonets and firing guns in the air.

To make matters worse, the Patriarch died only hours after the Concordat was ratified on 23 July, and rumours immediately spread that he had been poisoned by the regime.[124] The funeral was attended by thousands of mourners, including representatives of the Crown— but not the government—as well as representatives of Yugoslavia's Muslim leaders, the Bulgarian Orthodox Church, and Serbian opposition parties. The authorities banned a proclamation issued by the Serbian Church on the eve of the funeral, in which the Patriarch's death was compared to that of King Alexander: two great patriots

---

122 The Communists hoped to gain political ground during the period of intense popular dissatisfaction with the regime, realizing that the main opposition parties reacted relatively mildly. Milovan Djilas, *Memoir of a Revolutionary*, New York, 1973, 306.

123 'Black Flags in Yugoslavia: Concordat Bill Protests', *The Times*, 21 July 1937.

124 These rumours were unsubstantiated. Upon hearing that the Patriarch was seriously ill, Prince Paul immediately sent an emissary to Metropolitan Dositej, to ask about the Patriarch's health. Dositej told the emissary that the Patriarch's death was imminent, and that it was unfortunate he was dying on the same night when the Concordat was being voted in. 'But God is just!', Dositej added, raising his voice. BAR PPP, box 12, Vojislav Jovanović to Prince Paul, Belgrade, 23 July 1937.

who died for their cause, at the time they were most needed by their people.[125]

The government initially responded strongly. Despite the brutal police action, Stojadinović believed that in dealings with the Serbian Church a firmer position should be adopted.[126] Foreign newspapers reporting on the crisis were either bought up by the government or simply returned unsold,[127] while a long-serving Belgrade correspondent of Reuters was no longer welcome in the country.[128] The government allegedly also considered a clampdown on opposition leaders.[129]

Owing to public pressure, Stojadinović eventually backed down, withdrawing the document from further parliamentary procedure in late July 1937.[130] The Prime Minister explained his decision:

I therefore recommend that the question of the Concordat be taken off the agenda for the time being. We have shown good will and strong will to ratify the Concordat, but we wish the Concordat to pass [parliamentary procedure] while the atmosphere among the people is more positive and reconciliatory. If by signing the Concordat we sought to secure religious harmony in western regions of our country, it would not be wise to disturb

---

125 'Angered Church in Yugoslavia: Funeral To-Day of Patriarch', *The Times*, 29 July 1937. The Bulgarian Metropolitan Paul had attended the Theological College in St Petersburg together with the late Patriarch. Some leaders of the Islamic community in Yugoslavia openly sided with the Serbian Orthodox Church over the Concordat issue.

126 HIA, Dragiša Cvetković Collection, Prince Paul folder, Stojadinović to Prince Paul, Belgrade, 18 August 1937.

127 'Church and Cabinet in Yugoslavia', *The Times*, 5 August 1937.

128 'Processions Banned in Yugoslavia: Journalist to Leave', *The Times*, 22 July 1937.

129 'Alarmist rumours in Yugoslavia', *The Times*, 16 August 1937.

130 Radmila Radić, 'Religion in a Multinational State: The Case of Yugoslavia', in Dejan Djokić (ed.), *Yugoslavism: Histories of a Failed Idea, 1918-1992*, London and Madison, WI, 2003, 196-207, 201-02. For Stojadinović's account of the events see his *Ni rat, ni pakt*, 471-92.

religious harmony in eastern regions of the country by [ratifying] that same Concordat.[131]

Nevertheless, tensions remained high and clashes between the gendarmerie and opponents of the Concordat continued throughout the summer. One such incident took place on 15 August in Mladenovac, a small town south of Belgrade. When a crowd besieged the house of a local government deputy who had voted for the Concordat, the gendarmerie intervened brutally, killing two or three people (depending on the source) and wounding several.[132]

The three major Serbian parties joined the opposition to the Concordat partly because it seemed like a good opportunity to bring Stojadinović down. The Democrats were the first to criticise the Concordat, as early as December 1936, when Ivan Ribar, the most prominent Croat member of the party (as a member of the Executive Committee), entered into a debate with a Catholic newspaper.[133] However, during the 1937 crisis, the Serbian opposition leaders remained relatively passive—although this was a good opportunity to further destabilise the government—careful not to alienate the Croats. They wrote to Prince Paul, appealing to him to give mandate to a 'people's government', formed by the opposition. The Prince Regent never replied.[134]

The Concordat crisis showed that the relationship between the Serb-dominated government and Serb nationalism was not amicable. Seen in retrospect, the crisis was a prelude to the emergence of the Serbian question two years later. At the same time, however,

---

131 AJ 37/2/9-11, draft of Stojadinović's speech to the *skupština* (Belgrade), July 1937. Stojadinović claimed that throughout the crisis he had a full support from Archbishop Bauer and Coadjutor Archbishop Stepinac. HIA, Dragiša Cvetković Collection, Prince Paul folder, Stojadinović to Prince Paul, Bled, 26 August 1937.

132 'Alarmist rumours in Yugoslavia', *The Times*, 16 August 1937. The same article noted the government's warning to the public against spreading alarmist rumours.

133 Radojević, *Udružena opozicija*, 174.

134 Ibid., 174-5.

although the demonstrations seemed on the surface inspired by Serbian nationalism, many demonstrators simply wished to express their dissatisfaction with the regime.[135]

The crisis did not undermine significantly the relationship between the Croatian Peasant Party and the Serbian opposition. One reason was that Maček chose to stay out of the debate over the Concordat.[136] During the crisis, he sent a message to his Serbian counterparts, stating that if the opposition succeeded in forming a new government, he would propose taking the Concordat off the agenda. 'We Croats do not need a Concordat, nor do the Serbs,' Maček stated.[137] His behaviour was not surprising. Aware that Stojadinović's tactics were to win sympathies among the Croats and erode the support for his party in Croatia, the Croat leader did not wish to side with the Prime Minister in his conflict with the Serbian Orthodox Church. When Stojadinović mentioned, during their meeting in January 1937, that he intended to ratify the Concordat, Maček replied: 'I am not interested in that issue, but can tell you in advance: if you support the Concordat, I shall oppose it'.[138] Moreover, the Croat leader did not regard the Serb-Croat conflict as a religious one, and believed that religion had no place in politics. In an earlier statement, he explained that Croats were 'a Catholic, but not a clerical nation'.[139]

The Bloc of the National Agreement

The Concordat crisis fed the hopes of the opposition—in both Belgrade and Zagreb—that the government would fall. This led them to bury their differences and to begin negotiations on a common political programme. Maček believed that the opposition must do everything to secure Prince Paul's support. When Milan Gavrilović

---

135 Djilas, *Memoir of a Revolutionary*, 306.

136 Stojkov, *Opozicija*, 284.

137 Radojević, *Udružena opozicija*, 176.

138 Stojadinović, *Ni rat, ni pakt*, 517.

139 Vladko Maček, 'Hrvati su katolički, ali ne klerikalni narod', *Vodja govori*, 243-4.

travelled to Zagreb in early July to hold talks with the opposition leaders there, Maček asked him to appeal to his colleagues in Belgrade 'not to criticise the Prince [publicly]. We have to complete this together with him. Imagine if he died. [...] What would we do? It would be a disaster for both us and you.'[140] The Croat leader also wanted Paul to remain Regent beyond King Peter's eighteenth birthday. The following extract from the conversation between Gavrilović and Maček illustrates well the latter's view of the political situation in the country and his faith in Prince Paul:

[Maček]: A young man at the age of eighteen could not run my [farm at] Kupinec, let alone...

[Gavrilović]: ...the state.

[Maček]: The state, of course. Who knows who would then really govern...

[Gavrilović]: Petar Živković, [Jovan] Banjanin, and others.[141]

[Maček]: Yes, yes...That is why I think, and would argue that...we must extend the mandate of the Regency. We can and should work together with Prince Paul. I had the best possible impressions after the audience. When I returned [to Croatia], I gathered my friends, and when they asked me if there were any differences between the late King and this Prince Paul, I told them: [the King] hated Croats, [the Prince] does not hate them...That is why I cannot accept something in your [proposal]...You say here that if all the [party] leaders agree, then we would go to the Prince and tell him: We have reached an agreement. We have achieved what you thought we could not achieve...And if he rejected [the agreement], then we would fight. That is not good. It would seem like an ultimatum. It would be better to approach him more diplomatically.

---

140 AJ 80/31/151, [Izveštaj Milana Gavrilovića Jovanu Jovanoviću Pižonu], Belgrade [?], no date [ca. July 1937]. (This is a 6-page typed report to Jovanović Pižon, written by Gavrilović after he returned from Zagreb.)

141 Like Živković, Banjanin was a member of the JNS. This suggests that the opposition feared that the former government party could be brought into government by Prince Paul.

[Gavrilović]: You are absolutely right Mr President. I did not imagine it differently myself.[142]

Despite sharing Maček's belief in the importance of Paul's support, Serbia's opposition leaders were less enthusiastic about the Prince Regent. Gavrilović admitted that he had not been to the Royal Court since 1923, not even after Alexander's assassination.[143]

Maček, on the other hand, continued to keep contact with the government and the Royal Court. In early August Cvetković went to Zagreb to talk to the Croatian Peasant Party leaders (he met Pernar and Košutić,[144] but not Maček). Cvetković reported to Prince Paul that 'men close to Dr Maček have understood correctly the recent events. The political background of the entire campaign about the Concordat is completely clear to them.'[145] Cvetković emphasised that 'both they [the Croatian Peasant Party], and we, are threatened by one same danger coming from one side. I told them clearly that our collapse would result in their final collapse too. They realise this clearly. I think they will make significant concessions in the course of negotiations.'[146] Was he referring to external danger, or perhaps to an internal one, which had just nearly brought down the government—the Serbian nationalism?

---

142 AJ 80/31/151, [Izveštaj Milana Gavrilovića Jovanu Jovanoviću Pižonu], Belgrade [?], no date [ca. July 1937].

143 Ibid. Not that Prince Paul was too keen to receive Serbian opposition leaders. When Milan Grol requested an audience following his appointment as the new leader of the Democratic Party in February 1940, he had to wait several months before a reply arrived.

144 Košutić returned to the country in January 1937, after an eight-year exile. This was 'a further hopeful sign for the improvement of relations between the Serbs and Croats', in the aftermath of Maček's meetings with Prince Paul and Stojadinović, according to the London *Times*. 'Conciliation in Yugoslavia: Return of Exiled Croat', *The Times*, 30 January 1937. Košutić, and Krnjević, would leave the country once again in 1941, but that time as members of the Yugoslav government-in-exile.

145 BAR PPP, box 13, Cvetković to Prince Paul, Split, 7 August 1937.

146 Ibid.

On 29 August 1937 Prince Paul received Šubašić, who told him that Maček was worried by the political situation, was loyal to the Prince Regent and was willing to cooperate; apparently, Maček was disappointed in the Serbian opposition, because of its alleged links with the Serbian Church during the Concordat crisis.[147] The next day Cvetković informed Paul, following talks with 'friends from Croatia', that the situation was favourable for an agreement between the government and the Croatian Peasant Party.[148]

Nevertheless, talks between Maček's party and the Serbian opposition intensified simultaneously. On 16 September *Politika* somewhat prematurely reported that an opposition agreement had already been reached.[149] In fact, final discussions took place in Zagreb on 28 September.[150] The negotiations were slowed down by Maček's insistence that any resolution should clearly state that Serbs and Croats were two 'individualities', something the other parties were not so keen to emphasise. At the same time, in what appeared to be parallel negotiations, Šubašić met Korošec, while another member of Maček's party, Branko Pešelj, went to see Stojadinović.[151] Korošec told Šubašić that the government would not grant any concessions to the Croats outside the bounds of the Constitution, and that if anyone was offering them more, they were being unrealistic. Šubašić wanted to know what Prince Paul thought of the opposition talks, adding that Maček did not wish to lose the Crown's confidence. Korošec did not know Paul's opinion on the matter, but stated that if Maček were to lose the Prince Regent's support, the Croats would lose their 'greatest and most relevant friend', who sincerely wished

---

147 BAR PPP, box 5, Prince Paul's diaries, 29 August 1937.

148 BAR PPP, box 2, Cvetković to Prince Paul, Belgrade, 30 August 1937.

149 'U Zagrebu je juče zaključen prethodni sporazum izmedju beogradske Udružene opozicije i SDK', *Politika*, 16 September 1937.

150 Stojkov, 'O stvaranju Bloka narodnog sporazuma', 286. The Independent Democrats were conspicuously absent from the discussions.

151 BAR PPP, box 2, Korošec to Prince Paul, Belgrade, 29 September 1937; HIA, Dragiša Cvetković Collection, Prince Paul folder, Stojadinović to Prince Paul, Belgrade, 30 September 1937.

to meet Croat demands, but within the bounds of the Constitution, and not to the detriment of King Peter II and the state.[152]
The opposition agreement was finally reached on 2 October. By 8 October it was 'ratified' by the signatures of Davidović, Jovanović Pižon, Stanojević, Maček and Adam Pribićević, who thus formed the Bloc of the National Agreement (*Blok narodnog sporazuma*). The October agreement criticised both the 1921 and 1931 Constitutions, demanded the abolition of the latter and a return to democracy: 'Our parties [...] represent both the Serbian people and the Croatian people [and believe] that the moment has arrived to bring to an end once and for all the undemocratic regime and to enable the Croats, Serbs and Slovenes to run their state in mutual agreement.'[153] The opposition called for elections for a constituent assembly, which would work towards a constitution acceptable to the majority of Serbs, the majority of Croats, and the majority of Slovenes. Yugoslavia would remain a constitutional and parliamentary monarchy under King Peter II.[154] Although the regime publicly ignored the agreement, it followed the opposition activities closely.[155]

The long negotiations that preceded the agreement took place mostly in Zagreb, but also on Belgrade-Zagreb trains.[156] On 21 October 1937 the opposition leaders met to celebrate the agreement in the village of Farkašić, near one of the train stations not far from Zagreb.[157] It was agreed at the meeting that the agreement should be

---

152 BAR PPP, box 2, Korošec to Prince Paul, Belgrade, 29 September 1937.

153 AJ 37/10/60, 'Sporazum', Zagreb-Belgrade, 8 October 1937. For an insider's view and the text of the agreement in English see Lazar Marković, 'The Jugoslav Constitutional Problem', *Slavonic Review*, vol. 16, no. 47, January 1938, 356-69.

154 AJ 37/10/60, 'Sporazum', Zagreb-Belgrade, 8 October 1937.

155 BAR PPP, box 2, Cvetković to Prince Paul, Belgrade, 20 September 1937.

156 Note that both Zagreb and Belgrade are given as the places where agreement was signed.

157 Stojkov, 'O stvaranju Bloka narodnog sporazuma', 296-7; Maček, *In the Struggle for Freedom*, 180-81. Maček's claim that Farkašić was chosen because

presented to the Serbs, especially those from Serbia, as a clear sign
that the Croats recognised the common state and the dynasty. On
the other hand, the Croat population would be told that this was
the first act by which the Serbian leaders recognised Croats as equal
partners.[158] In a dinner address to the Farkašić meeting participants,
Maček said he was confident that Croats and Serbs would find a way
to overcome their differences. 'One day,' Maček continued, 'our children and grandchildren will find strange our arguments and various
quarrels. I am confident that we shall succeed and that our successors
[...] will remember us as the men who wished them well. To that,
may God give you all long life!'[159]

Was Maček confident in the Serb-Croat rapprochement also
because he maximised the chances for an agreement by continuing
to flirt with the regime? A month after the agreement was reached,
Pešelj told Stojadinović that the leadership of his party would wait a
little until the October agreement was forgotten and then continue
negotiations with the Crown and government, because that was
the only 'serious and realistic' option.[160] In January 1938 Cvetković
was told by Pernar that the Bloc of the National Agreement had
'definitely collapsed', and that Maček wished to see Prince Paul
to discuss the solution to the Croat question. Noting a degree of
'nervousness' among the leading members of the largest Croatian

---

the Serbian leaders refused to come to Zagreb is unconvincing as they visited
the Croatian capital throughout the summer. Historians sometimes refer to the
October 1937 agreement as the 'Farkašić agreement', although the agreement
had already been reached by the time of the Farkašić meeting, which served
mostly to discuss further tactics as well as to celebrate the successful conclusion
to the negotiations. I am grateful to Desimir Tošić for pointing this out to me.

158   Stojkov, 'O stvaranju Bloka narodnog sporazuma', 297.

159   AJ 37/10/60, 'Reč g. dr. Mačeka na večeri u Farkašiću', Zagreb, 23 October
1937.

160   HIA, Dragiša Cvetković Collection, Maček folder, Stojadinović to Prince
Paul, Belgrade, 11 November 1937.

party, Cvetković again concluded that the moment was opportune for negotiations.[161]

Maček in Belgrade

The Bloc of the National Agreement had not collapsed, however. After several quiet months, the Serb-Croat opposition came alive again in the summer of 1938, with Maček's visit to Belgrade. Maček arrived in the capital on 14 August and was greeted by tens of thousands of enthusiastic Serbs. In the spirit of the Farkašić meeting, the United Opposition portrayed Maček's visit as final proof that the Croats were in favour of Yugoslavia and of cooperation with Serbs.[162] The visit was to be the coronation of the October 1937 agreement. The Serbian opposition invited people to come to the Belgrade railway station to greet 'the Croat brothers', and to cheer the 'unity between Serbs and Croats' and the 'national agreement'.[163]

The visit was a success. Maček and other members of the Zagreb delegation –Košutić and Šutej of the Croatian Peasant Party, and the Independent Democrats Vilder, Budisavljević and Kosanović—were greeted by enthusiastic crowds along the route to Belgrade.[164] In the capital, tens of thousands of Serbs from all over Serbia turned up to cheer the Croat leader.[165] They were joined by Communists once again, Milovan Djilas describing the welcome given to Maček

---

161 BAR PPP, box 2, Cvetković to Prince Paul, Zagreb, 30 January 1938.

162 AJ 37/10/60, 'Obaveštenje prijateljima', pamphlet, Belgrade, ca. August 1938.

163 AJ 37/10/60, 'Živeo narodni sporazum! Živela sloga Srba i Hrvata! Živela sloboda!', pamphlet, Belgrade, 12 August 1938. Similar leaflets were distributed throughout Serbia, not just in Belgrade. See for instance AJ 37/10/60, 'Šumadinci', pamphlet, Kragujevac, August 1938.

164 *Trijumf misli narodnog sporazuma. Put Dra Mačka u Beograd*, Zagreb, 1938, 9.

165 The opposition claimed that more than 100,000 people gathered to greet the Zagreb delegation. Maček, *In the Struggle for Freedom*, 182.

as 'one of the most magnificent spectacles of mass action and mass passion.'[166]

The leaderships of the three parties of the United Opposition, headed by Davidović, Stanojević and Jovanović Pižon and joined by delegations of various associations, including veterans of the Salonika front, greeted the Zagreb delegation.[167] The guests were then taken to a private house in Svetosavska Street in central Belgrade, and it was from a balcony of this house that Maček and other opposition leaders addressed the crowd. Maček was touched and encouraged by the reception:

The public reception I received surpassed all expectations. The station at Belgrade was crammed with people, and along the streets, leading to my assigned quarters, a crowd of more than 100,000 had gathered to greet me. Surrounded by the different Serbian political leaders, I stepped out several times on the balcony of the house in which I was lodged to address the swaying multitude below. I stayed in Belgrade two days, and returned home full of optimism. I now believed that Serbia was ripe, if not quite yet for an equitable agreement with the Croats, at least for the definitive abolition of all dictatorship.[168]

Maček addressed the crowd, stating that he had come to Belgrade 'to continue the job which had started in Zagreb ten months previously'. He lamented that twenty years had been wasted in arguments. 'We Croats have suffered in blood and material [cost], and you Serbs have lost your freedom,' Maček told the crowd which broke into cheers of approval.[169] He concluded the speech by expressing his confidence that the 'united Croatian and Serbian people' would achieve mutual harmony to the satisfaction of 'both the Croatian people and

166 Djilas, *Memoir of a Revolutionary*, 307.

167 *Trijumf misli narodnog sporazuma*, 10.

168 Maček, *In the Struggle for Freedom*, 182. The HSS leader was somewhat disingenuous. As it has been argued, the Serbian leaders were above all concerned with ending the dictatorship, while Maček's main aim was to establish autonomy for Croatia, under the dictatorship if need be, as indeed happened in August 1939.

169 *Trijumf misli narodnog sporazuma*, 11.

the Serbian people'. He was then greeted by loud cheers of 'That's right!', 'Long live!' and 'Long live the *sporazum!*'[170] After the speech Maček went inside the house, but as the crowd called on him to return, he came out again and gave another speech, expressing regret that Stojadinović was not there to see in person the extent of popular support for a Croat-Serb agreement. Maček told the crowd:

When ten months ago leaders of the Serbian people, together with us Croats, laid the first foundations of the agreement (Loud cheers: Long live *sporazum!* Long live!), the government tried everything to show how the Serbian people does not want that agreement! (Loud screams: It does! It does!) What we are witnessing today here in Belgrade is proof that, if nothing else, those who came here want an agreement! (Thunderous cheers of approval: That's right! Long live agreement! Long live!) Serbian people, it is up to you, when you return to your homes, to send special regards to the Serbian peasant brothers from us Croats (Long and thunderous cheers of approval: Long live! Long live the Croats!) and to tell them: *a better future of both the Croatian and Serbian people lays only in an* agreement (Cheers of approval).[171]

It would be simplistic, if tempting, to conclude that Maček was speaking as a politician seizing an opportune moment to consolidate the evident support he enjoyed among Serbs. Nor was he simply carried away by his enthusiastic reception and let the occasion get the better of him. At a meeting of the delegations of all five opposition parties which was held behind closed doors, in Jovan Jovanović Pižon's house, the Croat leader repeated his belief that a Serb-Croat agreement was the only solution to the country's problems.[172] He stated that the reception the Zagreb delegation received was a sure sign that the politics of agreement, as formulated in October 1937, was supported by many Serbs. 'It took time before we reached this

---

170 Ibid. In a single sentence Maček talked both about the 'united Croatian and Serbian people' in the singular, while also referring to 'Croatian people *and* Serbian people'.

171 Ibid., 12. Emphasis in original.

172 Ibid., 13-14. 'I ask Dr Maček to consider that he is in his own house, his own Croatia', Jovanović Pižon said before inviting Maček to open the meeting.

point', Maček said. 'It has already been twenty years since we started living together and as you all know those twenty years have mostly been filled with various disagreements and even a serious conflict between the Croatian and Serbian population *in respect to their views of the common state*...it is time to put an end to this [conflict].'[173] The following extract from Maček's speech succinctly summarises his view of the Croatian question:

The Croatian people and the Serbian people have developed separately over [the period of] more than thousand years, each with its own separate national consciousness and each with its own separate understanding of the state. The Serbs managed to liberate themselves from Turkish rule and to create their own small state, which they strengthened, made more independent and slowly expanded. We Croats were part of the former Austro-Hungarian monarchy, but within it we preserved all the attributes of Croatian statehood. (Cheers: That's right!) It is another matter that those [state attributes] were not respected, but that is why we seceded from Austria-Hungary (Loud applause and cheers: That's right!) Look brothers, we separated from Austria-Hungary and entered the new system, the new state union ... we did not [do so] in order to have fewer rights and less freedom, but in order to gain more [rights and freedom] (That's right!)...Instead of attempting to find a way to satisfy the ambitions of both Croatian people and Serbian people inside the common borders, it turned out that the state had to be defended by the Law for the Defence of the State. First it had to be defended from individual Communists, then from Croat individuals, then from the whole Croatian people, and now, at the end, from the whole Serbian people (Loud and long cheers: That's right!!).[174]

Maček also offered an explanation of his party's position during the 1930s. Arguing that the dictatorship could be tolerated while it was 'open', because everyone believed it would only be temporary,

---

173 Ibid., 14. Emphasis added by D. Dj.

174 Ibid., 14-15. This echoed Radić's views of distinct historical developments of Serbs and Croats and the common self-perception among the Croats as a people with a 'thousand year-long' statehood. Although Croatia symbolically preserved some elements of statehood under Hungarian and later Austrian rule (namely its *sabor*), Maček was wrong to claim that 'all the attributes of Croatian statehood' survived following the end of independence in 1102.

he said that everything changed in 1931, when the Constitution was imposed by the King:

The main demand of the Croats, supported by representatives of the Serbian people, is the right of the people to create a constitution. The key point of our agreement is that this imposed Constitution be proclaimed invalid and that as soon as possible elections for a constituent assembly be called. Considering the mood of the Serbian people, which I have witnessed today, I believe that the whole work in a constituent assembly would be done quickly and smoothly'.[175]

At the end of the two-day summit in Belgrade, the opposition leaders issued a resolution, which hailed the 1937 agreement as a 'historic act' that marked the beginning of a 'new age in relations between Serbs and Croats'.[176] Apart from criticising the regime as 'undemocratic' and not true to the basic foundations of the Yugoslav state—freedom, democracy, social justice and the right to national self-determination—the resolution also warned of the danger coming from outside. Only a Yugoslavia based on a democratic regime and Serb-Croat unity 'could find moral, political and military strength, [powerful enough] to withstand temptations coming from everywhere.'[177]

Although there were suggestions to the contrary, the party rank and file appeared to have supported Maček's visit to Belgrade.[178] In the immediate aftermath of the visit, Filip Markotić, a member of Maček's party, told a large crowd in Slavonski Brod that the visit had been a huge success, with '150,000 people greeting Maček, includ-

---

175 Ibid., 15.

176 'Historijska rezolucija' [Belgrade, 15 August 1938], reproduced in ibid., 18-20, 18. The newspapers which published the text of the resolution had their whole circulation for the day seized by authorities.

177 Ibid., 20.

178 Leading members of the Croatian Peasant Party probably wished to reassure Prince Paul when they told Cvetković that Maček made the decision to go to Belgrade without consultation with other leading members of his party. BAR PPP, box 2, Cvetković to Prince Paul, Zagreb, 6 August 1938.

ing 27,000 peasants from Šumadija'.[179] Explaining that the opposition resolution called for a federation, even though not explicitly, Markotić reassured those present that rumours—presumably spread by the Ustaša—that Maček would betray the Croatian people were untrue. 'Croatian and Serbian people desire the organisation of this state in accordance with the best interests of the state itself and [in accordance with] the people's will,' Markotić declared, before stating that Maček was the only person who could save Yugoslavia, and that it would not be long before Stojadinović resigned.[180]

Several months later, during the election campaign, Maček issued a statement to 'Dear brothers Serbs!', stating that he would never forget the visit to Belgrade of August 1938, when he felt the spirit of 'heroic Šumadija'.[181] In August 1938 the Serbian people 'approved the path [...] towards the full national agreement in our common home.'[182]

Maček would be disappointed that the opposition did not receive more votes in Serbian areas in the December 1938 elections. 'My optimism was to be undone by those very citizens of Belgrade barely four months later,' he recalled.[183] The events of the summer of 1938 appeared favourable to the solution of the Croat question. Maček, however, believed that Croat autonomy could be achieved only with those Serbs who were in power. From his point of view, the opposi-

---

179   BAR PPP, box 13, Izveštaj prisutnog policijskog činovnika zboru koji je u Slav.[onskom] Brodu održao u četvrtak 18 o.m. [avgusta] Dr. Filip Markotić, kome je prisustvovalo oko 1500 ljudi.

180   Ibid. The report was written by an employee of the police; all public gatherings organised by the opposition had to be given a go ahead by the authorities, and attended by a representative of the regime, who had powers to interrupt the gathering if it were deemed to be against the unity of the state or against the dynasty. The gathering took place in the same town which witnessed the violent clashes between Maček's supporters and gendarmes in 1935.

181   AJ 37/10/60, Vladko Maček, 'Draga braćo Srbi!', pamphlet, Zagreb, 2 December 1938. Šumadija is a region in central Serbia, where the early nineteenth-century anti-Ottoman uprisings broke out.

182   Ibid.

183   Maček, In the Struggle for Freedom, 182.

tion's inability to win the elections marked the beginning of the end of the Bloc of the National Agreement, although it is tempting to suggest that the election results also provided Maček with an excuse to finally abandon his Serbian opposition partners. The Croat leader probably would not have minded if the United Opposition had formed a government together with the Peasant Democratic Coalition and the Yugoslav Radical Union. As it turned out, however, events were to show that a rapprochement between the Serbian opposition on the one hand and the Serb-dominated government and the Crown on the other could not be achieved. Once the Crown appeared willing to grant concessions Maček desired, there was little dilemma about which side would the Croatian Peasant Party would choose.

In 1937-8 a new government formed by the main opposition parties seemed more than just a distant possibility. Although Maček had not given up hopes of an agreement with the regime, following the failed talks with Prince Paul and Stojadinović, the cooperation with the Serbian parties improved. It also strengthened his position in the eyes of the Prince Regent, the only person, in Maček's view, who could grant Croatia autonomy. As for Prince Paul, Cvetković's increasingly frequent trips to Zagreb as the Crown's *de facto* emissary signalled that a deal was not definitely off, as well as that Stojadinović was being gradually sidelined. In hindsight, it also provided a taste of what was to come in 1939, when the three men finally reached an agreement that granted Croatia autonomy.

When in August 1938 Maček travelled to Belgrade, it was unlikely that he did not remember that more than eight and a half years previously he had taken the same train, but as a political prisoner being transferred to a Belgrade prison. In the years in between he had survived politically—although surviving literally was no mean feat either, considering the fate of his predecessor Radić and of King Alexander—and emerged as the somewhat reluctant leader of the united Serb-Croat opposition. In 1930 he was greeted by a smuggled cake sent by Dragoljub and Dana Jovanović. In 1938 all the major Serb opposition politicians, including Jovanović, as well as tens of thousands of ordinary Serbs, enthusiastically greeted him. Maček triumphantly proclaimed upon his return to Zagreb that 'the Serbian people now shares our honest and just beliefs [...] this is the beginning of an end of the tyranny.'[184] As events were to show, however, it was the beginning of an end of the Serb-Croat opposition.

---

184 *Trijumf misli narodnog sporazuma*, 22.

5
THE 1939 AGREEMENT

After the elections we will first try to find a solution to the Croat question. We want a brotherly agreement [*sporazum*]. But, because we are serious about [an agreement], and because we genuinely want to bring it to life, we know the boundaries beyond which we cannot go. Do we want an agreement? Convinced that I am speaking in the name of the whole party [JRZ], I hereby declare: we do. But, that very word, the very phrase—*sporazum*—... [means] that we could not accept it at any price.

Prime Minister Milan Stojadinović, 1938[1]

Certain parts of our homeland had in the past been culturally and geographically separated; they have developed their national individuality, which is still, twenty years after living in the common state, strongly manifested. We have to recognise this fact and seek a solution, within the borders of Yugoslavia, which will enable a normal coexistence.

Prime Minister Dragiša Cvetković, 1939[2]

[The Agreement] has laid the foundations for a free Croatia and [has] enabled the Croatian people, by developing its national individuality, to assume its deserved and rightful place in a unified Yugoslavia. After many disagreements, a basis has finally been found, [a basis] which will balance the interests of our inner homeland with [those of] our state of Yugoslavia. *In the national agreement of the Croats and Serbs, the [Croatian people] has found the only correct, the only realistic and the only possible way [forward].*

Ban of Croatia Ivan Šubašić, 1940[3]

---

1 AJ 37/10/59 (Papers of Milan Stojadinović), 'Vlada Dra. Stojadinovića i Hrvatsko pitanje', unknown author, ca. October–December 1938.

2 Dragiša Cvetković, 'Srpsko-hrvatsko pitanje i putevi *Sporazuma*', *Dokumenti o Jugoslaviji*, Paris, 1952, vol. 3, 20.

3 *Godišnjak Banske vlasti Banovine Hrvatske*, Zagreb, 1940, xi. Emphasis in original.

A day before the elections of 11 December 1938, Prime Minister Stojadinović spoke at a rally of Belgrade industrialists. The programme of his government, he explained, was short and simple: 'One king, one nation, one state, prosperity at home, peace on the borders'.[4] The slogan summarised the government's domestic and foreign policies very effectively, but it also highlighted the three major issues confronting it: the two aspects of the constitutional question—the opposition's challenge to integral Yugoslavism and to the continuation of the dictatorship; the economic crisis; and the international crisis.

Constitutionally Yugoslavia was a nation-state, yet this state of affairs was increasingly challenged not only by Croats, but also by Serbs cooperating with them in opposition. The 1930s were dominated by political contests between centralists and anti-centralists, and between advocates of integral Yugoslavism and advocates of what may be called 'agreement' Yugoslavism. Stojadinović's largely successful economic policies ('prosperity at home') were an important factor behind his relatively long three and a half years in office (long by Yugoslavia's interwar standards, at any rate).[5] However, the Yugoslav economy, like that of most of Europe, was affected by the international crisis. The Prime Minister was proud of his government's foreign policy, which was based on neutrality from the two military blocs, although Yugoslavia had under Stojadinović's premiership moved closer to Nazi Germany and Fascist Italy, and not only economically. Neutrality was, in Stojadinović's view, the only possible way to avoid the fate of Czechoslovakia.[6] However, it was increasingly becoming clear that it would be very difficult, if not im-

---

4 *Pravda*, 11 December 1938. Stojadinović's words in Serbo-Croat were: 'Jedan Kralj, jedan narod, jedna država, blagostanje unutra, mir na granicama.'

5 For an overview of Stojadinović's economic policies see John R. Lampe, *Yugoslavia as History: Twice There was a Country*, Cambridge, 2nd edn, 2000, 181-4.

6 And eventually of Yugoslavia itself, as Stojadinović later argued in his memoirs, the title of which—*Neither War, nor the Pact*—clearly suggests the author's view. Milan M. Stojadinović, *Ni rat, ni pakt: Jugoslavija izmedju dva rata*, Rijeka, 1970.

possible, for Yugoslavia to remain neutral in a Europe sharply polarised into three ideological blocs. Internal stability was therefore seen as essential at a time of international crisis. Both the government and the opposition, as well as the Prince Regent, hoped that the elections would be a first step towards achieving stability. Subsequent events would prove them right, although not many would have predicted the extent and pace of the changes.

The elections of December 1938

Stojadinović's election promise of course sounded uncomfortably similar to the infamous Nazi slogan.[7] Before the elections, the government party's 'Section for Internal Propaganda' published a pamphlet whose title echoed the government's motto.[8] It contained a selection of the Prime Minister's speeches and photographs from the election campaign, some of which show uniformed youth and even supporters of the Yugoslav Radical Union giving a fascist salute.[9] Although Stojadinović's flirtation with the far right has been noted by historians,[10] it is important to understand the Prime Minister's slogan both in the wider context of interwar Europe, and in the context of Yugoslav politics in the late 1930s and particularly of the government's election campaign in autumn 1938. The government and the opposition based their campaigns largely on Yugoslavia's national question. The government promoted King Alexander's integral Yugoslavism and a centralised state, and believed that it alone was capable of preserving Yugoslavia. The opposition coalition led by Vladko Maček, on the other hand, argued that it was their vision of a decentralised and preferably democratic Yugoslavia that guaranteed the country's unity—a unity that was especially needed during what

---

7 'Ein Volk, ein Reich, ein Führer!'

8 Milan Stojadinović, *Jedan kralj, jedan narod, jedna država*, Belgrade, 1939.

9 Ibid., *passim*.

10 Lampe, *Yugoslavia as History*, 185; Stevan K. Pavlowitch, *Yugoslavia*, London, 1971, 95-6; Joseph Rothschild, *East Central Europe between the Two World Wars*, Seattle, 1974, 257.

was clearly the most serious international crisis since the 1914-18 war. In other words, although one should not ignore Stojadinović's inclination towards authoritarian politics, nor his cordial relations with Berlin and Rome, his domestic discourse during the months leading up to the December elections and his eventual downfall in February 1939 should be understood primarily in the context of the internal political debate on the future of Yugoslavia.

That the question of Yugoslavia's internal structure was central to the government's election campaign is clear from speeches made by Stojadinović and other cabinet ministers during the election campaign. On the eve of the elections, Stojadinović warned that if the opposition won 'the new constitution would be a federal one, because Mr Maček believes that Serbs and Croats are not one but two nations. In other words, federation is [at the core of] Maček's programme.'[11] The Prime Minister stressed that the electorate could choose between his party, whose domestic and foreign policy guaranteed Yugoslavia's stability and integrity, and the opposition, which only offered internal divisions and uncertainties. 'One thing is certain,' Stojadinović argued, 'a federation would mean weakness, and very likely the disintegration of the country.'[12] Like King Alexander before him, the Prime Minister appeared to equate federation with a multi-national state, and hence argued that federalism was incompatible with integral Yugoslavism.[13] However, while Alexander was

---

11 *Pravda*, 11 December 1938.

12 Ibid.

13 There were prominent Yugoslavs not members of the government who believed that federalism would lead to disintegration of Yugoslavia. Less than two weeks before the elections, Jovan Plamenac, a former Prime Minister of Montenegro, wrote to Prince Paul to appeal on him to prevent the federalisation of the country, 'because in that case its collapse would be inevitable'. HIA, Dragiša Cvetković Collection, Prince Paul folder, Plamenac to Prince Paul, Belgrade, 29 November 1938. (Ironically, a Communist-dominated congress held on the same date in Jajce, Bosnia, in 1943, laid the foundations of the postwar federation.) Plamenac had in 1937 told the Yugoslav Consul General in Trieste that Yugoslavia should remain a dictatorship until a homogeneous Yugoslav identity developed and a liberal form of government could be introduced. (BAR

in all probability a genuine believer in the existence of a single Yugoslav nation, the same could not be said of Stojadinović, as explained in the previous chapter.

According to Stojadinović, Maček regarded the struggle for federalism as the essence of the Croat question. On the other hand, the Prime Minister believed that the Croat question should be seen as part of a wider Yugoslav national question, for which the Serbian government and the Serbs had fought at least since 1914. Before going on to accuse the United Opposition of entering a coalition with Maček out of pragmatic considerations, merely in order to take power, Stojadinović stated:

[Those of] you brothers who fought [in the First World War], surely still remember the Manifest of the late [King] Alexander, then the [Serbian Prince] Regent, and the [Serbian] government's declaration at Niš of [December] 1914, when we Serbs stated that our war aim was the liberation and unification of all our unliberated brothers, Serbs, Croats, and Slovenes. You see, brothers, the Croatian question dates back to that time. We were the first to raise it, but in doing so we sacrificed our lives and the lives of our children for the freedom not just of Serbs, but of Croats as well.[14]

The Prime Minister's discourse could be interpreted, on the basis of this extract, as Serb nationalist, rather than pro-Yugoslav, but that would be too simplistic, if perhaps not entirely incorrect. Most Serbs did not see much difference between Yugoslavism and Serbism; Yugoslavia to them was only a final phase of a struggle for Serb liberation which began in 1804. It was a state that united all Serbs, together with their previously 'unliberated brothers', Croats

PPP, box 12, Consul Životić to Stojadinović, Trieste, 30 October 1937.) His son John Plamenatz became a distinguished political theorist and philosopher who taught at Oxford University.

14 *Pravda*, 11 December 1938. The 'Manifest' to which Stojadinović referred was issued by Prince Regent Alexander on 29 July 1914, a day after Austria-Hungary declared war on Serbia. However, in it Alexander called upon Serbs to defend their 'homeland and the Serbian tribe', but no mention was made of Croats, Slovenes and other Yugoslavs. See 'Manifest regenta Aleksandra', Niš, 29 July (16 July O.S.), 1914, *Dokumenti o postanku Kraljevine Srba, Hrvata i Slovenaca, 1914-1919* (compiled by Ferdo Šišić,), Zagreb, 1920, 2-3.

and Slovenes. However, even if Stojadinović personally felt more Serbian than Yugoslav, he was far too pragmatic and shrewd a politician to let his private feelings be known at such a public gathering. His words probably say more about the way he perceived his audience than about his own views. Moreover, the speech appeared to be directed against the opposition, rather than against Croats *per se*. In the same speech he compared Maček unfavourably to Radić, who was in Stojadinović's opinion a Yugoslav patriot who recognised the state, the dynasty and the 1921 Constitution, and reached the agreement with Pašić in 1925.[15] The reference to the 1925 agreement also served to remind the audience that Stojadinović viewed himself as Pašić's legitimate successor and to suggest that after Radić's death, the Croats lacked a leader of similar qualities.[16]

Stojadinović also criticised the opposition's calls for federalism by employing economic arguments. He expressed a conviction that Yugoslavia's industrialists, businessmen and merchants would vote for the government because the opposition was offering a highly uncertain economic future, which could bring about a fragmented market, instead of a single, pan-Yugoslav one. Stojadinović argued that federal units would create a huge administrative burden on the state, weakening it not only politically but also economically, probably leading to the country's break-up.[17] Indeed, the government based its campaign partly on the argument that Maček's list was both incapable of running the state and opposed to its unity. The government party organ for the Savska *banovina* went too far when it described Maček as Yugoslavia's 'enemy no. 1', but Stojadinović's

---

15 *Pravda*, 11 December 1938. See also Stojadinović, *Ni rat, ni pakt*, 318, 467, 470.

16 See Stojadinović, *Ni rat, ni pakt*, 467.

17 *Pravda*, 11 December 1938. A fragmented market did pose a serious challenge for Yugoslavia's leaders from the second half of the 1960s onwards, and, it may be argued in retrospect, contributed to the country's disintegration. See John Lampe, 'The Two Yugoslavias as Economic Unions: Promise and Problems', in Dejan Djokić (ed.), *Yugoslavism: Histories of a Failed Idea, 1918-1992*, London and Madison, WI, 2003, 182-95.

whole campaign, more or less explicitly, accused the opposition of plotting to destroy the country.[18] The regime appears to have believed that the Serbian opposition was planning to incite upheavals, not unlike those during the Concordat crisis, and forcibly overthrow the government during the autumn.[19]

That it was the audience that often determined the content of speeches made by Yugoslav political leaders was manifested not only in Stojadinović's rhetoric. Addressing a pro-government rally in Paraćin (central Serbia), held on 7 November 1938, the Interior Minister Korošec emphasised that the Yugoslav Radical Union championed Yugoslav national unity, but that it also respected separate Serb traditions:

Who can demand from you to give up Serbdom? Serbian is your language, Serbian is your church, Serbian is your great past, Serbian is your glorious history and the unique heroism of the former Serbian army. Serbian are your customs and your tradition. But, above all, [before considering] Serbdom, Croatdom, Slovendom, we are good and loyal Yugoslavs who constantly care about and work for the progress and greatness of our common homeland, the Kingdom of Yugoslavia. ('Long live Yugoslavia!', 'Long live Dr Korošec!', 'Long live the JRZ!').[20]

However, when in Slovenia, Korošec would address matters relevant to Slovenes. During a meeting of the Dravska branch of the government party (essentially the former Slovene People's Party), Korošec replied to his critics, who accused him and the government of being anti-Slovene. He dismissed such accusations as untrue, adding that 'every Croat, Slovene or Serb knows that Korošec loves

---

18 *Obzor*, 9 December 1938, quoting from the article 'Maček neprijatelj Jugoslavije broj 1', published in *Glasnik JRZ za Savsku Banovinu* (Zagreb). The article particularly criticised the failure of the HSS headquarters to fly the state flag on 1 December, Yugoslavia's Unification Day.

19 BAR PPP, box 13, Police report, no date (ca. August 1938).

20 *Pravda*, 7 November 1938. Serbdom, Croatdom, Slovenedom are probably best English translations for *srpstvo*, *hrvatstvo*, and *slovenstvo*, which in Serbo-Croat and Slovene roughly mean a set of national, cultural, historical, spiritual and geographical values—similar to, but more than simply, national belonging.

his country Yugoslavia as well as his Slovenia.' After listing the establishment of a Slovene university and secondary schools and the Slovenian Academy of Arts and Sciences as only some of the major Slovene achievements in Yugoslavia, he argued that 'we would have never secured all that and much more if Dr Korošec and his followers had not been loyal to and if they had not loved their inner homeland.'[21] The 'inner homeland' he was referring to was Slovenia.

Similarly, Stojadinović began his speech at a government rally in Ljubljana held on 8 December by describing Slovenia as 'the ornament and pillar of our state: the land of beauty, culture and of an eternally lively national [Yugoslav] thought.'[22] The Prime Minister was equally 'adaptable' when he visited Bosnia on a pre-election tour. After stressing that Spaho was the only legitimate leader of Bosnia's Muslims, he told a crowd in Bijeljina, a town in eastern Bosnia with a mixed Serb and Muslim population, that 'the unity of the Orthodox and Muslims, which Nikola Pašić had always advocated, beautifully illustrates *the spiritual unity of all parts of Bosnia and Herzegovina.*'[23] Pašić's prime aim had been the settling of the 'Bosnian question', which he successfully managed.[24] Therefore, only the Croat question remained:

---

21 *Pravda*, 1 December 1938. It is not clear from the speech who exactly accused him of being anti-Slovene, but it was probably the opposition press.

22 *Politika*, 9 December 1938. The very reference to 'Slovenia', which of course did not officially exist in interwar Yugoslavia, is indicative in this context.

23 AJ 37/2/9 (Stojadinović papers), Predizborni govor Milana Stojadinovića u Bijeljini, 27 November 1938 (emphasis in original). See also *Obzor*, 29 November 1938. Fifty-four years later most Muslims of Bijeljina were to be either expelled or murdered by Serb paramilitaries, among whom there were supporters of Vojislav Šešelj, the leader of the Serbian Radical Party founded in 1991. Ironically, Šešelj, who is facing charges for crimes against humanity and war crimes at the International Criminal Tribunal for the former Yugoslavia at The Hague for the role of his paramilitaries in the wars in Croatia and Bosnia, regards his party as a successor of the old Radical Party.

24 Stojadinović clearly referred to the deal between Spaho and Pašić, by which the former agreed to support the 1921 Constitution in exchange for the preservation of Bosnia's historic borders within the new administrative division.

No one would be happier than me if we could find a solution [to the Croat question]. We want a solution, but not any solution. We don't want the solution proposed by Dr Maček. We simply cannot cross certain boundaries. *One King, one nation, one state—that is our programme.* We are willing to negotiate [with Maček], but only within the boundaries [of this programme]...[Otherwise] Dr Maček will have to stay in opposition for another 99 years.[25]

The Prime Minister often repeated similar arguments, most notably in a speech he gave in Belgrade on 16 October, at the start of the government's election campaign.[26]

That leading members of the government felt they had to reassure the public of the government's concern for preserving separate traditions, while also championing Yugoslav national unity, is a clear sign that they were aware that twenty years after the unification and almost ten years since King Alexander introduced the dictatorship, a single Yugoslav nation had still not been formed. Moreover, the Yugoslav National Party, the predecessor of the Yugoslav Radical Union as the government party, opposed the government. Led by a group of ex-Prime Ministers of the early dictatorship years, unquestionably supportive of integral Yugoslav ideology, the Yugoslav Nationalists had joined Maček's list, making it increasingly difficult for the government to argue that it alone stood for the country's unity.

The rivalry between the two parties preceded the election campaign. In October 1936, on the second anniversary of King Alexander's assassination, the gendarmerie prevented the Yugoslav Nationalists from holding a parallel commemoration at Oplenac, where King Alexander was buried, and where the government had organised its

---

25 *Obzor*, 29 November 1938 (emphasis in original). Stojadinović's reference to '99 years' in opposition was a response to Maček's previously made claim that he was willing to wait for 100 years for the solution of the Croatian question, if it proved necessary. See Dragoljub Jovanović, *Ljudi, ljudi...Vol. 2: Medaljoni 46 umrlih savremenika (sa fotografijama)*, Belgrade, 1975, 64.

26 AJ 37/2/9, Predizborni govor Milana Stojadinovića u Beogradu, 16 October 1938. Also AJ 37/10/59, 'Vlada Dra. Stojadinovića i Hrvatsko pitanje', unknown author, ca. October-December 1938.

own service.[27] In what was a good example of both this rivalry and the regime's way of neutralising political opponents, in the summer of 1938 Regent Stanković, probably in cooperation with Stojadinović, persuaded Jovan Banjanin, a leading Yugoslav Nationalist, to keep a low profile in exchange for a monthly fee. The regime's cause was helped by the fact that Banjanin fell out with Jevtić and Živković, two of the party's leaders.[28] Stojadinović had also attempted to win over Nikola Uzunović, another former Prime Minister and also a Yugoslav Nationalist, who allegedly did not get on with Živković.[29] The enmity between Stojadinović and Živković matched and even overshadowed the one between the Prime Minister and Maček, providing yet another example of an intra-ethnic, political conflict.[30]

In order to strengthen the 'integralist' bloc, the government encouraged the small but aggressively pro-Yugoslav and right-wing Yugoslav People's Party, led by Svetislav Hodjera, to join its list. Hodjera's followers were known as 'Yugoslav nationalists' and as *borbaši*, after the party organ *Borba* (Struggle).[31] On 10 October

---

27 BAR PPP, box 12, Milan Aćimović to Milan Antić, Belgrade, 10 October 1936. Oplenac is a small town in central Serbia where Karadjordje Petrović set up his headquarters during the First Serbian Uprising against the Ottomans (1804-13). The Karadjordjević kings later built a church in Oplenac, where remains of the deceased members of the family are kept. The church and the surrounding area serve today as a memorial to the Uprising but also as a shrine for those who support the restoration of the monarchy.

28 HIA, Dragiša Cvetković Collection, Prince Paul folder, Stojadinović to Prince Paul, Belgrade, 5 August 1938.

29 HIA, Dragiša Cvetković Collection, Prince Paul folder, Stojadinović to Prince Paul, Belgrade, 16 October 1938.

30 The diary of Milan Jovanović Stoimirović, editor of the pro-government newspaper *Samouprava* and in charge of the Central Press Bureau during Stojadinović's premiership, confirms this. The Prime Minister feared Živković and the Radicals around the Main Committee more than Maček or the Democrats and Agrarians. Milan Jovanović Stoimirović, *Dnevnik, 1936-1941*, Novi Sad, 2000, *passim*.

31 Not to be confused with the Communists' main newspaper of the same name, published in Belgrade to this day. The Yugoslav People's Party was founded in May 1933, by Hodjera, once the *Chef de Cabinet* to the former Prime Minister

Hodjera entered the government, as a minister without portfolio.[32] Stojadinović had hoped to unite all centralist forces under his leadership;[33] winning over Hodjera was a small coup for the Prime Minister. The leader of the *borbaši* had previously called on his followers to vote for Maček's list,[34] even though Hodjera campaigned against the federation as a form of state.[35]

The opposition presented two separate lists: Maček's and that of Dimitrije Ljotić. Political observers believed that Ljotić would do well if he secured 50,000 votes necessary for a seat in the parliament.[36] In the event, as in 1935, he failed even to get himself elected.

Maček's list united all major groups in opposition to the government. At its core were the Peasant Democratic Coalition and the United Opposition. The list was headed by Maček and it was a Serb-Croat coalition in all but name.[37] Its platform was based on the 1937 Bloc of the National Agreement. In the spirit of this agreement, it promised the electorate the abolition of the 1931 Constitution and a return to democracy, as well as the federalisation of the country. The opposition bloc was joined by the Yugoslav Nationalists and the

Živković. Its programme was based on King Alexander's integral Yugoslavism, and it enjoyed support among some Croats and Slovenes, as well as Serbs. See *Istorija gradjanskih stranaka u Jugoslaviji*, Belgrade, 1952, 377-82.

32   *Politika*, 11 October 1938.

33   Ljubo Boban, *Sporazum Cvetković-Maček*, Belgrade, 1965, 45-6.

34   Jovanović, *Političke uspomene*, vol. 5, 30.

35   AJ 14/22/536 (Papers of the Ministry of Interior of the Kingdom of Yugoslavia), pamphlet 'Borbaši i federacija', no date.

36   *Obzor*, 9 December 1938.

37   According to Dragoljub Jovanović, the opposition indeed modelled itself on the prewar Croat-Serb Coalition, which dominated South Slav politics in the Habsburg Monarchy between 1906 and 1918. *Političke uspomene*, vol. 5, 43.

small Socialist Party, led by Živko Topalović.[38] The influence of the Yugoslav Nationalists on Yugoslav politics had drastically declined since they had gone into opposition in 1935, and many of their supporters had joined the government party. However, Maček hoped that they would attract some of Stojadinović's supporters, while making less credible the government's accusations that the opposition was anti-Yugoslav. As the historian Ljubo Boban argued, 'to Maček, it was important to unite as many of Stojadinović's opponents as possible and widen the opposition camp.'[39] In fact, after the elections were announced, Maček invited both Ljotić and the Radical Party dissident Boža Maksimović into the coalition, to the dismay of the Serbian parties.

A working committee of the Bloc of the National Agreement eventually decided to invite Ljotić to join the united opposition list,[40] but he declined the offer, preferring instead to contest the elections on his own.[41] Ljotić's aggressive anti-government campaign earned him a prison sentence, but this did not detract him from taking part in the elections.[42] As the election results would show, both the govern-

---

38　In the later stages of the Second World War, Topalović joined General Mihailović when the latter attempted to broaden his movement to include more liberal political options and more non-Serbs. At first sceptical towards Mihailović, Topalović eventually became his chief political adviser and even presided over a congress at the Serbian village of Ba which was held in January 1944 and attended by representatives of other prewar parties, including the Croatian Peasant Party. It was meant to be an answer to the Partisans' Second Congress of the AVNOJ, held at Jajce in Bosnia, but like Mihailović's attempts to make his movement more inclusive, the Ba congress was too little, too late. For a first-hand, if pro-Mihailović, account of these events see Živko Topalović, *Srbija pod Dražom*, London, 1968.

39　MPHSS-1, 362.

40　*Politika*, 13 October 1938. The same body decided to issue an invitation to the JNS.

41　*Hrvatski dnevnik*, 19 October 1938.

42　Jovanović, *Političke uspomene*, vol. 5, 69-70; Jovanović Stoimirović, *Dnevnik*, 214-5. Ljotić was imprisoned on 26 October and released two weeks after the elections, on 24 December 1938. In a rather bizarre newspaper article he accused Stojadinović of being responsible for King Alexander's assassination, suggesting

ment and the opposition coalition overestimated Ljotić's strength.[43] Maksimović was never invited to join the opposition, because the Radicals' Main Committee refused to work together with their former party colleague. Maček even sent Juraj Šutej to Belgrade to try and persuade the Radicals to change their mind, but he was unsuccessful.[44] Instead, as in 1935, he asked the Croat voters to support Maksimović's list with signatures, so that he would be able to present a countrywide list.[45] The Croat leader believed that Maksimović would attract some of Stojadinović's potential voters.[46] This is another good example of the complexity of the Yugoslav political scene, emphasised throughout this book. Decisions by party leaders in interwar Yugoslavia were often motivated by tactics and pragmatism, not by nationalist feelings. The traditional argument, which tends to view the period simply in terms of a Serb-Croat conflict, does not

---

the existence of a joint plot between Stojadinović and Prince Paul to remove Alexander. Ljotić's followers also engaged in mini-terror against political opponents, both in government and in opposition. Thus, Dušan Bošković, a leading Independent Democrat from Vojvodina, who attended the November 1932 talks in Zagreb, was beaten up by the Ljotićists, while in Smederevo, Ljotić's powerbase, the gendarmerie regularly clashed with Ljotić's followers. 'Stojadinović plot': Jovanović, *Političke uspomene*, vol. 5, 51; Bošković: Jovanović Stoimirović, *Dnevnik*, 365.

43   Milan Jovanović Stoimirović wrote in his diary on 29 October that the government should not have arrested Ljotić, because this would only gain him popularity, adding somewhat pessimistically that 'we are not going to achieve an easy victory over Ljotić's supporters' (*Dnevnik*, 215). Similarly, Dragoljub Jovanović believed that Ljotić's arrest had boosted his popularity. Apparently, there had been rumours that he was secretly cooperating with the regime, but since these rumours were shown to be unfounded Ljotić's prestige had grown somewhat. (*Političke uspomene*, vol. 5, 51)

44   Hinko Krizman, 'Dnevnik', MPHSS-1, 362.

45   Jovanović, *Političke uspomene*, vol. 5, 66. In order to qualify for the elections, each list had to collect a certain number of 'signatures of support' from across the country. Dragoljub Jovanović suspected that Maček may well have done a similar favour to Ljotić, without Ljotić even knowing it.

46   Ibid. Maksimović would briefly return to government as Minister of Education in the Cvetković-Maček cabinet formed in August 1939.

account for developments such as this one, as Maksimović was once a symbol of everything the Croatian Peasant Party opposed.

Often, however, pragmatism was mixed with genuine ideals. An example was Maček's behaviour following the arrest of Dragoljub Jovanović on 1 October 1938. In a series of strong attacks on the regime, Maček stressed that prisons were full of Serbian peasants, including Dragoljub Jovanović, 'who was the first who had courage to call for a genuine agreement with Croats and had already spent a year in prison.'[47] Tomo Jančiković, a member of the Croatian Peasant Party, was Jovanović's lawyer. This was Maček's wish, and was 'not only an act of friendship, but also an act with political significance', according to Maček.[48] By asking Jančiković to defend Jovanović, the Croat leader obviously wished to emphasise the co-operation of Serbs and Croats in opposition to the regime, but also to lend support to someone who had in the past shown solidarity with him (e.g. the 'cake affair').

Only a few days before the elections, Korošec compared Maček's list with a 'cage of birds' of different sorts and sizes, which was carried by a 'tomcat' (the Slovene for tomcat is *maček*).[49] This was a clear reference to the diversity of parties and political views included in the opposition coalition. *Obzor*, a pro-Maček daily, appeared to confirm Korošec's view. In an editorial, published only two days before the elections, it claimed that:

---

47 Jovanović, *Političke uspomene*, vol. 5, 91. Dragoljub Jovanović was released only after the elections, in which he was unable to take part. This was in sharp contrast to Ljotić, who, although also under arrest during the elections (he was put in a cell next to Jovanović's), was allowed to run his party from his prison cell. Jovanović had previously been sentenced to one year in prison in October 1932 (Ibid., 115). See also Vladko Maček, *In the Struggle for Freedom*, University Park and London, 1957, 158n.

48 Jovanović, *Političke uspomene*, vol. 5, 91.

49 *Politika*, 9 December 1938. Korošec said this at a public meeting in Ljubljana.

Dr Maček and the HSS have concluded merely a technical coalition with the JNS and Dr Topalović's group, while with the SDS and the UO it also has a political agreement of 8 October 1937...but in reality the HSS primarily represents the Croatian national interests; it is the [main] political factor among the Croatian people.'[50]

The Croatian Peasants' cooperation with the Yugoslav Nationalists and the Socialists was indeed agreed for the purpose of elections, though it should not be forgotten that Maček had once regarded Živković his favourite negotiating partner within the official circles in Belgrade. It was also true that Maček's party was above all a Croatian party, which put Croatia's interests before all others. However, that did not mean that the Croatian Peasants' co-operation with the Independent Democrats and even the United Opposition was disingenuous. The Peasant Democratic Coalition had existed since 1927 and however improbable that seemed when it was first formed, it survived longer than any other coalition during the interwar period. Likewise, the cooperation between the Croatian Peasants and Serbian opposition lasted throughout most of the second half of the 1930s, despite many ups and downs.

It may be said that the opposition had a common aim, but not a single programme. As a result, its election campaign was not coordinated. 'In Serbia, as well as in other parts of Yugoslavia with a mixed population, the Serbian Opposition launched a large-scale electoral campaign,' Maček later recalled, 'while in Croatia things were quiet, as though no one were thinking of elections. There was no need for excitement, for everyone knew how to vote.'[51]

The Croat leadership saw the elections as a 'national plebiscite', believing that the elections presented the Croats with an opportunity to vote for the right to 'self-determination'.[52] Such tactics inevitably placed strains on Zagreb's relations with the United Opposition. This was possibly the reason why the parties united around the Maček

---

50 *Obzor*, 9 December 1938.
51 Maček, *In the Struggle for Freedom*, 183.
52 MPHSS-1, 366.

list did not issue a single joint election manifesto, just as they had failed to do so in 1935. The Serbian opposition, on the other hand, based its campaign on the October 1937 agreement, promising to democratise the country in the event of a victory. The federalisation part of the 1937 agreement was conveniently downplayed.[53] Internal divisions within the United Opposition—both between the different parties of the coalition and within the Agrarian party, divided into the 'left' and 'right' factions—posed additional problems.[54] Yet, once the votes had been counted, it emerged that Maček's list did surprisingly well, despite not winning the elections. The government list did not win as convincingly as its leaders and, more crucially, Prince Paul had expected. It received 1.6 million votes, against the opposition's 1.3 million votes. Just over 30,000 votes went to Ljotić.[55] In comparison to the 1935 elections the government lost over 100,000 votes, while the opposition gained nearly 290,000 votes.

It can be safely assumed that the majority of Croats voted for the opposition, just as the majority of Slovenes and of Bosnia's Muslims gave their votes to the government, or, more precisely, to its 'SLS' and 'JMO' components. A major shift occurred among the Serbian voters. Maček himself emphasised in his Orthodox Christmas message of 4 January 1939 that 600,000 Serbs had voted for him, including many from central Serbia.[56]

Nevertheless, the government's analysis of the election results confirmed Maček's later complaints that unlike the *prečani* Serbs, the Serbs of prewar Serbia, still predominantly voted for the govern-

---

53 Mira Radojević, *Udružena Opozicija, 1935-1939*, Belgrade, 1994, 183.

54 Jovanović, *Političke uspomene*, vol. 5, 35-6, 46-51.

55 The final results were as follows: the Stojadinović list: 1,643,783 votes (54.09 per cent of the total vote), the Maček list: 1,364,524 votes (44.9 per cent); the Ljotić list: 30,734 votes (1.1 per cent). *Službene novine*, 11 January 1939.

56 'Božićni pozdrav Dr. Vlatka Mačeka Srbima', Kupinec, 4 January 1939 (reproduced in full in Jovanović, *Političke uspomene*, vol. 5, 79). It is significant that Maček sent a Christmas message to Orthodox believers, but is unclear whether he did so in his capacity as leader of the SDK, or as a leader of the wider Serb-Croat opposition coalition, or, most probably, both.

ment. 'After the big demonstration against the regime during my visit four months earlier in which at least 100,000 people had taken part, I foresaw a sure Opposition victory,' Maček later wrote. In the aftermath of the December elections he felt disappointed with the Serbs who 'obviously did not dare vote openly against the regime, and neither did Macedonians, Germans and Magyars.'[57] On the territory of pre-1912 Serbia the government received 420,000 votes, while the three parties of the United Opposition got just over 160,000 votes.[58] With another 40,000 votes for the Yugoslav Nationalists, Maček received some 200,000 votes from Serbia 'proper'.[59]

A breakdown of election results in individual *banovinas* shows that the government lost in only two, predominantly Croat *banovinas*, Primorska and Savska, and won with a clear majority in all other *banovinas* except for Vrbaska, where there was a significant support for the Independent Democrats among local Serbs. An analysis of the election results produced by the Agrarians concluded that in total, 538,000 Serbs voted for the opposition, while 885,000 Serbs voted for the government. On the other hand, 767,000 Croats gave their votes to Maček, as opposed to 32,000 Croat votes for the government. The Agrarians' analysis included two new categories, 'Serbo-Croats' and 'Yugoslavs'; the former referred to all Serbo-Croat speakers (i.e. Serbs, Croats, Montenegrins and Bosnian Muslims), while the latter also included the Slovenes (i.e. all South Slavs, or Yugoslavs). More 'Serbo-Croats' voted for the opposition: 1,322,000 as opposed to just over 1 million votes for the government. Similarly,

---

57 Maček, *In the Struggle for Freedom*, 184-5.

58 AJ 37/47/722, 'Brojna snaga pojedinih stranaka sa liste dr. Stojadinovića na izborima od 11. XII 1938. u Srbiji' and AJ 37/47/723, 'Brojna snaga pojedinih stranaka sa liste dr. Mačeka na izborima od 11. XII 1938. godine u Srbiji'. The exact figures according to these analyses were: 419, 094 votes for the government (62.02 per cent of the total vote in pre-1912 Serbia), and 161, 352 votes for the UO, or 89,893 votes for the DS (13.3 per cent), 38,986 votes for the SZ (5.77 per cent) and 32, 473 votes for the Main Committee of the NRS (4.8 per cent).

59 AJ 37/47/723-725. The JNS in total received an impressive 122,755 votes, out of which 41,056 came from pre-1912 Serbia.

nearly 1,370,000 'Yugoslavs' gave their vote to Maček's list, while Stojadinović received nearly 1,240,000 'Yugoslav' votes. However, non-Slav minorities such as Germans, Hungarians and Albanians predominantly voted for the government; out of 434,000 'others' who voted, 406,000 gave their votes to Stojadinović.[60]

Essentially, however, while Croats predominantly voted for Maček's party, the government received almost two-thirds of the 'Serb' vote (including the peoples today called Macedonians and Montenegrins, who were at the time officially regarded as Serbs). Apart from Vrbaska, the opposition did reasonably well in Zetska *banovina*, where the so-called 'federalists', many of whom had been supporters of the exiled Petrović dynasty of Montenegro, were relatively strong.

The fall of Stojadinović

Despite winning the elections, the government fell on 4 February 1939. A group of five ministers, including Dragiša Cvetković, Mehmed Spaho and Miha Krek, resigned the previous day in protest at an apparently anti-Croat speech in the parliament by Bogoljub Kujundžić, the Education Minister.[61] In a reply to the Agrarian Branko Čubrilović, Kujundžić said that Yugoslavia's internal politics 'cannot be inspired by Kupinec, but by Oplenac', metaphorically rejecting federalism, advocated by Maček (who lived at his farm in Kupinec) and the opposition, in favour of integralism and centralism symbolised by the final resting place of members of the Karadjordjević family.[62] Stojadinović accepted their resignations, confident Prince Paul would give him another mandate.[63]

---

60 For a detailed analysis of the elections see Radojević, *Udružena Opozicija*, 66-76.

61 BAR PPP, box 13, Tekst ostavke petorice ministara, 3 February 1939.

62 Stojadinović, *Ni rat, ni pakt*, 522.

63 Ibid., 523-4.

However, Paul had already been secretly plotting to replace Stojadinović with Cvetković and the resignations, if not Kujundžić's speech, were undoubtedly instigated by the Prince Regent. He had sent Cvetković to Zagreb in the aftermath of the December elections, to talk to Maček.[64] Stojadinović, unaware of the plot, complained to the Prince Regent that Cvetković disobeyed his instructions not to talk to anyone from Maček's circle. The Prime Minister had been led to believe that the reason for his minister's trip to Zagreb was not 'political', but had received information that Cvetković unsuccessfully tried to see Maček.[65] Even the British minister to Belgrade, Ronald Hugh Campbell, was aware of the Prince Regent's plan.[66] Stojadinović apparently realised only after he had resigned that Paul had been plotting his downfall for some time.[67] One of the reasons for Stojadinović's ignorance may have been that he had become isolated from both his political allies and opponents towards the latter stages of his premiership—partly because of his authoritarian way of running the office and partly because he was allegedly spending too much time with his mistresses.[68]

Another factor behind the Prime Minister's fall was, in Campbell's words, Stojadinović's 'constantly growing hunger for power'.[69] Not

---

64 Jacob B. Hoptner, *Yugoslavia in Crisis, 1934-1941*, New York, 1962, 132.

65 BAR PPP, box 13, Stojadinović to Prince Paul, 24 December 1938.

66 FO 371/23875, Campbell to Halifax, Belgrade, 13 February 1939. Ronald Hugh Campbell should not be confused with Ronald Ian Campbell, who had been the previous British minister to Belgrade until 1 November 1939, when R.H. Campbell took over.

67 As he told Mario Indelli, Italy's minister to Belgrade. Galeazzo Ciano, *Ciano's Diary, 1937-1943*, London, 2002, 186. See also Stojadinović, *Ni rat, ni pakt*, 523.

68 Jovanović Stoimirović, *Dnevnik*, 143-4. Stojadinović's reputation as a womaniser was well known outside Yugoslavia. The Italians were prepared to use his 'weakness for pretty ladies to bring him further on our side...besides the official visits, I had prepared some dances with the most beautiful women of Rome society,' Ciano wrote in his diary on the eve of Stojadinović's visit in early December 1937 (*Ciano's Diary*, 33).

69 FO 371/23875, Campbell to Halifax, Belgrade, 13 February 1939.

only had he adopted the image of a fascist dictator, with uniformed followers who addressed him as *vodja* (leader), but 'it [also] seemed as if Stojadinović was going to be satisfied with nothing short of personal dictatorship.'[70] Prince Paul must have seen in Stojadinović a potential danger to his own authority and position. The Prince Regent was no doubt aware of Stojadinović's admiration for Fascist Italy, where Mussolini pushed the monarchy aside.[71] There were rumours that, unable to secure Maček's cooperation, Stojadinović was preparing, as an alternative, 'a semi-Fascist regime to be introduced by gradual stages.'[72] The former Prime Minister had failed to solve the Croat question and he was not very popular among Serbs either, mostly because of the government's pro-German foreign policy. Rebecca West, who travelled across Yugoslavia in the second half of the 1930s, noted a widespread hatred of Stojadinović 'throughout the length and breadth of the country'. 'He was hated chiefly because he was said to be a tyrant and an enemy of freedom,' according to West.[73] Rumours about Stojadinović's personal wealth and the corrupt nature of his government no doubt contributed to his unpopularity.[74] Increasing personal animosity between Stojadinović and Korošec, the Interior Minister and the second most powerful figure in the government, who enjoyed Prince Paul's confidence, did not help Stojadinović's position either.[75]

Reflecting on recent events, Jovanović Stoimirović wrote in his diary on 16 November 1939:

---

70 Ibid.

71 Ciano, *Cianno's Diary*, 33-4.

72 FO 371/23875, Rapp to Campbell, Zagreb, 11 February 1939.

73 Rebecca West, *Black Lamb and Grey Falcon: A Journey through Yugoslavia*, London, 1940, 478.

74 Jovanović Stoimirović records such rumours on several instances in his diary, noting his discomfort upon visiting the Prime Minister's very luxurious house with a group of Turkish journalists. *Dnevnik*, 186.

75 Ibid., *passim*.

Mr Stojadinović fell because he failed to grasp that it was the JRZ, and not he personally, that was seen as essential by the Crown. The Prince needed the JRZ so that history would say that he ruled with the help of the [Serbian] Radicals, Slovene People's Party and [Bosnian] Muslims. Mr Stojadinović wanted to turn the JRZ into his own party, and this would have led the Slovenes and Muslims to leave the party. The Prince's ideal was to add Maček to this combination. He [eventually] succeeded in this, but without Stojadinović.[76]

The first Cvetković government and the negotiations with Maček

On 10 March, one month after becoming Prime Minister, Dragiša Cvetković told the new parliament that the prime aim of his government was to re-establish the lost confidence of the Croats in the government, which could only be achieved if past mistakes were not repeated. This was the clearest sign yet that the regime was not going to continue to insist on integral Yugoslavism. Official Belgrade was finally ready to recognise the separate (though closely related) identities of Serbs, Croats and Slovenes. Cvetković said as much when he stated in the same speech that 'certain parts of our homeland had in the past been culturally and geographically separated; they have developed their national individuality, which is still, twenty years after living in the common state, strongly manifested.' Cvetković believed that the government had to recognise reality and to 'seek a solution, within the borders of Yugoslavia, which will enable a normal coexistence.'[77]

The speech could have been written by Maček and no wonder it received a genuine, if cautious welcome in Zagreb. 'For the first time

---

76 Ibid., 321-2.
77 Cvetković, 'Srpsko-hrvatsko pitanje', 20. However, years later, responding to accusations by Branko Miljuš, a Minister without portfolio in Cvetković's government, that he had abandoned integral Yugoslavism, Cvetković denied the charge. See Cvetković, 'Smisao, značaj i posledice srpsko-hrvatskog sporazuma', *Glasnik srpskog istorisko-kulturnog društva 'Njegoš'* (Chicago), no. 10, December 1962, 8-27, and Miljuš, *Sporazum 1939 godine*, Windsor, Canada, 1957.

since Yugoslavia had been created, the very existence of the Croatian Question had thus been officially recognized,' Maček later recalled of the government's new course. '[However] I did not react publicly to this and continued to wait for Belgrade to take the initiative.'[78] Maček was anxious to reach an agreement as soon as possible for two reasons: the growing international crisis and also his desire to neutralise the *Ustaša* opposition and more extremist elements within his own party. According to a report from Croatia written at the time of the Cvetković-Maček negotiations, the *Ustaša* activists were stepping up their propaganda campaign against the Croatian Peasant Party, which, according to the *Ustašas*, had 'sold the Croats to Jews and Serbs'.[79]

Following Cvetković's failed attempt to meet Maček in the immediate aftermath of the December 1938 elections, Prince Paul re-established contact with the Croat leader on 2 January, predictably through Šubašić.[80] Apparently, Paul told Šubašić that he was prepared to offer Maček 'all power in Croatia *via facti*', in exchange for Maček dropping his demands that the 1931 Constitution be abolished or revised.[81] On 10 January Maček replied, via Šubašić, that he would no longer insist on constitutional changes, and that he was ready to negotiate 'a triple [Slovene-Croat-Serb] division of the state'.[82]

Cvetković's statement of 10 March revealed the crucial concession that the government was now willing to make—the recognition of a separate Croat identity. By the late 1930s the Croatian Peasant Party, together with the Independent Democrats, had significant control on the ground in Croat territories, as Stojadinović pointed

---

78 Maček, *In the Struggle for Freedom*, 186.

79 BAR PPP, Izveštaj Zvonka Tomića o razgovoru sa Slavkom Cihlarom, ca. April-May 1939.

80 As Ilija Jukić, an emerging member of Maček's party, told R.W. Seton-Watson. FO 371/23875, R.W. Seton-Watson to Orme Sargent, 1 April 1939.

81 Ibid.

82 Ibid.

out to Prince Paul.[83] If Maček had been willing to follow Korošec and Spaho into the government, he would have had a free hand in Croatia. However, he demanded formal autonomy for Croatia. The Croat leader was willing to compromise on the Constitution, and even on territory, but would not accept the ideology of integral Yugoslavism. As Thomas Rapp, the British Consul General in Zagreb, concluded in a report to Campbell, Maček would settle for nothing less than the recognition of Croatian nationhood, a wide autonomy within Yugoslavia and equal status with Serbs.[84]

With Prince Paul seemingly willing to grant Croatia autonomy, Cvetković went to Zagreb in early April to negotiate the terms of an agreement. On 4 April Maček's office issued a communiqué stating that the Prime Minister and the president of the Croatian Peasant Party shared their views 'on the nature of the problems discussed', and that they agreed on 'the manner in which these problems should be solved'.[85]

With both sides prepared to compromise on the most important issues—Maček on the Constitution and Cvetković on integral Yugoslavism—only the question of boundaries of the future Croat entity remained to be decided. It would present a real test of the resolve of the Crown. The Prince Regent felt the Croats' territorial demands were unreasonable and ludicrous. When Šubašić demanded 'historic borders' for Croatia (meaning the inclusion of Bosnia-Herzegovina in Croatia) during an audience with Prince Paul in late March, Paul asked wryly: 'Do you mean the ninth or eleventh century [borders]'? Šubašić replied, apparently oblivious to Paul's sarcasm: 'No, the fourteenth century [borders],' to which the Prince Regent responded: 'Please, all [Catholic] friars [from Bosnia-Herzegovina] vote against

---

83 HIA, Dragiša Cvetković Collection, Prince Paul folder, Stojadinović to Prince Paul, Belgrade, 15 December 1938.

84 FO 371/23875, Rapp's confidential despatch to Campbell, Zagreb, 7 April 1939.

85 FO 371/23875, Enclosure to Mr. Rapp's despatch No. 9 of 7 April 1939.

Maček, despite Šutej spending most of his time in [Archbishop of Sarajevo] Šarić's office.'[86]

The Crown offered a union of Savska and Primorska—as well as the possibility of Maček forming the new cabinet—but the Croats wanted in addition at least the Croat-populated areas in Bosnia-Herzegovina.[87] Maček appears to have considered this a compromise on his part, since 'the fundamental contention of the Croats is that the Drina [river, separating Bosnia and Serbia] is their natural boundary.'[88] Hugh Seton-Watson (the son of R.W. Seton-Watson), who in 1939 'spent some months in Yugoslavia in close study of the situation', thought that Prince Paul, as 'the real director of the negotiation on the Serbian side', wanted to avoid political reforms by negotiating a territorial settlement with Maček.[89] Yet, as Seton-Watson observed in his memorandum, the territorial settlement was 'the most difficult question of all', because of the regions with a mixed

---

86 BAR PPP, box 13, Prince Paul's note on the meeting with Šubašić, Royal Palace, Belgrade, 24 March 1939. During the Second World War Archbishop Šarić collaborated with the *Ustaša* regime.

87 BAR PPP, box 13, Cvetković to Prince Paul, Belgrade, 19 April 1939. Maček was apparently not interested in being the Yugoslav Prime Minister.

88 FO 371/23875, Rapp's confidential despatch to Campbell, Zagreb, 7 April 1939. Even the Croat communist leader Andrija Hebrang apparently held this view when borders of federal republics in socialist Yugoslavia were discussed at the end of the Second World War. Since it had been decided that Bosnia-Herzegovina would be a separate republic, the question of Serb-Croat delineation in Vojvodina arose. Hebrang allegedly demanded those parts of Vojvodina that had been incorporated into the *Ustaša*-run Independent State of Croatia during the war, which included Zemun, a town on the outskirts of Belgrade. For more details see Milovan Djilas, *Vlast i pobuna*, Belgrade, 1991, 86-7 (first published in English as *Rise and Fall* in 1985). Djilas was in charge of a government-appointed commission for border demarcation.

89 FO 371/23875, Wickham Steed to Sir Robert Vansittart, London, 7 April 1939. Hugh Seton Watson's report on the situation in Yugoslavia was enclosed with Wickham Steed's letter to Vansittart, ibid. In his letter, Wickham Steed stressed to Vansittart that Britain 'ought to lose no time in putting pressure on the Prince Regent both diplomatically and (if possible) through more exalted channels' to solve the Croatian question.

Serbian and Croatian population, and especially because Bosnia's 'Mohammedans do not know whether they are Serbs or Croats.'[90]

Territorial settlement apart, there were other issues that proved difficult to negotiate, such as the question of military reforms. Maček accepted a common army, but demanded that Croatian conscripts serve in Croatia and asked for a proportional representation of Croats and Serbs among officer ranks.[91]

After a few weeks of intense negotiations, on 27 April Maček and Cvetković reached an agreement, which appeared to be acceptable to both sides. The agreement envisaged an autonomous Croatia that would consist of the Savska and Primorska *banovinas*, as well as the city and district of Dubrovnik (Zetska). The final boundaries of the *banovina* of Croatia would be determined after plebiscites in areas of Bosnia-Herzegovina where Croats lived, and in the Srem region of Vojvodina.[92] The central government was to have 'general powers only in respect of foreign affairs, national defence and Supreme Administration.'[93] A new Yugoslav government would include ministers from Maček's party, and its main task would be to 'prepare and carry out the re-organisation of the State', in which Serbs and Croats would be guaranteed full equality.[94] The Constitution of 1931 would remain, but the creation of the *banovina* of Croatia would be facilitated by Article 116 of the Constitution, which stated that in extraordinary circumstances the King may 'issue a royal decree calling for temporary, urgent and necessary measures to be applied in the whole kingdom or in some of its parts, regardless of constitutional

---

90   FO 371/23875, Hugh Seton-Watson's report on the situation in Yugoslavia.

91   FO 371/23875, Rapp's confidential despatch to Campbell, Zagreb, 7 April 1939.

92   FO 371/23875, Enclosure No. 1: Alleged text of the agreement reached between M. Tsvetkovitch and Dr. Matchek, enclosed with Campbell's letter to Halifax, Belgrade, 8 May 1939.

93   Ibid.

94   Ibid.

and legal regulations.'[95] Therefore, under the pretext of the growing international crisis Prince Paul could, in the name of the minor King Peter II, use Article 116 to proclaim an autonomous Croatia.

The proposed temporary nature of the agreement did not concern either side much. It was understood that the creation of an autonomous Croatia was only a first step towards a final internal settlement and a long-lasting solution to the national question in Yugoslavia. The agreement would come into effect 'on a date to be agreed upon', or, in other words, when and if the Prince Regent gave his consent.[96]

Failure of the April agreement

Because Cvetković's role in the negotiations with Maček was essentially that of the Crown's envoy Zagreb was optimistic about the agreement.[97] However, when no news came from Belgrade regarding Prince Paul's decision, Maček sent Šubašić to the capital on 1 May to explore the situation, instructing him to stay until a definite decision had been made.[98] Šubašić met both Cvetković and Prince Paul, but returned to Zagreb three days later without a clear answer.[99] This led Maček to conclude that the agreement was off: 'There remained only one interpretation, the one indicated in the German proverb *Keine Antwort ist auch eine Antwort*—no answer was a negative answer.'[100] Somewhat tactlessly, Maček issued a statement accusing Prince Paul of rejecting the agreement of 27 April.[101] The pro-Maček newspaper *Hrvatski dnevnik* (*Croatian Daily*) published the statement, but the

---

95 Boban, *Sporazum*, 194.

96 Ibid.

97 FO 371/23875, Rapp to Campbell, Zagreb, 7 April 1939.

98 BAR PPP, box 2, Cvetković to Prince Paul, Belgrade, 2 May 1939.

99 Boban, *Sporazum*, 165.

100 Maček, *In the Struggle for Freedom*, 189.

101 AJ 80/32/152 (Papers of Jovan Jovanović Pižon), 'Govor predsednika dra Vladka Mačeka održan na izvanrednoj sjednici Hrvatskog Narodnog Zastupstva', Zagreb, 8 May 1939.

whole issue was banned by the authorities.[102] The relations between official Belgrade and Zagreb reached a low point, despite Cvetković's claim in early May to both a journalist from *Politika* and Campbell that the 27 April agreement 'was still being studied'.[103] In fact, at this stage the government considered an overall agreement, by planning to divide up the country into four provinces: Slovenia, Croatia, Serbia and Bosnia, where 'Serbo-Croats are mixed with Muslims'.[104]

In order to put pressure on the Crown, 'The Croatian National Representation'—the *de facto* parliamentary HSS party which back in the years of boycott served as a Croatian quasi-parliament—issued a resolution accusing Belgrade of betraying the ideals of Yugoslavia, originally created as 'a State community which would give its three peoples the chance of independent national life and development'.[105] The Croat representatives gave a full vote of confidence to Maček to

Carry out all the necessary action in internal and also in *foreign* policy according to the future attitude of the Serbian people and the political situation in Europe, and the Croatian National Assembly, with the whole Croatian people, will follow and carry out those decisions, observing the principle that the existence and freedom of the Croatian people is above everything else.[106]

The resolution provides a good example of the Croatian Peasant Party tactics. The party leadership emphasised that it favoured a

---

102 Boban, *Sporazum*, 165.

103 FO 371/23875, Campbell's deciphered telegraph to the Foreign Office, Belgrade 6 May, 1939; *Politika*, 6 May 1939.

104 BAR PPP, box 2, Cvetković to Prince Paul, Belgrade, 2 May 1939. Cvetković spelled 'Muslims' with a small 'm', which in Serbo-Croat indicates a religious but not ethnic belonging. From the late 1960s, when Muslim Slavs of Bosnia and Sandžak were recognised by the communist authorities as a separate (Yugoslav) Muslim nation, the capital 'M' was introduced. A draft map of the internal division of Yugoslavia dating from this period and showing Bosnia as a separate unit is reproduced in Mihailo Konstantinović, *Politika Sporazuma. Dnevničke beleške, 1939-1941. Dnevničke beleške, 1944-1945*, Novi Sad, 1998.

105 FO 371/23875, Enclosure No. 2, Rapp to Campbell, Zagreb, 12 May 1939.

106 Ibid. Emphasis added by D. Dj.

common state, but because of Belgrade's policies, the Croats were apparently forced to seek international support for their cause and possibly even a solution to the Croat question outside Yugoslavia. This was the line which Radić first adopted in the early 1920s and Maček continued to follow, despite its clear failure to achieve significant results.

Whether the threats to internationalise the Croat question were empty or not, Italy was bound to feature prominently in any calculations, in both Zagreb and Belgrade. Maček's contacts in Berlin were told in March 1939 that Yugoslavia was in Italy's sphere of influence.[107] Rome, on the other hand, did not have a carefully developed policy towards Yugoslavia. At times it appeared willing to support Albanian irredentism in southern Yugoslavia, while at other times it wished to please Belgrade by permitting its Slovene minority to publish a Slovene-language newspaper.[108] As for the Croat question, Italy provided refuge for Pavelić's *Ustašas*, but following the rapprochement with Belgrade, during the Stojadinović premiership, Rome promised to keep the Croat extremists under surveillance.[109] The Italians, however, believed that there was a danger of a Serb-Croat civil war; and if Yugoslavia were to disintegrate, Italy wanted its share.[110]

A Croat of Italian origin, and a member of the Croatian Peasant Party called Carnelutti, visited the Italian Foreign Minister Count Ciano on 20 March 1939, claiming to be Maček's envoy. Maček apparently wanted Rome to put pressure on Belgrade to accept Croat demands for self-rule. If these demands were rejected, Croatia would rebel, proclaim itself a republic, and seek a customs and monetary union with Italy, as a first step towards a possible unification between the two countries. When Mussolini was informed about Carnelutti's

---

107 Hoptner, *Yugoslavia in Crisis*, 136.
108 Ibid., 139.
109 Ibid., 82.
110 Ibid., 138.

visit, he told Ciano to support the Croats.[111] When the negotiations between Belgrade and Zagreb broke off in early May, Carnelutti informed Ciano that Maček no longer wished to pursue an agreement with Belgrade; that he would continue his separatist movement; that he wanted a loan of 20 million dinars; and that within six months he would be ready to start an uprising.[112]

However, Maček's account of the Carnelutti mission differs from Ciano's. In a letter to Cvetković, written after Ciano's diaries were first published, Maček confirmed that Carnelutti was his contact with the Italians. When the negotiations between Belgrade and Zagreb broke off in May 1939, the Italians approached Carnelutti, asking whether the Croats would support the Italians in event of an Italo-Yugoslav war. There was apparently no mention of an uprising in Croatia. The Italians also proposed a personal union between Rome and Zagreb, through an Italian prince who would be crowned the King of Croatia. Maček rejected the offer.[113] Several years later, he gave a similar account to the historian Jacob Hoptner.[114]

Carnelutti was not the only Croat who approached Rome during this period.[115] On 30 March 1939 Ciano received the Marquis de Bombelles, a Croatian landowner, who spoke of unrest in Croatia and sought Italy's support for Croat independence. Ciano agreed to put him in touch with Pavelić.[116] On 5 April, the Italian Foreign Minister saw Bombelles once again. He hoped the Croat would secure a direct link with Maček and this time the two men discussed

---

111 Ciano, *Ciano's Diary*, 205.

112 Ibid., 232. Hoptner estimates that 20 million dinars was an equivalent of $400,000. Hoptner, *Yugoslavia in Crisis*, 140.

113 HIA, Dragiša Cvetković Collection, Maček folder, Maček to Cvetković, Washington, DC, 28 June 1949.

114 Hoptner, *Yugoslavia in Crisis*, 140-41. Maček told Hoptner that he did not remember any loan arrangements.

115 According to Hoptner, 'during the Second World War [Carnelutti] was of invaluable assistance to those who opposed the Ustaše terrorist regime. He disappeared after May, 1945.' *Yugoslavia in Crisis*, 141n.

116 Ciano, *Ciano's Diary*, 210, 212.

Italy's financial assistance for a propaganda campaign in Croatia.[117] Although Ciano told Bombelles in early May that it looked like Maček had reached an agreement with Belgrade and that Italy did not wish to weaken Yugoslavia, they kept up sporadic contacts over the next year. Bombelles went to see Ciano in the aftermath of Prince Paul's visit to Zagreb in January 1940, describing the visit as 'funeral during which no one took off his hat.' According to Ciano, Bombelles claimed that anti-Serb sentiments in Croatia were growing, making the situation ripe for a rebellion. 'Our proposed action plan should be the following: insurrection, occupation of Zagreb, arrival of Pavelić, appeal to Italy for intervention, formation of a kingdom of Croatia, and offer of the crown to the King of Italy,' Ciano told Bombelles, who agreed, adding that Italy's 'military effort will be at a minimum because the popular insurrection will be complete and the Serbs will be struck everywhere and implacably disposed of by the Croats themselves.'[118] But Rome's plans to exploit the connection with Bombelles suffered a serious blow when in May 1940 Ciano discovered through Pavelić that the Marquis had been working for the Yugoslav government all along.[119]

Maček was ready to exploit external factors in order to secure Croatian autonomy, preferably within Yugoslavia. When in April 1941 the country was invaded by Germany, Italy and their allies, the Axis powers proclaimed an independent Croatia, which incorporated the whole of Bosnia-Herzegovina and parts of Vojvodina. Maček refused the Axis' offer to govern such a Croatia, which opened the doors for Pavelić and consigned the Peasants' leader to house arrest and even a brief spell in the Jasenovac concentration camp. An Italian duke did become King Tomislav II of Croatia in May 1941, but

---

117   Ibid., 213.
118   Ibid., 314.
119   Ibid., 350. Bombelles was killed by the *Ustašas* when they came to power in Croatia in 1941.

he never set foot on the Croat soil, and 'abdicated' following Italy's withdrawal from the war in 1943.[120]

Prince Paul undoubtedly knew about Italy's keen interest in Croatia, and Maček's willingness to exploit it, but he rejected the April agreement primarily because of the Croat demands for more territory outside Savska and Primorska. The Prince Regent told Campbell on 4 May, before his trip to Rome, that the main problem with the agreement was the plebiscite issue. Paul feared that it would set an undesired precedent and that it could encourage ethnic Germans and Hungarians to demand plebiscites on autonomy for areas where they formed a majority. Paul also feared that by conceding too much to the Croats he was risking unrest among Serbs, especially if a large number of them were to end up living in a Croat *banovina*. This was a particularly delicate question in the light of Croat insistence that they be recognised as a separate nation and Zagreb's emphasis on a territorial delineation between Serbs and Croats.[121]

The British Minister in Belgrade also reported that the government had been under extreme pressure from 'various Serb bodies' not to accept the 27 April agreement. According to Campbell, 'even His Royal Highness had himself been warned by the Patriarch and by the General Staff that acceptance of the Croat demands in the present form would lead to something like a revolution in Serbia.'[122] It is quite possible that the Prince Regent was careful not to provoke another conflict with the Serbian Church which could have led to a crisis greater than the one over the Concordat. General Dušan Simović later claimed that the army was not consulted and that it played no role in the political negotiations between Belgrade and

---

120 See Stevan Pavlowitch's essay on Duke of Spoleto, who became Tomislav II, in his *Unconventional Perceptions of Yugoslavia, 1940-1945*, Boulder, CO, 1984.

121 FO 371/23875, Campbell to the Foreign Office, Belgrade, 5 May 1939.

122 Ibid.

Zagreb.[123] Nevertheless, in early May 1939 there were rumours that because of the continued failure to settle the Croat question, a new government would be formed by General Simović and by Milan Antić, the Minister of the Court.[124]

The Prince Regent felt that Cvetković had conceded to Maček more than he should have done.[125] During the negotiations, Cvetković was praised by the Zagreb press as the man who kept his word, 'who showed good will and understanding', and 'who put a lot of effort and energy trying to achieve promised results.'[126] But did he forget, amid all the praise, that he was little more than the Prince Regent's emissary? As Rapp reported to Campbell on 7 April:

The President of the Council [of Ministers] has certainly left the impression behind him that if he himself possessed the necessary authority the Croatian question would be quickly settled on the basis of the Croat proposals. How far this judgement is justified I have no means of judging, but it is not impossible that M. Cvetković wishes to make what political credit he can out of his role of honest broker. He would possibly like to pose as the man who honestly tried to solve the Croatian problem, if he cannot appear as the man who actually succeeded in doing so.[127]

Maček's demands even for territories where Croats were not in a majority certainly contributed to the deadlock. Each concession by the Cvetković team led to another demand by the Maček camp, while each stalemate would provoke renewed threats from the

---

123 In an interview with Ljubo Boban, who suspected that the army's influence must have been greater than Simović suggested. Simović apparently told Cvetković that he was against 'the partition of Bosnia' (*Sporazum*, 166n). Recalling the events of 1939, Maček believed the army was the greatest obstacle to the implementation of the agreement, as well as the main reason for 'our catastrophy', presumably referring to the short April war against Nazi Germany and Fascist Italy. HIA, Dragiša Cvetković Collection, Maček folder, Maček to Cvetković, Washington, DC, 15 July 1948.

124 Jovanović Stoimirović, *Dnevnik*, entry for 7 May 1939, 274.

125 Ibid. In Jovanović Stoimirović's opinion Maček 'toyed with Belgrade', and was responsible for breaking off the negotiations.

126 *Hrvatski dnevnik*, 2 April 1939.

127 FO 371/23875, Rapp to Campbell, Zagreb, 7 April 1939.

Croatian Peasant Party about the internationalisation of the Croat problem.[128] Campbell compared Maček to 'a peasant negotiating the sale of an acre of land', and believed that his demands had 'reached a level at which it is impossible for the Regency to concede without incurring the active hostility of the Serbs. It is useless to settle the Croatian problem by creating a Serbian one: it would merely divide the country more seriously than it is divided to-day.'[129]

It was not only the Prince Regent and his fear of Serbian reaction that led to Belgrade's rejection of the April agreement. Maček's demands were also rejected by both Spaho and Korošec, two influential, non-Serb members of the cabinet.[130] Spaho was particularly upset because Maček's proposal meant that large parts of the historic Bosnia-Herzegovina would be included in the Croatian *banovina*. 'For twenty years Maček has been bragging about justice [...] and now he wants to take over Muslim districts,' Spaho complained after Cvetković returned from Zagreb.[131] Korošec was equally critical of the Croat leader, whose aim to unite all Croats into a single entity he compared to Hitler's 'bandit-like' behaviour. Cvetković claimed that Maček had to insist on the plebiscites because of the pressure from Croatian nationalists, but personally did not expect Belgrade to consent.

---

128 FO 371/23875, Campbell to Halifax, Belgrade, 8 May 1939.

129 Ibid.

130 Korošec in particular was believed to be the most influential among ministers, owing to his prestige, experience and good relationship with the Prince Regent. Jovanović Stoimirović told Slobodan Jovanović that while Maček was the leader of the opposition, the government was in reality under Korošec's control—only the Serbs had no leader. *Dnevnik*, 245.

131 Konstantinović, *Politika Sporazuma*, diary entry for 1 May 1939, 20. Konstantinović's diary offers a valuable insider's account of the negotiations between Cvetković and Maček. However, Konstantinović, a member of the Serbian trio of legal experts engaged in negotiating and later drafting the text of the *Sporazum*, does not offer any other clue as to why the April agreement was rejected, except that Maček's demands had clearly seemed unacceptable to the government and presumably the Prince Regent.

Therefore, the agreement of 27 April failed because it was rejected by Prince Paul as well as by Korošec and Spaho, who felt that Maček's demands were unacceptable and that Cvetković had conceded too much. They also feared a Serb and Muslim backlash if all Croat claims, especially in regard to territory in Bosnia, were met.

The Cvetković–Maček agreement

Yugoslavia's international position during the first few months of 1939 had become even more precarious. Like the rest of the Balkans, with the partial exception of Greece and Albania (which was under Italy's sway), Yugoslavia was increasingly becoming economically dependent on Germany. After the *Anschluss* (the incorporation of Austria into Germany) of March 1938, Yugoslavia and Germany shared a border. Yugoslavia's traditional allies, France and Britain, were losing influence in the region. After the German intervention in Czechoslovakia in March 1939 and the Italian occupation of Albania the following month, it was becoming increasingly difficult for the Yugoslavs to remain neutral.

After his visit to Berlin in June 1939, Prince Paul concluded that a war of international proportions was inevitable.[132] He talked with marked antipathy about Germany and Nazism and, according to Campbell, 'it was impossible for anyone listening to him to doubt where his sympathies and wishes lie.'[133] At the same time, a 'reliable source' informed the Foreign Office that the Yugoslav Prince Regent was under pressure from Germany to join the Axis, and that the internal crisis could no longer be used as an excuse by Belgrade for its refusal to do so.[134]

Observers agreed that public opinion in Yugoslavia was unfavourably disposed to Berlin and Rome. For instance, at a football game between Yugoslavia and Italy, played in Belgrade in early June, home

---

132 Hoptner, *Yugoslavia in Crisis*, 147.
133 FO 371/23876, Campbell to Halifax, Bled, 8 July 1939.
134 FO 371/23876; Ingram to Shone, London, 26 July 1939.

supporters threw stones at Italian players giving the Fascist salute and booed Italy's flag. When, after the game, some supporters recognised the British Minister among the spectators, they surrounded and loudly cheered him, clearly expressing their sympathies for Britain.[135] Two months later a similar incident occurred, this time at a Davis Cup match between the tennis teams of Yugoslavia and Germany, which took place in Zagreb[136] (and which Yugoslavia won 3:2). Terence Shone, Britain's Chargé d'Affaires, believed, however, that anti-German sentiments in Zagreb were not as strongly manifested as anti-Italian sentiments expressed in Belgrade at the football game.[137] Anyhow, anti-German feeling in Croatia did not necessarily amount to Yugoslavism. While Belgrade celebrated the victory over Germany as *Yugoslavia's* victory, Zagreb's press proclaimed a victory for Croatia and Croats, because all the players in the Yugoslav team were actually Croats.[138] The Serb-Croat political rivalry often translated into the field of sport; for instance, the Yugoslav football team that came third at the 1930 World Cup in Uruguay was boycotted by players from Croatia.[139]

Although Maček periodically threatened Belgrade with seeking support for the Croats abroad, the growing European crisis reinforced his belief that a solution to the Croat question should be sought within the borders of Yugoslavia. A 'reliable source' informed Rapp that the Croat leader was 'extremely nervous about the possibility of war breaking out before the internal situation [in Yugo-

---

135   FO 371/23876, Campbell to Halifax, Belgrade, 3 June 1939. The Yugoslavs' hostile attitude may have been caused in part by their team's 1:2 defeat.

136   FO 371/23876, Shone to Halifax, Bled, 4 August 1939.

137   Ibid.

138   Josip Palada and Franjo Punčec played singles, while Punčec and Franjo Kukuljević played doubles for Yugoslavia.

139   The Yugoslav football federation was founded in Zagreb in 1919. Its headquarters moved from there to Belgrade following the proclamation of the dictatorship in 1929.

slavia] is clarified.'[140] Maček was aware that Prince Paul was 'friendly disposed towards Great Britain, [and] that Yugoslavia will not be able to remain neutral for long and will enter the war on the side of the democracies.'[141] He therefore instructed Krnjević to contact the Foreign Office and ask the British to put pressure on Belgrade to solve the Croat question. If a solution was not found, Krnjević should enquire what would the British position be in the event of Croatia declaring independence. The British refused to see Krnjević, but agreed to read his memorandum.[142] The FO did not wish to interfere in Yugoslavia's internal affairs; to see and even communicate with Krnjević directly would have certainly been interpreted that way in Belgrade.[143]

The Peasant Party leadership as a whole was in favour of finding a solution to the Croat question inside Yugoslavia. At a meeting of the party leaders from Bosnia, Juraj Šutej declared that in the light of the collapse of the negotiations with the Crown, the Croats faced two choices: they could either continue to work towards reaching an agreement with Belgrade, no matter how long it took, or seek foreign intervention in order to solve the Croat question. The meeting unanimously decided in favour of the first choice.[144] Therefore, although external factors accelerated developments in the country, internal factors also favoured a Serb-Croat agreement.

Both Belgrade and Zagreb understood the danger posed by the international crisis, but they also realised that regardless of external

---

140   FO 371/23876, Rapp's confidential despatch, enclosed with Shone's letter to Halifax, Bled, 13 August 1939.

141   Ibid.

142   FO 371/23876, The Foreign Office to the British Legation in Belgrade, London, 29 June 1939.

143   Victor Lennox, a *Daily Telegraph* journalist who acted as a liaison between the FO and Krnjević, was told by a Foreign Office official that 'it was a very delicate matter [...] to receive representatives of [a] minority in the Balkan states, as they invariably misrepresent the facts on their return and maintain that they had won official sympathy here for their cause.' Ibid. •

144   FO 371/23876, Shone to Halifax, Bled, 4 August 1939.

developments they had little choice but to continue negotiations. These gradually resumed in June. The demand for plebiscites was now dropped by Maček. Cvetković on his part offered to Maček several areas of Bosnia that had a Croat majority as well as parts of the Srem region in Vojvodina, in addition to Savska, Primorska and the city and district of Dubrovnik. It was also agreed that the final borders of the *banovina* would be drawn when the internal division of Yugoslavia was complete. The question of the respective jurisdictions of the new Croatian and central authorities—another bone of contention back in April—would be solved by a group of legal experts nominated by both sides.[145]

The Cvetković-Maček agreement was officially put into effect on 26 August 1939, with the formation of the Government of National Agreement (*Vlada narodnog sporazuma*) and the proclamation of the *banovina* of Croatia. Cvetković was appointed Prime Minister of the new government, with Maček as his deputy. Five other members of the Peasant Democratic Coalition entered the government (four Croatian Peasants and one Independent Democrat). The Democrats and the Radicals' Main Committee criticised the agreement, while the Agrarians supported it overall, although they too were critical of the fact that the non-democratic 1931 Constitution remained. The Agrarian Branko Čubrilović entered the government, not without opposition from his own party, as did Lazar Marković, who thus effectively ended his membership of the Main Committee of the Radical Party. Božidar Maksimović, another former Radical, who had throughout the 1930s pursued political action independent from

---

145 FO 371/23876, Rapp's confidential despatch on Serbo-Croat negotiations, enclosed with Shone's letter to Halifax, Bled, 13 August 1939. The Croatian side was represented by Ljudevit Filipinčić, the Secretary of the Bankers' Association and formerly a high official in the Habsburg government, Ivo Krbek, Professor of Law at Zagreb University, and Juraj Šutej, who in addition to being a prominent member of the HSS was also a lawyer. The Serbian team consisted of Mihailo Ilić, Mihailo Konstantinović and Djordje Tasić, all three eminent Professors of Law at Belgrade University.

both the Main Committee and the Yugolav Radical Union, joined the government as Education Minister.[146]

The *banovina* of Croatia had been formed by the amalgamation of the Savska and Primorska *banovinas*, with seven additional *kotari* (districts): Dubrovnik (formerly in Zetska *banovina*), Šid and Ilok (Dunavska), Gradačac and Derventa (Vrbaska), and Brčko, Travnik and Fojnica (Drinska). Its capital was Zagreb. In terms of area, it occupied just over one quarter of Yugoslavia's territory and was populated by a little over 4 million people (between one quarter and one third of the total population of Yugoslavia). Three quarters of its population was made up of Catholics (Croats), but almost 20 per cent were Orthodox (Serbs) and almost 4 per cent (Bosnian) Muslims.[147]

The Croatian *banovina* enjoyed full autonomy in the areas of agriculture, trade, industry, forests, mines, public works, social and health policy, physical education, justice, education and interior affairs. Only foreign policy and foreign trade, defence, public security, customs and finance remained under the jurisdiction of the central government in Belgrade. Legislative powers were to be jointly held by the King and the *sabor*, which was to be re-established and could only be summoned and closed by a royal decree. A royal decree would also be necessary to call fresh elections. Members of the *sabor* were to be

---

146 Members of the new government were: Dragiša Cvetković (Prime Minister), Vladko Maček (Deputy Prime Minister), Lazar Marković (Justice), Božidar Maksimović (Education), Miha Krek (Public Works), Džafer Kulenović (Forests and Mines), Jevrem Tomić (Physical Education), Nikola Bešlić (Transport), Aleksandar Cincar-Marković (Foreign Affairs), Gen. Milan Nedić (Army and Navy), Josip Torbar (Posts, Telegraphs and Telephones), Juraj Šutej (Finance), Bariša Smoljan (without portfolio), Ivan Andres (Trade and Industry), Srdjan Budisavljević (Social Policy and Public Health), Branko Čubrilović (Agriculture), Mihailo Konstantinović (without portfolio) and Stanoje Mihaldžić (Interior). Source: *Politika*, 26 August, 1939.

147 The exact figures were as follows: *territory*: 65,455,99 square kilometres (26.44 per cent of Yugoslavia's territory); *population*: 4,064,601 (28.88 per cent of Yugoslavia's population), including 3,020,685 Roman Catholics (75.06 per cent of the population of the *banovina*), 755,970 Serbian Orthodox (19.28 per cent) and 153,452 Sunni Muslim (3.81 per cent). Source: *Godišnjak Banske vlasti Banovine Hrvatske*, Zagreb, 1940.

elected by direct and secret ballot. Royal decrees relating to Croatia had to be jointly signed by the King and the *ban*. The latter's election had to be approved by the King.[148] Ivan Šubašić was appointed as the first (and as it turned out the only) *ban*. In a circular to all administrative, police, and gendarmerie authorities in the new *banovina*, Šubašić stated: 'Thanks to the trust of His Majesty the King I have been appointed *ban* of the *banovina* of Croatia. In accepting this duty, I am determined that affairs of the *banovina* will be [always] carried out [in a just manner] towards everyone, regardless of their nationality and religion, always in the name of the people.'[149]

The Serbian opposition and the Cvetković-Maček negotiations

On 8 February 1939, leaders of the United Opposition and the Peasant Democratic Coalition met in Jovan Jovanović Pižon's house in Belgrade (the same house where they hosted Maček the previous August), to discuss the political situation in the aftermath of the fall of Stojadinović. Maček did not travel personally, but sent his right-hand man Šutej, while Milan Kostić represented the Independent Democrats at the meeting, which was also attended by the Agrarians Jovanović Pižon, Milan Gavrilović, Branko Čubrilović and Miloš Tupanjanin, the Democrats Milan Grol, Božidar Marković and Božidar Vlajić, the Radicals Miloš Trifunović, Momčilo Ninčić and Lazar Marković, and two Yugoslav Nationalists: Bogoljub Jevtić and Grga Andjelinović. The meeting went well and the participants agreed on all issues discussed.[150]

The opposition leaders agreed that they should negotiate with the government jointly. The Croatian Peasants believed that the Belgrade opposition parties were more representative of the 'Serbian people' than Dragiša Cvetković and Serb members of the government. They

---

148 The full text of the Cvetković-Maček agreement is reproduced in Boban, *Sporazum*, 404-08.

149 HDA XXI/84/5698, Ban banovine Hrvatske Šubašić Dr. Ivan, Nastup dužnosti, Zagreb, 2 September 1939.

150 MPHSS-1, 20.

agreed to propose to Prince Paul the creation of a 'concentration government' that would include the Zagreb and Belgrade opposition blocs.[151]

Šutej travelled once again to Belgrade in late March to inform the opposition leaders there that Maček had decided to receive Cvetković, in his capacity as the Crown's envoy, and that he had also demanded that 'the real representatives of the Serbian people, that is the UO and not the JRZ, take part in the negotiations'.[152] A leader comment published on 29 March in the *Hrvatski dnevnik* explained:

The politics of national agreement cannot be carried out without the representatives of the Croatian and Serbian people. That principle dominated the agreement of 8 October 1937, and it dominates today in Croatia. The United Opposition and the Croatian Peasant Party, as the representative of the Croatian people, are both loyal to that principle. They both put all their energy in settling the relations between the Croatian and Serbian people.[153]

The Serbian opposition parties seemed happy with this view, but they soon found themselves out of the main picture, mostly because Prince Paul was opposed to their inclusion in the government. He was said to fear that bringing another coalition into the negotiations would slow the whole process down, and perhaps make an agreement impossible. The Prince Regent was in a hurry to settle the Croatian question because of the growing international crisis. But, most importantly, he felt that he could not accept the United Opposition's calls for an end to the dictatorship. Because Maček sought autonomy for Croatia, not necessarily democracy for Yugoslavia, an agreement between him and the Crown was possible. With the United Opposition's principled stance on the demand for the abolition of the 1931 Constitution and a return to a genuine parliamentary democracy, a compromise between the Serbian opposition parties and the government and the Crown proved impossible. The Serbian parties'

---

151 Ibid., 22.

152 Ibid., 31.

153 Ibid., 21. Note the failure to mention the SDS, which was largely sidelined during the negotiations between Cvetković and Maček.

demand that Cvetković and the governing party should be excluded from the negotiations was unrealistic. Both Prince Paul and Maček rejected this proposal. Once Maček realised that the Crown had serious intentions, he was ready to abandon his Serbian allies.[154]

The Independent Democrats attempted in vain to achieve a mini-agreement between the Croatian Peasant Party and the United Opposition during Maček's negotiations with Cvetković. Ideologically, the Independent Democratic Party was closer to Serbia's opposition parties, particularly the Democratic Party. When the 27 April agreement fell through, the Independent Democrats saw a good chance for a rapprochement between the two sides. While the United Opposition objected to Maček's tactics—concerned exclusively with achieving autonomy for Croatia—the Independent Democrats came up with a proposal for an overall agreement, which they hoped would be acceptable to the Serbian opposition.

Srdjan Budisavljević, the author of the proposal, envisaged the internal division of Yugoslavia into three *banovinas*: Slovenia (Dravska), Croatia (Savska, Primorska, and Vrbaska) and Serbia (Dunavska, Moravska, Drinska, Zetska and Vardarska). Maček accepted the proposal, but the United Opposition rejected it, because it offered more territory to Croatia than Cvetković was willing to give, and because the proposal did not address the issue of democratisation of the country. The Independent Democrats wished to include Vrbaska in the future Croatian *banovina* because that way most of their voters would be inside Croatia; moreover, with more Serbs included in Croatia, the position of the Serb minority would be potentially less vulnerable. The Independent Democrats' initiative, however, could not prevent the deterioration of the relations between Maček and his Serbian counterparts. To the Serbian opposition Maček was a

---

154 Ibid., 31-9. Boban believed that Prince Paul refused to consider democratisation because he feared it would have a negative impact on Yugoslavia's good relations with two major non-democracies: Germany and Italy. However, this seems unlikely. Germany in particular was not so interested in Yugoslavia's internal politics, so long as Belgrade's foreign policy was 'cooperative'.

traitor, as Vlajić angrily stated.[155] To Maček, the Serbian parties had simply become an unnecessary burden.

The immediate aftermath of the agreement and Croat reactions

Reactions to the Cvetković-Maček agreement among the population could generally be described as follows: most Croats enthusiastically supported it, while many Serbs opposed it. However, as in other respects, the situation with the Serbs was not straightforward: Serb leaders of the Yugoslav Radical Union officially supported the Cvetković-Maček agreement, but many of the party's Serb members began to argue for the creation of a Serbian *banovina* that would include Serb-populated areas of Croatia. Bosnian Muslims generally rejected the agreement, because they opposed the inclusion of 'Bosnian' districts into Croatia. Although Bosnia as a separate administrative entity had ceased to exist in 1918, the sense of Bosnian identity and the memory of Bosnia's historic borders clearly remained strong among local Muslims.

The 1939 agreement was certainly one of the turning points of Yugoslavia's interwar history, and yet in many respects initially it did not change significantly the situation on the ground in terms of Serb-Croat relations. Although there were incidents involving Croats on the one side and Serbs and 'integral Yugoslavist' Croats on the other, this was also true of the period prior to 26 August 1939. For instance, a police report recorded that on 15 July someone broke the windows of the house of a Zagreb pensioner, Pavle Galić, because he failed to fly the Croatian flag on the occasion of Maček's birthday. The following day, windows of the house of Josip Komerički, a carpenter working for the state rail company and a member of the Zagreb branch of the government party, were also smashed.[156] It was enough to be known as a member of the government party to risk intimida-

---

155 Ibid., 61-2. See also BAR PPP, box 13, Dragiša Cvetković to Prince Paul, Belgrade, 19 April 1939.

156 HDA XXI/82/5645, Izveštaj o političkim prilikama i dogadjajima u mesecu julu, Zagreb, 5 August 1939.

tion. Thus, Lajoš Kozma from the village of Reftal, near Osijek, had his windows broken in the night of 5-6 August 1939, for no apparent reason other than his political affiliation.[157]

However, things changed after the agreement in several ways. The intimidation against pro-government individuals and organisations, both Serb and Croat, in areas with a Croat majority intensified. Nikola Vučković, a corporal of the Varaždin gendarmerie, was beaten up on 10 September by a group of locals in the village of Mačkovac near Varaždin. The report on this incident provides an insight into the life of a Yugoslav gendarme, the possible motive behind the attack, and the cooperation between the new authorities and the gendarmerie:

On 10 September 1939 the corporal of gendarmerie Vučković P. Nikola of the gendarmerie station at Ivanec, of the Varaždin gendarmerie unit, went to a football game, having been issued with a permission to leave the station until 20:00 hours by the station commander; he stayed at the game until 16:00 hours and then left the stadium [...] hoping to meet a girl in order to have fun.

After he failed to find a suitable girl, at 1:30 hours on 11 September he went to the nearby village of Mačkovac [...] to attend a party organised by [local] miners. At around 2:00 hours he was approached by two soldiers [...] who asked him for cigarettes, and at the same time was attacked by a group of miners [...] one of whom hit his head and back several times with a stick; [the gendarme briefly] fell unconscious, during which time [the attackers] took his pistol with seven bullets, his knife and belt and ran away. When the corporal regained consciousness he returned to the station around 2:30 hours and according to the gendarme on duty, Travar Dmitar, went straight to his bed and fell asleep while still in a drunken state; the station commander found him still sleeping in the morning.[158]

---

157 HDA XXI/83/5655, Političke prilike, izvještaj za mjesec kolovoz, Kraljevska banska uprava Savske banovine, Zagreb. The author of this report, probably written in September, used the Croatian word 'kolovoz' and not the Serbian 'avgust', whereas the previous report was dated 'jul', and not 'srpanj' (see the previous footnote). Although the report was typed on the paper which had the old heading of 'Savska banovina', this was an example of the 'Croatisation' of the official discourse in the new banovina.

158 HDA XXI/84/5730, Štab Savskog žandarmeriskog puka Banskoj vlasti banovine Hrvatske (Odjelu za unutarnje poslove), Zagreb, 18 September 1939.

The report concluded that the wounds Vučković received had not been serious, while the motive for the attack was 'apparently hatred of the gendarmerie', an institution which symbolised the old, Serb-dominated regime.[159] The *banovina* authorities asked the commander of the Savska gendarmerie battalion to move Vučković to another station, because after the incident the gendarme had 'completely lost any authority' among the local population, and 'similar incidents occurring again could not be discounted.'[160] The commander, Colonel Stanković, duly responded, sending Vučković to another post.[161]

In addition to the gendarmerie, prominent members of the former regime also came under attack. In another, unrelated incident, which occurred in October, Ivan Ruljančić, the president of the local Serbian Orthodox community and the former mayor of the town of Vis, on the island of Vis, was badly beaten by a group of unknown culprits. The reason for the attack was allegedly the legacy of his years in power. Ruljančić, a former Radical who had joined the Yugoslav Nationalists, had apparently been particularly harsh with Maček's local supporters. Moreover, he had also encouraged the conversion of Croats to Serbian Orthodoxy, which worsened the relationship between Serbs and Croats on this Adriatic island.[162] Ruljančić's name suggests that he was probably of Croat origin and therefore could have been a convert himself.[163]

---

159 Ibid.

160 HDA XXI/84/5730, Banska vlast banovine Hrvatske, Odjeljak za državnu zaštitu Komandantu Savskog žandarmeriskog puka, Zagreb, 9 October 1939.

161 HDA XXI/84/5730, Komandant pukovnik Mil. M. Stanković Banskoj vlasti banovine Hrvatske, Zagreb, 13 October 1939.

162 HDA XXI/83/5660, Izvještaj o političkoj situaciji i raspoloženju naroda, Ispostava Banske vlasti u Splitu Banskoj vlasti banovine Hrvatske, kabinetu gosp.[odina] Bana, Split, 16 November 1939.

163 According to the report, there were some 200 Croats in Vis who had converted to Orthodoxy. HDA XXI/83/5660, Izvještaj o političkoj situaciji i raspoloženju naroda, Ispostava Banske vlasti u Splitu Banskoj vlasti banovine Hrvatske, kabinetu gosp.[odina] Bana, Split, 16 November 1939. There is no evidence that the government encouraged conversions, although it probably did not oppose them either.

Attacks on gendarmes as well as on well-known supporters of the former regime acquired a different significance in the new context. The changed circumstances certainly made those intimidated feel more insecure and unprotected. Another report noted that in the aftermath of the Cvetković-Maček agreement the population of Split and surrounding areas might be divided into two groups: Maček's supporters, whose rights were protected and who felt safe and free, and 'Serbs and Yugoslav Sokols,[164] who effectively cannot count on protection, while some members of the HSZ [Croatian Peasant Defence] and HSS supporters threaten and attack them; even innocent children are not spared [intimidation]'.[165]

Because of their strong links with Alexander's dictatorship, the Sokol societies were particularly targeted in areas dominated by the Croatian Peasant Party, regardless of whether the Sokol members in question were Serb or Croat. On 2 September Dragutin Kramer, 'a prominent member of the Sokols', was murdered in Zagreb when returning home at night, in what was believed to be a politically-motivated murder.[166] The murder of Kramer was exceptional, but there were many instances of physical attacks on Sokols. Martin Car and Mate Katnić, leading members of the Sokol society in the overwhelmingly Croat town of Crikvenica,[167] complained about in-

---

164 Sokol societies were Slav nationalist athletic organisations dating back to Habsburg days. In 1929 the Croatian and Slovene Sokol organisations were replaced by a single, Yugoslav one, which played an important role in the dictatorship's attempts to create a single Yugoslav identity. See Nikola Žutić, Sokoli: Ideologija u fizičkoj kulturi Kraljevine Jugoslavije, 1929-1941, Belgrade, 1991.

165 HDA XXI/84/5734, Izveštaj o političkoj situaciji, Primorski žandarmerijski puk ispostavi banske vlasti, Split, 15 October 1939.

166 HDA XXI/85/5796, Uprava policije u Zagrebu, Kriminalni otsek, Kraljevskoj banskoj upravi Savske [sic!] banovine, Odeljku za državnu zaštitu, Zagreb, 2 September 1939.

167 According to the 1931 population census, there were 11, 709 Roman Catholics and 98 Orthodox among the Serbo-Croat speakers living in the Crikvenica district. Bogoljub Kočović, Etnički i demografski razvoj u Jugoslaviji od 1921. do 1991. godine (Po svim zvaničnim a u nekim slučajevima i korigovanim popisima), Paris, 1998, 2 vols, vol. 1, 58.

timidation by Maček's followers to the headquarters of the Yugoslav *Sokol* Association in Belgrade, which then forwarded their complaint to the Ministry of Physical Education.[168]

In this letter, members of the Crikvenica *Sokol* society complained that on the same day that the agreement was concluded a campaign against *Sokol* members and their families began. Leading members of the local *Sokol* organisation were beaten up or had their windows smashed. Stjepan Car, Martin's brother, suffered severe head injuries and ended up in hospital. On 3 September Ljubo Škiljan, the head of the local municipality and leader of the HSS-controlled Croatian Peasant Defence, forcibly took over the *Sokols'* building in Crikvenica, virtually making the society's activities impossible.[169] The letter concluded with a plea in the name of 'all male and female *Sokols*, and all Croats and Serbs of Yugoslav orientation to [...] make public our difficult position.'[170] Another report noted several cases of vandalism against *Sokol* properties in the Šibenik area and on the island of Hvar during October, but also stated that the situation was generally good and that the agreement was accepted by population at large.[171]

Croats who supported the previous regime came under attack as much as their Serb counterparts. The reasons for intimidation were often complex and had much to do with local context and the behaviour of victims, as the incidents in Mačkovac, Vis and Crikvenica show. In that respect, particularly revealing is a report sent by the Zagreb police to the new *banovina*'s Office for State Protection, in regard to the latter's concern that Serbs and pro-Yugoslav Croats were being exposed to a 'state of terror'. The author(s) of the report stated that:

---

168   HDA XXI/84/5729, Savez Sokola Kraljevine Jugoslavije, Ministarstvu fizičkog vaspitanja naroda, Belgrade, 7 September 1939.

169   Ibid. The attached letter from Car and Katnić, 4 August [should be September] 1939.

170   Ibid.

171   HDA XXI/83/5660, Izvještaj o političkoj situaciji i raspoloženju naroda, Ispostava Banske vlasti u Splitu Banskoj vlasti banovine Hrvatske, kabinetu gosp.[odina] Bana, Split, 16 November 1939.

It is true that for some time, since the establishment of the Croatian *ba-novina*, there have been incidents, but those incidents have not had an [anti-Serb and anti-Yugoslav] character, nor could they be described as an organised action 'against all Serbs and Croats of Yugoslav orientation', for the [simple] reason that in most cases the motive behind incidents have been personal vendetta and hatred, and the personal settling of scores.

Incidents have been taking place mostly in suburbs, among minor, primitive people, so the psychosis felt already in 1935[172] is now being repeated against so-called '*Četniks*' [...] The psychosis has only been magnified by the international crisis which demanded a partial mobilisation [of army conscripts], as well as by various rumours designed to spread panic [...] which often affected intelligent and well informed people, let alone backward people [living] on the periphery.[173]

The report also commented on allegations that around 200 persons had moved from Zagreb to Belgrade since the creation of autonomous Croatia:

Even if [it were true that] 200 people fled Zagreb for Belgrade, one cannot conclude on the basis of this that terror is carried out in Zagreb against all Serbs and Yugoslav-oriented Croats, because, as is well known, a large number of Serbs of all professions live in Zagreb, as well as a large number of Croats of Yugoslav orientation, and nothing whatsoever has happened to any of them, but they all live and work peacefully.[174]

Although the Zagreb police statement betrayed a sense of understanding if not outright sympathy for the perpetrators, who were according to this view no more than ignorant people understandably seeking revenge, the report makes a very important point: the conflict in the Croatian *banovina* was in many aspects personal and

---

172 The author probably referred to the election campaign that year, when tensions ran high and violent clashes between the opposition and government supporters were not uncommon.

173 HDA XXI/84/5724, Redarstveno ravnateljstvo u Zagrebu, Banskoj vlasti banovine Hrvatske, Odjelku [*sic*!] za državnu zaštitu, Zagreb, 26 October 1939. The '*Četniks*' referred to in the report were members of the Serbian veteran *Četnik* organisations, some of whom had actually been aggressively pro-Yugoslav. The term acquired a different, more pejorative meaning after the Second World War and during the Yugoslav wars of the 1990s.

174 Ibid.

ideological, not necessarily 'ethnic'. Croats of different ideological persuasions, especially those who had participated in former regimes, were targeted as much as Serbs.

Nevertheless, it would be simply wrong to argue that there was an absence of ethnically-inspired conflict. When two gendarmes from the village of Aleksandrovo, on the island of Krk, attempted to search a group of twenty young men, after shots were heard in the neighbourhood, the men ran away, swearing at the gendarmes' 'Serbian mother' and warning the gendarmes that they would 'not be searching [people] for much longer.'[175] Chasing the men, the gendarmes entered a nearby house, without realising that a wedding party was going on inside. Probably provoked by the uninvited guests, Nikola Franolić and Mate Mrakovčić ordered the gendarmes to leave immediately, because they now lived in a 'free Croatia and did not need any *opančari* around'.[176] The gendarmes were forced to back down, because they were heavily outnumbered, but later managed to arrest one of the men, who illegally possessed a gun.[177]

The physical intimidation of Serbs and pro-Yugoslav Croats was exclusively limited to the local level. The Croatian Peasant Party leadership was not directly involved. It was in its interest to maintain order, although some of its policies alienated the Serb population. Its first test came on 6 September, the birthday of King Peter II. Birthday celebrations for the Karadjordjević dynasty or Maček always carried a high potential for conflict between political opponents. Yet, 6 September 1939, the first in the *banovina* of Croatia, was remarkably calm. In the Split area no incidents 'except a small one in Omiš' were reported.[178] Šubašić ordered all state buildings to fly Yugoslav

---

175 HDA XXI/84/5721, Aleksandrovo: incident izmedju žand.[armerijske] patrole i grupe mladića, Sresko načelstvo u Krku, Banskoj vlasti banovine Hrvatske, Odjeljku za državnu zaštitu, Krk, 14 October, 1939.

176 Ibid. *Opančari* means those who wear *opanci*, peasant shoes traditionally worn in central Serbia.

177 Ibid.

178 HDA XXI/82/5606, Sresko načelstvo Split, Mjesečni izvještaj o unutrašnjoj situaciji za mjesec septembar 1939, Split, 28 September 1939.

and Croat flags. Post offices, customs offices, port authorities and gendarmerie stations had only Yugoslav flags put out, while schools had both Yugoslav and Croat flags. Private houses were decorated by Yugoslav, Croatian and Serbian flags, although the Croat ones predominated.[179]

Although careful not to incite 'tribal' conflict, the leadership of the Croatian Peasant Party intensified its Croat-centric discourse following the creation of the Croatian *banovina*. A good example was the ceremony on the first anniversary of the death of Ante Trumbić on 19 November 1939, in Trumbić's home town of Split, organised by Maček's party. According to a police report, the whole ceremony appeared to have turned into celebration of Croat nationalism, with Croatian flags all over the town. Trumbić was exclusively described as a champion of Croat rights, while his key role in Yugoslav unification was completely ignored.[180] Yet, the event was deemed not 'nationalist' enough by the Frankists, who held a separate memorial on the premises of their 'Ante Trumbić' society in Split.[181] Frankists commemorated death anniversaries of other prominent Croat historical figures, such as Eugen Kvaternik and Ante Starčević,[182] separately from the Croatian Peasant Party, reflecting the divided historical memories among Croats and other South Slavs. Pro-Yugoslav Croats, Serbs and Slovenes regarded figures such as Trumbić and even Starčević as the prophets of Yugoslavism.

Soon after the Cvetković-Maček agreement a large number of *Ustaša* émigrés went back to Croatia. According to a police report, by mid-October as many as 213 *Ustašas* had returned to the territory of the former Primorska *banovina* from Italy—out of a total number

179 Ibid.

180 HDA XXI/83/5661, Mjesečni izvještaj o stanju javne bezbednosti i političkoj situaciji na području Redarstvenog ravnateljstva Split za novembar 1939, Split, 4 December 1939.

181 Ibid.

182 HDA XXI/83/5660, Izveštaj o političkoj situaciji i raspoloženju naroda, Ispostava banske vlasti u Splitu, Banskoj vlasti banovine Hrvatske, Kabinetu gosp.[odina] Bana, Split, 16 November, 1939.

of 391 *Ustaša* members or sympathisers born in the territory of Primorska who were based in Italy.[183] The same report stated that most of them had kept a low profile since returning, and it appears that some were even given jobs in local government institutions.[184]

Nevertheless, the months following the agreement witnessed increasing rivalry and clashes between members of the Croatian Peasant Party and Frankists and *Ustašas*, as well as between Maček's and Communist sympathisers.[185] While in opposition, the Croatian Peasant Party had enjoyed virtually unchallenged support among Croats. Even after entering the government the party still commanded a strong majority support among Croats. 'A vast majority of Croats [living] on the territory of the [Split] region are supporters of the HSS,' an official report stated. 'They are all entirely satisfied with the present situation in the country [as a whole] and in the *banovina* [of Croatia]. Supporters of this party are disciplined, and blindly follow instructions from the [party] leadership in Zagreb.'[186]

However, once in power, Maček's party found it more difficult to maintain its monopoly in Croatia, the challenge coming from both the left and the right. In addition, splits occurred within the party. The main reasons were the rivalry over positions in local government and dissatisfaction of some more radical members of the Croatian Peasant Party with the agreement of August 1939.[187] The Split branch of the party faced a particularly strong challenge from

---

183 HDA XXI/84/5734, Izveštaj o političkoj situaciji, Primorski žandarmerijski puk ispostavi banske vlasti, Split, 15 October 1939. In all probability, not all those branded by the authorities as *Ustašas* formally belonged to the organisation, though they may have shared the *Ustašas'* anti-Yugoslavism and anti-Serb sentiments.

184 Ibid.

185 HDA XXI/83/5660, Izvještaj o političkoj situaciji i raspoloženju naroda, Ispostava Banske vlasti u Splitu Banskoj vlasti banovine Hrvatske, kabinetu gosp.[odina] Bana, Split, 16 November 1939.

186 Ibid.

187 HDA XXI/83/5660, Izvještaj o političkoj situaciji i raspoloženju naroda, Ispostava Banske vlasti u Splitu, Banskoj vlasti banovine Hrvatske, kabinetu gosp.[odina] Bana, Split, 16 November 1939.

rival political groups. The Frankists were led by Edo Bulat, a former Maček supporter, Ivo Cuzzi and Ivo Bulić, and were popular among the youth and shop assistants, as well as among some peasants.[188] By May 1940 there were as many as 60 dissident Croatian Peasant Party groups in the Split area alone.[189]

One of the reasons for the internal divisions was that the Croatian Peasant Party was for the first time truly in a position to divide the spoils of office, as the following contemporary account suggests:

While [local] HSS leaders had during the previous regimes organised the party cells throughout the population, some of them, wishing to assume a leading role in decision-making purely out of personal ambitions, have come into conflict with their comrades; in many places now there are personal conflicts [between HSS leaders] which have had a [negative] effect among the [party] supporters. [The party followers] are beginning to group around different factions, for or against certain [local] leaders [...] The conflict between the Split-based HSS leaders, the deputy Dr Josip Berković and Paško Kaliterna, should be particularly mentioned, because it has *de facto* divided the party in the Split region into two groups.[190]

Kaliterna's conflict with the Split branch of the party facilitated an even closer cooperation between the Croatian Peasants and the Independent Democrats at the local level. The leader of the Independent Democrats in Split, Edo Leontić, never got on well with Kaliterna. After Kaliterna virtually became an HSS dissident, Leontić became the most loyal ally of the Split branch of Maček's party.[191] Another prominent local politician and another ethnic Croat, Grgur-Grga Andjelinović—Leontić, too, was a Croat—was the leader of the Yugoslav Nationalists' Split branch. An integralist Yugoslav,

---

188 Ibid.

189 Ljubo Boban, 'O političkim previranjima na selu u Banovini Hrvatskoj', *Istorija XX veka: Zbornik radova*, vol. 2, Belgrade, 1961, 243.

190 HDA XXI/83/5660, Izvještaj o političkoj situaciji i raspoloženju naroda, Ispostava Banske vlasti u Splitu, Banskoj vlasti banovine Hrvatske, kabinetu gosp.[odina] Bana, Split, 16 November 1939.

191 Ibid.

Andjelinović kept a relatively low profile after August 1939.[192] Like other integralist Yugoslavs, he did not necessarily oppose the idea of a Serb-Croat agreement, but was against the abandonment of the integral Yugoslav ideology.[193]

The political situation in Split in the late 1939 illustrated well the complexity of Yugoslav politics and the impossibility of reducing it to a Serb-Croat conflict. In the case of Split the conflict was as much among Croats as it was between Croats and Serbs. Similar situation emerged in other parts of the *banovina*. However, the Serb-Croat dimension did represent an important element of the political contest in post-1939 Yugoslavia. Soon after the Cvetković-Maček agreement, the Serbs began to unite around calls for a Serbian *banovina*, which, they argued, should include Serb-populated areas of the newly established autonomous Croatia.

---

192 Ibid.

193 See for instance Prvislav Grisogono, 'Sporazum i jugoslovenski nacionalni elementi', *Vidici*, no. 15-16, 10 September, 1939, 386-9. For a more critical view of the Cvetković-Maček agreement as an act of betrayal of the Yugoslav ideal see Niko Bartulović, 'Sporazum i Jugoslovenstvo', *Vidici*, no. 17-18, 25 September 1939, 434-7. Integralist Yugoslav authors, gathered around the journal *Vidici*, were equally critical of all Yugoslav particularistic nationalisms, including the calls for a Serbian *banovina*—see Milan Marjanović, 'Suština našeg problema', *Vidici*, no. 1-2, 25 January 1940, 2-4 .

6

THE AFTERMATH

The whole country [...] has been witnessing for the past eight months the regulation of Serb-Croat relations [...] without the participation of the Serbs...While under the leadership of their undoubtedly legitimate representatives, [and] in complete freedom, [...] the Croats have been organising their Croatian *banovina* and marking its boundaries in the mixed area bordering Serb [populated areas], the Serbs have been standing aside, their hands tied, [and] their mouths [blocked].

A statement by the Democratic Party, 1939[1]

On 14 January 1940, just before 3:00pm, a royal train from Belgrade arrived at the main Zagreb railway station. The train, whose passengers included Prince Paul, Princess Olga[2] and Prime Minister Cvetković, had left Belgrade the same morning at exactly 8:00pm, briefly stopping at the Croatian towns of Vinkovci and Slavonski Brod, where the royal and government passengers were greeted by local officials and 'ordinary' people. The two towns' train stations were decorated with flowers and Croatian and state flags, and on the platform there were representatives of all local societies, ranging from various Croatian cultural, political and professional associations to the Yugoslav *Sokols*.[3] In Zagreb, the royal party was welcomed by

---

1 *Demokrati o današnjem stanju u zemlji*, Belgrade, November 1939.

2 Olga, Princess Paul of Yugoslavia (1903-1997), was the daughter of Prince Nicholas of Greece and Denmark and Grand Duchess Helen Vladimirovna of Russia. She married Paul in 1923. Her sister Marina (1906-1968) married the Duke of Kent in 1934.

3 'Zagreb je svečano i oduševljeno dočekao Nj. Kr. Vis. Kneza Namesnika i Kneginju Olgu', *Politika*, 15 January 1940.

Maček, Šubašić, Archbishop Stepinac, leading members of the Peasant Democratic Coalition, and thousands of people. Flowers were everywhere, and so were flags, both Yugoslav and Croatian. In addition to many Zagrebians, 'tens of thousands [of] disciplined peasants, loyal to Dr Maček, came to Zagreb...from their villages...to greet His Royal Highness the Prince Regent and Princess Olga', braving a cold January day.[4]

While the Prince Regent inspected an army unit commanded by General Nedeljković, in charge of a regional army corps, Maček entertained Princess Olga who held a large bouquet of flowers. After Prince Paul completed the military inspection, the Croat leader walked towards a podium with microphones to give what would undoubtedly become a historic speech, if for no other reason than the occasion. This was the first visit to Croatia by the man many Croats regarded as most responsible for their newly acquired autonomy. 'Your Royal Highness,' Maček began, 'I am filled with joy to be in a position to welcome Your Royal Highness together with [...] Princess Olga to the *capital of Croatia and of all Croats*, in the name of *all Croats*.'[5] He continued:

Your Royal Highness is blessed with three virtues that can only rarely be found in a single person. The first is [...] justice, the second wisdom, and the third is courage. We should be grateful to your sense of justice that you were perhaps the first to realise that demands of the Croatian people were justified. It is thanks to your wisdom that you realised that the Kingdom of Yugoslavia could only be saved by granting the Croats their demands, and it is thanks to your courage that you acted like a real man by cutting the Gordian knot in a single blow. It is for these reasons that the Croatian people welcomes you today with open arms and wishes you, through me, a happy stay [in Croatia]. Long live the Prince Regent, long live Princess Olga![6]

---

4 Ibid.

5 Ibid. (Emphasis added by D. Dj.).

6 Ibid. Maček clearly saw himself as the leader of all Croats, including those living outside the Croatian *banovina*, while Zagreb was, in his view, the capital of all Croats, and not only of the *banovina*. Although made in a different context, similar claims by Franjo Tudjman and Slobodan Milošević, the presidents of Croatia and Serbia respectively, would provoke in the late 1980s and early 1990s

Maček's emotional speech was greeted by loud cheers. The Prince Regent shook the Croat leader's hand and took the podium, replying briefly: 'I am particularly touched by your words and unusually happy to be in Zagreb today.'[7] Paul's short speech was greeted by loud cheers and was followed by Šubašić's somewhat longer address welcoming the Belgrade guests and praising the 1939 agreement. The Croats apparently did not mind Paul's brevity, which often led Serbs to accuse him of being cold and 'too English'.[8] Hardly anybody noticed that it was also the day when New Year was celebrated according to the old, Julian calendar, still kept by the Serbian Orthodox Church.

The visit was arranged in order to show to the public that the Serb-Croat conflict was over.[9] If this had still not been achieved in reality, the genuinely warm reception the Prince Regent received on his first trip to autonomous Croatia signalled that the Crown had regained the confidence of many Croats. Although Maček, like perhaps most Croats, was concerned primarily with Croatia—as his speech clearly showed—Yugoslavia as a state had become more acceptable to the Croats following the Cvetković-Maček agreement. Prince Paul's visit to Zagreb certainly helped restore Croatian support for Yugoslavia, but, as one contemporary observer noted, it also

---

endless discussions and arguments, as both these leaders saw themselves as representatives of their nations, not their republics, thus breaking the accepted norm in socialist Yugoslavia.

7   Ibid.

8   Milan Jovanović Stoimirović, who accompanied Prince Paul to Rome in May 1939, noted that Paul was very warmly greeted at the Vatican, by Croat and Slovene monks, but feared that the Prince's cold manner might have insulted Mussolini. Milan Jovanović Stoimirović, *Dnevnik, 1936-1941*, Novi Sad, 2000, 277. In a marked contrast to Paul's reserved, elegant appearance, the Foreign Minister Aleksandar Cincar-Marković appeared to have adopted Stojadinović's way of communicating with foreign officials. During the same visit by the Yugoslav delegation to Rome, Cincar-Marković and his Italian counterpart Count Ciano spent a great deal of time flirting with women, even when at the theatre. Ibid., 278.

9   Neil Balfour and Sally Mackay, *Paul of Yugoslavia: Britain's Maligned Friend*, London, 1980, 185.

helped to cement support for the Croatian Peasant Party among the population at large.[10]

It seemed, not merely from the point of view of high politics, that the country as a whole as well as Croatia, as its only autonomous province, faced a more stable future, as *ban* Šubašić stated in his welcoming address.[11] Yet, a careful observer might have noticed that the main reason for the Croats' newly-found enthusiasm was undoubtedly, to some extent, the Croatian *banovina*'s transformation into a quasi-nation-state. Maček welcomed the Prince Regent to 'the capital of Croatia and all Croats, in the name of all Croats'. In January 1940 alone, the month of Paul's visit to Zagreb, eleven new associations had been registered on the territory of the *banovina*, most of them 'Croatian' and none 'Yugoslav'. Another eight associations were registered the following month, all with the prefix 'Croatian'.[12] At the same time, attacks on organisations and individuals closely connected with the previous regime, whether they were Serb or Croat, intensified after August 1939.

A Serb reaction was perhaps inevitable. By the time of Prince Paul's visit to Zagreb, many Serbs from the *banovina* had joined in what had grown into a pan-Serb 'movement', encouraged, if not organised, by the Serbian Orthodox Church, the Serbian Cultural

---

10   HDA XXI/87/6013, Sresko načelstvo Split, Komandantu Jadranske divizijske oblasti, mjesečni izvještaj o unutrašnjoj situaciji za mjesec siječanj 1940. god.[ine], Split, 26 January 1940.

11   'Zagreb je svečano i oduševljeno dočekao Nj. Kr. Vis. Kneza Namesnika i Kneginju Olgu', *Politika*, 15 January 1940.

12   HDA XXI/87/6021, Izvještaj o poslovanju za I tromjesečje 1940. i o političkim prilikama i dogadjajima u istom tromjesečju. Redarstveno ravnateljstvo, Zagreb, banskoj vlasti banovine Hrvatske, Odjeljenju za unutarnje poslove, Odjelku za državnu zaštitu u Zagrebu, Zagreb, 4 April 1940. Among the new societies registered in January were: the Croatian Football Association, the Croatian Bowling Association, the Association of Croatian Mountaineering Societies, the Croatian Table Tennis Association, and even the First Croatian Association of Newspaper Salesmen. The Assocation of Croatian Teachers' Societies, the Croatian Library Association, the Association of Croatian Dance Teachers and the Croatian Association of Restaurant-owners were among those associations registered in February 1940.

Club and most 'Serb' political parties. The movement was unofficially known as 'Serbs, rally together!'. By early 1940 it had gathered such a momentum that on 11 March that year the *banovina* of Croatia authorities requested all regional civilian and police officials 'within three days, regardless of reports sent hitherto, to produce reports about the "Serbs, rally together" movement, that is about the movement for the secession of Serbian districts from the territory of the Croatian *banovina*.'[13]

The Serbian question

The Serbian question was inseparably linked with the Croatian question. Croat demands for greater autonomy within Yugoslavia were chiefly motivated by their fear of Serbian domination. At the same time the Serbs, scattered through Bosnia and Croatia, felt that any concession to Croats would be at their expense. Such fears seemed confirmed after the Cvetković-Maček agreement was announced and an autonomous Croatia that incorporated a large number of Serbs was established.

It could be argued that the Serbian question had already emerged before August 1939. The resentment against Serbs among non-Serbs, particularly Croats, because of the Serbian domination of the state fed Serb arguments of betrayal and of the ungratefulness of non-Serbs. It also led to occasional violence against the Serb population in predominantly Croat areas, usually at the time of elections. A journalist close to the Stojadinović government described to Milan Jovanović Stoimirović in late August 1936, three years before the establishment of autonomous Croatia, the growing anti-Serb sentiments among Catholics and Muslims, which he encountered while on a trip to Bosnia. 'In Bosnia the *Serbian question* is emerging, Mr

13 HDA XXI/89/6129, Naredba svim sreskim načelstvima, ispostavama, gradskim redarstvima i redarstvenim ravnateljstvima od banske vlasti banovine Hrvatske, Zagreb, 11 March 1940.

Jovanović, and that question is more dangerous than all others.'[14] Jovanović Stoimirović agreed. Following the conversation with the journalist he wrote in his diary that he had always foreseen 'the Serbian reaction' to the 'Catholic action'. 'Korošec cares about Ljubljana only. Behmen[15] [is interested] only in the Muslims...[Non-Serbs] interfere in Serbian affairs and interests, while nobody allows the Serb to say anything in this country, and yet they talk about Serbian hegemony.'[16]

A somewhat less obvious factor behind the emergence of the Serbian question was the conflict between Serb nationalism and the Yugoslav state. During the 1930s, an increasing number of Serbs came to believe that Serb 'interests' clashed with the Yugoslav integral ideology promulgated by the regime. Dragoljub Jovanović remembered discontent among Serbian peasants over additional '*banovina* taxes' they were required to pay after the *banovinas* were established on 3 October 1929. Jovanović recalled a popular song he heard among peasants of the Moravska *banovina* at the time: 'You [Serbia] used to be an Empire, then a Kingdom, and now you are merely a *banovina* [followed by a particularly vulgar swearword]'.[17] Dissatisfaction with the new order may have been triggered by a social-economic factor, but there were also those who lamented the disappearance of the 'Serbian name' following the King's 'Yugoslavicising' measures. For example, Serbian and Montenegrin army officers bemoaned the

---

14 Jovanović Stoimirović, *Dnevnik*, entry for 29 August 1936, 70. Emphasis in original. Stijepo Kobasica, the journalist, compared the situation he encountered in Bosnia to the summer of 1914. Then anti-Serb sentiments were widespread following the assassination of Archduke Francis Ferdinand in Sarajevo on 28 June, by Gavrilo Princip. Despite all the tension that Kobasica must have witnessed, this was a highly exaggerated statement.

15 Šefkija Behmen, a Bosnian Muslim leader and Minister without portfolio in the Stojadinović government.

16 Jovanović Stoimirović, *Dnevnik*, 70-71.

17 In Serbo-Croat: '*Ti si bila carevina, pa postade kraljevina, a sada si banovina, p... li ti materina!*' The '*banovina*' in this context was probably Moravska, which included most of central Serbia. Dragoljub Jovanović, *Političke uspomene*, Belgrade, 1997, 7 vols, vol. 2, 171.

abolition of their old military flags in 1929. The clash between Serbism and Yugoslavism was an important and yet usually overlooked conflict.

A warning of what was to come after the creation of the *banovina* of Croatia came in the summer of 1937, during the Concordat crisis. Yet, the signs were there even earlier. On 14 January 1937, six months before the crisis over the Concordat escalated, responding to rumours of an impending deal between the Yugoslav state and the Holy See Patriarch Varnava warned in his New Year's address:

The patience of the Serbian tribe is coming to an end. Our pride no longer allows us to keep silent. We are the tribe that has suffered greatly. We have liberated this country and established order only to be hated and denied equality [in that same country]. We sacrificed everything: our flag, coat of arms...We demand equality. Otherwise, I shall sacrifice my head for my flock.[18]

The speech was directed against the government, and was immediately banned by Stojadinović after it was first broadcast on radio.[19] Yet, this probably mattered little to non-Serbs, who must have felt threatened by the Patriarch's tone.

Three factors led to the emergence of the Serbian question in the aftermath of the 1939 Agreement. First, a large number of Serbs were included within the boundaries of the *banovina* of Croatia. Second, what started on 26 August 1939 was clearly the federalisation of the country, which to many Serbs amounted to a prelude to disintegration. Third, the agreement marked the effective end of integral Yugoslavism. The Serbs, as the largest and geographically the most scattered Yugoslav 'tribe', were generally happier than other Yugoslavs to live in a centralised state in which only one, Yugoslav, nation

---

18 Cited in Jovanović Stoimirović, *Dnevnik*, 97. It is not clear whether the Patriarch was actually suggesting that he was ready for an armed clash with the authorities if necessary.

19 Ibid. Jovanović Stoimirović, who listened to the radio broadcast of the speech, could hear loud cheers and applause from those present when the Patriarch gave the speech.

officially existed. With the abandonment of integral Yugoslavism, the question of a Serb identity within Yugoslavia arose.

The following general aspects of the Serbian question in the late 1930s may be identified:

(a) Calls for a Serbian banovina. Advocated by all, including the Croatian Peasant Party, which hoped it would cement the *de facto* federalisation of the country.

(b) Calls for the secession of Serb-populated areas from the banovina *of Croatia*. The Serbian Church and the Serbian Cultural Club were among the most prominent advocates of such a scenario which was at the core of the 'Serbs, rally together!' movement.

(c) Criticism of the Cvetković–Maček agreement as an anti-democratic act. The Serbian opposition, in particular the Democrats, criticised the agreement on the grounds that it put an end to the Bloc of the National Agreement and thus to calls for the return to democracy and the abolition of the 1931 Constitution. The Independent Democrats voiced similar concerns, despite participating in the new government.

Towards a Serbian banovina?

In 1965 the historian Ljubo Boban published for the first time a document entitled 'Draft decree on organisation of the Serbian Lands'. Boban believed that the document was drafted by Professors Mihailo Konstantinović, Djordje Tasić and Mihailo Ilić, the Serbian constitutional experts who advised Cvetković during the negotiations with Maček. They apparently produced the document some time in late 1939, after receiving instructions from Cvetković.[20]

---

20 Ljubo Boban, *Sporazum Cvetković–Maček*, Belgrade, 1965, 314. Boban acquired the document from Vaso Čubrilović, also a historian and the younger brother of Branko, a minister in the Cvetković-Maček government. Vaso Čubrilović claimed he was given the document by Cvetković personally in 1943. The text of the document is published in full in ibid., 412-18, while its most important extracts are reproduced in JF-1, 569-70.

On 16 December 1939 Konstantinović, a Minister without portfolio in the Cvetković-Maček government, was received by Prince Paul, to whom he handed his 'project on the *banovina* of the Serbian lands'.[21] As there are only minor differences between this draft and the document published by Boban, Konstantinović was almost certainly the author of the document, probably together with Ilić and Tasić, his close collaborators.[22] The government, or at least its Serbian members, worked towards the creation of a Serbian *banovina*; it is unlikely that Konstantinović could have drafted such a document and presented it to the Prince Regent without Cvetković's knowledge.

The document published by Boban envisaged the formation of a third 'ethnic' *banovina*—the Dravska being for practical purposes Slovenia; this would be a *banovina* of the 'Serbian lands'. It would involve the unification of Vrbaska, Drinska, Dunavska, Moravska, Zetska and Vardarska *banovinas* into a single province, the capital of which was to be Skopje (Belgrade would remain the capital of Yugoslavia).[23] The *banovinas* entering this new Serbian *banovina* would be turned into semi-autonomous regions, and would maintain their existing boundaries, names and regional capitals. The future Serbian entity would enjoy the same level of autonomy from the central government in Belgrade as the Croatian *banovina*. In other words, it would be in charge of its finances, justice, education and social policies, while the central government would be responsible for defence, customs and foreign policy.[24] It remains unclear whether the authors of the document envisaged the inclusion in a future Serbian

21 Mihailo Konstantinović, *Politika Sporazuma. Dnevničke beleške 1939-1941; Londonske beleške 1944-1945*, Novi Sad, 1998, 83.

22 See ibid., 578.

23 Skopje—or Skoplje in Serbian—was the capital of the medieval Serbian empire, designated as the future capital of the Serbian *banovina* most probably in order to emphasise the apparently Serbian character of 'south Serbia', the region contested by Bulgaria, and populated by Slavs whose language was closest to Bulgarian, ethnic Albanians, ethnic Turks and Roma.

24 Boban, *Sporazum*, 412-8; JF-1, 569-70.

banovina of those territories previously parts of Vrbaska, Zetska and Dunavska which since August 1939 had formed part of the *banovina* of Croatia.

With the formation of autonomous Croatia one thing was certain: the rest of the country would be further divided up according to ethnic and/or historic criteria, effectively reversing the King Alexander-inspired division of October 1929. The same day as the Cvetković-Maček agreement was concluded a ruling on implementing the decree on the formation of the *banovina* of Croatia in relation to the rest of the country was also issued. It stated that the decree 'of 26 August 1939 could be extended to other *banovinas* by royal decrees. In such a case, *banovinas* could [either] unite, or their territories could [be subject to] changes.'[25] The extent of the autonomy of future *banovinas* would equal the level of autonomy of Croatia. However, it was unclear how many new *banovinas* there would be and where their boundaries would be drawn.

Because Dravska included virtually all Slovenes of Yugoslavia, the potential for disagreement in regard to the territory of the future Slovene *banovina* was minimal. The only exception was the inclusion of Draga and Osilnica, two Slovene-populated municipalities, in the Croatian *banovina*. Karel Škrulj, a former Clerical deputy and leading member of the Yugoslav Radical Union from the Kočevje region, paid a visit to Draga and Osilnica after the agreement, in order to collect signatures for a petition supporting the inclusion of the two municipalities in Dravska. It was only a matter of time before Dravska was transformed into the *banovina* of Slovenia, Škrulj told the local Slovene population, virtually all of whom signed the petition.[26]

---

25 MPHSS-2, 227.
26 HDA XXI/84/5726, Sresko načelstvo u Čabru, banskoj vlasti banovine Hrvatske, Odjeljak za državnu zaštitu, 10 October 1939. The two municipalities had previously belonged to the Kočevje district in Dravska. Present-day Croatia and Slovenia are involved in a border dispute over the Bay of Piran.

Immediately after the creation of the *banovina* of Croatia, Korošec suggested that a Slovene *banovina* should be proclaimed as well.[27] A special working group was formed within the government, to prepare for the creation of an autonomous Slovenia. Its members were Miha Krek, Mihailo Konstantinović, Lazar Marković and Stanko Majcen, the vice-*ban* of Dravska.[28]

However, a Slovenian *banovina* was not proclaimed because Croats and Serbs regarded all other issues as secondary to the Serb-Croat question. If Dravska was turned into Slovenia, then how could the government continue to postpone the creation of a Serbian *banovina*, and would the rest of the country not have automatically become *de facto* a greater Serbia? Maček always believed that Serbs and Croats formed the main axis in Yugoslavia. Therefore, sorting out their relations was of utmost importance; all other issues could wait, including the question of the Slovene *banovina*.[29] Similarly, Serb members of the government wanted to wait for an agreement on the Serbian *banovina* first, before 'upgrading' Dravska, possibly at the same time. Cvetković told Konstantinović that Krek's insistence on a Slovene *banovina* was nothing less than 'blackmail' and that the Slovene politician 'did not have a [wider] feeling for the state'.[30] In the Prime Minister's opinion, the moment was not right for the proclamation of autonomous Slovenia. The Croats had their *banovina*, the Slovenes had for practical purposes had theirs in the form of Dravska since 1929, but 'what have the Serbs got?', Cvetković asked Konstantinović.[31]

---

27   Ibid., 49.

28   MPHSS-2, 231; Konstantinović, *Politika sporazuma*, 50. Krek would 'succeed' Korošec as the leading Slovene in the government. (Most leading Slovene politicians in the twentieth century had a surname which began with 'K': Anton Korošec, Miha Krek, Albert Kramer, Fran Kulovec, Edvard Kardelj, Boris Kidrič, Stane Kavčič, Sergej Krajger and Milan Kučan.)

29   Boban, *Sporazum*, 262.

30   Konstantinović, *Politika sporazuma*, 50. Entry for 19 September 1939.

31   Ibid. Konstantinović, too, had some reservations about a Slovenian *banovina*, but mainly because of potential legal implications.

The Slovenes, however, felt in the late 1930s that their loyalty to the state had not been rewarded properly. Both Krek and Marko Natlačen, *ban* of Dravska, told Konstantinović that since the Cvetković-Maček agreement many ordinary Slovenes criticised Korošec, complaining that 'the Croats are against this state, and still they got everything, whereas we are loyal to the state [*državotvorni*] but got nothing!'[32]

The key question was where to draw the borders of the Serbian *banovina*. Would it include the whole of Yugoslavia, minus Slovenia and Croatia? This was clearly Cvetković's plan, and certainly many Serbs, though not all, argued in favour of such an outcome. At the same time, Maček was keen to emphasise that the boundaries of the Croatian *banovina* were temporary and that he was looking to add more territory. He used the opportunity of Prince Paul's visit to Zagreb to raise the question of the territorial expansion of the Croatian *banovina* into six unnamed districts in Bosnia and Vojvodina, but it is unclear what Paul's response was.[33]

Maček may have been under pressure from more radical elements within his party and from the Frankist opposition to try to extend Croatia's territory further. The pro-Maček press argued that the *banovina* of Croatia should incorporate Bosnia and parts of Vojvodina, although Maček was personally apparently satisfied with the terms of the 1939 agreement. This is what Stanoje Mihaldžić, the Minister of the Interior and a former vice-*ban* of Savska and Zagreb police chief, told Milan Jovanović Stoimirović.[34] The latter felt that 'it was a shame that Maček was smeared [by the Serbian public] without

---

32 Ibid., 49, 51.

33 MPHSS-2, 158. Boban's source is a report by Italy's Consul General to Zagreb, Giovanni Gobbi, whose own sources of information had been 'two persons, very close to Dr Maček'. Unfortunately, the Prince Regent's personal diaries do not shed any light on this issue.

34 As the head of the Zagreb police, Mihaldžić arrested Maček in January 1933, during the political crisis which followed the 'Zagreb points' of November the previous year.

much evidence' and that various statements and deeds were being ascribed to him, presumably by his political opponents.[35]

The status of Bosnia-Herzegovina posed a major difficulty. As the Yugoslav Muslim Organisation began to demand autonomy for Bosnia, was there going to be a fourth, Bosnian *banovina*, as Ljuba Davidović proposed back in early 1933, and as the government considered briefly in 1939?[36] Most Croats and Serbs seemed to prefer a division of Bosnia among themselves. The Croats believed that the so-called 'Turkish Croatia' (most of Vrbaska) should be joined to the Croatian *banovina*. Although the area did not have a Croat majority, the Croat 'state right' argument was employed to justify Croat demands, as well as economic and geographical factors. On the other hand, virtually all Serbs argued that Bosnia should be part of a future Serbian *banovina*. The Serbian Cultural Club, whose representative in Banja Luka was Stevan Moljević,[37] was most radical in this respect; according to Moljević and his colleagues, Bosnia was undoubtedly a Serbian ethnic territory. Only the Democrats were prepared to offer autonomy to Bosnia. In a 'Letter to Bosnians and Herzegovinians', Davidović repeated his argument of February 1933 that Bosnia should be a separate province, which would act as a buffer between Serbs and Croats, possibly together with southern Dalmatia. At the same time, the Yugoslav Muslims, now under Kulenović's leadership (following Spaho's death in late June 1939, the same month as Jovanović Pižon died), started a campaign for a Bosnian *banovina* and the restoration of historic Bosnia.[38]

---

35 Jovanović Stoimirović, *Dnevnik*, 323.

36 BAR PPP, box 2, Cvetković to Prince Paul, Belgrade, 2 May 1939. See also Konstantinović, *Politika sporazuma*, 516-8.

37 During the Second World War an adviser to the *Četnik* leader Mihailović.

38 See Mira Radojević, 'Bosna i Hercegovina u raspravama o državnom uredjenju Kraljevine (SHS) Jugoslavije 1918-1941. godine', *Istorija XX veka*, no. 1, 1994, 7-41. Kulenović became deputy prime minister in the *Ustaša* government during the Second World War, when the whole of Bosnia-Herzegovina was incorporated into the Independent State of Croatia.

The Croatian Peasant Party also argued that parts of Vojvodina should be added to the Croatian *banovina*, on the basis of both ethnic and historic rights. Vojvodina had been another bone of contention during the negotiations between Cvetković and Maček, but because it had played an important role in Serbian nineteenth century history, and also because of a large number of Serbs living there, all Serb parties and groups regarded it as part of a future Serbian *banovina*.[39]

A specially convened meeting took place on government premises on 3 November 1939 to discuss the future reorganisation of the country.[40] Among those present were Cvetković, the ministers Kulenović, Lazar Marković, Konstantinović, Krek, Senator Korošec and Milan Gavrilović, the new leader of the Agrarians—represented in the government through Čubrilović—since Jovanović Pižon's death in June that year. Notably, no Croats took part. Cvetković and Marković were in favour of postponing further changes until a more opportune moment, while Korošec and Gavrilović wanted an immediate proclamation of the *banovinas* of Slovenia and Serbia, respectively. Kulenović, as it was to be expected, demanded the creation of a Bosnian *banovina*. Gavrilović agreed that Bosnia's autonomy should be recognised, but within the Serbian unit. The following extracts from the discussion illustrate well the essence of the debate among Yugoslav leaders in the post-1939 period:

Cvetković: The question of the reorganisation of the state could wait until the King comes of age. These things can therefore be postponed.

Korošec: They cannot be postponed, because the reality demands a solution

Marković: If there is to be no postponement, then not only Slovenia but Serbia, too, should be granted a new status.

Korošec: I am not only a Slovene, but also a Yugoslav, and that is why [I believe] these things need to be put on the agenda, so that we see what be-

---

39   See Mira Radojević, 'Srpsko-hrvatski spor oko Vojvodine 1918-1941', *Istorija XX veka*, no. 2, 1996, 39-73.

40   BAR PPP, box 13, minutes from the meeting, 3 November 1939.

longs to [individual] tribes and what to [country as a] whole. All these issues demand a simultaneous solution, otherwise it will not be known where is the whole and what is left of it.

[…]

Cvetković: I cannot accept a separate Croatia, a separate Slovenia […], and that only Serbia remains Yugoslavia.

Gavrilović: […] What has been done for the Croats should be done for the others, as well, in order to save Yugoslavia and Yugoslavism…If the Serbian question escalates fully, it would destroy the agreement with the Croats. It is indeed difficult to solve the [problem] of the restructuring of the state, difficult because of Bosnia, because of Montenegro, even Vojvodina, but a solution is possible as well as necessary…Therefore, let us solve the legal status of Slovenia straight away, but [also and] especially the Serbian question. We should call for local elections immediately; in Serbia everyone expects local elections, but the ballot should be secret, and not open, as Mr Korošec demands. [...]

Kulenović: Local elections are necessary…[But] if we create three provinces on the [Slovenia-Croatia-Serbia] basis, that would kill the whole [i.e. Yugoslavia]…We must respect the feelings, customs and wishes of the people. For that reason, Bosnia and Herzegovina must be a separate unit. It had lived in the past and through centuries its own, separate life. And it wants to again. [...]

Gavrilović: I am for trialism, with a separate status for Bosnia within one of the composing parts.

Cvetković: In that case the Croats should give back those municipalities taken from Bosnia and Herzegovina.

Konstantinović: During the negotiations they said they would do it. But, only if in addition to Croatia and Slovenia [and Serbia], a fourth unit is created.

Marković: What fourth [unit]? Like Croatia? No, that cannot be.

Kulenović: [...] Bosnia and Herzegovina is a mini Yugoslavia. Therefore, it should be separate [within Yugoslavia]. If there is no separate Bosnia and Herzegovina, than there is no Yugoslavia.

Gavrilović: Not even one per cent of Bosnian Serbs would accept that.

Kulenović: When Serbian deputations [from Bosnia] start arriving here [in Belgrade] you will realise you are mistaken.

Gavrilović: The Croats have gathered together on the basis of ethnicity. Today, we cannot solve any of these questions any other way. Mr Kulenović says there is no Yugoslavia without a separate Bosnia and Herzegovina, but I say that there is no Yugoslavia if it is not held together by Serbia. And Serbia will not do that if there is to be a parcelling out of the Serbs.

Cvetković: The ultimate answer to these questions will be provided by freely elected representatives from the whole country; we should not, for now, insist on defining these problems any further, because by doing so we could bring down the government.[41]

'Serbs, rally together!'

It is not clear who first coined the rallying call. Ljubo Boban argued that it was not a new slogan and that it could be heard as early as 1918.[42] Whereas the idea that Serbs should rally together in the face of various external threats certainly goes back well before 1918—one may indeed argue that the Serb support for Yugoslavia was motivated by this idea—the 'Serbs, rally together!' slogan only became widely used in the aftermath of the Cvetković-Maček agreement. It even became the semi-official name of the 'movement' that campaigned for the secession of Serb-populated and, in some cases, of Muslim-populated areas of the Croatian *banovina*.[43] Even the authorities used

---

41 Ibid.

42 Boban, *Sporazum*, 255n.

43 In cases where Serbs claimed that Bosnian Muslims were in fact Serbs.

the name to describe 'the movement for the secession of [predominantly] Serbian districts from the territory of *banovina* Croatia.'[44] The 'movement' emerged across the *banovina* soon after August 1939. Serbian Orthodox priests were often among its leaders, petitioning for the secession of predominantly Serb areas or areas they perceived as Serb from the Croatian *banovina*. Father Zdravko Borisavljević, a priest from the village of Vinjska, was a key speaker at a Serb rally held in the northern Bosnian town of Brčko on 26 January 1940, a day before St Sava's Day, a major Serbian national and religious holiday. He claimed that in the post-agreement Yugoslavia:

Serb freedom is forbidden, the Serb *gusle*[45] are forbidden, the Serbian song is forbidden, even in Belgrade, but not by Serbs. Serbs must fight against being insulted and against being a minority, but Serbs are insulted when they read [...] that in 'Gradska elektrana' in Osijek all but Serbs had their wages raised, so that Serbs are [now] paid 4.50 dinars per hour, while non-Serbs 5.50 dinars per hour.[46]

Local politicians, merchants and other leading Serbs from Derventa, Brčko, Bosanski Šamac and Gradačac also spoke at the rally. Most speeches were similar in tone, although none so blatantly nationalistic as Father Borisavljević's. The meeting was opened by Milorad Kostić, whose speech outlined the main complaints and demands of those Serbs who opposed the Cvetković-Maček agreement, as well as their position vis-à-vis Yugoslavism and Serbism. Kostić began by explaining the motives for the meeting: the international crisis and 'the question of saving Yugoslavia's unity and a strong Serbdom, because without a strong Serbdom there would be

---

44 HDA XXI/89/6129, Naredba svim sreskim načelstvima, ispostavama, gradskim redarstvima i redarstvenim ravnateljstvima od banske vlasti banovine Hrvatske, Zagreb, 11 March 1940.

45 A single-stringed instrument traditionally played by Serbs, Montenegrins, and Croats and Muslims from the Dinaric regions of the former Yugoslavia.

46 HDA XXI/89/6129, Sresko načelstvo u Brčkom, banskoj vlasti banovine Hrvatske, Otsjek za državnu zaštitu, Brčko, 26 January 1940.

no [Yugoslav] state.'[47] Kostić emphasised that the person who spoke in the Serbs' name—Dragiša Cvetković—was not their legitimate representative. He added that Serbs were not against an agreement with Croats, because without it Yugoslavia could not survive, but that they wanted an agreement which would ensure they were equal to Croats. Therefore, they should be united in a Serbian *banovina* which would include all areas of Bosnia populated by Serbs and by Muslims, because according to Kostić the latter were in fact Serbs: 'Under the terms of the current agreement, a number of Serbian districts have been joined to the *banovina* of Croatia [...], among them the districts of Brčko, Gradačac and Derventa, where alongside Serbs there are 55,000 Muslims whom [we] Serbs regard as Serbs.'[48]

Apart from arguing for the secession of the three districts from Croatia on ethnic grounds—an argument which gained legitimacy following the creation of the Croatian *banovina*—Kostić also believed that the three Bosnian districts should 'unite with Serbia' because the people of the region fought in the First World War for the creation of Yugoslavia and unification with Serbia. This was a common belief among many Serbs, who often did not distinguish between the notion of Yugoslav and Serb unity. The Serbs tended to regard Yugoslavia as their own state, which they liberated and created. 'Dr [Juraj] Krnjević called the Serbs a minority, but they cannot be that in their own state,' Kostić said, before rejecting any possibility of autonomy for Bosnia: 'The Serbs [of Bosnia] fought for the unification with Serbia, so there cannot be an autonomous Bosnia.'[49]

Where the 'ethnic' argument could not apply, those who called for the secession of areas they regarded as 'Serb' employed 'historic' arguments. Referring to the Serbian sacrifices of the First World War

47 Ibid.

48 Ibid.

49 Ibid. Many Bosnian—and Croatian—Serbs fought against Serbia and the unification, as soldiers in the Habsburg army. The argument that Serbs could not be a minority in Yugoslavia reemerged in the late 1980s and early 1990s. See Jasna Dragović-Soso, *'Saviours of the Nation': Serbia's Intellectual Opposition and the Revival of Nationalism*, London, 2002.

was not the only 'historic' argument used by Serb opponents of the agreement. Some Serbs from the municipality of Mostar, where at the time there lived '8,844 Muslims, 5,764 Croats and 5,502 Serbs', called for the secession of the region and its inclusion in the Serbian *banovina* on the basis of Herzegovina's apparent mediaeval Serbian past. 'As the sons of the Vojvodina of St Sava, we demand the secession of the city of Mostar from the Croatian *banovina*,' an unpublished resolution drafted by a group of Mostar Serbs stated.[50]

The pan-Serb movement spread beyond the Bosnian-Herzegovinian districts of Croatia with a large Serb population. Serbs from the Glina area south of Zagreb, led by two local priests and a teacher, issued in November 1939 a resolution calling for the secession of the region from Croatia. The following month they held another meeting, but this time issued a more moderate statement, demanding merely full equality with Croats in the *banovina*.[51] Niko Novaković, a former Minister without portfolio, led a campaign among the Serbs of Knin, Benkovac, Obrovac and Šibenik for the secession of predominantly Serb areas and their unification with the Vrbaska *banovina*. Novaković was apparently acting in collaboration with Senator Petar Zec, whose plan was to present to Prince Paul a petition from local Serbs demanding their secession from the *banovina* of Croatia.[52]

---

50 HDA XXI/89/6129, Sresko načelstvo u Mostaru, banskoj vlasti banovine Hrvatske, Odjeljak za državnu zaštitu, Predmet: Pokret 'Srbi na okup', Mostar, 16 March 1940. Herzegovina means Duchy ('Vojvodina' in Serbo-Croat). The whole region was named after a fifteenth century Duke, who assumed the title the Duke of St Sava. Nevertheless, Duke Stefan Vukšić Kosača is also claimed by Croats (who call him *Stjepan Vukčić* Kosača).

51 HDA XXI/89/6129, Sreski načelnik u Petrinji banskoj vlasti banovine Hrvatske, Odjeljak za državnu zaštitu, Predmet: Pokret 'Srbi na okup'[,] otcepljenje i odvajanje pojedinih srezova sa područja banovine Hrvatske, Petrinja, 13 March 1940. Glina was the site of the infamous 'church massacre'of August 1941, when the *Ustašas* gathered the local Serb population inside an Orthodox church and massacred them. The whole region around Banija, Lika and Knin witnessed some of the worst fighting in the Second World War and was also one of the areas where the Yugoslav war of the 1990s began.

52 HDA XXI/85/5784, Primorski žandarmeriski puk, Komandantu žandarmeriske brigade banovine Hrvatske, Split, 12 December 1939.

Although the movement was widespread in areas of the *banovina* where large numbers of Serbs lived, its supporters usually had local goals. Thus, the Serbs from Vukovar had ever since the creation of autonomous Croatia demanded the transfer of their district to the jurisdiction of the Dunavska *banovina*. Their leader was Nikola Teodorović, a secondary school teacher and a leading member of the local branch of the Yugoslav Radical Union.[53] However, the 'Serbs, rally together!' movement failed to attract a mass following in the Vukovar area,[54] just as it eventually failed to attract mass support elsewhere.

According to an official report from Vukovar a serious mistake had been made when nothing was done to strengthen the Independent Democrats' local branch after August 1939. The party had always been weak in Vukovar, partly because its members had been 'persecuted [by the former regime] more than even the HSS members.' However, after the agreement many Serbs would have joined the Independent Democratic Party 'out of opportunism' if for no other reason, as the party was now in the government. However, the chance was not seized because the party was poorly organised and divided into two factions, between the older and younger members. As a result a Croat, presumably not a member of either faction, was elected president of the local branch of the Independent Democrats. He was 'an honourable and good man [but] Serbs do not and cannot accept him as their leader', because they were looking for a Serb to provide leadership. It did not help the local Independent Democrats that their relationship with the Vukovar branch of the Croatian

---

53 HDA XXI/89/6129, Sresko načelstvo u Vukovaru banskoj vlasti banovine Hrvatske, Odjelu za unutarnje poslove (Za odjeljak za državnu zaštitu) u Zagrebu, Predmet: Vukovar srez, političke prilike, Vukovar, 2 January 1940. Vukovar, with its mixed Croat-Serb population, was the site of one of the most brutal conflicts in the former Yugoslavia in the 1990s. By the end of 1991 it was taken over by the Yugoslav People's Army and Serbian paramilitaries, who had previously almost completely destroyed it and who committed atrocities against Croat civilians upon entering the city. Following the end of the war in Croatia in 1995 it was peacefully reintegrated into Croatia.

54 Ibid.

Peasant Party was not very close. The Croat party looked down on its small coalition partner, although it, too, was divided into several factions.[55]

In those areas where the Independent Democrats were well-organised and had significant support there was much less opposition to the agreement and Serb-Croat relations tended to be significantly better. This was not surprising, as the party genuinely supported a Serb-Croat agreement and had, publicly at least, always stood by the Croatian Peasants, even though Maček merely kept his coalition partners informed of the latest developments during the negotiations with Cvetković, rather than consulting them.[56] On the day Croatia became autonomous, the Independent Democrats' leadership issued a statement praising the agreement, describing it as the 'crowning of our efforts'.[57] In areas dominated by the Independent Democrats even local priests, generally among the most radical advocates of the Serb cause, supported the agreement. Thus for instance a report on the political situation in the central Bosnian town of Bugojno, written in December 1939, stated that:

Relations between Croats and Serbs are very good, even cordial. The leader of the local Serbs, most of whom are supporters of the SDS, is a priest, Jovo Popović, who has established an honest and brotherly cooperation with [local] Croat representatives [...] so that their relationship is virtually ideal.[58]

Authors of the reports noted divisions among local Muslims. Some were pressurised into joining the Croatian Peasant Party, while others, members of the Yugoslav Radical Union, simply did not know where their allegiances belonged any more. In any case, many hoped

---

55 Ibid.

56 Boban, *Sporazum*, 275.

57 Cited in Ivan Jelić, 'O nekim odjecima sporazuma Cvetković-Maček medju Srbima u banovini Hrvatskoj', *Historijski zbornik Slavonije*, vol. 3, 1965, 153.

58 HDA XXI/87/5979, Načelstvo sreza Bugojnskog, mjesečni izvještaj o javnoj sigurnosti i političkoj situaciji za mjesec prosinac 1939. g., Bugojno, 6 January 1940.

that Bosnia would achieve some form of autonomy, perhaps even its own *banovina*.[59]

After the initial wave of protests across Serb areas in Croatia, when petitions were signed, resolutions issued and delegations sent to Belgrade to demand secession from Croatia, the situation calmed down. Once it became clear that the 'Serbs, rally together!' movement had failed to change the situation significantly, it lost its appeal. Virtually all reports note that after the busy autumn, by the spring of 1940 activities of those calling upon Serbs to 'rally together' decreased markedly.[60] Another reason for the calming down of the situation was that once the initial shock was over, many Serbs came to accept the new order. However, this did not mean that dissatisfaction among them went away—it was still there, as many reports noted, but was not as visible as it had been during the first few months following the 1939 agreement.[61] One of the reasons was a more sensitive approach by the Croat authorities. Aware that the politically motivated change of civil servants and other personnel had gone too far, Šubašić sent a circular in June 1940 to all local civilian and police authorities ordering them to cease firing staff using excuses such as: 'in the interest of the people', 'for political reasons' and 'on suspicion of being a communist', but without any 'concrete facts'. Those who ignored the circular 'would be held responsible' for a serious breach of conduct and risked being removed themselves from their positions.[62]

The Croat leadership had done little to prevent the often indiscriminate removal of Serb personnel from the local administration, police and schools. The aforementioned transfer to another post of

---

59 Ibid.

60 HDA XXI/89/6129, Predmet: Ocjepljenje [sic] i odvajanje pojednih [sic] srezova od banovine Hrvatske u vezi sa pokretom 'Srbi na okup', Zagreb, 13 April 1940. (The document is a summary of all reports sent to the *banovina*'s Department for State Protection; author unknown.)

61 Ibid.

62 HDA XXI/88/6053, Ban Šubašić Ispostavi banske vlasti Split, Redarstvenim ravnateljstvima, Zagreb, Split, svim sreskim načelstvima, etc., Zagreb, 7 June, 1940.

Nikola Vučković was understandable and inevitable and was carried out in cooperation between the gendarmerie and the civilian authorities.[63] However, there were many examples of the contrary. The replacement of a Serb teacher Bogojević by another teacher, Josip Vuksan, an ethnic Croat, in Veliko Korenovo, a predominantly Serbian village near Bjelovar, a town east of Zagreb, was much harder to justify. It caused a small rebellion among the population of the village, who occupied the school and refused to leave until their old teacher was reinstated.[64] The villagers insisted they had nothing against the Croats in general nor against the new, Croat, teacher personally, but were only protesting 'against those few [Croats] who wanted to get rid of Bogojević for their own, *personal* and *material* reasons'.[65]

The official report on the incident concluded that the villagers' protest was justified and that it was hard to understand why Bogojević was removed. The authorities were eventually able to end the protest by promising to investigate the whole case properly.[66] Although the Bjelovar authorities tackled the crisis with tact and fairness, Bogojević's case caused enough damage and gave credence to the frequently heard calls for Serbs to unite in common action. An article that appeared in *Srpski glas* (*Serbian Voice*), the organ of the Serbian Cultural Club published in Belgrade, correctly argued that Serb dissatisfaction with the post-agreement order was not simply invented from above. While acknowledging that there were certain advocates of the Serbian cause who were not well qualified to represent Serbian interests, the author of the article argued that 'those

63 HDA XXI/84/5730, Štab Savskog žandarmeriskog puka banskoj vlasti banovine Hrvatske (Odjelu za unutarnje poslove), Zagreb, 18 September 1939.

64 HDA XXI/88/6048, Sresko načelstvo Bjelovar, banskoj vlasti banovine Hrvatske, Odjeljku za državnu zaštitu, Bjelovar, 2 March 1940.

65 Ibid. (Emphasis added by D. Dj.)

66 Ibid.

who think that the present mood among Serbs is an artificial product of the propaganda' were seriously mistaken.[67]

There were cases where Serbs initially did not oppose the creation of autonomous Croatia, but the new authorities' aggressive and insensitive policies created Serb resentment. The head of the Benkovac district reported that local Serbs increasingly complained that:

We accept the *banovina* of Croatia, we support the agreement of 26 August 1939 and accept it as the basis of the future reorganisation of the [Yugoslav] state, we accept and welcome every word by the Croatian *ban* Dr Ivan Šubašić, but we cannot accept what the [...] HSS activists are doing on the ground. [68]

Parallels with the immediate post-1918 period were striking, with the roles between Serbs and Croats reversed.

The authorities of the new *banovina* made unsuccessful attempts to Croatise the language, which even some leading members of the Croatian Peasant Party described as 'stupid'.[69] Maček wanted a Croatian coat of arms for the new *banovina*, and even the introduction of Croatian currency.[70] Although none of these proposals was

---

67 S.M.D. [Slobodan M. Drašković], "'Velikosrpstvo'", *Srpski glas*, no. 3, 30 November 1939. The author was the son of Milorad Drašković, the Interior Minister assassinated by Communists in 1921.

68 HDA XXI/89/6129, Načelstvo sreza benkovačkog, banska vlast, odjeljak za državnu zaštitu, Predmet: Pokret 'Srbi na okup' [,] otcepljenje i odvajanje pojediniih sreza [sic!] sa područja banovine Hrvatske, Benkovac, 16 March 1940.

69 Konstantinović, *Politika sporazuma*, 170. Šutej told Konstantinović in August 1940 that he was in favour of the preservation of the 'phonetic' style, and against the introduction of the so-called 'etymological' style of writing (the latter would be introduced less than a year later by the *Ustašas*). 'They are doing stupid things' ('*Oni rade gluposti*'), Šutej told Konstantinović.

70 Apparently, the Croat leader wanted half a *dinar* to be renamed *novčić*, 10 *dinars* a *banica* and 20 *dinars* a *banovac*, while 100 *dinars* was to be renamed *kuna* (marten); Jovanović Stoimirović, *Dnevnik*, 314-15. Konstantinović (*Politika sporazuma*, 105) recalls a conversation with Maček, who demanded a separate coat of arms for the Croatian *banovina*. Konstantinović argued that while it would not mean much to Croats, the introduction of a separate coat of arms would feed Serb fears of Croatian separatism. Besides, the Yugoslav coat of arms already

implemented in practice, rumours that they would be led to a rise in tensions among the Serbs, already ultra-sensitive following the formation of autonomous Croatia.

Economic factors contributed to the dissatisfaction of ordinary Serbs, as well as Croats, with the new authorities. In Croatia, like in the rest of the country, small landowners formed the vast majority of the land-owning peasantry. The percentage of small landowners in Croat areas was even higher than in Serb areas of the country. Thus, in Savska landholdings under 5 hectares formed 75.9 per cent of all land, while in Primorska it was as high as 86.5 per cent (in comparison, in Moravska it was 64.2 per cent and in Dunavska 62.8 per cent). The peasants were heavily in debt: the percentage of owners of plots of land under 10 hectares who were in debt was over 93 per cent in Savska and as high as 97 per cent in Primorska (by comparison, in Dunavska it was 83.4 per cent and in Drinska 84 per cent).[71] On top of the problem of debt, the price of food in Croatia rose by between 50 per cent (beef) and 100 per cent (flour, potato, beans) in the period between August 1939 and August 1940.[72]

Remarkably, the new authorities did little to address this problem. Although the Croatian Peasant Party was above all concerned with the national question, functioning more like a national movement than a political party, it had also based its campaign against Belgrade and the local gentry on the argument that Croatia was economically exploited. So it was highly ironic that when a group of Croat peasants forcibly entered Maček's farm at Kupinec in August 1940 in

---

consisted of the Croatian, Serbian and Slovenian coats of arms. Konstantinović could not remember how the conversation eventually ended, but recalled it as 'an awkward' discussion. *Kuna* was the currency of the Independent State of Croatia (NDH) during the Second World War and is Croatia's currency today. When it was re-introduced in the early 1990s (following an earlier adoption of the old Croatian chequerboard flag, used in the NDH, but also long before), by the then government of Franjo Tudjman, it led to strong Serb objections.

71   Ljubo Boban, 'O političkim previranjima na selu u banovini Hrvatskoj', *Istorija XX veka: Zbornik radova*, vol. 2, Belgrade, 1961, 227.

72   Ibid., 231.

order to cut down forest trees, Maček called upon the once hated
gendarmerie to get rid of intruders, his own Peasant Defence having
refused to intervene against the peasants.[73] Later that year, a public
rally organised by Maček's party in Podgora was disrupted by dissatisfied peasants who complained that the party had promised that,
once the Croatian question was solved, they would not have to pay
tax and that the number of bureaucrats would be trimmed down,
but that in reality '[we] are today hungry and don't have enough
bread.'[74]

The economic crisis and the failure of the Croatian Peasant Party
to deal with social issues unsurprisingly made people sympathetic to
the Communists. Reports from the period particularly note growing
'communist action'.[75] Some however went over to the other extreme,
joining the *Ustašas* in the case of Croats, or various Serb groups that
were united under the 'Serbs, rally together' banner in the Serbian
case. The regime's brutal measures against political opponents could
not halt the growing dissatisfaction with the governing party in
Croatia.

The situation was additionally complicated by the governing Yugoslav Radical Union's support of and even direct involvement in
the 'Serbs, rally together!' movement. Although the party formed
the backbone of the Cvetković-Maček government, many of its Serb
members worked to undermine the Croatian *banovina*. Teodorović,
the aforementioned leader of the Vukovar Serbs, who campaigned
for the secession of the town from Croatia, was a member of the
party with close links to its senior members.[76] The support for the
Serb cause by the Yugoslav Radical Union, which often contradicted

---

73 Boban, 'O političkim previranjima na selu', 238-9.

74 Ibid., 250.

75 For instance HDA XXI/87/6021, Redarstveno ravnateljstvo Zagreb,
banskoj vlasti banovine Hrvatske, Izvještaj o poslovanju za I tromjesečje 1940 i o
političkim prilikama i dogadjajima u istom tromjesečju, Zagreb, 4 April 1940.

76 HDA XXI/89/6129, Sresko načelstvo u Vukovaru banskoj vlasti banovine
Hrvatske, Odjelu za unutarnje poslove (Za odjeljak za državnu zaštitu) u
Zagrebu, Predmet: Vukovar srez, političke prilike, Vukovar, 2 January 1940.

the 1939 agreement, was not limited to local party officials. Even Cvetković himself apparently sponsored and gave editorial suggestions to *Srpska riječ* (*Serbian Word*), a newspaper of the Croatian Serbs that openly criticised the agreement he reached with Maček.[77] One of the reasons for Cvetković's action could be his dissatisfaction with the way the Croat press close to Maček reported Yugoslav politics, and the 1939 agreement in particular, insisting that it was only a 'first step'—leaving open to interpretation what the next step would be for Croatia.[78]

The rivalry between 'Serb' parties for leadership among Serbs, which intensified after the agreement, was not limited to those parties participating in the government. Božidar Vlajić, a leading Democrat, believed that his party was best suited to unite the Serbs. At the time of Prince Paul's visit to Zagreb, Vlajić conceded that gathering the Serbs in a united front was 'outside the scope of regular party business.' However,

Somebody has to take the initiative...Who is better qualified than our party [the Democratic Party], which has been and has remained among Serbs the embodiment of opposition to all regimes which lacked the people's support and which has always advocated with utmost belief the solution to our state problem in the form of a representative government and the agreement between the Serbian people and Croatian people.[79]

Vlajić's discourse betrayed the Democrats' post-1939 dilemma: democracy or nationalism?

It was a non-party organisation - or, in Stevan Pavlowitch's words, a 'think tank' of the Serbian intellectual and professional élite[80] - which came closest to representing the pan-Serb cause in the late 1930s. The Serbian Cultural Club (SKK) was founded in Belgrade in

---

77   Konstantinović, *Politika sporazuma*, 104.

78   Ibid., 171.

79   *Politika*, 14 January 1940.

80   Stevan K. Pavlowitch, *Serbia: The History behind the Name*, London, 2002, 134.

late 1936, early 1937.[81] Its members included leading Belgrade intellectuals, such as Slobodan Jovanović and Isidora Sekulić, as well as Dragiša Vasić and Vladimir Ćorović, a Serb historian from Bosnia. Initially its activities were mostly cultural, but this changed following the agreement. After August 1939, a number of local branches sprang up across the Serb-populated areas of Croatia, Bosnia and Vojvodina.[82] At this time the Club's main, if not sole aim was to define and defend Serbian interests in Yugoslavia.[83]

The Club's mouthpiece was the Belgrade-based weekly *Srpski glas*, edited by the sometime left-wing writer Dragiša Vasić.[84] Its first issue came out on 16 November 1939 and the last on 13 June 1940, when it was banned by the authorities, for its criticism of the 1939 agreement.[85] While stating that it was not opposed to an agreement between Serbs and Croats, 'which has always been necessary', the newspaper criticised the Cvetković-Maček agreement for endangering the state unity and for being incomplete; it claimed that, unlike the Croats, the Serbs were not properly represented in the government.[86] Moreover, the paper called on all 'Serb' parties to halt interparty rivalry, for which 'there was a place in prewar Serbia, and which may have its place in a [future] separate Serbian unit, if Yugoslavia is eventually turned into a federation, but such rivalry does not have

---

81 It was probably formed in late 1936, as it was formally registered with the Ministry of Interior in January 1937. The exact date of its formation is not known. For the history and activities of the Club see Ljubodrag Dimić, *Kulturna politika Kraljevine Jugoslavije*, Belgrade, 1996-97, 3 vols., vol. 1, 507-61, and Nebojša A. Popović, 'Srpski kulturni klub (1937-1941)', *Istorija XX veka*, vol. VII, no. 1-2, 1989, 109-40.

82 Dimić, *Kulturna politika*, vol. 1, 512.

83 Pavlowitch, *Serbia*, 134. See also Dimić, *Kulturna politika*, 509-12, and Jelić, 'O nekim odjecima sporazuma', 147.

84 Like the lawyer Moljević, Vasić would eventually become a close collaborator of General Mihailović during the Second World War.

85 Miodrag Jovičić, 'Reč unapred', in *'Jako srpstvo-jaka Jugoslavija'. Izbor članaka iz 'Srpskog glasa', organa Srpskog kulturnog kluba 1939-1940*, Belgrade, 1991, 5.

86 Editorial, *Srpski glas*, no. 1, 16 November 1939.

a place at the moment when the question of Serb-Croat relations is raised.'[87]

The newspaper argued that just like the Croats, who approached politics from a national point of view, the Serbs should agree on a single national programme, which might be possible without all the parties uniting into a single one.[88] This was not far from Maček's view that the Serbs, like the Croats, should have a single party or leader who would represent their interests. While the Croat press had often in the past accused the monarchy, the army and the government of being 'Serb', none of them had actually represented Serbs, certainly not in the same way the Croatian Peasant Party represented Croats, as Maček was well aware.

The Serbian Cultural Club rejected integral Yugoslavism, and called instead for Serb unity and a return to old 'Serbian' values—the same values which had apparently characterised the Serb nation before Yugoslavia was formed. The editors of *Srpski glas* argued:

Recently, one can hear from different sides the slogan 'Serbs, rally together'. We too believe that Serbs should rally together, but we hasten to add that merely rallying together is not going to be enough unless at the same time the old spirit does not wake up inside the Serbs the same spirit which used to inspire their strength and greatness in the past, that same faith in the national ideals and that same manly decisiveness to sacrifice everything else for the sake of those ideals. What we need today is a moral revival. Within its limited powers, our paper will serve that revival.[89]

Despite an increasingly Serb nationalist discourse and the rejection of integral Yugoslavism, the Serbian Cultural Club did not reject Yugoslavia as a state. Its members argued that Yugoslavia could only be strong if 'Serbdom' was strong, not weak and divided. Indeed, the motto of *Srpski glas* was 'Strong Serbdom—strong Yu-

---

87 Ibid.
88 Ibid.
89 Ibid.

goslavia'.[90] Slobodan Jovanović, the Club's chairman, argued in an article published in the newspaper that Serbs had a twofold role in post-1939 Yugoslavia: to defend Serbian interests, but also to make sure that the central government functioned and that Yugoslavia became stronger, not weaker.[91] In the same article, he also argued that Yugoslavism was not incompatible with Serbian and Croatian nationalism. He saw Yugoslavism as a *state idea*, whereas Serbianism and Croatianism were *national ideas*.[92] Jovanović believed that Serbs and Croats should revert to the original Yugoslavism of the Illyrian movement, which was a reaction against a threat from a larger nation (Hungarians). According to him, Yugoslavia should be based on the self-interest of Serbs and Croats to live in a common state, which would best protect them from their neighbours and bigger powers.[93] Again, this was not unlike Maček's own view of Yugoslavia—a union of close, but separate peoples, not a Yugoslav nation-state.

Yet, even in the post-agreement atmosphere, when the Serbian question virtually replaced the Croatian one, the position *Srpski glas* took—another article began with 'It is time for a pure Serbian voice to

---

90 Similar arguments could be heard in the 1980s, during the revival of Serbian nationalism in the last decade of socialist Yugoslavia. For thorough analyses of the rise of Serbian nationalism among the intellectuals see Dragović-Soso, *'Saviours of the Nation'* and Audrey H. Budding 'Serb Intellectuals and the National Question, 1961-1991', unpublished PhD thesis, Harvard University, 1998.

91 Slobodan Jovanović, 'Jugoslovenska misao', *Srpski glas*, no. 8, 4 January 1940. The article was based on Jovanović's lecture given at the Club's premises the previous December. Jovanović became one of two Deputy Prime Ministers in the government of General Dušan Simović, formed on 27 March 1941, when the Cvetković government was overthrown because it had signed the Tripartite Pact two days previously. (The other Deputy Premier was Maček.) He was the Prime Minister of the London-based Yugoslav government-in-exile between January 1942 and August 1943 and Deputy Premier once again between August 1943 and June 1944. He died as an émigré in London in 1958.

92 Ibid. It is unclear whether Jovanović believed that state idea was possible without a 'state nation' (*Staatsvolk*).

93 Ibid. See also Aleksandar Pavković, *Slobodan Jovanović: An Unsentimental Approach to Politics*, Boulder, CO, 1993, 199-204.

be heard'[94]—provoked strong criticism from a number of prominent Serbs. The paper started a polemic with a rival publication *Napred* (Forward), published by a group of Serbian federalists led by Mihailo Ilić, one of the three Serbian constitutional experts who helped draft the Decree for the Formation of the *banovina* of Croatia and a vocal proponent of federalism. Arguing that most Yugoslavs—but particularly Serbs—did not understand the real meaning and advantages of a federation, the group around Ilić compared the situation in Yugoslavia to the one in the United States in 1787, when leading thinkers debated the federation and explained its meaning to the public.[95] Aware that most Serbs probably feared that the federalisation would weaken the state's unity and could even lead to its disintegration, editors of *Napred* argued that,

Conscious of all political, national and cultural components [that have formed] our country and [as] defenders of their rights and aspirations, we remain supportive of a single and strong state [...] which would preserve and encourage all different [identities]. We have always been, like the old *Federalist* once was in America, for this form [of state, i.e. federation], because it means a desire for unity all those groups which do not want and cannot accept unitarism. Because now, as then [in 1787], 'federalism means a true unity and leads to a more complete national harmony', as [Alexander] Hamilton said.[96]

Slobodan Jovanović and Dragoljub Jovanović perhaps best symbolised the two different views among the Serb intellectual and political elite as regards the national question. The former was a leading Serbian intellectual who had stayed outside politics until his involvement with the Serbian Cultural Club, while the latter was a leading opposition politician. In January 1940 the two men had a

---

94 [Ed.], 'Naša reč', *Srpski glas*, no. 1, 16 November 1939.

95 [Mihailo Ilić], 'Smisao i zadaci federacije', *Napred*, 28 October 1939.

96 Ibid. Hamilton, together with James Madison and John Jay, was the editor of *The Federalist*, and one of the authors of the US Constitution (the *Napred* article also mentions Madison and Jay). For more on the views of the *Napred* group see also [Mihailo Ilić], 'Federacija, nacija i nacionalizam', *Napred*, 13 December 1939.

253

long conversation about Yugoslav politics.[97] Dragoljub was a former student of Slobodan's and had a great respect for his old professor, whom he called 'our Voltaire'.[98] However, just as he fell out with his party leadership over the course the party was taking,[99] Dragoljub would openly question the political judgement of his former professor. Because their conversation was almost entirely centred around the question of Serb-Croat relations, the 1939 agreement and the activities of the Serbian Cultural Club, it merits a brief analysis.

After Dragoljub told Slobodan that he and his friends could not forgive his involvement with *Srpski glas*, the conversation moved on to the 'national question', when Slobodan suddenly became serious, as usual when the topic was raised, according to Dragoljub.[100] Dragoljub said that he would not mind if the Croats received more Bosnian territory or if Muslims eventually became Croats, rather than Serbs—otherwise they might declare themselves as Turks. Slobodan replied that in that case the Croats would leave Yugoslavia at the first opportunity, a possibility which Dragoljub rejected.[101] 'The more Serbs live in Croatia,' Dragoljub said, 'the harder it will be for it [Croatia] to separate from Serbia. I am, for instance, in favour of the incorporation of Vrbaska into [the *banovina* of] Croatia [...] If the Serbs are really threatened in Croatia, it will be easier for them to defend themselves if there are more of them.'[102] Slobodan insisted

---

97 Jovanović, *Političke uspomene*, vol. 5, 303-12. See also Nadežda Jovanović, 'Slobodan Jovanović i Dragoljub Jovanović: Prilog proučavanju njihovih uzajamnih odnosa', *Tokovi istorije* (Belgrade), no. 1-2, 1996, 117-65.

98 Jovanović, *Političke uspomene*, vol. 5, 303.

99 In February 1940 the Left Agrarians formed a new party, the People's Peasant Party. Jovanović, *Političke uspomene*, vol. 5, 326.

100 The following section is based on and all citations are taken from ibid., 304-11.

101 In interwar Yugoslavia it was widely accepted that Muslims were still undecided about their national identity. What is interesting however is that neither of the Jovanovićs mentioned the possibility of Muslims becoming Yugoslavs. This was another indication that by 1940 the idea of Yugoslavism in the 'ethnic sense' was largely dead.

102 This view was shared by the Independent Democrats.

that Serbs were endangered in Croatia, quoting a Croatian newspaper which argued that Croatian Serbs would get all their rights, but that they must regard Croatia as their homeland. Dragoljub replied that there was nothing wrong with this, as Croatia was indeed their homeland. When Slobodan mentioned that a number of Serbs had fled Croatia since August 1939, Dragoljub argued that only those who had done injustice to Croats during the previous order had to flee, but that most Serbs had no reasons to feel they were forced to leave.

Dragoljub revealed that a member of his party was writing an open letter to Slobodan Jovanović in which he would remind him of Julien Benda's *La Trahison des clercs*.[103] 'They [the Agrarian youth] see in you yet another intellectual who betrayed his ideals. Someone who stayed outside politics all his life, but in his old age has started to contribute to the Serb-Croat conflict.' Slobodan strongly denied he had anything against Croats, but was finally provoked enough to start talking about his involvement with the Serbian Cultural Club, which he had previously avoided.

Slobodan explained that it was not true he was persuaded to join the Serbian Cultural Club by Bosnian Serb intellectuals who lived in Belgrade. The formation of the Club was in fact his own idea, after a trip several years previously to Dalmatia and Bosnia. He had realised then that Serbs seemed 'confused [about their identity] and that their cultural institutions were in ruins.' What had started as a cultural action increasingly turned into a political one, especially after the Cvetković-Maček agreement, but Slobodan denied that the Club's aim was to form an all-Serb party:

I cannot form a Serbian party, but neither can you [form] a pure peasant party. A single idea is not enough. They[104] have only a national [idea], and you only a social one. You must emphasise more the national aspect. Only those movements which managed to form an amalgam of several ideas be-

---

103 First published in Paris in 1927.

104 Although it is unclear, it seems that he was referring to more nationalist members of the SKK.

came successful. Hitler managed to create such an amalgam. Maček as well. Small streams need to unite to form a river. You should form a Serbian Peasant Party. That might be successful.

Slobodan believed that the Serbs' mistake was not making any concessions to the Croats for so long and then all of a sudden conceding too much in August 1939. Dragoljub agreed, adding that Serbs suffered from a 'complete lack of trading spirit. The Slovenes would have done it differently.'[105] The older Jovanović then talked of how Croats looked down upon Serbs as if these were a lower race, but his former student rejected this, accepting that perhaps only the Catholic church held such views. 'We are not giving you up,' Dragoljub told Slobodan. 'You are a great Serb, but you must not become a Greater Serb [nationalist].'[106]

Slobodan Jovanović's discourse was not more 'Serbian' than Maček's discourse was 'Croatian'. However, by the late 1930s his views were clearly considered too radical by some of his friends, such as Dragoljub Jovanović and Mihailo Ilić. Dragoljub evidently felt that, with his great prestige, Slobodan could have done more to promote Serb-Croat cooperation.

In the afternoon of 1 January 1940, only days before he met Dragoljub, Slobodan had a meeting with Mihailo Konstantinović. He told the minister that there existed three different opinions among Serbs. The unitarists believed that the situation should remain as it was until the war was over, when the Cvetković-Maček agreement must be annulled. Some Serbs were in favour of the immediate formation of a Serbian *banovina*. The third group argued that the status quo should remain indefinitely. He supported the second opinion: a Serb entity should be formed as soon as possible. Among other reasons, this was because it would prevent further 'autonomist tendencies in

---

105 This is another example of national stereotypes among Yugoslavs, referred to previously.

106 In original: 'Vi ste veliki Srbin, ne smete biti velikosrbin.'

provinces in the Serbian part (Macedonia, Vojvodina, Montenegro, Bosnia).'[107]

A month after the meeting with Slobodan Jovanović, Dragoljub Jovanović formally left the Agrarians to form the People's Peasant Party. One of those Agrarians who followed him, Milan Milošević, published his open letter to Slobodan Jovanović.[108] Milošević accused Slobodan of failing to see the historic significance of the 1939 agreement, despite being a leading historian, and of not realising that 'the Croatian question is not the cause but a consequence of the Serbian question'. He was disappointed to see Slobodan Jovanović cooperating with the 'hegemonistic and corrupt Belgrade clique' instead of 'directing his friends towards Mirogoj,[109] where Stjepan and Pavle Radić, [Djuro] Basariček and other Croatian martyrs are buried' and where Slobodan's friends 'would maybe understand why Croats are not interested much in centralism.'[110] Milošević branded the Serbian Cultural Club as 'chauvinistic' and opposed to Serb-Croat cooperation. Its members had kept quiet during the dictatorship, but raised their voices now that Croat demands had finally been met. Therefore,

Neither you nor your friends have the right to speak in the name of the Serbian people [...] That should have been done during the dictatorship [when you should have] raised the banner of freedom against violence and lawless-

---

107 Konstantinović, *Politika sporazuma*, 89.

108 Miloš M. Milošević, *Otvoreno pismo gospodinu Slobodanu Jovanoviću, profesoru Univerziteta, akademiku, predsedniku Srpskog kulturnog kluba i uvodničaru Srpskog glasa: Odgovornost Slobodana Jovanovića za defetizam Srpskog glasa*, Belgrade, 1940. Key sections are reproduced in Jovanović, *Političke uspomene*, vol. 6, 64-8. Milošević was an admirer of Julien Benda, whom he met while a student in Paris. See his portrait in Dragoljub Jovanović, *Ljudi, ljudi...Medaljoni 94 političkih, javnih, naučnih i drugih savremenika*, Belgrade, 2005, 350-5.

109 The Zagreb cemetery.

110 Jovanović, *Političke uspomene*, vol. 6, 66. In the aftermath of Stjepan Radić's death, in August 1928, Milošević wrote a moving article 'In front of the open grave of Stjepan Radić' (*Pred otvorenim grobom Stj. Radića*) in *Novosti*, an Agrarian paper which he edited. In the article he strongly condemned the murder 'in the name of free Serbia, in the name of the Serbian peasants', accusing the regime and its supporters, who were now mourning Radić's death, of insincerity. Jovanović, *Političke uspomene*, vol. 2, 123.

ness [...] Now only when the danger is over you have started shouting that 'the time has come for Serbdom to have its manly and decisive say.[111]

The 1939 agreement as an end of the Serb-Croat opposition

In the aftermath of the fall of Stojadinović, when Cvetković and Prince Paul first made a concrete approach to Zagreb, the Croatian Peasant Party kept the Serbian United Opposition informed of its contacts with the regime. But an agreement that would involve all three sides proved impossible. The main reason was that in 1939 the gulf between the two 'Serb' sides—the UO and the Serb component of the governing Yugoslav Radical Union—proved more difficult to bridge than differences existing between the government and Maček's party. The efforts by the Independent Democrats to bring the Serbian opposition into the picture proved fruitless, not least because the Serbian parties felt betrayed by Maček.[112] While the Cvetković-Maček government included a semi-dissident Agrarian (Branko Čubrilović) and two dissident Radicals (Lazar Marković and Boža Maksimović), no Democrats entered the cabinet.

Perhaps somewhat surprisingly, the initial criticism of the agreement by the United Opposition was moderate. The main reason for this was that none of the three parties was opposed to the idea of an agreement with the Croats, while the Democrats and the Agrarians accepted the federalisation of Yugoslavia. By the late 1930s the Democrats had began to argue openly that the official ideology of integral Yugoslavism had failed. A month before the Cvetković-Maček agreement Milan Grol had stated that Serbs, Croats and Slovenes were 'three national individualities', although he also believed that Yugoslavia was an 'organic whole', made up of the three groups.[113] In their first statement following the agreement, issued on 28-29 Au-

---

111 Cited in Jovanović, *Političke uspomene*, vol. 6, 66-7.

112 BAR PPP, box 13, Dragiša Cvetković to Prince Paul, Belgrade, 19 April 1939.

113 MPHSS-2, 285.

gust 1939, the Democrats criticised the agreement because it went against the principles of the 1937 Bloc of the National Agreement, but did not oppose the idea of an agreement.[114]

In November 1939 the Democratic Party offered a more detailed verdict on the agreement and on post-*sporazum* Yugoslavia.[115] A manifesto, entitled *The Democrats on the Current State of the Country*, repeated the accusation that the Cvetković-Maček *sporazum* fundamentally contradicted the agreement of October 1937. The main criticism of the 1939 agreement was that it reduced Yugoslavia's problems to the question of the territorial division of the country, ignoring the key problem, the need to return to democracy. Furthemore, the Cvetković-Maček agreement stated that the borders of the Croatian *banovina* were only temporary, therefore creating the potential for a more serious Serb-Croat conflict over disputed territories in Bosnia and Vojvodina. The Democrats also complained that not only did the August 1939 agreement reduce the Serb-Croat question to a demarcation of Croat territories, but the real representatives of the Serb people—the United Opposition—had not been consulted. Unlike the Croats, who, under the leadership of their true representatives, were free to organise their own *banovina*, the Serbs remained without democratic representation and were helpless to change anything.[116]

The Democrats therefore opposed the Cvetković-Maček agreement on two grounds: it was undemocratic and it put an end to the joint Serb-Croat opposition bloc, which had emerged in the second half of the 1930s. They also argued that the agreement, while virtually solving the Croat question—by giving autonomy and a democratic government to Croats—had left the Serbs in limbo: still under

---

114 'Saopštenje užeg Glavnog odbora Demokratske stranke', *Politika*, 30 August 1939.

115 *Demokrati o današnjem stanju u zemlji*, Belgrade, November 1939.

116 Ibid., 4-9. The new authorities in the *banovina* of Croatia may have been 'true representatives' of the people, but by reaching the agreement with the Crown they lent their support to the dictatorship and did not introduce a liberal democracy in Croatia.

dictatorship and unclear where the borders of their own *banovina* would be drawn. Moreover, the Democrats had argued long before August 1939 that the Croat question was part of a wider, social and economic crisis in Yugoslavia, and that it was mistake to reduce it to a question of territory and politics.[117] During the Second World War, remembering the events of the 1930s, Milan Grol wrote in his diary that:

Davidović had twice sacrificed party unity for the sake of an agreement with the Croats. In 1932, in the middle of the dictatorship, the DS argued for a complex state, and recognised the Croats their right to autonomy [...] We fought for an agreement with Dr Maček, at a heavy price. Even our criticism of Cvetković's agreement was not against the very act but against its spirit [...] the consequences of which were the breakdown of *solidarity*, without which agreements between Serbs and Croats are worthless.[118]

Whereas the Agrarians continued to support the federalisation, the Radicals reverted to their old centralist platform after August 1939. In late November that year, the Main Committee of the Radical Party officially applied to the Ministry of Internal Affairs to be formally registered, after the government promised to regulate the status of political parties.[119] In the application it stated that its programme would call for preservation of the 'unity of the nation and state'—a somewhat ill-calculated move in the light of the changes in the official discourse after August 1939. It is no wonder that it never received a reply from the Ministry.[120] In the immediate

---

117 Mira Radojević, 'Demokratska stranka o državnom preuredjenju Kraljevine Jugoslavije (1935-1941)', *Istorija XX veka*, no. 1-2, 1991, 45.

118 Milan Grol, *Londonski dnevnik, 1941-1945*, Belgrade, 1990, 81. Emphasis in original. It is not clear how Davidović 'sacrificed party unity', considering that there was no significant opposition within the party to its leadership's course of action during the 1930s.

119 MPHSS-2, 289. Although all pre-1929 parties, except the Communists, openly resumed their activities under Prince Paul's regency, they were still formally banned. Thus, the Yugoslav press was obliged to refer to them with the prefix 'b', for '*bivša*' (former); this requirement was gradually dropped in the late 1930s.

120 Ibid., 289-90.

aftermath of the Cvetković-Maček agreement the Agrarians issued a statement 'unanimously welcoming the great achievement that is the agreement and wishing that [both] the state and national welfare are built on that basis'. They especially greeted the entry of the Croatian Peasants into the government, 'hoping that together with them it would be possible to fulfil the principles of the agrarian movement and achieve democracy throughout the country.'[121] However, in a private conversation with Hinko Krizman, Milan Gavrilović admitted that the Agrarians could not continue to support the government for much longer, because of the ongoing conflict with the Yugoslav Radical Union, which continued despite Čubrilović's entry into the government.[122] Immediately after the 1939 agreement, there were rumours that a government reshuffle would soon take place, in order to open the door to the United Opposition. Could that be another reason why the Serbian parties hesitated before increasing the volume and tone of their criticism of the agreement? The Radicals' Main Committee held negotiations with Cvetković over the 'reunification' of the Radical Party in late 1939 and early 1940, but these proved ultimately unsuccessful, just like several other earlier attempts.[123] The government, and especially Maček, wanted to include more Serbs in the cabinet, in order to weaken the opposition to the agreement. To that effect, Maček encouraged two younger members of the Democratic Party, Dragomir Ikonić and Dragoljub Milovanović Bena, to join the government, but failed. Once again, the Prince Regent objected to the Serbian opposition parties entering the government. He feared that the government would be less stable as a result, and was opposed to the United Opposition's insistence on the democratisation of the country, which would inevitably mean the

---

121 *Politika*, 4 September 1939.
122 Krizman, 'Dnevnik', 26-30 December 1939, MPHSS-2, 292.
123 BAR PPP, box 14, Mita Dimitrijević to Milan Antić, Belgrade, 15 February 1940.

abolition of the 1931 Constitution.[124]

As explained previously, the Independent Democrats officially adopted a federalist platform in 1932, in order to strengthen their coalition with the Croatian Peasant Party. However, while they supported Croatia's autonomy and criticised state centralism, once it became clear in 1939 that a Croatian *banovina* would be established, the Independent Democrats did not wish to see it become too independent from the central government in Belgrade. Like the Serbian United Opposition, the junior partner in the Peasant Democratic opposition primarily campaigned for the democratisation of the country, while federalism came second. The Independent Democrats preferred a genuine Serb-Croat agreement, not simply a compromise between Maček and the Crown. They were perhaps the most genuine Yugoslavs, whose support for Serb-Croat unity came with no conditions attached.

The diary of Hinko Krizman offers an invaluable insight into the thinking of a leading Independent Democrat. Less than two weeks before the Cvetković-Maček agreement was finally reached, Krizman wrote:

Maček must try to achieve a success this way, because the people are impatient and because he cannot and does not wish to pursue the politics of catastrophe [i.e. secession]. The Regency is also in favour of an agreement, so long as it keeps the JRZ as the main instrument of its policies. [It is a] difficult situation for the SDS because we have to accept any agreement Maček negotiates and because it would be good for the country if the HSS entered

---

124 MPHSS-2, 292-6. Because of the flirtation with the regime, Ikonić was expelled from the DS in January 1940, unlike Milovanović who managed to persuade the party that although he was approached by the government, he would not have joined it without prior agreement from the party leadership. Ikonić eventually became a cabinet minister, for less than two days, between 25 March 1941, when several ministers resigned in protest at the government's decision to join the Tripartite Pact, and 27 March when the government was deposed in a military coup. Milovanović was shot by Nazis in the Kragujevac massacre of October 1941.

the government and accepted some responsibility, but the political side of such an agreement is bound to be shaky and incomplete.[125]

Krizman was aware that the forthcoming agreement was likely to solve only one question—that of Croat autonomy—but would leave the question of the democratisation of the country open. He urged that:

The external and internal situation demands an urgent agreement and that the HSS be given an opportunity to have [state-wide] political responsibility. The satisfaction of Croat demands has become a primary issue, but it would be a disaster for the future [of the country] to negotiate an agreement with Cvetković and the JRZ; the price is the survival of the [political] system and the imposed Constitution. [Such an agreement] would be a step forward only if the HSS does not fail and if the future government does not repeat the weaknesses of the Pašić-Radić government of 1925-1927.[126]

Other leading Independent Democrats were more pragmatic. At a meeting of the party executive council, held in order to discuss Maček's agreement with Cvetković, Krizman was alone against participation of the party in the new government. Others shared his reservations, including Srdjan Budisavljević, Adam Pribićević's successor as the party leader, but believed that entering the government was vital for the party's interests. After the agreement was signed, Krizman wrote in his diary that this was 'not a government of national agreement, but a coalition government between the HSS and JRZ.'[127]

The Independent Democrats competed with the Yugoslav Radical Union for supremacy in Serbian areas of Croatia.[128] Even when Budisavljević entered the government, the rivalry between him and the Prime Minister Cvetković reflected the rivalry between the two

---

125 Hinko Krizman, 'Dnevnik', 15 August 1939, ibid., 192-3.
126 Ibid., 193.
127 Krizman, 'Dnevnik', 26-27 August 1939, ibid., 193.
128 Jelić, 'O nekim odjecima sporazuma', 153.

parties. Maček, the Croat, often found himself mediating between his two Serb colleagues.[129]

Maček's coalition partners could not afford to appear less supportive of the 1939 agreement than the Yugoslav Radical Union. Their support for the agreement secured the continued coalition with the Croatian Peasant Party; the party's position would have been significantly weaker if the Peasant Democratic Coalition had broken apart. Following the 1939 agreement, the conflict between the Independent Democrats and the Yugoslav Radical Union intensified. Using its position as Maček's coalition partner, the SDS replaced a number of JRZ administrators in the newly formed *banovina*. Thus for instance, the authorities in the municipalities of Vrlika, Knin, Obrovac and Kistanje, all belonging to the Yugoslav Radical Union, were replaced in March 1940 by Independent Democrats.[130] Although the fired personnel had all declared themselves loyal to Cvetković after Stojadinović was forced to resign, this was clearly not enough to save their jobs.[131] It was also possible that among them there were pro-Yugoslav Croats loyal to the government—there had been some in virtually every town—who may have been replaced by Serb members of the Independent Democratic Party. The 'defenders' of 'Serb interests', such as the Serbian Cultural Club, ignored such cases.

Cvetković was aware that support for the Yugoslav Radical Union in Serbia was weak, so he aimed to strengthen the party's position among Serbs outside Serbia. He even personally toured Croatia, addressing a Yugoslav Radical Union rally in Ogulin in December 1939.[132] Maček tolerated the activities of the Union for two reasons. First, he was keen to keep cordial relations with Cvetković. At a dinner party attended by cabinet ministers, Maček toasted Cvetković with 'Long live Dragiša!', and jumped up from his seat after Cvetković

---

129 Konstantinović, *Politika sporazuma*, 91.
130 Boban, 'O političkim previranjima na selu', 241.
131 Ibid.
132 MPHSS-2, 272n.

suggested that he should resign soon, as his main aim was achieved. 'No, you can't [do that], we must finish what we have started,' Maček told Cvetković.[133] Maček was, according to Konstantinović, in a very good mood those days. At a dinner he hosted, the Croat leader stated that they were all working for the good of the Serbs, the Croats and their common homeland, Yugoslavia. 'We Croats are like that,' Maček said. '[W]hen we fight, we fight, but when we like someone, we really like them!'[134]

The second reason why the Croat leader preferred that Serbs who were not members of the Independent Democratic Party joined the Yugoslav Radical Union was that this was a far preferable option to their joining organisations which opposed the Cvetković-Maček agreement. Although Cvetković's party colleagues often joined the 'Serbs, rally together!' movement, the party as a whole was not opposed to the agreement and did not wish to see the *banovina* of Croatia dismembered.

The Kingdom of Yugoslavia has been usually seen by historians as a Serb-dominated state. As Ivo Banac put it:

After the unification, the denial of the national individuality of each South Slavic nation, a position inherent in the precepts of unitaristic Yugoslavism, greatly facilitated the introduction of centralism. Under the conditions that prevailed, with all the institutions of the former Serbian state virtually intact, centralism was the system least likely to foster national identity. Instead, it furthered the goals of Serbian supremacy, reflected in the dominant position of the Serbs in all spheres of public affairs.[135]

It would be hard to dispute the above verdict. One needs only look at the names of Yugoslavia's numerous prime ministers in the inter-

---

133 Konstantinović, *Politika sporazuma*, 55. Entry for 4 and 5 October 1939.
134 Ibid.
135 Ivo Banac, *The National Question in Yugoslavia: Origins, History, Politics*, Ithaca, NY, 4th edn, 1994, 407.

war period, all but one of whom were Serbs, to agree with the main thrust of the argument. However, as argued throughout the book, the complexity of Yugoslavia's history requires a particularly nuanced and careful approach. Was there really a 'Serbian supremacy...in all spheres of public affairs'? The Serbs, especially those of pre-1912 Serbia, enjoyed a clear domination in the political and military spheres. However, by the second half of the 1930s non-Serbs were becoming more prominent in the army. If it had not been for the war and the country's dismemberment, an ethnic balance, extending to the highest military posts, might have been achieved.[136]

Even in the field of the economy, Croat accusations of Serb hegemony are hard to sustain. By the late 1920s, more than half of Yugoslavia's bank resources were based in Zagreb,[137] while Croatia, alongside Slovenia, remained the richest part of the country. This might explain why many Croatian industrialists and businessmen were loyal to Belgrade, although in some cases their genuine Yugoslav identity played a role.[138] Croatia's economic progress in the interwar period is particularly remarkable given that before the First World War its industry was barely more developed than Serbia's. In 1910 almost 70 per cent of enterprises were small, family-run businesses, while less then 1 per cent employed more than 20 workers.[139] While Croats popularly believed that they were being exploited by Belgrade, many Serbs saw Croatia as 'the Trojan horse of their

---

136 Stevan K. Pavlowitch, 'How many non-Serbian Generals in 1941?', *East European Quarterly*, vol. 16, no. 4, January 1983, 447-52. See also the work by Mile Bjelajac on the history of the Yugoslav army, listed in the bibliography.

137 Leslie Benson, *Yugoslavia: A Concise History*, Basingstoke, 2001, 49.

138 For example Božo Banac, the director of Yugoslav Lloyd, financially supported the Yugoslav Committee and remained a believer in Yugoslavism all his life. See Vane Ivanović, *LX: Memoirs of a Jugoslav*, New York, 1977. When the Second World War began Banac and his stepson Vane Ivanović placed a number of ships under the British flag, even though Yugoslavia was still neutral. See Dejan Djokić, 'Yugoslav anti-Axis Resistance, 1939-41: The Case of Vane Ivanović', *Slavonic and East European Review*, vol. 79, no. 1, January 2001, 127-41.

139 Ivo Goldstein, *Croatia: A History*, London, 1999, 106.

former enemies', because of Zagreb's economic dominance, largely due to its trade with Austria and Hungary.[140]

As for cultural politics, no Serbian organisation or prominent individual argued for a Serb cultural model to be imposed on non-Serbs (with the exception of Macedonians). Not even the Radicals, usually seen as the 'Greater Serbian' party. The work of Miroslav Krleža, the leading Croatian, left-wing writer, appeared more frequently in Belgrade than in Zagreb.[141] Yugoslavia's intellectuals were interested in promoting a 'synthetic' Yugoslav culture, a blend of Serbian, Croatian and Slovene traditions, as Andrew Wachtel has convincingly argued.[142] At the same time, individual cultures, including the Croatian one, developed during the period.[143]

Croats were the only Yugoslav 'tribe' which, after 1939, achieved formal autonomy within Yugoslavia. The *banovina* of Croatia was larger and enjoyed a greater degree of self-rule than either Croat territories in the Habsburg Monarchy or the post-1945 Socialist Republic of Croatia (up until the mid-1970s at least). At the same time, the leadership of the Croatian Peasant Party, which had so long campaigned for the federalisation of Yugoslavia, never considered granting autonomy to areas with a Serb or Bosnian Muslim majority inside Croatia.

In August 1939, for the first time since unification, the boundaries of an internal administrative unit were expressly drawn according to ethnic criteria (the partial exception had been Dravska). Unlike King Alexander's *banovinas*, Croatia was a *banovina* of a single Yu-

---

140 Benson, *Yugoslavia*, 183n. See also John Lampe, *Yugoslavia as History: Twice there was a Country*, Cambridge, 2nd edn, 2000, 187-9.

141 Pavlowitch, *Serbia*, 137.

142 Andrew B. Wachtel, 'Ivan Meštrović, Ivo Andrić and the Synthetic Yugoslav Culture of the Interwar Period', in Dejan Djokić (ed.), *Yugoslavism: Histories of a Failed Idea, 1918-1992*, London and Madison, WI, 2003, 238-51. See also Wachtel's *Making a Nation, Breaking a Nation: Literature and Cultural Politics in Yugoslavia*, Stanford, CA, 1998.

143 For cultural politics during the interwar period see Dimić, *Kulturna politika*.

goslav tribe, the Croats—although it included a significant number of non-Croats. The creation of autonomous Croatia marked a significant departure from the 6 January order, if not its end. The 1939 agreement did not just provide for Croat territorial autonomy; it also recognised that the Croats had developed a separate identity, which in turn meant the effective end of integral Yugoslavism.

Debates over the internal division of the country, in particular over the creation of a Serbian *banovina* and the final territorial scope of the *banovina* of Croatia, dominated the political discourse of post-1939 Yugoslavia. This was the period when the Croatian question was virtually solved, certainly from the perspective of the leadership of the Croatian Peasant Party. At the same time, the period witnessed the emergence of the Serbian question. After the Cvetković-Maček agreement, the positions of Serbs and Croats were somewhat reversed. The Serbs were now unsure of their status in Yugoslavia; many demanded autonomy, while some even questioned how 'just' this Yugoslav state was.

It would be too simplistic, however, to describe even this period as an era of Serb-Croat conflict. The debate was often Serb-Serb, and even Croat-Croat, because following the 1939 agreement, the Croatian Peasant Party's virtual monopoly over Croat opinion somewhat lessened. For all its flaws, the agreement marked a positive step toward finding a Serb-Croat compromise.

CONCLUSION

'The Yugoslavs,' said an Italian lady to me in London, and her beautiful lips looked as if they could scarcely bring themselves to pronounce the name, 'the Yugoslavs' she said, 'are very wild and black.' If I have given the impression in this book that they are white, my fault will be much greater than the lady's, since I am not quite a stranger to them.[1]

Despite the internal instability, interwar Yugoslavia did not disintegrate from within, as did its socialist successor in the early 1990s. It was destroyed by Nazi Germany, Fascist Italy and their allies in a short war of April 1941.

When the Second World War broke out in September 1939, Belgrade proclaimed neutrality. The stark reality of the Yugoslavs' situation meant that they had to deal with Italy and Germany without the help of their French and British allies. The failure by the League of Nations to condemn Italy, following the assassination of King Alexander in 1934, for providing refuge to the *Ustašas* was a clear indication that small European countries could not count on much support from the democratic Powers. Although Yugoslavia achieved an uneasy rapprochement with Italy during the Stojadinović premiership, and even though Germany may not have been interested in its territory, after the 1938 *Anschluss* the Balkan state found itself squeezed between two large, aggressive neighbours. Germany and Italy also happened to be Yugoslavia's major trading partners. It was only a matter of time before neutrality would no longer be an option.[2]

---

1 Henry Baerlein, *The Birth of Yugoslavia*, London, 1922, 2 vols, vol. 2, 392.
2 For a comprehensive account of the Yugoslav entry into the war see Jacob Hoptner, *Yugoslavia in Crisis, 1934-1941*, New York, 1962, 170-292.

On 25 March 1941 Yugoslavia joined the Tripartite Pact (concluded the previous year between Germany, Italy and Japan), after sustained pressure from Berlin and Rome. Britain tried hard to persuade Belgrade not to do so, but without a concrete offer of help the British could not have hoped to influence even the Anglophile Prince Paul.[3] The day after the Pact was signed by Prime Minister Cvetković and Foreign Minister Cincar-Marković in Vienna, Paul left Belgrade for his mountain retreat in Slovenia. What he did not know was that a military coup was about to take place in the capital city. A group of Serb officers of the Yugoslav Army, led by Generals Borivoje Mirković and Dušan Simović, overthrew the government and the Royal Regency on 27 March, and proclaimed King Peter II of age six months before his eighteenth birthday.[4]

The conspirators had popular support. As soon as the news from Vienna reached the country, thousands of people went out on the streets of Belgrade and other Serbian and Slovenian towns to demonstrate against the signing of the Pact. 'Better War than the Pact!' and 'Better Grave than [being] a Slave!' were the slogans of the day. As in the 1937 anti-Concordat demonstrations, the Communists joined in. This time they played a more prominent role, even if they did not organise and lead the demonstrations, as the post-1945

---

3 Both King George VI ('Bertie', as he was called by friends, who included Prince Paul) and British Foreign Minister Anthony Eden wrote personally to Paul several times, urging him to refuse to sign the Tripartite Pact. BAR PPP, box 2, Eden to Prince Paul, Athens, 4 March 1941; Eden to Paul, Cairo, 17 March 1941; King George VI to Prince Paul, n.d. [ca. March 1941]; King George VI to Prince Paul, 23 March 1941.

4 The officers were joined by one civilian: Radoje Knežević of the Democratic Party, whose brother Major Živan Knežević also took part in the conspiracy. For an insider's view of the coup, which complements Hoptner's account well, see Dragiša N. Ristić, *Yugoslavia's Revolution of 1941*, University Park, 1966 (Ristić was General Simović's *aide-de-camp*). For an update on the British role in the events of late March see Sue Onslow, 'Britain and the Belgrade *Coup* of 27 March 1941 Revisited', *Electronic Journal of International History*, March 2005 (http://www.history.ac.uk/ejournal/Onslow.pdf).

Yugoslav historiography claimed.[5] Croatian towns remained largely quiet. Maček and the Croatian Peasant Party feared that to refuse to sign the Pact would mean certain war for which Yugoslavia was not ready and in which Croatia would suffer the most.[6]

Prince Paul had found pressures of the regency at times so challenging that he nearly resigned several months before Yugoslavia was drawn into the war.[7] Yet, he was bound by a sense of duty towards the country and his young nephew, King Peter II. Regardless of whether one agrees with the then Yugoslav leadership's decision to join the Tripartite Pact or not—this author does not—Paul genuinely believed that it was the best, if not the only option.[8] The Axis powers offered Yugoslavia what seemed like very favourable terms: they guaranteed to respect Yugoslavia's territorial integrity and sovereignty; Belgrade would not be asked to provide military assistance; and the Yugoslav territory would not be used for the transit of Axis troops during the war. Moreover, a secret note promised that Yugoslavia's interests in the Aegean, namely the control of the Greek port of Salonika, would be taken into account when territorial adjustments to frontiers in the Balkans were made.[9]

Whether Hitler and Mussolini would have respected these terms is impossible to tell, but Berlin failed to honour treaties even with much more powerful countries such as the Soviet Union. Although written with Britain's interests in mind first and foremost, Anthony Eden's letter to Prince Paul in early March 1941 shows that contemporaries can sometimes see beyond the short-term future:

---

5 Milovan Djilas provides a first hand account of the demonstrations in *Memoir of a Revolutionary*, New York, 1973, 367-74.

6 Vladko Maček, *In the Struggle for Freedom*, University Park and London, 1957, 205-07.

7 BAR PPP, box 14, Prince Paul's resignation speech, handwritten, no date (Paul later wrote in the top margin: 'late 1940, early 1941').

8 BAR PPP, box 4, Princess Olga's diary, Belgrade, 24 March 1941.

9 Hoptner, *Yugoslavia in Crisis*, 240-41. An English translation of the protocol of adherence to the Pact is published in ibid., 304-06.

I am so certain that a passive Yugoslavia once completely surrounded will be subjected to all the well-known German methods of bleeding and disruption, that I have no hesitation in urging you most earnestly to decide to resist this evil and to join with us and Greece in an attempt to withstand it. What, Sir, would the result of the other course be? To endure German rule now in its most contemptuous form, and at the end of the war to lie for many years under the evil after-effects of a German occupation rendered all the more pernicious and disruptive because it has not been resisted. In such conditions the soul of a people must suffer. In choosing the alternative to resist with us, hard though it may be for the moment, you and your people will at least know that you have done all in your power to avoid the far worse fate that has befallen Roumania and Bulgaria. You will then be able to face the future with the greater courage and hope, rooted as they will be in your own splendid traditions and brave deeds. Could this not be made plain to any who, in some parts of your country, fail to see matters in their true light?[10]

Even if Yugoslavia survived the war intact, as an ally of the Axis its post-war status in the Soviet-dominated Eastern Europe might well have resembled that of Bulgaria and Romania. Yugoslavia found its soul on 27 March, in Churchill's famous words, but would soon lose its 'body', both metaphorically and literally. Yet, it re-emerged in 1945, victorious and with a prestige similar to the one enjoyed by Serbia at the end of the First World War. Admittedly, a Communist government was soon established, but Yugoslav democracy had been marginalised even before the war, as epitomised by the introduction of the royal dictatorship in 1929 and the collapse of the Serb-Croat democratic opposition ten years later.

Although some participants in the Belgrade coup continued to be opposed to the Cvetković-Maček agreement, the new cabinet, formed by General Simović, included the Croat leader as one of two deputy Prime Ministers (the other one was Slobodan Jovanović), and several other Croat ministers. The Simović government was representative of all the major parties, including the Democrats. Faced with an imminent attack, the government tried to reassure Berlin that it would respect the 25 March agreement. It also signed a Treaty of Friendship with the Soviet Union and declared Belgrade an open

---

10   BAR PPP, box 2, Eden to Prince Paul, Athens, 4 March 1941.

city. These were the measures borne out of desperation which proved too little too late, from Hitler's point of view. In the early hours of Sunday 6 April, German aircraft bombarded the Yugoslav capital, marking the beginning of a decisive Axis' attack. Eleven days later the Yugoslav Army capitulated, but not before the King and members of the government fled the country, eventually reaching the safety of London.

The Kingdom of Yugoslavia therefore officially continued to exist, though in reality the country was partitioned following the invasion. Croatia, which incorporated the whole of Bosnia-Herzegovina and parts of Vojvodina, became an *Ustaša*-ruled state within the Nazi order, while the rest of what had been Yugoslavia was either occupied or annexed. A fratricidal, Serb-Croat war went hand in hand with an ideological and often intra-ethnic struggle between two resistance movements and various collaborationist groups. By the end of the war in May 1945, when the country was liberated (largely) by the Communist-led Partisan army, around one million Yugoslavs had died, half of them Serbs.[11] Despite the harsh nature of the foreign occupation, most Yugoslavs were probably killed by other Yugoslavs.

The Yugoslav civil war of the 1940s should be understood within the wider context of the Second World War, and in any case it should not obscure the fact that Yugoslavs themselves had formed a united state at the end of the First World War. The unification of Yugoslavia in December 1918 was by no means certain until the later stages of the war, but its creators could present the act of union as the fulfilment of a century-long Yugoslav idea. The creation of this state (formally a nation-state) was facilitated by President Wilson's advocacy of the right of nations to self-determination. In reality, however, the

11   See Bogoljub Kočović, *Žrtve Drugog svetskog rata u Jugoslaviji*, London, 1985, and Vladimir Žerjavić, *Gubici stanovništva Jugoslavije u Drugom svjetskom ratu*, Zagreb, 1989.

Kingdom of Serbs, Croats, and Slovenes was a 'complex' state. Serbia and Montenegro had been independent since 1878, though large parts of their territories (Macedonia, Kosovo and Sandžak) had not been 'liberated' from the Ottoman Empire until the Balkan Wars of 1912-13. Slovenia and Dalmatia had been Austrian-governed territories, while Croatia-Slavonia and Vojvodina had formerly been under the Hungarian administration. Bosnia-Herzegovina had been jointly governed by Vienna and Budapest between 1878 and 1918. Yugoslavia incorporated different monetary, economic, legal and education systems, and several transport networks. It was a mosaic of cultures and traditions, pieced together by historic circumstances, political will, and ethnic and linguistic kinship—not necessarily in that order.

Most Serbs, whose nineteenth century was marked by national and political emancipation from the Ottoman Empire, understood Yugoslavia as an extended Serbia—a centralised nation-state. As (sometimes self-perceived) liberators of Croats and other South Slavs, they could not quite understand Zagreb's demands for de-centralisation and autonomy. Moreover, they felt betrayed by the Croats' inability to accept the new state as enthusiastically as they had done. On the other hand, the Croats, among whom the Yugoslav idea had originated in the early nineteenth century, were used to historic rights and Habsburg-style dualism. Their policy of boycotting state institutions proved fruitless and only helped, rather than hindered, Serb domination.

Conflicting visions of Yugoslavia among Serb and Croat political leaderships emerged during the formative period (1918-21). However, the contest between (mostly Serb) centralists and (mostly Croat) federalists was but one aspect of the contest. Inter-party and even intra-party conflicts and alliances—regardless of ethnic affiliation—made a crucial impact. Rather than being set prior to the unification, the views of leading Serb and Croat politicians on the Serb-Croat question evolved during the 1920s. Radić advocated republicanism and a boycott of the Belgrade parliament in the early 1920s, but also negotiated with Davidović, who increasingly distanced himself from the state centralism championed by Pašić and Pribićević. In 1925 Radić entered Pašić's government—an event hailed by its supporters as a breakthrough in Serb-Croat relations—and this prompted Pribićević's resignation. Two years later, in an even bigger U-turn, Radić joined Pribićević in opposition, to form the Peasant Democratic Coalition, which called for a federal monarchy.

Following Radić's assassination in summer 1928, Yugoslavia's young democratic institutions entered a final crisis. On 6 January 1929 King Alexander abolished the Constitution, the parliament and political parties, and introduced a royal dictatorship.

In the early 1930s the regime sought to reach a compromise with the Croatian Peasant Party, but the two sides could not agree. Belgrade wanted Maček, Radić's successor, to publicly support the government and, preferably, join it before any changes *within* the existing order could be made. Maček's position, on the other hand, was that a separate Croat identity must be recognised by granting Croatia wide autonomy. At this time he also demanded free elections for a constituent assembly that would eventually adopt a constitution acceptable to the majority of Croats. Effectively, Maček sought a return to the starting point of 1918-19, when, ironically, his party had chosen to boycott the provisional institutions.

A series of resolutions—sparked off by the 'Zagreb points' of November 1932—signalled the beginning of a united Serb-Croat opposition front. Yet, its birth was slow, partly because of disagreements among the Serbian opposition parties. After the assassination of King Alexander in October 1934, the royal dictatorship was relaxed and political parties were able to function more or less freely. In the May 1935 elections the Democrats and the Agrarians presented a joint list with the Peasant Democratic Coalition and the Yugoslav Muslim Organisation. The list was headed by Maček and, although it failed to win the elections, the opposition did better than it had been expected. This prompted Prince Regent Paul, Alexander's *de facto* successor, to bring about a change of government and to start negotiations with Maček. The new government included the Radicals' pro-regime faction, the Slovene Clericals and the Yugoslav Muslims, who would soon merge into a single party—the Yugoslav Radical Union. However, Milan Stojadinović, the new Prime Minister, was unable and possibly unwilling to persuade the Croatian Peasant Party to join the Union or the government. Maček met the Prince Regent on several occasions during this period, but their talks came to nothing. After the failure of negotiations with the regime, the Croat leader turned again to the Serbian opposition, but maintained contacts with Prince Paul. The cooperation between the Peasant Democratic Coalition and Serbia's United Opposition would reach its peak in 1937-8 and would contribute to the fall of Stojadinović in February 1939, although the Yugoslav Radical Union remained the government party.

Eventually, Maček reached a compromise with the Crown in August 1939. An autonomous Croatian *banovina* was set up, and the Peasant Democratic Coalition entered the government. However, rather than a Serb-Croat agreement, the Cvetković-Maček *sporazum* was but a rapprochement between the largest Croatian party (in coalition with the Independent Democrats, who were supported by many Croatian Serbs), on the one hand, and the Crown and the government, on the other. The 1937 Bloc of the National Agreement between the Zagreb and Belgrade opposition and even the Pašić-Radić pact of the mid-1920s were political compromises arguably more deserving of the label 'Serb-Croat'.

The Cvetković-Maček agreement satisfied a majority of Croats, if not their far right and far left. It also led to the escalation of the Serbian question. Many Serbs—both those living in autonomous Croatia and those in the rest of Yugoslavia—sought to 'rally together' all their compatriots in a Serbian unit, while the Slovenes and Bosnian Muslims called for the creation of their own *banovinas*. Integral Yugoslavism, which had been introduced in 1929 to save Yugoslavia, was eventually, ten years later, abandoned by most Yugoslavs, even by many of its most enthusiastic supporters, the Serbs. Thus, within a relatively short time-span the country of the South Slavs underwent a transition, in political discourse as well as in institutional structure, from a nation-state to a multi-national state.

If the solution of the Croat question led to the opening-up of the Serbian one, and put an end to the democratisation of the country, the beginning of federalisation promised to bring long-term stability. By the late 1930s a decentralised state became acceptable to many Serbs, not only to non-Serbs. It is probable that had the Yugoslav kingdom not been formed along such strict centralist lines, the interwar period would have been less volatile. When Yugoslavia re-emerged after the Second World War, it was as a federation, albeit a Communist one. Tito's Partisans were able to attract support from among all Yugoslav groups partly because they promised a decentralised, federal Yugoslavia after the war. However, the ultimate and tragic end of the Yugoslav state in the 1990s raises the question whether federalism was indeed appropriate, at least in its communist form.

It has been argued throughout the book that the traditional 'ethnic conflict' approach fails to explain a number of political developments in the interwar period. Ethnic and political conflicts coexisted and were often intertwined. If this work has concentrated more on the latter, it is because these tend to be overlooked by most scholars. Even in a society presumably deeply divided by a history of ethnic conflict, it is too simplistic to approach the subject assuming that there existed homogeneous Serb and Croat opinions. Intra-ethnic struggles went hand in hand with inter-ethnic contests, particularly in the case of Serbs.

Interwar Yugoslavia offers a constructive example to all those engaged in studying conflict management in multinational states. The former Yugoslav region may be perceived as perpetually violent with some justification, but, as this book has shown, there was a period when the Yugoslavs made sustained attempts to overcome ethnic and political conflicts by searching for a compromise. Indeed, the existence of Yugoslavia through much of the twentieth century went against the ostensible Balkan norm. It was only after the demise of a united Yugoslav state—in the 1940s and in the 1990s—that the region experienced a violent 'balkanisation'.

Despite constant political crises, Yugoslavia was not uniquely unstable, nor more undemocratic than most other countries of interwar East-Central Europe, nor was the national question the only reason for its instability. The constitutional debate between centralists and federalists was characteristic of the whole region and only in Austria and Germany did the federalists prevail, after a long political struggle.[12] Czechoslovakia resembled Yugoslavia in respect of both its diversity and its centralist form of government. In Poland Józéf Piłsudski carried out a coup d'état in order to put an end to several years of inter-party rivalry and unstable government coalitions, three years before King Alexander did the same in Yugoslavia. As in the case of Yugoslavia, the Polish 1921 Constitution was highly centralist, but unlike the Yugoslav 1921 Constitution, it effectively provided for assimilation of national minorities.[13] Leaders of postwar Romania found it as difficult as their Yugoslav counterparts to integrate former Habsburg territories—regardless of whether those territories were populated by ethnic Romanians or by members of a large Hungarian minority—with the pre-war kingdom.[14] Not that there had existed a great deal of integration between various components of the late Dual Monarchy. The merging of the formerly

---

12 Mark Mazower, *Dark Continent: Europe's Twentieth Century*, London, 1998, 7.

13 Joseph Rothschild, *East Central Europe between the Two World Wars*, Seattle, 1974. Czechoslovakia: 73-135; Poland: 34, 46. Incidentally, R.W. Seton-Watson, the leading contemporary specialist on interwar East-Central Europe, regarded King Alexander and Piłsudski as relatively benign dictators. He thought Mustafa Kemal Atatürk and King Zog of Albania to be more authoritarian rulers, though not quite as dictatorial as Mussolini and Primo de Rivera. 'Jugoslavia and Croatia (Address given on January 29th, 1929)', *Journal of the Royal Institute of International Affairs*, March 1929, 129. Admittedly, Seton-Watson's verdict on Alexander was made only several weeks after the dictatorship was introduced.

14 However, unlike Romania, Yugoslavia was not simply an extension of a prewar state.

Austrian-controlled Czech lands with the Slovak territories that had once belonged to the Hungarian half of the Monarchy met a number of obstacles, too.[15]

By the second half of the 1930s all countries in East-Central Europe, with the exception of Czechoslovakia, became dictatorships. Even Czechoslovakia's democracy was not without its limitations. While the Yugoslav dictatorship was relaxed after 1934, Bulgaria (in 1935), Greece (in 1936), and Romania (in 1938) all turned to authoritarianism.[16]

No extreme right-wing ideology enjoyed significant support in Yugoslavia.[17] The far left was a marginal force, too, in spite of the Communists' brief rise in the early 1920s and a partial revival in the late 1930s. Overall, however, Yugoslavia went through political challenges similar to those experienced by the rest of the continent during the interwar period, famously described by E.H. Carr as the *Twenty Years' Crisis*.[18]

The events of the 1930s may help explain the Yugoslav Communists' appeal during the war and in its aftermath. In retrospect, a power vacuum began to appear even before Yugoslavia was drawn into the Second World War. Party life was re-established under Prince Paul's regency, although the dictatorship was never fully abandoned and political freedoms remained seriously limited. However, after an initial recovery of party politics after 1934, by the end of the decade the

---

15 Rothschild, *East Central Europe*, 86.

16 Rothschild's book (ibid.) remains the best study of interwar East-Central Europe.

17 Robert Kaplan's views notwithstanding. Kaplan wrote in the early 1990s, during the war in Bosnia, that 'Nazism, for instance, can claim Balkan origins. Among the flophouses of Vienna, a breeding ground of ethnic resentments close to the southern Slavic world, Hitler learned how to hate so infectiously.' *Balkan Ghosts: A Journey through History*, London, 1994, xxiii.

18 E.H. Carr, *Twenty Years' Crisis, 1919-1939*, London, 1939.

old parties were suffering from a crisis of identity, caused partly by a loss of leadership.[19]

Yugoslavia lost most of its political elite by the end of the second interwar decade. Following Svetozar Pribićević's untimely death in exile in 1936, Anton Korošec (1872-1940), Mehmed Spaho (1883-1939), Ljuba Davidović (1863-1940) and Jovan Jovanović Pižon (1869-1939) all died of natural causes in quick succession. Aca Stanojević (1852-1947) lived for another several years, but his career was clearly coming to an end.[20] Moreover, Stojadinović's political career ended for all intents and purposes in February 1939. While historians have noted the gap left after Pašić's death in 1926 and the assassinations of Radić in 1928 and King Alexander in 1934, few have noticed that this loss of leadership was arguably a more serious blow to Yugoslavia's politics. Korošec was succeeded by Miha Krek, who was incomparably less influential within the government, and Spaho by Džafer Kulenović, a more nationalist politician who would end up as a vice-premier of the *Ustaša* government. Dragoljub Jovanović left the Agrarians in 1940 to form a new party, and although the Democrats managed relatively successfully to replace Davidović by Milan Grol, the latter lacked both Davidović's charisma and his ability to compromise.

As if to signal the end of an era several initiatives emerged that proposed the formation of new political parties. Already in 1927, before the formation of the Peasant Democratic Coalition, Radić allegedly planned to spread his movement to non-Croat areas, by forming the People's Peasant Party.[21] The post-1929 order is usu-

---

19 According to Dragoljub Jovanović, Slobodan Jovanović believed that the royal dictatorship did not destroy the old political parties but merely announced their death, which had already taken place during the 1920s. *Političke uspomene*, Belgrade, 1997, 7 vols, vol. 5, 33.

20 Stanojević spent the war in his home town Knjaževac, refusing to cooperate with the collaborationist Serbian regime of General Milan Nedić. After the war, he briefly resumed his long and distinguished political career, before dying at the age of 95.

21 Milan Marjanović, *Stjepan Radić*, Belgrade, 1937, 168-9.

ally known for its suppression of political parties, yet it also created two government parties: the Yugoslav National Party (which grew out of the Yugoslav Radical (Peasant) Democracy) and the Yugoslav Radical Union. The latter was in fact a close coalition between Stojadinović's Radicals, Korošec's Clericals and Spaho's Muslims. When Stojadinović realised that Maček would not join the Union, he hoped the Croatian Peasants would unite with the Serbian opposition in a single, federalist bloc. In late 1934 and early 1935 Korošec and Stanojević negotiated closer cooperation and possibly the creation of a new party. Not long before the creation of the Yugoslav Radical Union in summer 1935, General Živković unsuccessfully proposed to Maček a merger of the Croatian Peasants, the Radicals, the Yugoslav Muslims and the Slovene Clericals.

In the aftermath of the 1939 agreement, Cvetković considered replacing the Yugoslav Radical Union with a countrywide peasant party. At the same time, the Democrats, the Independent Democrats, and the Yugoslav Nationalists briefly contemplated merging into a single party. Even the 'Serbs, rally together!' movement was symptomatic of this attempted reconfiguration of the political scene. Only weeks before the war broke out in Yugoslavia, Srdjan Budisavljević proposed the (re)unification of the Democrats and Independent Democrats in a public talk in Belgrade, attended, among others, by Desimir Tošić, the leader of the youth section of the Democratic Party.[22] There were also plans to broaden the government by including the Democrats. However, a broad coalition government would only be formed on 27 March, under Simović's premiership.

That same day Prince Paul made his last train journey from Slovenia to Belgrade, his holiday cut short by the news of the coup in Belgrade. He was formally requested to return to the Royal Palace by General Nedeljković, whose troops Paul had inspected in January 1940 while on a triumphant first visit to autonomous Croatia. As he was passing through Croatian towns, the Prince Regent must have recalled how only 14 months previously he had made the trip in the

---

22 I am grateful to Mr Tošić for this information.

opposite direction, greeted by flags and flowers along the route and hailed as the saviour of Yugoslavia.

Already not very popular among Serbs, Prince Paul had pursued a foreign policy that resulted in his being ousted from power. Upon arriving in Belgrade in the evening, Paul calmly resigned as regent and advised Peter to formally approve the new government and assume his duties as King.[23] The other two regents also stepped down. Cvetković was released following a brief spell in captivity, while Maček joined the Simović cabinet, albeit after some hesitation. The new, all-party government was meant to symbolise national unity, but within weeks the country would disappear from the map of Hitler's Europe.

Whether Yugoslavia could have been saved in 1941—regardless of who was in power—remains of course an open question.

---

23 BAR PPP, box 4, Princess Olga's diary, Belgrade, 27 March 1941. The Prince and his family spent the war in Kenya and South Africa, effectively as prisoners of the British government. Ironically, Stojadinović shared their destiny, although he was sent to Mauritius. Cvetković and Maček remained in Serbia and Croatia, respectively, playing no part in politics. Maček resigned from the government, choosing to remain in Croatia, but his party continued to be represented in various cabinets formed in exile. The *Ustašas* sent him briefly to a concentration camp and he spent most of the war under house arrest.

BIBLIOGRAPHY

PRIMARY SOURCES

Unpublished

(1) Arhiv Srbije i Crne Gore (Archives of Serbia and Montenegro, formerly Archives of Yugoslavia [Arhiv Jugoslavije – AJ], Belgrade)
AJ 14 Fond Ministarstva Unutrašnjih poslova Kraljevine Jugoslavije (Papers of the Ministry of the Interior of the Kingdom of Yugoslavia)
AJ 37 Milan Stojadinović Papers
AJ 38 Fond Centralni presbiro Kraljevine Jugoslavije (The Central Press Bureau Papers)
AJ 74 Fond Kraljev Dvor (The Royal Court Papers)
AJ 80 Jovan Jovanović Pižon Papers
AJ 83 Sava Kosanović Papers
AJ 102 Stanislav Krakov Papers
AJ 138 Fond Ministarski savet Kraljevine Jugoslavije (Papers of the Council of Ministers of the Kingdom of Yugoslavia)
AJ 335 Vojislav Jovanović Marambo Papers
(2) Bakhmeteff Archive of Russian and East European Culture (BAR), Columbia University, New York
Papers of Prince Paul, Prince Regent of Yugoslavia (1934-41)
Papers of Jacob Hoptner
(3) Hrvatski državni arhiv (HDA – Croatian State Archives, Zagreb)
Grupa XXI: Politička situacija, 1910-1941 (Group XXI: Political situation)
Fond 157: Banovina Hrvatska, Odjel za unutarnje poslove (Collection 157: *Banovina* of Croatia, Office for internal affairs)
(4) Hoover Institution Archives (HIA), Stanford University, Dragiša Cvetković Collection

(5) National Archives, Kew (formerly Public Record Office – PRO) FO 371 – Foreign Office Papers, General Correspondence from 1906: Southern European Department

Published

Dokumenti o postanku Kraljevine Srba, Hrvata i Slovenaca, 1914-1919 (compiled by Ferdo Šišić), Zagreb: Matica Hrvatska, 1920

Vodja govori: Ličnost, izjave, govori i politički rad vodje Hrvata Dra. Vladka Mačeka (compiled by Mirko Glojnarić), Zagreb: Danica, 1936.

Godišnjak Banske vlasti Banovine Hrvatske, Zagreb: Tisak zaklade tiskare Narodnih novina, 1940.

[Hrvatska seljačka stranka], *Ustav 'Neutralne Selj.[ačke] Republike Hrvatske i Program Hrvatske seljačke stranke*, London, 1946.

'Jako srpstvo-jaka Jugoslavija': Izbor članaka iz 'Srpskog glasa', organa Srpskog kulturnog kluba 1939-1940 (compiled by Miodrag Jovičić), Belgrade: Naučna knjiga, 1991.

Jugoslovenski federalizam: Ideje i stvarnost. Tematska zbirka dokumenata (compiled and edited by Branko Petranović and Momčilo Zečević), 2 vols, Belgrade: Prosveta, 1987.

Kingdom of Yugoslavia, 1919-1929, Belgrade: The Central Press Bureau of the Presidency of the Ministerial Council, 1930.

Korespondencija Stjepana Radića (compiled by Bogdan Krizman), 2 vols, Zagreb: Institut za hrvatsku povijest, 1972-73.

Pašić, Nikola, *Sloga Srbo-Hrvata*, Belgrade: Vreme knjige, 1995 (edited by Djordje Stanković).

Radić, Stjepan, *Politički spisi: Autobiografija, članci, govori, rasprave* (compiled by Zvonimir Kulundžić), Zagreb: Znanje, 1971.

R. W. Seton-Watson and the Yugoslavs: Correspondence, 1906-1941, 2 vols, London: British Academy and Zagreb: Institute of Croatian History, 1976.

Srpski Ustavi od 1835. do 1990. godine (Sa Ustavima Kraljevine SHS i Kraljevine Jugoslavije), Belgrade: Gramatik, 2004.

Yugoslavia through Documents: From its Creation to its Dissolution (compiled by Snežana Trifunovska), Dordrecht: Martinus Nijhoff Publishers, 1994.

Zapisnici sa sednica Ministarskog saveta Kraljevine Jugoslavije 1929-1931. (edited and compiled by Ljubodrag Dimić, Nikola Žutić and

Blagoje Isailović), Belgrade: Službeni list SRJ, 2002.

Memoirs, diaries and recollections

Ciano, Galeazzo, *Ciano's Diary, 1937-1943*, London: Phoenix Press, 2002 (*Diary 1937-1938* was first published in 1952 and *Diary 1939-1943* was first published in 1947).

Cvetković, Dragiša, 'Srpsko-hrvatsko pitanje i putevi Sporazuma', *Dokumenti o Jugoslaviji*, vol. 3, Paris: D. Cvetković and Časlav Nikitović, 1952.

——, 'Jugoslavija izmedju dva rata. Unutrašnja i spoljna politika Jugoslavije', *Dokumenti o Jugoslaviji*, vol. 4, Paris: D. Cvetković and Časlav Nikitović, 1953.

——, 'Namesništvo. Unutrašnja i spoljna politika Jugoslavije', *Dokumenti o Jugoslaviji*, vol. 5, Paris: D. Cvetković and Časlav Nikitović, 1954.

——, 'Smisao, značaj i posledice srpsko-hrvatskog sporazuma', *Glasnik srpskog istorisko-kulturnog društva 'Njegoš'* (Chicago), no. 10, December 1962, 8-27.

Djilas, Milovan, *Memoir of a Revolutionary*, New York: Harcourt Brace Jovanovich, 1973.

[Dožić, Gavrilo], *Memoari Patrijarha srpskog Gavrila*, Belgrade: Sfairos, 1990.

Godeša, Bojan and Ervin Dolenc (eds), *Izgubljeni spomin na Antona Korošca. Iz zapuščine Ivana Ahčina*, Ljubljana: Nova revija, 1999.

Grol, Milan, *Londonski dnevnik, 1941-1945*, Belgrade: Filip Višnjić, 1990.

Henderson, Neville, *Water Under the Bridges*, London: Hodder and Stoughton, 1945.

Ivanović, Vane, *LX: Memoirs of a Jugoslav*, New York: Harcourt Brace Jovanovich, 1977.

Jovanović, Dragoljub, *Ljudi, ljudi...*, 2 vols; vol. 1: *Medaljoni 56 umrlih savremenika*; vol. 2: *Medaljoni 46 umrlih savremenika (sa fotografijama)*, Belgrade: published by author, 1973-5.

——, *Ljudi, ljudi...Medaljoni 94 političkih, javnih, naučnih i drugih savremenika* [vol. 3, edited by Nadežda Jovanović], Belgrade: Filip Višnjić, 2005.

——, *Političke uspomene*, 7 vols, Belgrade: Arhiv Jugoslavije and

Kultura, 1997.

Jovanović, Slobodan, *Moji savremenici* (ed. by Radoje Knežević), Windsor, Canada: Avala, 1962.

——, *Zapisi o problemima i ljudima, 1941-1944*, London: Udruženje srpskih pisaca i umetnika u inostranstvu, 1976.

Jovanović Stoimirović, Milan, *Dnevnik, 1936-1941*, Novi Sad: Matica srpska, 2000.

Konstantinović, Mihailo, *Politika Sporazuma. Dnevničke beleške, 1939-1941. Dnevničke beleške, 1944-1945*, Novi Sad: Agencija 'Mir', 1998.

Maček, Vladko, *In the Struggle for Freedom*, University Park and London: The Pennsylvania State University Press, 1957.

Meštrović, Ivan, *Uspomene na političke ljude i dogadjaje*, Zagreb: Matica Hrvatska, 1993 (first published in Buenos Aires, 1961).

Miljuš, Branko, *Sporazum 1939 godine*, Windsor (Canada): Avala, 1957.

Pavlović, Kosta St., *Onakvi kakve sam ih znao* (Priredio Stevan K Pavlowitch), Belgrade: Otkrovenje, 2004.

Pešelj, Branko M., *U vrtlogu hrvatske politike: Sjećanja i pogledi. Poseban osvrt na pitanje Bosne*, Zurich: Bošnjački Institut, 1989.

Pribićević, Svetozar, *Diktatura Kralja Aleksandra*, Belgrade: Prosveta, 1953 (first published as *La dictature du roi Alexandre*, Paris, 1933).

Ribar, Ivan, *Iz moje političke suradnje (1901-1963)*, Zagreb: Naprijed, 1965.

Sforza, Count Carlo, *Makers of Modern Europe: Portraits and Personal Impressions and Recollections*, Indianapolis: The Bobbs-Merrill Company, 1928.

Stojadinović, Milan M., *Ni rat ni pakt: Jugoslavija izmedju dva rata*, Rijeka: Otokar Keršovani, 1970 (first published in 1963).

Tito, Josip Broz, *Sabrana djela*, Belgrade: Komunist and BIGZ and Zagreb: Naprijed, 1982, vol. 5: September 1939 - September 1940.

Contemporary publications and pamphlets

Andjelinović, Grga, *Svima prijateljima i političkim istomišljenicima u Primorskoj Banovini!*, Split, 1936.

Andrassy, Juraj, *Novo ustavno uredjenje Hrvatske*, Zagreb: Tiskara 'Merkantile', 1940.

Armstrong, Hamilton Fish, *The New Balkans*, London and New York: Harper and Brothers, 1927.

———, 'The Royal Dictatorship in Yugoslavia', *Foreign Affairs*, vol. 7, no. 4, July 1929, 600-615.

———, 'After the Assassination of King Alexander', *Foreign Affairs*, vol. 13, no. 2, January 1935, 204-25.

Baerlein, Henry, *The Birth of Yugoslavia*, 2 vols, London: Leonard Parsons, 1922.

Bartulović, Niko, *Od Revolucionarne Omladine do Orjune*, Split: Splitska društvena tiskara, 1925.

Buchan, John (ed.), *Yugoslavia*, London: Hodder and Stoughton, 1923.

Beard, Charles A. and George Radin, *The Balkan Pivot: Yugoslavia. A Study in Government and Administration*, New York: Macmillan, 1929.

Bićanić, Rudolf, *Ekonomska podloga Hrvatskog pitanja*, Zagreb: Vladko Maček, 1938.

Carr, E.H., *Twenty Years' Crisis, 1919-1939*, London: Macmillan, 1939.

Ćorović, Vladimir, *Istorija Jugoslavije*, Belgrade: Narodno delo, 1933.

Demokrati o današnjem stanju u zemlji, Belgrade: Sekretarijat Demokratske stranke, November 1939.

Dimitrijević, Mita, *Mi i Hrvati. Hrvatsko pitanje (1914-1939): Sporazum sa Hrvatima*, Belgrade: 1939.

Dvorniković, Vladimir, *Borba ideja*, Belgrade: Službeni list SRJ, 1995 (first published by Geca Kon in 1937).

———, *Karakterologija Jugoslovena*, Belgrade: Geca Kon, 1939.

Glojnarić, Mirko, *Borba Hrvata: Kronika dvaju desetljeća političke povijesti (1919-1939)*, 2nd edn, Zagreb: Naklada Antuna Velzeka, 1940.

Graham, Jr, Malbone W., 'The "Dictatorship" in Yugoslavia', *The American Political Science Review*, vol. 23, issue 2, May 1929, 449-59.

Graham, Stephen, *Alexander of Jugoslavia: Strong Man of the Balkans*, London: Cassell & Co., 1938.

Gunther, John, *Inside Europe*, London: Hamish Hamilton, 1936.

Horvat, Josip, *Politička povijest Hrvatske*, 2 vols, Zagreb: August Cesarec,

1990 (First published as *Politička povijest Hrvatske, 1918-1929*, Zagreb, 1938).

Jančiković, Tomo, *Hrvati u izborima 11. prosinca 1938.*, Zagreb, 1939.

Jovanović, Slobodan, *Ustavno pravo Kraljevine Srba, Hrvata i Slovenaca*, Belgrade: Službeni list SRJ, 1995 (first published by Geca Kon in 1924).

——, 'Je li federalizam kod nas mogućan?', *Srpski književni glasnik* (*Nova serija*), Belgrade, vol. 1, 1920, 435-41.

[Jovanović, Slobodan], 'The Yugoslav Constitution of 1921', *Slavonic [and East European] Review*, vol. 3, no. 7, June 1924, 166-78.

Marjanović, Milan, *Stjepan Radić*, Belgrade: Jugo-Istok, 1937.

Marković, Lazar, *Politika*, Belgrade: Geca Kon, 1925.

——, *Jugoslovenska država i Hrvatsko pitanje (1914-1929)*, Zagreb: Komisiona naklada 'S. Kugli', 1935.

——, 'The Jugoslav Constitutional Problem', *Slavonic [and East European] Review*, vol. 16, no. 47, January 1938, 356-69.

Novak, Viktor, *Antologija jugoslovenske misli i narodnog jedinstva, 1390-1930*, Belgrade: Štampa državne štamparije, 1930.

Orr, Dorothea, *Portrait of a People: Croatia Today*, New York and London: Funk & Wagnalls Company, 1936.

Patton, Kenneth S., *Kingdom of Serbs, Croats and Slovenes (Yugoslavia): A Commercial and Industrial Handbook*, Washington, DC: US Government Printing Office, 1928.

Primedbe i prigovori na projekat Konkordata izmedju naše države i Vatikana, parafiranog 25.VII. 1935. god., Sremski Karlovci: Patrijaršiska štampa, 1936.

Protić, Stojan M., *Naša spoljna i unutrašnja situacija (Konferencija održana u Klubu beogradskih Radikala 2-X-1919)*, Belgrade: Geca Kon, 1920.

——, *Uoči Ustavotvorne skupštine*, Belgrade, 1920.

Radošević, Mijo, *Osnovi savremene Jugoslavije. Političke ideje, stranke i ljudi u XIX i XX veku*, Zagreb: Štampa zadružne štamparije, 1935.

Seton-Watson, R.W., *The Southern Slav Question and the Habsburg Monarchy*, London: Constable, 1911.

——, 'Jugoslavia and Croatia (Address given on January 29th, 1929)', *Journal of the Royal Institute of International Affairs*, March 1929,

117-33.

——, 'The Background of the Jugoslav Dictatorship', *Slavonic [and East European] Review*, vol. 10, no. 29, December 1931, 363-76.

——, 'Jugoslavia and the Croat Problem', *Slavonic [and East European] Review*, vol. 16, no. 46, July 1937, 102-12.

Šišić, Ferdo, *Jugoslovenska misao: Istorija ideje narodnog ujedinjenja i oslobodjenja od 1790-1918*, Belgrade: Balkanski institut, 1937.

South-Eastern Europe: A Political and Economic Survey, London: The Royal Institute of International Affairs and Oxford University Press, 1939.

South-Eastern Europe: A Brief Survey, (Information Department Papers, no. 26), London: The Royal Institute of International Affairs and Oxford University Press, 1940.

Spomenica Ljubomira Davidovića, Belgrade: Glavni odbor Demokratske stranke, 1940.

Stojadinović, Milan M., *Jedan kralj, jedan narod, jedna država*, Belgrade: Izdanje sekcije za unutrašnju propagandu JRZ, 1939.

Stojanović, Ljubomir, *Nekolike misli o našem novom državnom uredjenju*, Belgrade: Štamparija 'Merkur' Milorada Stefanovića, 1919.

Šuklje, Franjo, 'Centralism and Autonomy in Jugoslavia', *Slavonic [and East European] Review*, vol. 2, no. 5, December 1923, 328-35.

Tomašić, Dinko, 'Constitutional Changes in Yugoslavia', *Political Science Quarterly*, vol. 55, no. 4, December 1940, 582-93.

Trijumf misli narodnog sporazuma. Put Dra Mačka u Beograd, Zagreb: Demos, 1938.

Vojnović, Lujo, *Vaskrs Hrvatske*, Zagreb, 1939.

West, Rebecca, *Black Lamb and Grey Falcon: The Record of a Journey Through Yugoslavia in 1937*, London: Macmillan, 1941.

[The Yugoslav Committee], *The Southern Slav Library*, nos. 1-6, London, 1915-16.

Newspapers and journals

Arhiv za pravne i društvene nauke (Belgrade)
Dom (Zagreb)
Hrvatski dnevnik (Zagreb)
Javnost (Belgrade)
Jugoslovenski glas (Zagreb)

Jugoslovenska zastava (Novi Sad)
Napred (Belgrade)
Naša reč (Paris and London)
Nova Evropa (Zagreb)
Nova riječ (Zagreb)
Novo doba (Split)
Obzor (Zagreb)
Politika (Belgrade)
Pravda (Belgrade)
Riječ (Zagreb)
Samouprava (Belgrade)
Seljački glas (Zagreb)
Seljačko kolo (Zagreb)
Srpski glas (Belgrade)
Srpski književni glasnik (Belgrade)
The Times (London)
Vidici (Belgrade)
Vreme (Belgrade)

SECONDARY SOURCES

Unpublished doctoral theses

Budding, Audrey Halfant, 'Serb Intellectuals and the National Question, 1961-1991', unpublished PhD thesis, Harvard University, 1998.
Hepburn, Phillip Anthony, 'The Failure of Centralism: The Centralist System and Political Relations in Yugoslavia, 1934-1939', London School of Economics and Political Science, 1987.
Nielsen, Christian Axboe, 'One State, One Nation, One King: The Dictatorship of King Aleksandar and His Yugoslav Project, 1929-1935', Columbia University, New York, 2002.
Nikolić, Irina Aleksandra, 'Anglo-Yugoslav Relations, 1938-1941', University of Cambridge, 2001.

Books and monographs

Allcock, John B., *Explaining Yugoslavia*, London: Hurst, 2000.
Anderson, Benedict, *Imagined Communities: Reflections on the Origin and*

Spread of Nationalism, London: Verso, revised and extended ed., 1991.

Bakić, Jovo, *Ideologije jugoslovenstva izmedu srpskog i hrvatskog nacionalizma, 1914-1941. Sociološko-istorijska studija,* Zrenjanin: Gradska narodna biblioteka 'Žarko Zrenjanin', 2004.

Balfour, Neil and Sally Mackay, *Paul of Yugoslavia: Britain's Maligned Friend,* London: Hamish Hamilton, 1980.

Banac, Ivo, *The National Question in Yugoslavia: Origins, History, Politics.* Ithaca, NY: Cornell University Press, 4ᵗʰ ed., 1994 (first published in 1984).

——, *Protiv straha: Članci, izjave i javni nastupi, 1987-1992.,* Zagreb: Slon, 1992.

Benson, Leslie, *Yugoslavia: A Concise History,* London: Palgrave, 2001.

Berend, Ivan T., *Decades of Crisis: Central and Eastern Europe before World War II,* Berkeley and Los Angeles, CA: University of California Press, 1998.

Bilandžić, Dušan, *Historija Socijalističke Federativne Republike Jugoslavije: Glavni procesi, 1918-1985,* Zagreb: Školska knjiga, 3ʳᵈ revised ed., 1985.

Biondich, Mark, *Stjepan Radić, the Croat Peasant Party, and the Politics of Mass Mobilization, 1904-1928,* Toronto University Press, 2000.

Bjelajac, Mile, *Vojska Kraljevine SHS, 1918-1921,* Belgrade: Institut za savremenu istoriju Srbije, 1988.

——, *Vojska Kraljevine SHS/Jugoslavije, 1922-1935,* Belgrade: Institut za savremenu istoriju Srbije, 1994.

——, *Jugoslovensko iskustvo sa multietničkom armijom, 1918-1991,* Belgrade: Udruženje za društvenu istoriju, 1999.

Boban, Ljubo, *Sporazum Cvetković-Maček,* Belgrade: Institut društvenih nauka – Odeljenje za istorijske nauke, 1965.

——, *Svetozar Pribićević u opoziciji, 1929-1936,* Zagreb: Institut za hrvatsku povijest, 1973.

——, *Maček i politika Hrvatske seljačke stranke. Iz povijesti hrvatskog pitanja, 1918-1941,* 2 vols, Zagreb: Liber, 1974.

——, *Kontroverze iz povijesti Jugoslavije,* 3 vols, Zagreb: Školska knjiga and Stvarnost, 1987-1990.

——, *Dr. Tomo Jančiković. HSS izmedju zapadnih saveznika i jugoslavenskih komunista,* Zagreb: Školska knjiga, 1996.

Božić, Ivan, Sima Ćirković, Milorad Ekmečić and Vladimir Dedijer, *Istorija Jugoslavije*, Belgrade: Prosveta, 1972.

Brubaker, Rogers, *Nationalism Reframed: Nationhood and the National Question in the New Europe*, Cambridge University Press, 1996.

Cipek, Tihomir, *Ideja hrvatske države u političkoj misli Stjepana Radića*, Zagreb: Alinea, 2001.

Ćirković, Sima M., *The Serbs*, Oxford: Blackwell, 2004.

Clissold, Stephen (ed.), *A Short History of Yugoslavia: From Early Times to 1966*, Cambridge University Press, 1966.

Cornwall, Mark (ed.), *The Last Years of Austria-Hungary: Essays in Political and Military History, 1908-1918*, University of Exeter Press, 1990.

Cornwall, Mark, *The Undermining of Austria-Hungary: The Battle for Hearts and Minds*, Basingstoke: Macmillan, 2000.

Crampton, R.J., *Eastern Europe in the Twentieth Century – and After*, London and New York: Routledge, 2nd ed., 1997.

Čulinović, Ferdo, *Slom stare Jugoslavije*, Zagreb: Školska knjiga, 1958.

——, *Jugoslavija izmedju dva rata*, 2 vols, Zagreb: JAZU, 1961.

Dedijer, Vladimir, *The Road to Sarajevo*, London: MacGibbon and Kee, 1967.

Dimić, Ljubodrag, *Kulturna politika u Kraljevini Jugoslaviji*, 3 vols, Belgrade: Stubovi kulture, 1996.

——, *Srbi i Jugoslavija: Prostor, društvo, politika (Pogled s kraja veka)*, Belgrade: Stubovi kulture, 1998.

Dimitrijević, Sergije *et al.* (eds), *Iz istorije Jugoslavije, 1918-1945: Zbornik predavanja*, Belgrade: Nolit, 1958.

Djilas, Aleksa, *The Contested Country: Yugoslav Unity and Communist Revolution, 1919-1953*, Cambridge, MA: Harvard University Press, 3rd ed., 1996 (first published in 1991).

Djokić, Dejan (ed.), *Yugoslavism: Histories of a Failed Idea, 1918-1992*, London: Hurst and Madison, WI: University of Wisconsin Press, 2003.

Djordjević, Dimitrije (ed.), *The Creation of Yugoslavia, 1914-1918*, Santa Barbara, CA and Oxford: Clio Books, 1980.

Dolenc, Ervin, *Kulturni boj. Slovenska kulturna politika v Kraljevini SHS 1918-1929*, Ljubljana: Cankarjeva založba, 1996.

Dragnich, Alex N., *The First Yugoslavia: Search for a Viable Political*

System, Stanford, CA: Hoover Institution Press, 1983.

Dragović-Soso, Jasna, *'Saviours of the Nation': Serbia's Intellectual Opposition and the Revival of Nationalism*, London: Hurst, 2002.

Dugandžija, Nikola, *Jugoslavenstvo*, Belgrade: Mladost, 1985.

Ekmečić, Milorad, *Ratni ciljevi Srbije, 1914*, Belgrade: Prosveta, 1990, 2nd ed. (first published in 1973).

———, *Stvaranje Jugoslavije, 1790-1918*, Belgrade: Prosveta, 1989.

Gellner, Ernest, *Nations and Nationalism*, Oxford: Blackwell, 1983.

Gligorijević, Branislav, *Demokratska stranka i politički odnosi u Kraljevini Srba, Hrvata i Slovenaca*, Belgrade: Institut za savremenu istoriju, 1970.

———, *Parlament i političke stranke u Jugoslaviji, 1919-1929*, Belgrade: Institut za savremenu istoriju and Narodna knjiga, 1979.

———, *Kralj Aleksandar Karadjordjević*. 3 vols, Belgrade: Zavod za udžbenike i nastavna sredstva, 2002.

Goldstein, Ivo, *Croatia: A History*, London: Hurst, 1999.

Gross, Mirjana, *Povijest pravaške ideologije*, Zagreb: Institut za hrvatsku povijest, 1973.

Hobsbawm, Eric J., *Nations and Nationalism since 1780: Programme, Myth, Reality*, Cambridge University Press, 2nd ed., 1992.

Hoptner, Jacob, *Yugoslavia in Crisis, 1934-1941*, New York and London: Columbia University Press, 1962.

Howarth, David, *Discourse*, Milton Keynes and Philadelphia: Open University Press, 2000.

Hroch, Miroslav, *Social Preconditions of National Revival in Europe: A Comparative Analysis of the Social Composition of Patriotic Groups among the Smaller European Nations* (translated by Ben Fowkes), Cambridge University Press, 1985.

Istorija gradjanskih stranaka u Jugoslaviji, vol. 1, Belgrade, 1952. [Author(s) unknown]

Janković, Dragoslav, *Jugoslovensko pitanje i Krfska deklaracija 1917. godine*, Belgrade: Savremena administracija, 1967.

Jareb, Jere, *Pola stoljeća hrvatske politike, 1895-1945*, Buenos Aires: Knjižnica Hrvatske revije, 1960.

Jelavich, Charles, *South Slav Nationalisms: Textbooks and Yugoslav Union before 1914*, Columbus, OH: Ohio State University Press, 1990.

Jovanović, Nadežda, *Politički sukobi u Jugoslaviji, 1925-1928*, Belgrade:

Rad, 1974.

———, *Život za slobodu bez straha: Studija o životu i delu dr. Dragoljuba Jovanovića*, Belgrade: Institut za noviju istoriju Srbije, 2000.

Jović, Dejan, *Jugoslavija: Država koja je odumrla. Uspon, kriza i pad četvrte Jugoslavije*, Belgrade: Samizdat B92 and Zagreb: Prometej, 2003.

Judah, Tim, *The Serbs: History, Myth and the Destruction of Yugoslavia*, New Haven, CT: Yale University Press, 1997.

Kitchen, Martin, *Europe between the Wars: A Political History*, London and New York: Longman, 10th impression, 1997.

Kočović, Bogoljub, *Etnički i demografski razvoj u Jugoslaviji od 1921. do 1991. godine (po svim zvaničnim a u nekim slučajevima i korigovanim popisima)*, 2 vols, Paris: Dialogue, 1998.

Krestić, Vasilije Dj., *Srpsko-hrvatski odnosi i jugoslovenska ideja u drugoj polovini XIX veka*, Belgrade: Nova knjiga, 1988.

———, *Iz istorije Srba i srpsko-hrvatskih odnosa*, Belgrade: BIGZ, 1994.

———, *Genocidom do Velike Hrvatske*, Novi Sad: Matica srpska and Belgrade: Arhiv Srbije, 1998.

Krizman, Bogdan, *Vanjska politika jugoslavenske države 1918-1941*, Zagreb: Školska knjiga, 1975.

———, *Hrvatska u Prvom svjetskom ratu: Hrvatsko-srpski politički odnosi*, Zagreb: Globus, 1989.

Lampe, John R., *Yugoslavia as History: Twice There was a Country*, Cambridge University Press, 2nd ed., 2000 (first published in 1996).

Lampe, John and Mark Mazower (eds), *Ideologies and National Identities: The Case of Twentieth-Century Southeastern Europe*, Budapest: CEU Press, 2004.

Lederer, Ivo J., *Yugoslavia at the Paris Peace Conference: A Study in Frontiermaking*, New Haven, CT: Yale University Press, 1963.

Livezeanu, Irina, *Cultural Politics in Greater Romania: Regionalism, Nation Building, and Ethnic Struggle, 1918-1930*, Ithaca, NY: Cornell University Press, 1995.

MacKenzie, David, *The 'Black Hand' on Trial: Salonika, 1917*, Boulder, CO and New York: East European Monographs (distributed by Columbia University Press), 1995.

Matković, Hrvoje, *Svetozar Pribićević i Samostalna demokratska stranka*

BIBLIOGRAPHY

do šestojanuarske diktature, Zagreb: Institut za hrvatsku povijest, 1972.

———, *Svetozar Pribićević: Ideolog, stranački vodja, emigrant*, Zagreb: Hrvatska sveučilišna naklada, 1995.

———, *Povijest Jugoslavije: Hrvatski pogled*, Zagreb: Naklada Pavičić, 1998.

Mazower, Mark, *Dark Continent: Europe's Twentieth Century*, London: Penguin, 1998.

Miller, Nicholas J., *Between Nation and State: Serbian Politics in Croatia before the First World War*, University of Pittsburgh Press, 1997.

Mills, Sara, *Discourse*, London and New York: Routledge, 1997.

Milosavljević, Olivera, *U tradiciji nacionalizma (ili stereotipi srpskih intelektualaca XX veka o 'nama' i 'drugima')*, Belgrade: Helsinški odbor za ljudska prava u Srbiji, 2002.

Mitrović, Andrej, *Jugoslavija na Konferenciji mira*, Belgrade: Zavod za izdavanje udžbenika SR Srbije, 1969.

———, *Vreme netrpeljivih. Politička istorija velikih država Evrope, 1919-1939*, Belgrade: Srpska književna zadruga, 1974.

———, *Srbija u Prvom svetskom ratu*, Belgrade: Stubovi kulture, 2004 (first publ. in 1984).

———, *Vreme destruktivnih*, Čačak: Čačanski glas, 1998.

Pavković, Aleksandar, *Slobodan Jovanović: An Unsentimental Approach to Politics*, Boulder, CO and New York: East European Monographs (distributed by Columbia University Press), 1993

Pavlović, Kosta St., *Vojislav Marinković i njegovo doba, 1876-1935*, 5 vols, London: published by author, 1955-60.

Pavlowitch, Stevan K., *Yugoslavia*, London and New York: Benn, 1971.

———, *Unconventional Perceptions of Yugoslavia, 1940-1945*, Boulder, CO and New York: East European Monographs (distributed by Columbia University Press), 1984.

———, *The Improbable Survivor: Yugoslavia and its Problems, 1918-1988*, London: Hurst, 1988.

———, *A History of the Balkans, 1804-1945*, London and New York: Longman, 1999.

———, *Serbia: The History behind the Name*, London: Hurst, 2002.

Perović, Latinka (ed.), *Srbija u modernizacijskim procesima 19. i 20. veka*.

Uloga elita, Belgrade: Čigoja štampa, 2003.

Petranović, Branko, *Istorija Jugoslavije, 1918-1978*, Belgrade: Nolit, 1980.

———, *Jugoslovensko iskustvo srpske nacionalne integracije*, Belgrade: Službeni list SRJ, 1993.

Petrovich, Michael Boro, *A History of Modern Serbia*, 2 vols, New York and London: Harcourt Brace Jovanovich, 1976.

Politički život Jugoslavije, 1914-1945: Zbornik radova (Sveske Trećeg programa), Belgrade: Radio Beograd, 1973.

Polonsky, Antony, *The Little Dictators: The History of Eastern Europe since 1918*, London: Routledge & Kegan Paul, 1975.

Purivatra, Atif, *Jugoslovenska muslimanska organizacija u političkom životu Kraljevine Srba, Hrvata i Slovenaca*, Sarajevo: Svjetlost, 1974.

Radan, Peter and Aleksandar Pavković (eds), *The Serbs and Their Leaders in the Twentieth Century*, Aldershot: Ashgate, 1997.

Radojević, Mira, *Ujedinjena opozicija, 1935-1939*, Belgrade: Institut za savremenu istoriju Srbije, 1994.

Rogel, Carol, *The Slovenes and Yugoslavism, 1890-1914*, Boulder, CO and New York: East European Monographs (distributed by Columbia University Press), 1977.

Rothenberg, Gunther E., *The Military Border in Croatia, 1740-1881: A Study of an Imperial Institution*, University of Chicago Press, 1966.

Rothschild, Joseph, *East Central Europe between the Two World Wars*, Seattle and London: University of Washington Press, 1974.

———, *Ethnopolitics: A Conceptual Framework*, New York: Columbia University Press, 1981.

Šarac, Nedim, *Uspostavljanje Šestojanuarskog režima 1929. godine, sa posebnim osvrtom na Bosnu i Hercegovinu*, Sarajevo: Svjetlost, 1975.

Seton-Watson, Hugh, *Eastern Europe between the Wars, 1918-1941*, Cambridge University Press, 1946.

Seton-Watson, Hugh and Christopher, *The Making of a New Europe: R.W. Seton-Watson and the Last Years of Austria-Hungary*, London: Methuen, 1981.

Singleton, Fred, *A Short History of the Yugoslav Peoples*, Cambridge: Cambridge University Press, 1985.

Smith, Anthony D., *Theories of Nationalism*, London: Duckworth, 1983.
——, *The Ethnic Origins of Nations*, Oxford: Blackwell, 1986.
Stanković, Djordje, *Nikola Pašić i jugoslovensko pitanje*, Belgrade: BIGZ, 1985.
——, *Nikola Pašić i Hrvati (1918-1923)*, Belgrade: BIGZ, 1995.
——, *Istorijski stereotipi i naučno znanje*, Belgrade: Plato, 2004.
Stefanovski, Mirjana, *Ideja hrvatskog drzavnog prava i stvaranje Jugoslavije*, Belgrade: Draganić, 1995.
Stokes, Gale, *Three Eras of Political Change in Eastern Europe*, New York and Oxford: Oxford University Press, 1997.
Stojanović, Dubravka, *Srbi i demokratija. Istorijska studija o 'zlatnom dobu srpske demokratije' 1903-1914*, Belgrade: Udruženje za društvenu istoriju, 2003.
Stojkov, Todor, *Opozicija u vreme šestojanuarske diktature, 1929-1935*, Belgrade: Prosveta, 1969.
——, *Vlada Milana Stojadinovića, 1935-1937*, Belgrade: Institut za savremenu istoriju, 1985.
Sugar, Peter F. and Ivo J. Lederer (eds), *Nationalism in Eastern Europe*, Seattle: University of Washington Press, 1969.
Sugar, Peter F. (ed.), *Eastern European Nationalism in the Twentieth Century*, Washington, DC: The American University Press, 1995.
Terzić, Velimir, *Slom Kraljevine Jugoslavije 1941: Uzroci i posledice poraza*, Belgrade: Narodna knjiga, Belgrade-Ljubljana: Partizanska knjiga and Titograd: Pobjeda, 1982.
Tešić, Dragan, *Jugoslovenska radikalna zajednica u Srbiji, 1935-1939*, Belgrade: Institut za savremenu istoriju, 1997.
Tomasevich, Jozo, *Peasants, Politics and Economic Change in Yugoslavia*, Stanford University Press and London: Geoffrey Cumberlege, Oxford University Press, 1955.
Tošić, Desimir, *Srpski nacionalni problemi*, Paris: Oslobodjenje, 1952.
——, *Stvarnost protiv zabluda: Srpsko nacionalno pitanje*, Belgrade: Slobodan Mašić (Nova 122), 1997.
——, *O ljudima: Eseji, zapisi, sećanja*, Belgrade: Slobodan Mašić (Nova 160), 2000.
——, *Demokratska stranka 1920-1941*, Belgrade: Službeni list Srbije i

Crne Gore and Fond 'Ljuba Davidović', 2006.

Trgovčević, Ljubinka, *Naučnici Srbije i stvaranje jugoslovenske države, 1914-1920*, Belgrade: Srpska književna zadruga, 1986.

Tudjman, Franjo, *Hrvatska u monarhističkoj Jugoslaviji, 1918-1941*, 2 vols, Zagreb: Hrvatska sveučilišna naklada, 1993.

Vilder, Većeslav, *Bika za rogove. Gde je izvor spora srpsko-hrvatskog? Gde je rešenje?*, London: Demos, 1957.

Vučetić-Mladenović, Radina, *Evropa na Kalemegdanu: 'Cvijeta Zuzorić' i kulturni život Beograda 1918-1941*, Belgrade: INIS, 2003.

Vujović, Dimitrije, *Ujedinjenje Crne Gore i Srbije*, Titograd [Podgorica]: Istorijski institut NR Crne Gore, 1962.

——, *Podrgorička skupština 1918.*, Zagreb: Školska knjiga, 1989.

Wachtel, Andrew Baruch, *Making a Nation, Breaking a Nation: Literature and Cultural Politics in Yugoslavia*, Stanford University Press, 1998.

Zečević, Momčilo, *Na istorijskoj prekretnici: Slovenci u politici jugoslovenske države 1919-1929.*, I, Belgrade: Prosveta and Institut za savremenu istoriju and Ljubljana: Inštitut za zgodovino delaveskega gibanja, 1985.

Živojinović, Dragoljub, *America, Italy and the Birth of Yugoslavia, 1917-1919*, Boulder, CO and New York: East European Monographs (distributed by Columbia University Press), 1972.

Žutić, Nikola, *Sokoli: Ideologija u fizičkoj kulturi Kraljevine Jugoslavije, 1929-1941*, Belgrade: Institut za savremenu istoriju, 1991.

Journal articles and chapters in edited volumes

Banac, Ivo, 'Historiography of the Countries of Eastern Europe: Yugoslavia', *The American Historical Review*, vol. 97, no. 4, October 1992, 1084-1104.

——, 'The Fearful Asymmetry of War: The Causes and Consequences of Yugoslavia's Demise', *Daedalus*, vol. 121, no. 2, 1992, 141-74.

——, 'Nationalism in Southeastern Europe', in Charles A. Kupchan (ed.), *Nationalism and Nationalities in the New Europe*, Ithaca, NY: Cornell University Press, 1995, 107-21.

Biber, Dušan, 'O padu Stojadinovićeve vlade', *Istorija XX veka. Zbornik radova* (Belgrade), vol. VIII, 1966 (Belgrade), 5-71.

Boban, Ljubo, 'O političkim previranjima na selu u Banovini Hrvatskoj', *Istorija XX veka. Zbornik radova*, vol. 2, 1961, 225-66.

——, 'Zagrebačke punktacije', *Istorija XX veka. Zbornik radova*, vol. IV, 1962, 309-64.

——, 'Oko Mačekovih pregovora s grofom Ćanom', *Istorija XX veka. Zbornik radova*, vol. VI, Belgrade, 1964, 303-57.

——, 'Iz historije odnosa izmedju Vl. Mačeka i dvora u vrijeme šestojanuarskog režima (Odnosi do oktroiranog Ustava od 3. IX 1931), *Historijski zbornik* (Zagreb), vol. XVIII, 1965, 47-67.

——, 'Iz historije odnosa izmedju Vl. Mačeka i dvora u vrijeme šestojanuarskog režima (Odnosi od Septembarskog ustava do marseljskog atentata), *Zbornik Historijskog instituta Slavonije* (Osijek), vol. 4, 1966, 167-238.

——, 'Iz historije odnosa izmedju Vl. Mačeka i dvora u vrijeme šestojanuarskog režima (Odnosi od marseljskog atentata do petomajskih izbora), *Zbornik Historijskog instituta Slavonije*, vol. 3, 1965, 167-201.

Bogdanov, Vaso, 'Historijski uzroci sukobu izmedju Hrvata i Srba', *Rad*, Knjiga 311, Zagreb: JAZU, 1957, 353-477.

Bracewell, Wendy, 'National Histories and National Identities among the Serbs and Croats', in Mary Fulbrook (ed.), *National Histories and European History*, London: UCL Press, 2nd impression, 1994, 141-60.

Djilas, Aleksa, 'Hrvatsko-srpski sukob i liberalna demokratija', in A. Djilas (ed.), *Srpsko pitanje*, Belgrade: Politika, 1991, 163-79, and in A. Djilas, *Raspad i nada: Eseji, članci i intervjui, 1991-1994*, Belgrade: Princip, 1995, 9-27.

——, 'Fear Thy Neighbor: The Breakup of Yugoslavia', in Charles A. Kupchan (ed.), *Nationalism and Nationalities in the New Europe*, Ithaca, NY: Cornell University Press, 1995, 85-106.

Djokić, Dejan, 'Yugoslav anti-Axis Resistance, 1939-41: The Case of Vane Ivanović', *Slavonic and East European Review*, vol. 79, no. 1, January 2001, 127-41.

Dobrivojević, Ivana, 'Sudstvo i sudije u doba šestojanuarskog režima Kralja Aleksandra (1929-1935)', *Tokovi istorije* (Belgrade), no. 3-4, 2005, 28-53.

Dragnich, Alex N., 'The Anatomy of a Myth: Serbian Hegemony', *Slavic*

Review, vol. 50, no. 3, Fall 1991, 659-62.

Gaković, Milan, 'Savez zemljoradnika (Zemljoradnička stranka) i sporazum Cvetković-Maček', *Zbornik za istoriju Bosne i Hercegovine* (Belgrade), 1997, 275-94.

Gligorijević, Branislav, 'O pitanju ulaska predstavnika HRSS u Davidovićevu vladu 1924. i o krizi i padu te vlade', *Istorija XX veka. Zbornik radova*, vol. VII, 1965, 345-406.

———, 'Politička previranja u Demokratskoj stranci na pitanju taktike prema Hrvatskom bloku u drugoj polovini 1922.', *Istorija XX veka. Zbornik radova*, vol. VIII, 1966, 165-269.

———, 'Razlike i dodirne tačke u gledištu na nacionalno pitanje izmedju Radikalne i Demokratske stranke, 1919-1929.', *Jugoslovenski istorijski časopis*, (Belgrade), no. 4, 1969, 153-58.

———, 'Neki aspekti na odnose izmedju Demokratske stranke i Hrvatske republikanske seljačke stranke (1919-1925), *Istorija XX veka*, vol. XII, 1972, 355-74.

———, 'Uloga vojnih krugova u "rešavanju" političke krize iz 1924. godine', *Vojnoistorijski glasnik* (Belgrade), vol. 23, no. 1, 1972, 161-86.

———, 'Jugoslovenstvo izmedju dva rata', *Jugoslovenski istorijski časopis*, vol. XXI, no. 1-4, 1986, 71-97.

———, 'Stvaranje prečanskog fronta u Hrvatskoj i političke posledice (1927-1941)', *Jugoslovenski istorijski časopis*, vol. XXX, no. 1, 1997, 91-116.

———, 'King Aleksandar I Karadjordjević', in Peter Radan and Aleksandar Pavković (eds), *The Serbs and Their Leaders in the Twentieth Century*, Aldershot: Ashgate, 1997, 140-57.

Gross, Mirjana, 'Croatian National-integrational Ideologies from the end of Illyrism to the Creation of Yugoslavia', *Austrian History Yearbook*, vol. 15-16, 1979-1980, 3-33.

Janković, Dragoslav, 'Ženevska konferencija o stvaranju jugoslovenske zajednice 1918. godine', *Istorija XX veka. Zbornik radova*, vol. V, 1964, 225-62.

Jelavich, Charles, 'Serbian Nationalism and the Question of Union with Croatia in the Nineteenth Century', *Balkan Studies*, vol. 3, no. 1, 1962, 29-42.

Jelić, Ivan, 'O nekim odjecima sporazuma Cvetković-Maček medju

Srbima u Banovini Hrvatskoj', *Historijski zbornik Slavonije*, vol. 3, 1965, 147-66.

Jovanović, Nadežda, 'Slobodan Jovanović i Dragoljub Jovanović: Prilog proučavanju njihovih uzajamnih odnosa', *Tokovi istorije*, no. 1-2, 1996, 117-65.

Lederer, Ivo J., 'Nationalism and the Yugoslavs', in Peter F. Sugar and Ivo J. Lederer (eds), *Nationalism in Eastern Europe*, Seattle: University of Washington Press, 1969, 396-438.

Linta, Miodrag, 'Vlada Milana Stojadinovića 1935-1936. i Srbi u Hrvatskoj', *Ljetopis Srpskog kulturnog društva 'Prosvjeta'* (Zagreb), vol. 2, 1997, 168-92.

MacKenzie, David, 'Dragutin Dimitrijević-Apis', in Peter Radan and Aleksandar Pavković (eds), *The Serbs and Their Leaders in the Twentieth Century*, Aldershot: Ashgate, 1997, 58-94.

Martić, Miloš, 'Dimitrije Ljotić and the Yugoslav National-Movement Zbor, 1935-1945', *East European Quarterly*, vol. 14, no. 2, Winter, 1981, 219-39.

Matković, Hrvoje, 'Veze izmedju Frankovaca i Radikala od 1922-1925.', *Historijski zbornik*, vol. XV, 1962, 41-59.

———, 'Hrvatska zajednica: Prilog proučavanju političkih stranaka u staroj Jugoslaviji', *Istorija XX veka. Zbornik radova*, vol. V, 1963, 5-136.

———, 'Stjepan Radić i Svetozar Pribićević u jugoslavenskoj politici od ujedinjenja do šestojanuarske diktature', *Jugoslovenski istorijski časopis*, no. 4, 1969, 148-53.

Miletić, Aleksandar, 'Unutrašnja trgovina u Kraljevini SHS 1919. godine', *Tokovi istorije*, no. 3-4, 2003, 7-20.

Nedelcovych, Mima S., 'The Serb-Croat Controversy: Events Leading to the *Sporazum* of 1939', *Serbian Studies*, vol. 1, no. 3, Fall 1981, 3-29.

Pavlowitch (Pavlović), Kosta St., 'Yugoslav-British Relations, 1939-1941 (as seen from British sources)', *East European Quarterly*, vol. 12, Fall 1978, 309-39, and vol. 12, Winter 1979, 425-41.

Pavlowitch, Stevan K., 'Jugoslavia in Perspective', *Review of the Study Centre for Jugoslav Affairs* (London), no. 9, 1970, 750-67.

———, 'How Many non-Serbian Generals in 1941?', *East European Quarterly*, vol. 16, no. 4, January 1983, 447-52.

————, 'Jugoslavija 1918-1991: Poraz jednog identiteta i jedne nestabilne političke kulture', *Istorija XX veka*, vol. XIV, no. 1, 1996, 7-20.

Pešelj, Branko, 'Serbo-Croatian Agreement of 1939 and American Foreign Policy', *Journal of Croatian Studies* (New York), vol. XI-XII, 1970-1971, 3-82.

Popović, Nebojša A, 'Srpski kulturni klub (1937-1941)', *Istorija XX veka*, vol. VII, no. 1-2, 1989, 109-40.

Radojević, Mira, 'Demokratska stranka o državnom preuredjenju Kraljevine Jugoslavije (1935-1941), *Istorija XX veka*, vol. IX, no. 1-2, 1991, 37-63.

————, 'Sporazum Cvetković-Maček i pitanje razgraničenja u Sremu', *Istorija XX veka*, vol. X, no. 1-2, 1992, 61-72.

————, Bosna i Hercegovina u raspravama o državnom uredjenju Kraljevine (SHS) Jugoslavije 1918-1941. godine', *Istorija XX veka*, vol. XII, no. 1, 1994, 7-41.

————, 'Srpsko-hrvatski spor oko Vojvodine 1918-1941', *Istorija XX veka*, vol. XIV, no. 2, 1996, 39-73.

————, 'Srpska gradjanska opozicija i Srbi u Hrvatskoj', *Tokovi istorije*, no. 1-2, 1996, 21-32.

Rusinow, Dennison, 'The Avoidable Catastrophe', in Sabrina P. Ramet and Ljubiša S. Adamović (eds), *Beyond Yugoslavia: Politics, Economics and Culture in a Shattered Community*, Boulder, CO.: Westview Press, 1995, 13-37.

————, 'The Yugoslav Peoples' in Peter F. Sugar (ed.), *Eastern European Nationalism in the Twentieth Century*, Washington, DC: The American University Press, 1995, 302-411.

Stanković, Djordje, 'Neuspeh Stojana Protića u okupljanju političkih snaga radi rešavanja hrvatskog pitanja 1921. godine', *Istorijski glasnik* (Belgrade), no. 7, 1971, 7-34.

————, 'Kriza radikalsko-demokratske koalicije 1921. godine i hrvatsko pitanje', *Jugoslovenski istorijski časopis*, no. 1-2, 1972, 79-91.

————, 'Nacionalizam i politička kultura (istorijsko iskustvo prvih godina jugoslovenske države)', *Tokovi istorije*, no. 1-2, 1993, 111-22.

————, 'Reforma prosvete u banovini Hrvatskoj i Srbi u Slavoniji', *Godišnjak za društvenu istoriju* (Belgrade), vol. IV, no. 2-3, 1997, 233-40.

————, 'Srbi Slavonije u "Državnoj vlasti" i "Unutrašnjoj upravi" za vreme diktature', *Godišnjak za društvenu istoriju*, vol. VI, no. 2, 1999, 156-63.

Stojkov, Todor, 'Gradjanska opozicija i skupštinski izbori od 8. novembra 1931. godine', *Istorija XX veka. Zbornik radova*, vol. IV, 1962, 251-307.

——, 'O stvaranju Bloka narodnog sporazuma', *Istorija XX veka. Zbornik radova*, vol. VI, 1964, 245-302.

——, 'O takozvanom Ličkom ustanku 1932.', *Časopis za suvremenu povijest* (Zagreb), vol. II, no. 2, 1970, 167-80.

Tomašić, Dinko, 'Hrvatska u europskoj politici', *Društvena istraživanja* (Zagreb), no. 8, November-December 1992, 907-38 (originally publ. as 'Croatia in European Politics', *Journal of Central European Affairs*, April 1942, 63-85).

Trifković, Srdjan, 'The First Yugoslavia and Origins of Croatian Separatism', *East European Quarterly*, vol. 26, no. 3, September 1992, 345-70.

——, 'Yugoslavia in Crisis: Europe and the Croat Question, 1939-41', *European History Quarterly*, vol. 23, no. 4, October 1993, 529-61.

——, 'Prince Pavle Karadjordjević', in Peter Radan and Aleksandar Pavković (eds), *The Serbs and Their Leaders in the Twentieth Century*, Aldershot: Ashgate, 1997, 158-202.

Vucinich, Wayne, 'Interwar Yugoslavia', in Wayne Vucinich (ed.), *Contemporary Yugoslavia: Twenty Years of Socialist Experiment*, Berkeley and Los Angeles: University of California Press, 1969, 1-58.

Zečević, Momčilo, 'Neki pogledi u Srbiji na političku delatnost Dr Antona Korošca 1918-1940.', *Istorija XX veka*, no. 1-2, 1990, 117-38.

Zelenjin, V.V., 'Kralj Aleksandar Karadjordjević (1888-1934)', in *Zarobljenici nacionalne ideje*, Belgrade: Filip Višnjić, 1996 (first published by the Russian Academy in 1993; translated by Gordana Barjaktarević), 136-59.

Zlatar, Zdenko, 'The Yugoslav Idea and the First Common State of South Slavs', *Nationalities Papers*, vol. 25, no. 3, September 1997 (Special issue: *The Disintegration of Yugoslavia: Inevitable or Avoidable*, guest-edited by Aleksandar Pavković), 387-406.

Žutić, Nikola, 'Ideologija Jugoslovenstva i njeno raspadanje, 1929-1939 (s posebnim osvrtom na vladu M. Stojadinovića), *Istorijski glasnik*, 1988, 63-91.

INDEX